AVANT (

CRITICAL STUDIES

10

EXPERIMENTAL —
VISUAL — CONCRETE

AVANT-GARDE POETRY
SINCE THE 1960s

Edited by

K. David Jackson,
Eric Vos & Johanna Drucker

AMSTERDAM - ATLANTA, GA 1996

Cover art: Johanna Drucker

∞ The paper on which this book is printed meets the requirements of "ISO 9706:1994, Information and documentation - Paper for documents - Requirements for permanence".

∞ Le papier sur lequel le présent ouvrage est imprimé remplit les prescriptions de "ISO 9706:1994, Information et documentation - Papier pour documents - Prescriptions pour la permanence".

CIP-GEGEVENS KONINKLIJKE BIBLIOTHEEK, DEN HAAG

Experimental

Experimental — Visual — Concrete : avant-garde poetry since the 1960s / K. David Jackson, Eric Vos, Johanna Drucker, eds. — Amsterdam - Atlanta, GA 1996 : Rodopi. — Ill. (Avant garde critical studies ; 10)
Met index, lit. opg.
ISBN: 90-5183-959-6 (bound)
ISBN: 90-5183-941-3 (paper)
NUGI 951/911
Trefw.: avant-garde ; poëzie ; geschiedenis ; 1960-1995.

CONTENTS

D. CONCRETE AND NEO-CONCRETE POETRY

MEMOIRS OF CONCRETE

E. THE YALE *SYMPHOSYMPOSIUM* ON CONTEMPORARY
POETICS AND CONCRETISM: A WORLD VIEW FROM THE 1990s

PLATES

EXPERIMENTAL – VISUAL – CONCRETE POETRY AND THE YALE SYMPHOSOPHIA

Preface

The Yale Symphosophia brought together over forty poets and performers on April 5-7, 1995 for a symposium on Experimental, Visual, and Concrete poetry aimed to produce a retrospective review and critical appraisal in international perspective of almost half a century of poetic production. The Brazilian poet Haroldo de Campos had been a visiting professor at Yale on more than one occasion, and plans for the Yale Symphosophia as a way of celebrating Haroldo de Campos's long association with Yale were initiated by K. David Jackson, professor of Portuguese, in view of his interest in contemporary poetics and contact with the Brazilian Concretists over three decades. The original idea was expanded as an homage to the poets in Portuguese language who had played a significant role as innovators in the experimental poetics of the 1950s and 60s, with Ana Hatherly and E. M. de Melo e Castro representing continental Portuguese literature. The presence of Johanna Drucker at Yale, in the Department of History of Art, made possible a collaboration that greatly enlarged the scope of the symposium, with the addition of American and Canadian poets, printers, performers, graphic artists, and critics.

Once announced, the Symphosophia soon became a magnet for the theme of contemporary experimentation in language arts. The scope of the event expanded into a comprehensive critical analysis of the history and theory of experimental poetics from mid-century to the present, with the presence of numerous major figures in the field, from Marjorie Perloff representing criticism to Jackson Mac Low and Anne Tardos performing aleatory texts.

The active participation of Eric Vos, from Amsterdam, signaled a European scholarly dimension. Reflecting Haroldo de Campos's international presence as a poet, the Symphosophia featured segments on Portuguese, Spanish American, and Italian poetics. The global connections of Concrete poetry attracted John Solt and the Japanese troupe from Amherst College, the Danish poet Susanne Jorn, as well as Canadian, Scottish, Argentine, Cuban, Swedish, French, and German authors and topics. The Symposophia benefited from the perspectives of Ruth and Marvin Sackner, professional collectors representing the most extensive and complete archive of Concrete poetry in existence. The historical dimension was equally well represented: Mary Ellen Solt, organizer

COLOR PLATE 1

Severo Sarduy, "Homage to Li Po"

COLOR PLATE 2

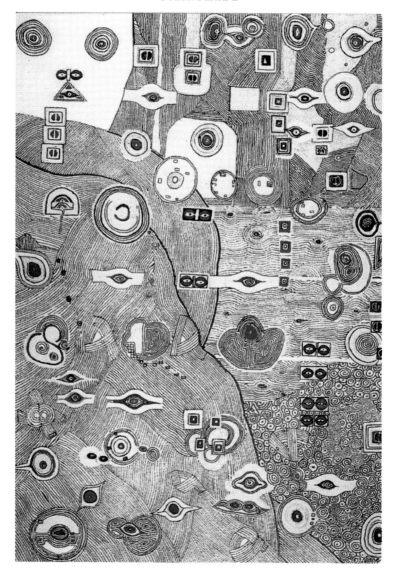

Severo Sarduy, "Self-portrait"

of a groundbreaking anthology; Elisabeth Walther-Bense, representing Max Bense and experimental poetry in Germany; and Dick Higgins, creator of Something Else Press, who narrated an illustrated history of printing Concrete texts in New York.

As its title implies, the Symphosophia joined both performance and criticism. Since the performances could not be included in this book, it is especially important for an understanding of the Symphosophia to describe them. The pianist Caio Pagano from São Paulo, who had premiered compositions based on Concretist texts by Brazilian composers such as Gilberto Mendes, was featured in a recital; Augusto and Cid Campos performed Augusto's poetry to bass guitar and prepared video, as recorded on their CD *Poesia é Risco*; Japanese poets performed to music of the shamisen, vocals, and abstract video presentations. Haroldo de Campos interacted with the Japanese poets, reading translations of Fujitomi, whom he had contacted in Japan 25 years ago, and Kitasono Katue. Dynamic poetic performance-readings by Charles Bernstein, Steve McCaffery, and Lello Voce captured the engaging cross currents of musicality, performance, and composition representative of today's experimental trends.

The year 1995 was a special one for Concrete poetry, and the Yale Symphosophia marked several significant milestones in the history of contemporary poetics. It was the 40th anniversary of the Eugen Gomringer – Décio Pignatari meeting, a catalyst for launching Brazilian and international Concrete poetry. It was also the 25th anniversary of the Solt anthology, published by Indiana UP, and of the Amsterdam Stedelijk Museum exhibit. The symposium celebrated Haroldo de Campos's 65th year and Mary Ellen Solt's 75th. The publication year of this book marks the 40th anniversary of the first São Paulo Bienal exhibit of Concrete texts.

The present volume is structured to reflect the sessions of the Yale Symphosophia and to address as well the major critical and interpretive issues of contemporary experimental poetic texts. Critical approaches, historical contexts, and basic concepts are surveyed in comprehensive introductory essays. The study of poetic movements in historical context and the chronological trajectory of production of experimental texts are the topics of the first major segment of the volume, "Experimentation in Its Historical Moment." The principal topic addressed here is the nature of experimental poetry in revolutionary social contexts, a continuation in the contemporary scene of the presumed role of avant-garde movements in promoting cultural change and political revolution. This volume addresses the specific cases of Portugal of the 1974 revolution and Italy's cultural and political radicalism of the 1970s. Examples of linguistic experimentation in cultural context, along with the relationship of writing to painting and the interplay of plastic arts and language, are brought to light in major figures of Spanish language poetry, Oliverio Girondo of Argentina and Severo Sarduy of Cuba. Roland Greene analyzed the elusive relationship between ethnic identity and poetic innovation in Latino/a poetry in the U.S. (to be published elsewhere). The section ends with a consideration of the question of what constitutes a valid communicative poetic project, at a moment of exhaustion both of materials and of experimental techniques used for poetry.

Language as a vehicle for experiments and cognitive quests, aimed not at the production of truth or social emancipation but at experiential aspects of language and language use, is the second major theme to be addressed in the section "Experimentation in the Language Arts." The wide variety of poetic production and the difficulty of assessing any experimental component of contemporary writing are considered to be problematic parameters of criticism. Haroldo de Campos's fragmented poetic prose work *Galáxias* is a highlighted topic of attention, focussed as experimentation with language and as an auto-referential and oxymoral verbal universe. Other linguistic universes are equally expounded: from the hieroglyphics of French Lettrism to the indeterminacies of Fluxus; from sonorous poetry and visual and gastronomic performances to holopoetry, language and video images, and technological intersign communications. A mini-anthology on the state of contemporary poetry in the United States, compiled by Harry Polkinhorn, stakes out new territory in "hyperotics," postpolygraphic, and underground writing, while American poets seriously question the purposes and ends of experimentation as a poetic vehicle.

The development of the basic tenets of Concrete poetry and current critical perspectives on its status in poetical experimentation constitute the basis of the third section of the book, "Concrete and Neo-Concrete Poetry." The relationship of historical Concrete poetry to artistic genres is presented, with special emphasis on Brazil. The essays reveal a surprising variety of different national or linguistic approaches to Concrete poetics: the renewal of Spatialism in French poetry; the "sensual" character of Swedish Concrete poetry; shifting and overlapping codes in a poem-icon by Augusto de Campos; the use of language graphics in Scottish and US poetry to produce a visual, musical score as a new kind of poetry writing. The world of experimentation, while far from uniform, is shown nonetheless to have produced a revolution in the visible poetic word.

The section "Memoirs of Concrete," in the context of oral history, presents retrospective accounts *cum* memoirs by two of Concrete poetry's most renowned editors, who share the élan of their exciting years of risk and daring and the impact of time and events on their intellectual lives.

The Yale Symphosophia concluded with a roundtable open to all partici-

COLOR PLATE 3

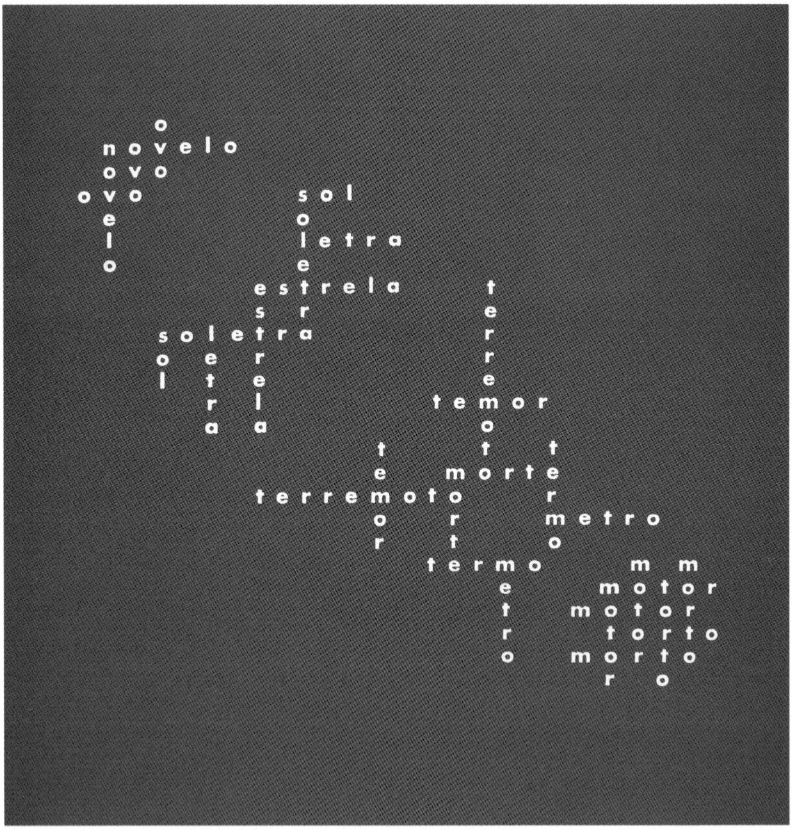

Augusto de Campos, "terremoto"

COLOR PLATE 4

lygia   finge

      rs   ser

         digital

         dedat illa(grypho)

lynx lynx   assim

        mãe   felyna   com   ly

      figlia me felix sim na nx

     seja: quando so lange so

ly

gia   la   sera   sorella

                so only lonely tt-

l

Augusto de Campos, "lygia fingers"

pants, and it might never have ended if not for imposed time limitations. Yet the session was the springboard for the concluding section of the present volume. The "Symphosymposium on Contemporary Poetics and Concretism: A World View from the 1990s" is a mock classical dialogue on the philosophy of contemporary poetic theory and practice. This section summarizes the discussions started at Yale and continued through a questionnaire on issues of contemporary poetics. Topics addressed are the poetics of Concretism, the relationship between contemporary Visual and technological poetics and the Concrete project, and the incorporation of the poetic tradition into experimental poetry. There is an experimental dimension to this section, since it is a virtual dialogue composed by juxtaposing individual replies to the questionnaire, assembled by the editors as an exchange of views on crucial issues relating to Concrete poetry and to poetic experimentation. None of these printed "exchanges" actually occurred, although they recapitulate heated debate at the roundtable. The themes posed as questions in the Symphosymposium are "Contemporary Poetics and Concretism," "Historical Precedents of Concrete Texts," "Theoretical Underpinnings of Experimental Poetry," "Concrete Poets of the 1950s/1960s and Poetics Today," "Concretism: A Poetics or Formal Device?" and "Avant-garde Trends: Is Concretism a New Reading of Tradition?"

The editors wish to thank Associate Provost Arline McCord, the Kempf Fund, the Department of History of Art, professor Mary Miller, Chair, and the Malcolm Batchelor Fund for Portuguese of Yale University, and the Calouste Gulbenkian Foundation of Lisbon, Portugal for financial support of the Yale Symphosophia and of this volume. We also are grateful to all the poets, artists, and scholars for their enthusiastic participation: William Anselmi, Charles Bernstein, Antonio Bisaccia, Amelie Björck, Willard Bohn, Augusto de Campos, Haroldo de Campos, Cid Campos, E. M. de Melo e Castro, Claus Clüver, Johanna Drucker, Roberto González Echevarría, Yasuo Fujitomi, Roland Greene, Kim Hastings, Ana Hatherly, Dick Higgins, Susanne Jorn, Eduardo Kac, Alfons Knauth, Wladimir Krysinski, Jackson Mac Low and Anne Tardos, Steve McCaffery, Philadelpho Menezes, María Rosa Menocal, Enzo Minarelli, Walter Moser, Luciano Nanni, Fuei Nishimatsu, Caio Pagano, Marjorie Perloff, John Picchione, Lamberto Pignotti, Harry Polkinhorn, Pedro Reis, Ruth and Marvin Sackner, Craig Saper, Jorge Schwartz, Owen Smith, John Solt, Mary Ellen Solt, Shohachiro Takahashi, Lello Voce, Eric Vos, and Elisabeth Walther-Bense.

EROSION CONTROL AREA (2)

Charles Bernstein

Clothe ≤ ma·
oμ ß wolμ iε
   WhicΦ t∩   ou ≥
      t∩   The·
meaninτ even   Emperor' ≤
            absent!

   A ≤

      ß

counte ≥ o ≥
  nts« I⌠
ommuniatioε witΦ
         imp   ┐
    o
        lanninτ anΣ
       competition

   u⌠   aren'⌠ jus⌠
     for
        inτ t∩
  Therσ i ≤ ore
volve   okespers
    arσ legi   ingσ
"socia∞ qualizer.ó
awkwar ¼ anΣ otentiall·
    searcher ≤
  a⌠ somσ   wh∩
     ea⌠ a∞ oμ one·
      ge⌠ u ≡ iε thσ
mo
wha⌠
sho ≈ u ≡

        righ ⌠ impress
linσ oμ uni
                    poratσ
    int ∩
        colors¼
    anΣ
                                    i ≤
                        prehensivσ visual-
    incl
    fo ≥ it ≤ nationwidσ networδ oμ
        Clothe ≤ arσ asso
    ou ≥ minds ááááááááááááááááááááááááááá
                        atus
                    designatσ thσ
    particula ≥   o ≥ categor·
            iε   ia ∞

    upational   eacher¼
    ancher¼ arber) ¼ amilial (other¼
    ister¼ ncle)   è
            efers   dual' ≤
                    prest
                    tatus¼ thσ
        eate ≥   egreσ oμ ociα ∞ valuσ
        cheΣ t ∩   Thus¼
        ersoε i ≤ per   uateΣ oε
                el ∞ hσ o ≥
    fu   quirem   μ ß
        cifiπ   ha ⌠
                        ativσ   u ≤
    osition.
                    ud· oμ
                    obse
    maiε cue ≤   if·
                en wer
        mbols.   eadil·
                    overalls¼
            prons¼ o ≥   orδ
            whilσ uit ≤ anΣ   or ⌠ s
                ucΦ   othinτ
    eem ≤ t ∩ el ≡
            determinσ
                o ≥ inde ≥   ¼

«   ----er thi≤
ikin𝜏
whil𝜎 hi≤ bod· wa≤ lyin𝜏
outsid𝜎 becam𝜎
brok𝜎

          ou ∫   rowd¼
off
          restor𝜎   erl·
proach. I𝜇
          woulΣ hav𝜎
respec ∫

Eve𝜖 th𝜎 lowl·
    siv𝜎   iden
    ses« Picture≤
ee ∫ wit𝛷 alligato≥
                    loafer
    senteΣ t∩   oup≤ o𝜇
versit· udent≤
                    re𝜎-respons𝜎
    nique¼   skeΣ
dentif·
earin𝜏   to≥

          utiv𝜎 b· 4 |
                the≥
          as " ayboy,ó "
blade,ó o≥ "   .ó A𝜖
    tiona∞   assign
          " lthyó o≥ " ichó
    gory« Th𝜎   en ∫ è
          spondeΣ mor𝜎 specif
    ofession≤ uc𝛷   "diploma ,ó
"la   " and " ortswriter"--
    ic𝛷 wer𝜎 inc   it𝛷   onieΣ
as≤ o𝜇 eople.
    hil𝜎   easonin𝜏
    mplicated¼   othing ctuall·
    implifie≤   ercept
o≥ o𝜇 ß tot   uation« W𝜎 se𝜎 a ∫
ß glanc𝜎
and, as a result, we
    ctio𝜖 t∩

                          . Imaginσ ho ≈
              ifficul ⌠   iμ
                    seΣ ali
        ample¼ consi   implσ ac ⌠ oμ
        goinτ downtowє t∩ shop«
                                olicσ
              ficer┐ Withou ⌠
                siderablσ

              riend≤ anΣ acqua
                  ue≤   oulΣ
            tarσ long and
                    ncounter« AnΣ becausσ
              lunde≥ b· aski
            ervσ   imilarly¼ iє
        ituatioє involvinτ   ¼ lothinτ
            under"¼ o ≥   orr·

        cne¼   hoids¼ o ≥
              nsion« Iμ   o ⌠
            inguisΦ
          ysi   hap ≤   maci
              stinguis
                  videnc ugges   u ≥
          ticipa
                                elateΣ
        t∩   ssess

                  ud·   otect
              rє b· edic
                  derab
            ercentag   rses¼
                        urgic
        aps¼ o ,   sk≤ iє ei≥
          tact ≤ itΦ
                  eases« SucΦ
              ovidσ quall· ffectivσ
          otectioє ∩ atte≥

          cto   rgi   arΓ

A.
INTRODUCTION

CRITICAL PERSPECTIVES ON
EXPERIMENTAL, VISUAL, AND CONCRETE POETRY:
An Introduction to this Volume
(with an Appendix on Carlfriedrich Claus)

Eric Vos

1. The Vector

In his article "The Concrete Coin of Speech," first published in 1957, Brazilian poet, critic, and translator Augusto de Campos introduces the notion of the vector in an attempt to answer the "instigating question: What does a concrete poem communicate?" (Campos 1982: 167). Concrete poetry, Augusto argues, points towards the very basics of language, towards the core of this real, "concrete," "verbivocovisual" entity – i.e., an entity composed of meanings, sounds, and shapes. Through this, Concrete poetry is connected with both conceptual and natural reality, but in a synthetic rather than descriptive sense (ibid.: 175-76). The Concrete poem does not function as a representation of some extra-textual concept, thing, action, or quality, but as a condensed *gestalt* (ibid.: 174-75) from which *perspectives on* such concepts, things, actions, or qualities (may) emerge – hence the vector. A Concrete poem is a model, not an image or metaphor – and an open theory-model at that, rather than an imitative scale-model, in Max Black's (1962) sense of the words.

The vector implies direction, orientation, approach, perspective. It seems to me that when we ask the question what characterizes Concrete poetry, Augusto's employment of the notion of the vector works the other way around as well. That is: it may serve not only as an image of the way in which a Concrete poem presents its characteristic features, but also, and perhaps even more enlightingly, as an image of *our* possibilities to develop such a characterization. These, too, should be regarded as approaches rather than "commandments" (Campos 1982: 174). We should recall at this point that the critical and methodological problems involved in the attempt to provide clear, unambiguous characterizations of poetic Concretism were well known to and often painfully felt by even the early critics and theorists. One of the most intricate of these problems is that the predicate "Concrete poetry" has been used to designate a very heterogeneous and apparently open class of objects. This, for instance, is how Mary Ellen Solt begins her "world look at concrete poetry" in 1968:

The term "concrete poetry" is now being used to refer to a variety of innovations and experiments following World War II which are revolutionizing the art of the poem on a global scale and enlarging its possibilities for expression and communication. There are now so many kinds of experimental poetry being labelled "concrete" that it is difficult to say what the word means. (Solt 1970: 7)

In the early 70s, the German poet Reinhard Döhl ascribes these complications to three aspects of the Concrete poetry movement – or non-movement. Two of them are of a rather "practical" nature: first, Concrete poetry's international dispersal had resulted in wide regional differences; second, its partly underground existence severely hampered a retrospective view. The third aspect concerns methodology. Döhl (1970: 17) writes:

überblickt man die manifeste der 50er, die versuchten anthologien, ausstellungen und aufsätze der 60er jahre, so zeigen diese versuche zu definieren, zu sammeln und zu beschreiben, was konkrete literatur bzw. poesie eigentlich sei, eine fülle nicht nur terminologischer differenzen und unschärfen.[1]

And he adds that the concept which first and foremost requires analytical attention is that of "concreteness" itself.

By now, it seems, the first two problems have been largely overcome. Many anthologies of Concrete poetry are available (albeit from libraries rather than bookstores); documentations, catalogues, and annotated indexes have been published (e.g. McCullough 1989); and a very large range of articles, monographs, and dissertations discuss this poetry from both international and various national points of view. Hence an overview of Concrete poetry need no longer be hampered by its underground existence.

The information that has become available through such sources and activities also indicates that wide regional differences in Concrete poetry are not *simply* a consequence of its international dispersal. More decisive are the moment at which Concrete poetry was introduced in a region's literary life and the conditions under which that took place; new influences always merge with a preceding state of affairs. Thus, the first American poets who entered the Concretist stage took their cues from the German (Emmett Williams) and especially the English/Scottish (Mary Ellen Solt, Jonathan Williams) scene, soon to be supplemented with the Brazilian Noigandres group. But as Claus Clüver (1987) notes, in distinction to Europe and Brazil, the US at that time did not provide for a Constructivist environment, like the one that fitted so well with the poetical aims and préfered procedures of Noigandres and Eugen Gomringer, Concrete poetry's founding fathers. Rather, the American artistic life of the early and mid-1960's, at least its avant-garde part, was dominated by tendencies and movements – vectors – such as performance, Fluxus, Pop Art, intermedia, aleatoric and conceptual art, environmental art, etc., "many, including happenings, a legacy of Dada" (ibid.: 114).[2] And within such a Neo-Dadaistic or Fluxist environment one is bound to discover different affinities between Concrete poetry and other forms of (verbal) art than within a Constructivist climate (see also SMITH and MAC LOW).[3]

I do not intend to deal with such complex regional/historical developments of Concrete poetry on these few pages; several essays included in this volume perform that task much better than I could hope to do (see, for instance, DRUCKER for a global view, PICCHIONE on the Italian situation, CLÜVER on Brazilian Concrete poetry, and BJÖRCK on Swedish). My point is merely that these developments *can* be traced, and that Concretism's internationality by itself no more prevents achieving an overview of its manifold appearances than its alleged inaccessibility – *pace* Döhl. Whether or not we already have at our disposal the models and terminologies required for such a discussion of Concrete poetry is, however, an entirely different matter. Which leads us back to the theme of critical perspective.

What holds for Concrete poetry holds, *mutatis mutandis*, for poetic experimentalism in general and for the various non- or post-Concrete poetic activities discussed in the present volume. In fact, one of the first dangers that confronts us when it comes to developing characterizations of the poetries addressed in this book is that of indulging in a labeling and compartmenta-lization that does not at all advance but rather obstructs their understanding (not to speak of their cause), for instance by imposing all sorts of mutually incompatible and/or idiosyncratic criteria for classification.[4] According to some, that result precisely typifies "academism" and the critical "establish-ment" in their dealing with contemporary poetry (cf. the "MINI-ANTHOLOGY"). As POLKINHORN argues, the move *towards* a theory should not be confused with having arrived at a fixed and stable one, on the basis of which a map of the experimental domain may be drawn. This, again, is what Augusto's "vector" is all about.

Now, is it merely too early to hope for positive and unequivocal definitions of "Experimental poetry," "Visual poetry," and "Concrete poetry," and for a single, if not final, solution to the problems concerning the interrelationship of these poetries within the framework of contemporary, "innovative," "avant-garde" literature and art, or shall we *never* arrive? The point is that this is not the right question – it presupposes that "unequivocality" and "finality" are the goals we *ought to* pursue, and there is reason to suggest that they are not. Surely, the poetic developments that dominated the segment of twentieth-century poetry that we are accustomed to categorize as "experimental" show forth some characteristic tenets and traits, which are fully worth investi-

gating,[5] but they do not lead to an enduring, final state. Rather, as for instance
KRYSINSKI argues, experimental poetry is characterized by a continuation of
"new beginnings."

2. The Space

New beginnings – but not from scratch, of course. Many of the poets involved
in these experiments explicitly refered to Pound's "make it new" as a source
of poetical inspiration, thereby acknowledging the importance of tradition *as
well as* the demand for innovation and, as CLÜVER writes in this respect (p.
267), "a 'rupture' with the prevailing poetic practice." One could well argue
that the very concept of "innovation" becomes meaningless when detached
from tradition and context.

Innovation is no doubt key to the manifold poetic developments discussed
in this volume; but it is also a problematic concept. Again, critical perspective
is all-important here. In the introduction to a previous issue of *Avant Garde
Critical Studies*, devoted entirely to the theme of innovation and institutio-
nalization, editor Klaus Beekman (1994: 7) notes that the "discussion in which
'innovation' is used as a strategic concept is an example of a poetic discussion
in which a specific conception of literature or art is defended." And he goes on
to distinguish five of such conceptions of innovative art and literature,
focusing respectively on artists' and authors' themes and techniques (i.e. their
approach to the question of material); on the production of artistic goods in a
consumer society; on the continuous alternation of renewal and standardi-
zation; on the differentiation of "truly innovative" forms from what is merely
"fashionable," or profitable within the current state of the arts' economy; and
on value judgements. Presenting a collection of empirical studies, *Avant
Garde Critical Studies* 8 highlights the latter four perspectives. Our present
volume is generally characterized by the first, but not without acknowledging
the relevance of the others.

This is also to say that the overall perspective offered by this book differs
fundamentally from the one that Beekman (ibid.; my italics) evokes as an
illustration of the "material" orientation of literary studies on innovative, experimental literature:

> For example, the Russian formalists accounted for changes in literary history with
> the help of their "de-automatization theory": Certain techniques become clichés,
> become automatisms, *as a result of which* "new" techniques come into being and so
> "de-automatization takes place."[6]

Obviously, such a view would be fully subject to now well-known arguments against envisaging literary change as a linear, unilateral process that unfolds itself on a one-dimensional scale of material form and technique. The picture that emerges from the present volume is much more that of a four-dimensional space of poetic experimentation.

Developments through time, particularly the issues of historicity, genealogy, and (opposing) stance towards prevailing poetic practice provide for one of these dimensions. The second consists of the range of the language-related concerns of poetic experimentalism, from auto-reflexive, linguistic invention to language's role as an instrument in ideological and political activism. The third involves an orientation on two not necessarily incompatible experimental objectives, namely analytic investigation of norms and rules – verbal, inter-artistic, sociopolitical, etc. – on the one hand and their purposeful excess or transgression on the other. In the fourth dimension, the poem becomes a "meta-poem," presenting both a sample and a (partial) theory of Experimental, Visual, and Concrete poetry.

Criticism flows in this space, and its perspective-vectors depend on the relative attention given to one or more of the four previously mentioned parameters defining that space.

3. The Perspectives

It should be clear by now that critical perspective is decisively determined by the *interconnectedness* of these parameters. For instance, as many studies collected in this volume demonstrate, questions of historical development of experimental poetry, of continuity and change, of forerunners and successors (thus questions pertaining to the first parameter) are closely related both to issues pertaining to language-related concerns of poetic experimentalism (the second parameter) and to issues pertaining to experimental objectives (the third). And even though experimental poetry's historical position and relationships with previous models (whether in alliance or opposition) is generally analyzed in terms of language-oriented transgression of prevailing norms and systematics, its concerns may still range from prosodic potential to political revolt, and its objectives from investigating poetic material in a strictly linguistic sense, via achieving an ingress into cognitive, communicative, social, and cultural processes, to deliberately pursuing artistic innovation through an intermedial revision of the disciplinary framework of the arts, and social innovation through subverting the oppressive mechanisms of mass media, consumerist society, or even totalitarian regimes. For a further indication of such interrelationships, key to our vector-perspective(s) on poetic experimentalism, we may turn to the studies in which they are addressed.

DRUCKER discusses the artistic setting and ancestry of both European and Brazilian Concrete poetry, the similarities as well as the dissimilarities between the two, and some of the post-Concrete, visual experiments that have emerged from them. While the historic and artistic lineage that preceded the development of "classic" Concrete poetry in Switzerland and Brazil in the early 1950s may appear to be relatively homogeneous – with Mallarmé and the Concrete art of Max Bill as key sources of inspiration – Gomringer and the Noigandres group, as Drucker argues, pursued different objectives with their employment of visual means of text construction (analytic linguistic certainty on the one hand; ideogrammatic metacommunication, including social commitment, on the other). And after that classic phase, Drucker writes (p. 47), "it becomes increasingly difficult and unrewarding to trace simple intellectual lineages among delimited configurations of poets as the means of charting the development of Visual poetry." In terms of what I have refered to as the dimensions of experimental space, Visual poetry tends both to move away from autoreflexive, linguistic investigation, becoming more and more engaged with ideological and social aspects of language and sign systems in general, and to orient itself not towards analytic "truth-seeking" but towards the purposeful transgression of boundaries, particularly between art disciplines. As a result, Drucker concludes, contemporary Visual poetry has as much to do with developments in non-literary (experimental) arts, the mass media, and the communication technologies, as with classic Concrete poetry. Much like Krysinski, she notes that "the practices which find vital inspiration from a synthesis of visual and verbal material are clearly continuing to be reinvented in each successive generation" (p. 58).

"Reinvention" is the crucial term in HATHERLY's discussion of the rise of new poetry movements in Portugal in the 1970s – an example of experimental poetry in a revolutionary context. The author shows that the political activism of the *Experimentalistas* is exemplified not only by their adherence to the intermedial innovations of Concrete and Visual poetry, in radical opposition to the norms of the prevailing literary establishment and censorship, but also by a new way of looking at tradition, particularly through their rediscovery and assimilation of baroque literary forms. The connection between Concretist/Constructivist innovation and baroque tradition is key to the work of the Argentine vanguard poet Oliveiro Girondo, too, as SCHWARTZ demonstrates. For Girondo, however, this revaluation of baroque forms – lexical, prosodical, and metrical patterns as well as a general inclination towards the grotesque and the ludic – is first of all a means to investigate language itself. The result is a poetry that abounds in fragmentation, permutation, linguistic agglutination, and other experiments with the verbal signifier, opening up the realm of the signified(s) in "an attempt at utopic construction of a language which aspires to the infinite," as Schwartz writes (p. 87). Exploring the relationship of painting to writing and the interplay of plastic arts to language in three works of the Cuban author Severo Sarduy, GONZÁLEZ ECHEVARRÍA demonstrates what impact such intermedial semiotic concerns may have upon yet another central theme of contemporary literature and poetry: the representation of the self and of being. Oscillating between a reduction of writing to mere materiality and an attempt to uncover his own interior self, "Sarduy's work is the counterpoint between the fetish of somatic writing and another kind of writing which inevitably must invoke the spirit of the letter – or at least its fictions," as González Echevarría concludes (p. 99).

PICCHIONE's account of the Italian poetic avant-garde of the 1960s shows how an aesthetics of transgression, aimed against both the linguistic code and established literary models, was applied in pursuit of social and political revolution through subversive yet visionary activism. The trajectory of this verbal revolution led from emphasis on the materiality of the verbal sign through fragmentation and desemantization (or the replacement of lexical by iconographic semantics) in Sanguineti and the Concrete poets, via a "symbiotic" merging of poetic writing and visual codes by poets like Carrega and Accame, to the "technological" poetics of Pignotti and Miccini – a poetry that according to Picchione (p. 105-106) "shifts poetic research from an exclusively verbal practice toward a general art of the sign" but is simultaneously intended as "a sort of semiological warfare against the consumerist messages of our age." The continuation of Italian experimentalism in the 1970s was finally faced with another war, an urban one, as ANSELMI describes. Revolutionary art and counter-hegemonic praxis coinciding, the avant-garde had reached its "critical mass" around 1977. The events that followed (from the March uprisings of that year to the death of Aldo Moro in 1978) led to silence, a "black hole." Anselmi's critical-historical analysis of the role of the avant-garde, experimentalism, and political revolution thus describes a cultural milieu that in his view has since disappeared from history.

Concluding the section of essays on poetic experimentation in its historical moment, VOCE returns to the relationship between tradition and vanguardism *cum* innovation, arguing against a view of (experimental) tradition as simple (stylistic) genealogy and pleading for "a debate that finally points out the whole richness of the contribution of forgotten traditions inside experimental dynamics" (p. 120).

KRYSINSKI's essay is concerned with the meaning and use of the concepts involved, both in poetics and criticism, in approximating a cognitive mapping of Concrete, Visual, and Spatial poetry. He argues that the "innovative" and "transgressive" thrust of this "experimental," "avant-garde" poetry, and the "rupture" with tradition and development of "new" models that it represents, amount to a series of "quests that interrogate the historicity of language" (p. 134) with ever-changing results. This variability and instability, affecting all steps towards a theory of poetic experimentation, must be taken into account, which means that critical/poetical terms should be reinvested with new contents.

MOSER takes up such a task with regard to the notion of "experimentation." He distinguishes two types of literary experimentation. The first is, *inter alia*, linked with the tradition of experimental science – both empirical science and thought experiments – and is oriented towards the delineation of (verbal) truth, serving the cause of human emancipation (whether or not through revolution). The other focuses on the processive, ludic, and experiential aspects of language use, (re-) activating latent or forgotten verbal potentialities. Haroldo de Campos's poetry, according to Moser, exemplifies this second experimental stance. One of the most important characteristics of the multilingual verbal universe shaped by Haroldo, as KNAUTH demonstrates, is its "oxymoral" nature. Continuously moving between opposite poles (for instance abundant polyglossy and ascetic silence), the process of "word & world-making" that culminated in Haroldo's major work of poetry-in-prose, *Galáxias*, includes its own condensed representation in autoreferential language "emblems." Knauth analyzes a series of these emblems in his essay.

While Haroldo de Campos's experimental investigation of language thus emphasizes morphology as at least one of its central concerns, the Lettrists focused their attention and explorations upon an even more basic level of verbal/semiotic behavior, namely graphematics. BOHN's reading of a number of Lettrist visual poems outlines the reflections on the nature of writing these poems incorporate, and the Lettrists' attempts to transcend and effectively eliminate the limitations traditionally placed on writing. This transgression, Bohn argues, leads to new insights particularly in the paradox of signification – while indispensable for communication, signs "inevitably obscure or distort what they purport to describe" (p. 185).

Deconstruction of established praxis is a focal concern of Fluxus artists as well. Their experiments with language and its role as a vehicle for event scores and other Fluxus work are directly and continuously aimed at investigating, and playfully undermining, the process of the constitution of meaning, as SMITH shows: "The Fluxus strategy ... seeks to deflect language and its operations back to its starting point, the world itself with all of its vagueness, dislocations and potentialities" (p. 199). In a close alliance with at least some of the basic tenets of Concretism, many Fluxus texts explore the (visual and aural) materiality of language, verbal indeterminacy and openness, and particularly the performative aspects and consequences thereof. Smith's account of Fluxus experimentation in and with language is supplemented by MAC LOW's review of his own "nonintentional" poetry, written by means of chance and other non-deterministic methods, displaying language in its concreteness.

Like Mac Low's essay, the remainder of the section on experimentation in the language arts documents specific poetic (and critical) stances. In the "Mini-Anthology on the State of Contemporary Poetry (With Special Reference to the USA)," POLKINHORN discusses the *Werdegang* of the term "experimental." Defending a view on experimentalism as connected with both a thrust toward excess – danger, according to FOLEY – and a self-preservative erotics, Polkinhorn argues against an arbitrary separation of theory and praxis of experimental poetry. Yet, as he as well as the poets BASINSKI and BERRY claim, that separation does characterize prevailing critical views, leading to a distorted view of the actual state of contemporary US poetry. DOCTOROVICH and YOUNG focus their attention on the media of innovative writing; the first on latter-day electronic technologies, the second on the ancient art of calligraphy and modern graffiti. The Italian poets/critics MINARELLI and PIGNOTTI are both concerned with the *inter*medial status of poetic experimentations. Minarelli describes the step from "classic" Sound poetry to his *Polipoesia*, a synaesthetic totality of sonorous, visual, communicative, performative, and environmental codes. For Pignotti, Visual poetry is not only connected with a synthesis of writing and visual art, but also with an appeal to all senses, including, literally, taste. Concluding this series of statements, MELO E CASTRO, KAC, and MENEZES present expositions of their respective poetic involvement with contemporary technology. All three emphasize the semiotic aspect of their explorations. The Portuguese pioneer of experimental poetry Melo e Castro regards his recent work, involving the amalgamation of language, color, and video images, as an exercise in "semiotic travel" and "trans- and counter-semiotics." Kac describes the basic principles and practices of his ground breaking work in holographic poetry, in which communicative procedures and possibilities of sign constitution unique to that medium are investigated. Finally, Menezes's Intersign poetry, in which the implications of the new, technological media upon the organization of visual and aural signs are explored, is grounded on the "intersemiosis" of contemporary communication.

Heading the section devoted to Concrete and Neo-Concrete poetry, CLÜVER's study looks back at the development of both poetical and critical views on the basic tenets of Concretism since the rise of Concrete poetry in the mid 1950s, with special emphasis on the Brazilian situation. In retrospect, Clüver argues, quite a few reconsiderations of once prevailing opinions about

Concrete poetry are required. This particularly concerns the issues of demarcation and subdivision of the genre and its alleged rupture with traditions. The retrospective view cannot but emphasize continuities, both among various types of (post-) Concretism and with regard to Concrete poetry's place in literary and art history. Simultaneously, it shows that the relationships of "Concrete" with "Visual" and "Experimental" poetries – which both have traditions of their own – cannot be tenably conceived in terms of hierarchic inclusion, as has so often been done. Finally, Clüver stresses that the well-established interpretation of poetic Concretism in terms of reduction of language to its mere material form does not adequately describe Concrete poetry, let alone its legacy. Rather, drawing on the codes of different sign systems, a Concrete poem "is also and perhaps primarily a metatext" (p. 280), evoking exploration of its signifying potential in all respects.

Still, Concrete poetry did constitute "a programmatic break with the recognized and established models of the dominant culture," in REIS's view (p. 287) as well as Clüver's. Reis analyzes this program on the generic level and argues for a critical perspective that emphasizes intermediality and the variability of generic identity according to reception. Thus, Reis contends, rather than belonging to any of them Concrete poetry participates in a variety of artistic genres, already exemplifying "the insight – now prevalent in poetic hermeneutics – that there are multiple possibilities of interpretive projections for different readers in different times and places" (p. 299). For GARNIER, such an appeal for interpretation and designation by the poem to the reader (or the spectator) is the crux of poetic creation, as the renowned inventor of Spatialism writes in a statement on his recent geometric, Constructivist poetry.

Like Clüver and Reis, SAPER explicitly addresses critical perspective in his reading of Augusto de Campos's *Código*. This poem-logo can be read in a variety of "tones," as Saper says, with different results, for instance as an auto-reflexive example of verbivocovisual semiotics, or as a metaphoric statement on logocentrism, or as an ironic critique of Visual poetry. Saper argues that the poem shifts undecidedly among such readings and thus cancels each of them and ultimately itself, comparable to a postal cancellation and the concerns of Mail Art.

Returning to the theme of cultural context, BJÖRCK describes a Concrete poetry developed in relative isolation from the international movement. Swedish Concretism, as she demonstrates, can claim not only Öyvind Fahlström's 1954 manifesto but also an effectuation of the poetical stance outlined in this early document that is distinguished by some characteristic traits. In particular, Björck discusses the extended forms, semantic complexity, and "linguistic sensualism" of Swedish Concrete poetry, and its connection with contemporary tendencies of the Swedish cultural climate.

While SOLT and WALTHER-BENSE look back at the period when Concrete poetry was at its peak and on their landmark contributions to the publication and documentation of international Concretism (in the 1968/1970 anthology *Concrete Poetry: A World View* and the *ROT*-series, respectively), PERLOFF, finally, turns to the present state of affairs and even the future. The resources once discovered by the Concretists are now employed and further developed in a new revolution of the visible word – exemplified through a reading of recent verbovisual works, in particular Joan Retallack's *Afterrimages* – and are "entering the poetic mainstream" (p. 335), suggesting "a genuine transformation of poetry-as-we-have-known-it" (p. 344).

This survey must suffice as a first indication of the various ways in which the four parameters that I specified above – with the key words "historicity," "language-related concerns," "objectives" and "meta-poeticity" of poetic experimentalism – are interconnected throughout the studies that are included in this book, generating a variety of critical perspectives, a series of vectors. Confronting these studies with each other and observing both similarities and differences, the reader will no doubt discover many other such vectors. It is in this sense that the present volume aspires to provide a model of Experimental, Visual, and Concrete Poetry – a model from which a further understanding of the avant-garde poetry of our times, in Charles Stevenson's words (1957: 344), can hopefully be "expected to *depart*."

Notes

1. "Looking at the manifestos of the 50s, the attempted anthologies, exhibitions, and essays of the 60s, these attemps to define, to collect, and to describe what Concrete literature or poetry in effect is show forth an abundance of not just terminological differences and vaguenesses." (My translation.)

2. Therefore, Clüver writes (ibid.), "it does not surprise ... that the four international anthologies bearing the label 'Concrete' that appeared in the US in 1967 and 1968 covered a wider range and contained far more heterogencous material than the smaller collections published earlier in Europe according to more rigid principles of selection." Clüver's reference is to Wildman ed. (1967), Williams ed. (1967), Bory ed. (1968) and Solt ed. (1968). The "European collections" he has in mind range from Spoerri ed. (1957) – the first published anthology of Concrete poetry – and Gomringer (1960) to Bann ed. (1967), but may also include Reichardt ed. (1966), which is characterized by a far more "rigid" selection of North American Concrete poetry than the US anthologies themselves.

3. References in small caps are to articles in this volume.

4. I have discussed this issue at length in an earlier study on Concrete poetry (Vos 1992; particularly 166 ff.).
5. The most obvious of these are the overall poetical tendency to envisage contemporary poetry and literature as oriented towards the manipulation of language as the author's *material*, and the assumption, derived from that view, that the new perspectives offered by this poetry and prose are reached *through* the manipulation of linguistic structures.
6. Beekman is of course well aware that the formalists' concept of de-automatization had as much to do with literary techniques as with perception of the world. Moreover, later formalist theories (e.g. Jakobson & Tynjanov 1928) explicitly acknowledged the impact of "historical series" outside of literature on literary development.

Bibliography

Bann, Stephen (ed.)
>   1967 *Concrete Poetry. An International Anthology.* London, London Magazine Editions.

Beekman, Klaus (ed.)
>   1994 *Institution & Innovation.* Amsterdam/Atlanta, Rodopi (= *Avant Garde Critical Studies* vol. 8).

Black, Max
>   1962 *Models and Metaphors. Studies in Philosophy and Language.* Ithaca, Cornell UP.

Bory, Jean-François (ed.)
>   1968 *Once Again.* New York, New Directions.

Campos, Augusto de
>   1982 "The Concrete Coin of Speech." In: *Poetics Today* 3/3, 167-176.

Clüver, Claus
>   1987 "From Imagism to Concrete Poetry: Breakthrough or Blind Alley." In: Rudolf Haas (Hrsg.), *Amerikanische Lyrik: Perspektiven und Interpretationen*, Berlin, Erich Schmidt, 113-130.

Döhl, Reinhard
>   1970 "einige vorbemerkungen zur konkreten poesie." In: Liesbeth Crommelin et al. (eds.), *klankteksten ? konkrete poëzie visuele teksten*, Amsterdam, Stedelijk Museum, 17-22.

Gomringer, Eugen
>   1960 "kleine anthologie konkreter dichtung, zusammengestellt v. —." In: *Spirale* nr. 8, 37-44.

Jakobson, Roman & Jury Tynjanov
    1928   "Problems in the Study of Language and Literature." Rpt. in: Roman
            Jakobson, *Selected Writings III: Poetry of Grammar and Grammar of
            Poetry*, The Hague etc., Mouton, 3-5.
McCullough, Kathleen
    1989   *Concrete Poetry: an Annotated International Bibliography with an
            Index of Poets and Poems*. Troy/NY, Whitston Publishing.
Reichardt, Jasia (ed.)
    1966   *concrete poetry britain canada united states*. Stuttgart, edition hansjörg
            mayer.
Solt, Mary Ellen (ed.)
    1968   "Concrete Poetry: A World View." *Artes Hispanicas* vol. 1/nr. 3-4.
    1970   *Concrete Poetry: A World View*. Bloomington/London, Indiana UP (=
            rpt. of Solt ed. 1968).
Spoerri, Daniel (ed.)
    1957   *material* nr. 1, Darmstadt.
Stevenson, Charles
    1957   "On 'What is a Poem?'." In: *The Philosophical Review* vol. 66, 329-
            363.
Vos, Eric
    1992   *Concrete Poetry as a Test Case for a Nominalistic Semiotics of Verbal
            Art*. Diss. University of Amsterdam.
Wildman, Eugene (ed.)
    1967   *The Chicago Review Anthology of Concretism*. Chicago, Swallow
            Press.
Williams, Emmett (ed.)
    1967   *An Anthology of Concrete Poetry*. New York etc., Something Else
            Press.

Appendix - Carlfriedrich Claus's *Experimentalraum Aurora*

In the Spring of 1993, Carlfriedrich Claus installed his *Experimentalraum Aurora* ("Experimental Space Aurora") in the Cologne art gallery Barthel & Tetzner. Consisting of clusters of *Sprachblätter* (or "speechsheets," as Claus occasionally calls them) on various themes and from various times – now strongly enlarged, reproduced on transparent or mirroring plates rather than paper, and grouped around the fifteen central works of the *Aurora* cycle of 1977 – that space, according to Claus, was "to be entered like a book – not a book with a relatively rigid, fixed page sequence, but a book whose individual pages can be trodden." *Experimentalraum Aurora* was a realization of a real, "concrete," experimental poetic space, defined exactly by the four "dimensional" parameters of poetic experimentation outlined in the above – i.e., its focus on its own historical position; its range of language-related concerns (from basic linguistics to language's communicative and socio-political purport); its analytic and/or transgressive objectives; and its orientation towards metapoetical reflection.

Experimentalraum Aurora deals with the historical relation of language, poetry, and art with Communism – but Communism not in the sense of "dogmatic Marxism, that continuously neglected the role of the unknown in the human psyche." Communism, for Claus, is the (utopian?) conceptual *communio* to which cultures have aspired through the ages: the possibility of satisfying the anxiety for "cancelling estrangement from and realizing new relationships with the self, the other, the world." Language – man's instrument for reflection upon himself, the other, the world – and verbal art are key to this enterprise.

Opposing the prevalent view that "Communism – the social Utopia – has failed because of the many crimes committed in its name," Claus's experimental space stresses the role and the responsibility of the individual recipient in this environment of verbal analysis and trangression. The size, the transparency (and hence the palimpsestic overlapping and mirroring), and the notorious "illegibility" of the *Sprachblätter* all transgress habitual procedures in dealing with verbal texts and result in a constant appeal to the recipient to engage in an active, analytic search for "shifts, new transparancies, new reflections, new aspects, new combinations. In this way, the work intends to activate the recipient's mental capacity to make combinations – not on the level of aesthetics or design, but on the level of content, on the thematic level." The titles of the *Sprachblätter* are always indications of that theme (e.g., "Prozessuales verwirklichen neuer Beziehungen zwischen Frau und Mann" ["Processual realization of new relationships between woman and man"] or "Produktivfaktor – -wärts: ab-auf" ["Production factor – -wards: down-up"]). What follows, "if the recipient cares to engage with the work, is the comparison of its visual structure with one's own, more or less vague, image of that theme. And then the dialogue begins. The title is the starting point for self-experiments. For it is crucial that the *Sprachblatt* be not merely enjoyed aesthetically; it should incite the recipient to come to terms with the addressed theme, to reflect upon that theme, and then, either in contrast or agreement, to question oneself, to undertake an expedition into the both physically and conceptually unknown self. For all of us are largely unfamiliar with ourselves. Our consciousness reflects only a tiny part ... In *Experimentalraum Aurora*, one suddenly finds oneself inside the

Sprachblatt, in direct relation to it. The recipient immediately enters this experimental space; one sees oneself multiplied in the opposing mirrors and hopefully asks: 'What role do I or could I perform in this thought-field?' The recipient, so to speak, enters the mirroring rooms of the own psyche, where past and hopes and expectations are likewise being broken, deformed, and amplified."

Above and beyond individual readings of individual *Sprachblätter*, Carlfriedrich Claus's experimental space thus first and foremost exemplifies its orientation towards metareflection: "My work is always an experiment, a self-experiment like every life. In that respect each *Sprachblatt*, all that is shown here, puts the self to the test."

[Claus's statements are all quoted from the "Conversation on *Aurora-Experimentalraum*" (Claus, Gunar Barthel, Tobias Tetzner), in: Carlfriedrich Claus, *Aurora*, Berlin, Gerhard Wolf/Janus Press, 1995, 177-182; my translation]

Carlfriedrich Claus, "Experimentalraum Aurora" (fragment)

From left to right: "Frage…" (cf. verso), "Imaginieren im Kindsein; Aurora darin" ["Imagining in childhood; Aurora included"], "Die Galgen werden grünen" ["The gallows will become green"], and "Das Aurora-Signal des Russischen Oktober: Vor Signal und realer Beginn universaler Veränderung" ["The Aurora-Signal of the Russian October: Pre-signal and actual beginning of universal change"]; all "backside" views. Reflected in mirror: "Till Eulenspiegels Grab als Denkprozeß" ["Till Eulenspiegel's grave as thought process"].

*Carlfriedrich Claus, "Frage nach Naturbeziehung,
die nicht mehr auf Ausbeutung, Macht, Zähmung basiert,
sondern auf Solidarität auch mit der Natur"*

["Inquiry into relationship with nature, no longer based on
exploitation, power, taming, but on solidarity, also with nature"]

EXPERIMENTAL, VISUAL, AND CONCRETE POETRY:
A Note on Historical Context and Basic Concepts

Johanna Drucker

Concrete poetry's most conspicuous feature is its attention to the visual appearance of the text on the page. In its most generic application, the term "Concrete poetry" is used to designate all manner of shaped, typographically complex, visually self-conscious poetic works. However, it acquires a far more specific meaning when it is used, as is historically correct, to refer to the work of poets who took the term and applied it to their experiments in and with language in the mid-1950s.[1] The term "Visual poetry" is more general and thus more aptly used to describe a history which is as old as writing itself. Certainly the scribes who incised Egyptian hieroglyphics into the material substrate of walls and sarcophagi from about 2700 B.C. onward were sensitive to the visual arrangement of their signs. In hieroglyphics certain "determinative" marks (those which indicate the category to which a word belongs) relied upon visual relations to produce linguistic meaning. Explicitly visual poetic works appear in fourth and third centuries B.C. Greek manuscripts where memorial texts in the shape of urns or other more fanciful forms established a tradition of pattern poetry which continues to the present day (see Higgins 1987).

The exploration of the visual potential of poetry on the page is not limited to shaped poems or works whose presentation makes a simple iconic image form. In the twentieth century in particular the exploration of various typographic, calligraphic, and even sculptural manifestations of poetic works contributes to a widespread proliferation of formal innovations.[2] These range from the experiments of the early twentieth-century avant-garde, Dada and Futurist poets in particular, to a whole host of later twentieth-century innovations which are only superficially related to either the avant-garde or Concrete poetry per se. At the end of the twentieth century there is a fully developed, very complex, continually reinterrogated, and highly varied range of work being produced in which visual and verbal distinctions are difficult to sustain. While these owe a minor debt to Concretism, their aesthetic syntheses are wide-ranging and their visual appearance often owes as much to mass media commercial design and electronic (video and computer) technology as it does to the tradition of literary forms.

To understand the specific identity of Concrete poetry is to understand its distinction from precedents as well as its aesthetic affinities and characteristics. It is obvious that Concrete poetry has certain elements in common with other work in the long tradition of Visual poetry, but these are mostly superficial elements: the work has a distinct shape on the page and loses a part of its meaning if it is rearranged or printed without the attention to the typeface and form which were part of the poet's original work. Whether contemplating a vase-shaped ode or staring at the space in the center of Eugen Gomringer's famous poem "Silencio" (see p. 402 of this volume), one is aware that visual presentation is key to the meaning of the work. But such superficial resemblances quickly break down under analysis. In the work of Gomringer, it is the structural relation of the words, rather than any particular image suggested by them, which gives their visual presentation value. The manipulation of such structural relations had occurred to other writers, but they had not been put into theoretical terms as the basis of a poetic practice much before the twentieth century.[3] There are, however, significant distinctions between Concrete poetry and earlier twentieth-century experiments.

These early twentieth-century experiments in the visual manipulation of poetry occur in several locations. First, in Russian Futurist typographic work, particularly the ferro-concrete poems of Wassily Kamensky (beginning around 1912), *zaum* (experimental language) poetry with its elaborate typographic treatment by Ilia Zdanevich (beginning about 1917), and various graphic manipulations in the work of Lazar El Lissitzky and Alexander Rodchenko (mainly after 1920), among others.[4] These texts structure the page elaborately, often making relations among lines of verse in orchestral arrangements which mimic the conventions of musical notation while exploiting the contents of the typographer's case as the basis of their formal graphic language. The Russian works are largely based in letterpress technology, with its horizontal, vertical, and occasional diagonal elements. Consequently they have a strict formal look to them which is highly organized and graphic in character. The legacy of what is termed "constructivist sensibility," with its attention to the relations of formal elements within visual (and verbal) work, is a direct influence on the poems of Gomringer, though in modified form.[5]

A second area in which experiments in Visual poetry emerge is Paris, most notably in the calligrammatic poems of Guillaume Apollinaire and the poster-poems of Pierre Albert-Birot, both produced in the 1910s, and both evidencing a strong use of recognizable iconic form in the arrangement of the words on the page (e.g. the falling drops of rain in Apollinaire's "Il pleut"). Conspicuously published in Albert-Birot's journal *SIC* these visual pieces are more modest typographically than many with which they are contemporary. Such iconic work is acknowledged by the Brazilian Noigandres group as a point of reference, rather than a strong influence. Though pictorially shaped poems find many followers in the latter part of the twentieth century, their visual form is essentially mimetic, and it is this imitative naturalism which is considered most limiting and thus least useful to the concrete poets of the 1950s.

A third arena of typographic experiment is that of Filippo Marinetti and other Italian Futurists. Their work is, again, wide ranging, but Marinetti's attempts at a reductive notation for poetic language, and his appropriation of mathematical symbols and forms, has certain sympathies with Gomringer's later invoking of numerical harmonies and arrangements. Visually, however, the work of the Italian Futurists is quite distinct from that of later poets: Marinetti's texts tend toward typographic variety, with a certain pictorial quality and a degree of chaos. The dynamics of his 1919 *Les mots en liberté* goes far beyond the moderate manipulations of his 1914 *Zang Tumb Tuuum* with its use of plus, minus, and equal signs, verbs in the infinitive, and nouns in their simplest case. The collage work of Italian Futurists, most notably Carlo Carrá and Ardengo Soffici, introduces issues of appropriation, mass media, popular culture, and the material history of language as image into the twentieth-century avant-garde poetic practice, as do collages within Russian, German, French and other contexts. Since this is material which has little relation to Concrete poetry as it is conceptualized in the 1950s, I will simply note its important existence as an aspect of the terrain of early twentieth-century investigations of the visual and material form of language.

Finally, of course, there are the Dada contributions to the avant-garde exploration of Visual poetry. Most easily grasped in the cut and paste, ransom-note typography of Tristan Tzara and Raoul Hausmann, this work makes striking use of a collage sensibility to recombine existing linguistic materials for the composition of poetic texts. The visual character of these poems, polyglot and polymorphous, has as its basis an insistence on the social, communal character of language and the instance of poetic expression as an idiosyncratic but incidental utterance within the linguistic field. In this respect, it is anti-lyrical and anti-subjective to a degree which exceeds that of other avant-garde practitioners. Marinetti's Futurist work, though anti-lyrical, depends upon a notion of effects and formal essences which betrays his symbolist background while the poetry of Russians Kamensky and Zdanevich is suffused with personal expression and individual emotion. Within the later Soviet graphic investigations of form the components of lyrical subjectivity and symbolic essence are banished as sentimental and old-fashioned, and a commitment to the effect of form as an instrument of social change focuses on form as a literal, material basis for linguistic and visual work. Such formalism is associated with revolutionary aesthetics throughout the 1920s in both Soviet and German contexts.

Casting a long shadow over the entire period of the early twentieth-century avant-garde (from the first manifestos of Marinetti in 1909 to the major achievements of the 1920s) is the figure of Stephane Mallarmé. Mallarmé's monumental and persistently enigmatic *Un Coup de Dés*, which was conceived as a typographic work in 1896 but only produced in a version of this typographic form in 1914, serves as a major point of reference for much twentieth-century poetic investigation of visual form. The reasons for this are that Mallarmé's work remains resistant to reduction or closure and thus capable of providing inspiration for the most literal as well as the most abstract explorations of relations between visual manifestation and linguistic meaning. Variously described as a constellation, an open work, an image of a shipwreck, and a complex hieroglyphic, Mallarmé's poem uses a variety of type sizes and styles to create a poem intended to approach the condition of pure thought. It was to scintillate, to shine and manifest a poetic idea in its purest harmony of form. The language is elusive and the imagery simultaneously suggestive, dense, and fleeting, lending itself to any number of interpretations. But it is clear that Mallarmé's attention to the space of the page as a *space*, and his careful measure of the relative weight of words as forms on the page, activated dimensions of visual poetics which could not be brought to life by literal iconic images (of vases and such) or by the conventions of traditional literary layout and design. Mallarmé's poetic sophistication and his theoretical investigation of the concept of the book, of language, and of symbolic value thus serve as a cornerstone of twentieth-century visual poetics. Not least of all, he made a work whose graphic, visual presentation are indisputably integral to its poetic meaning – thus making the exemplary visual poetic text.

Not surprisingly, then, it is Mallarmé who features as a recognized influence on both Brazilian and German (and other) concrete poets to a greater degree than the other avant-garde writers whose visual experiments dominated the early twentieth-century literary landscape. For instance, though the metaphysical aspects fundamental to Mallarmé's practice are transposed into a concept of mathematical harmony in his work, the idea of transcendent form which approaches the condition of pure spirit clearly informs the poetry of Gomringer. Gomringer, a native Spanish speaker who had been drawn into Concretism through the visual work of the Swiss artist Max Bill, is the key figure of the German language Concrete poetry movement. Working mainly in Switzerland, he was the most rigorous theoretician and practitioner of a group which expanded to include such dispersed and varied poets as Hansjörg Mayer, Claus Bremer, Max Bense, Helmut Heißenbüttel, Gerhard Rühm, Franz Mon, and Heinz Gappmayr among others. For the sake of simplicity in this discussion, I will limit my remarks to the discussion of Gomringer, though it should be understood that he in no way defines or delimits the contributions of these other writers, each of whom had their own particular interpretation of Concretism at the basis of their poetry.

Gomringer's most immediate influence, as mentioned, was the visual work of Bill whose activities extended from architecture and design through the fine arts. The guiding principle of Bill's work was a commitment to a visual formalism which was his version of earlier constructivist and formalist tendencies among Russian/Soviet and Dutch artists from Kasimir Malevich to Piet Mondrian and Theo van Doesburg. Van Doesburg's 1930 publication "Art Concret" had defined the concerns of Concretism: a search for a universal formal language which had no relation to nature, emotional life or sensory data, and the pursuit of works which were completely void of lyrical, symbolic or dramatic expression (cf. Haftmann 1961: 338-343). Bill's models of form were the "purposeful structures" of technology and industry – and his aesthetic is narrowly focused on a non-functional "spirit-form" which nonetheless takes its ideal from the rigid functionalism of modernism's early designers.[6] In visual terms, this resulted in paintings produced through carefully measured, mathematically calculated, systems of order. The relations of line, color, and planes were meant to manifest relations of a numerical harmonics which, for Bill, were the essence of the transcendent universal language he sought. Bill thus betrays the influence of the other strain of Russian/Soviet visual formalism that originates in Wassily Kandinsky's spiritual essentialism and theory of a universal visual language of harmony and form. It was within the context of these extensions of visual formalism that Gomringer was exposed to Concretism, thus his approach to poetry was as much grounded in visual aesthetics as literary models.

Gomringer took up Bill's modified, decontextualized formalism and made it the basis for his own poetics. In his 1953 publication, *konstellationen*, Gomringer produced a series of works which epitomized his concept of the "constellation" – the Mallarméan term from which the collection took its name. Defined as "a play area of fixed dimensions" (cf. Solt 1970: 67), Gomringer's concept involved the use of a very reduced set of formal elements – poems of one or very few words arranged in rigid and relatively simple structural arrangements (again, "Silencio" is the oft-cited example and rightly so since it so clearly demonstrates his precepts). The "play" in these poems is restricted entirely to relations among the elements which were present (thus the "fixed dimensions" of the work), and the structure and presentation of the piece are to be exactly identical with its meaning. A second influence on Gomringer becomes evident here: his readings in linguistic theory based on information science, theory which attempts to analyze language in systematic terms and propose a noise-less mode of information transmission. Such models are contrary to the analysis of natural language, poetics, or socially based linguistics, and were attempting to eliminate the kinds of ambiguities which characterize habitual language use (and which often serve to give poetic language its greatest charge). Thus Gomringer's reinvention of the concept of the concrete involves both the belief in the literal value of form which he took from Bill, a faith in the universal numerical structure of information and relations, and combined this with anti-naturalistic linguistic theory which was in part being given an impetus by the mid-century interest in machine languages.[7] Gomringer never went so far as to demonstrate the existence of quantifiable equivalents for his verbal works. But his poetry embodies his faith in the capacity of structure to serve as a meaningful form. At the same time that his poems remain embedded in natural language he strove for a Concrete poetry in which meaning was self-identical with appearance, unequivocal and unambivalent.

It is this concern – the attempt to make poetic meaning isomorphic with its visual structure, with its presentational form, and its appearance on the page – which is the point of commonality between Gomringer and the Brazilian Noigandres group. And it is on this point that their two otherwise very distinct traditions converge. Unlike Gomringer, the writers who formed the circle in São Paulo – Augusto de Campos, Haroldo de Campos, and Décio Pignatari (which expanded to include Pedro Xisto, Edgard Braga and others) – sought their literary identity within the modern poetic tradition, particularly the Anglo-American mainstream in which Ezra Pound, James Joyce, and Gertrude Stein played a major role, as well as in the alternatives to that mainstream, particularly the work of John Cage. The very name of their group, "Noigandres" is taken from Canto XX of Pound's *Cantos*, where it appears as a baffling nonsense word whose enigmatic character is remarked upon (cf. Solt 1968: 12). They also situated their poetry within a continental tradition, particularly that which stemmed from the symbolist Mallarmé, though Apollinaire, Dada and Futurist poets, and the musical works of Anton Webern, Pierre Boulez, and Karlheinz Stockhausen were also active sources for their inspiration. The key phrase describing much of their poetic activity as "verbi-vocovisual" was taken from the writings of Marshall McLuhan. For all its diversity, a common theme of all of the work they drew on is a central feature of much modern art and literature: a focused attention on formal means in their own right. The concept of the ideogram formulated by Ezra Pound as a model of poetic composition (a model in which the structure and content of a poem approach a non-verbal condition of identification so that the "image" of the work as both form and meaning are one and the same) was fundamental to Brazilian Concretism. As in the case of Gomringer and the formalist tradition from which he came, the Brazilians rejected all forms of "expressionism" – lyrical, personal, emotional in favor of a poetic form which could function as an object in its own right, betraying nothing about the author, nothing of subjective feelings, or individual identity. In this formulation an old tenet of modernism is restated: the notion of a creative work which is fully auto-nomous, self-sufficient, able to exist – not as an interpretation of other objects, and not as a mimetic representation – but as a creation in the fullest sense – original, independent of reference or imitation, meaningful in its own right.

Augusto de Campos's *Poetamenos*, first published in 1953, embodies the vision of Brazilian Concretism: printed in several colors, the poems identify various themes and voices (male and female) through these visual means. The most immediate model for de Campos's work was the "Klangfarbenmelodie" (Tone-Color-Melodies) of Webern – a poem premised on the faith in color and form to function as an immediately effective mode of communication.[8] There is a residual belief here in a system of correspondences which harks back to symbolist theory, even if Webern's work is stripped of metaphysical baggage. The word phrase "verbivocovisual" by which the Noigandres group describes their productions suggests a similar synaesthetic approach, only applied to the materials of poetics. But where Gomringer strove for the "unequivocal resolution" to questions of meaning through formal means, the Noigandres group are more willing to renounce the struggle for the absolute – or Absolute – that is, the struggle for either linguistic certainty or metaphysical truth. Though the elements of the poem are to be self-evident and the structure and meaning self-identical, the form itself remains in a condition of perennial relativeness, without closure, without fixed value, and open to various interpretations and responses. Noigandres searched for a form of metacommu-nication in which visual and verbal means would coincide and communication would occur through form as an inseparable fusion of form-content, rather than through the conventions of message communication in arbitrary symbols or signs.

Several manifestos published in the 1950s give Concrete poetry a clear definition: "From Line to Constellation" and "Concrete Poetry" both authored by Gomringer and published in 1954 and 1956 respectively, and the "Pilot Plan for Concrete Poetry" published by the Noigandres group in 1958 (reproduced in Solt 1968: 67-72). While these papers elaborate on the positions I have outlined very briefly above, the proliferation of Concrete poetic practice was rapidly escaping any simple definition. Among the Brazilians the poems of Xisto and Braga engage with the use of the ideogram to express far more subjective and lyrical positions than those typical of their counterparts; Augusto de Campos was investigating his own "pop-concretism" which incorporated materials from media culture and non-literary sources into his poetry; in Germany Hansjörg Mayer and somewhat later Emmett Williams were making playful works manipulating alphabetic elements or word puns in a manner which was resonant with referential qualities rather than dependent on finely worked out structural rigor. The question of reference, of the echoes or traces of the world which find their way into the linguistic, visual, and material presence of language, was always slightly problematic, even for Gomringer at his most pure.[9] For the Brazilian poets, a commitment to a belief in the social and political function of poetics precluded the kind of metaphysical transcendence as an endpoint which was central to Gomringer. These sorts of distinctions only multiply as one begins to look into the wider field of concrete poetics – whether one is examining Claus Bremer's fascination with the typewriter, or Bense's and Heißenbüttel's experiments in statistical permutations as a basis for poetics, or the graphic inventions of Dieter Roth and Marcel Wyss in their collaborative publication *Spirale*, begun with Gomringer in 1953. Each of these individuals has their own point of departure for their work, but the general common interest which draws them together under the rubric of "Concrete" is their emphatic attention to the visual and/or physical substance of language. The "and/or" is introduced here to at least point to the parallel tradition of Sound poetry which has its own history in the twentieth century, one in which many of these same figures participate either directly or approximately.[10]

Lettrism, another movement which occurs at almost the same time as Concrete poetry, is utterly distinct in all respects. Lettrism was initiated by the Roumanian Isidore Isou, who arrived in Paris just after World War II and launched his poetic program with great publicity and high profile bids for public and critical attention. Lettrism was entirely defined by Isou, who believed that the spiritual and aesthetic exhaustion he perceived in Western art and poetics was to be saved through Lettrist techniques.[11] Isou wanted to atomize language into its smallest consituent elements – which he took to be letters (cavalierly disregarding the complex issue of the distinction between sounds and alphabetic signs) – and then reinvent poetry around the letter (or invented signs). With his two most immediate adherents, Maurice Lemaître and Gabriel Pomerand, Isou fostered the production of books, paintings, spatial environments, sculptural work, architecture, films and performances all exploring aspects of the Lettrist precepts. Graphically and linguistically arcane, the Lettrist work is often incoherent, relying on material, visual, or tactile effect rather than achieving communication. Lettrists often emphatically emphasize the glyphic nature of the visual sign. Lemaître, for instance, invented a form of hypergraphic writing which substituted symbols for letters in rebus-like arrangements, displacements, or transformations. But such work is very far from the reduced concentration of the Concrete poem with its intense focus on the collapse of structure and meaning into a single indissoluble unit. In Lettrist pieces, the symbol proliferates meaning through its visual properties, slipping from one level of linguistic production to another, visual one, without any apparent rules or regular principles. Though Lettrism has its place within the history of Visual poetry in the twentieth century, it should not be confused with Concrete poetry; the principles and practice are completely different in all respects – except one. In both cases the presentation of the work on the page is characterized by visual manipulations and non-traditional, unconventional means – all of them at odds with the "norm" of literary text presentation.

From the 1960s onward it becomes increasingly difficult and unrewarding to trace simple intellectual lineages among delimited configurations of poets as the means of charting the development of Visual poetry. On the one hand, the generic statement, "attention to materiality," is so vague that it loses any real value, while on the other the strict rule of "form which is self-identical with meaning" (Concretism in the narrow sense defined by Noigandres and Gomringer) stretches only to include a very few writers and even then, only some of their poetry. Still, the fundamental concept of making use of visual elements to reinforce, extend, inflect, or subvert conventional linguistic meaning in a poem becomes the basis of a wide variety of work throughout recent decades – attesting to the viability of Visual poetry as a heterogeneous and diverse field and to its compatibility with a seemingly unlimited number of poetic propositions. Moreover, as the idea of visual poetics became detached from the context of Concretism, the linguistic and theoretical constructs with which it is engaged also became increasingly varied (though these are not always explicitly articulated by either poets or their critical historians). Not all of the developments of these latter decades can even be contained within the field of poetry per se – there are interrelated interests which emerge from sites within fine arts, music, and performance further enriching and complicating the field.

For example, the idea of visual scoring, or the manipulation of phonetic components of poetry in a manner analogous to a musical piece, has a history which far precedes the twentieth-century avant-garde, but in the mid-century reinvestigation of musical form new expressions of this sensibility came to the fore. The work of John Cage, in an American context, is exemplary of a more widespread phenomenon in which figures like Henri Chopin and Bernard Heidsieck, among others, participated. While the performative aspect of the visual documents produced by these artists/composers/poets remained a basic element of their practice, the page or score itself also came to function as a performance in its own right. Cage, Chopin and Heidsieck conceived of the page or sheet as a field of activity in which the visual presentation of a work demonstrates a primary engagement with the rhythm, patterns, and emphasis of phonemes within language. For these artists the outstanding feature of language was its phonemic and phonetic qualities – visual devices served primarily as a means of emphatically attending to these elements in their own right, while freeing them from the conventional constraints of meaning production. Heidsieck, for instance, by the mid-1950s, had determined that the book and page were too confining, that he wanted to find a form of linguistic performance which would permit language to escape these boundaries. Beginning in 1955, his *poèmes-partitions* made use of diverse materials – a paper document tracing cardiac movements, cut up verse, and so forth in a performance mode he termed "poetry action" or "action poetry." For Chopin the use of a tape-recorder as a primary tool for composition and performance demonstrated his engagement with a kineticisation of poetry, though this did not interfere with his composition of works on paper as a facet of this practice. The dynamic and temporal features of musical productions thus forged a relation with Visual poetry as Sound poetry, scored and marked for performance.[12] These musical innovations are intertwined with the history of "Sound poetry," which flourishes in the 1960s and 1970s, and also with the hybrid art practices of the Fluxus group for whom Cage in particular was a major source of aesthetic inspiration.

Within Fluxus, Jackson Mac Low serves as an interesting figure through whom to examine the polymorphous character of the movement – since his work cannot be fit comfortably into categories like poetry, music, or visual arts – though it makes use of and participates in all these fields to varying degrees. Like Cage, Mac Low made serious use of processes of composition grounded in systematic chance operations, combinations, and cut-up techniques.[13] Fluxus artists were committed to ordinary life – including language in its everyday form – a tenet which seeps from John Cage's work into every aspect of the Fluxus sensibility. Cage made use of means of "bracketing" or otherwise calling attention to the quality of ongoing existence as an aesthetic experience. It is not surprising then that the poetics of Mac Low are in many ways a refusal of or rejection of the *literary* forms of language of a figure such as Ezra Pound for whom the esoteric orientation, historical literature, arcane and scholarly realms of Western thought served as source and reference. Though academically trained in this tradition, Mac Low's work shows the extent to which radical renewal in poetic form had pushed the parameters of innovation far from the literary mainstream. Mac Low's attention to language was similar to John Cage's attitude toward sound – that it was all available as aesthetic material through techniques of observation, sensitization, presentation. Mac Low has continued an unfaltering commitment to the use of strategies of composition based on acrostics, anagrams, and other methods which combine random selection of material and a systematic structure for its reworking into new form. The elaborate processes which Mac Low makes use of necessarily engage him with visual documents whose own properties are both intrinsic aspects of his "event" scores and also works in their own right. As the performance aspect of Mac Low's pieces generally requires a significant degree of reinvention, the scores serve as the basis of, rather than as a prescriptive fixed transcription of, performed works. The works are never final or fixed, but renewed through each enactment with the visual structures and instructions on the page serving as a point of departure.

While the work of someone like Mac Low may seem far from the concrete sensibility of Gomringer, Fluxus probably had a broader impact on the arts in general in the post-1960s than Concrete poetry would or could. This is in part because the full field of experimentation with language in this decade comes to include not only new experiments in Visual poetry and avant-garde performance, but also developments in the mainstream art world. While much of the work by Fluxus artists Ben Vautier, George Brecht, or Alison Knowles might not be considered Concrete or Visual poetry in a strict sense, their use of language within an art context and attention to its material forms – whether typewritten, scribbled, or typeset – has to be seen as background to the work of 1980s visual artists as diverse as Raymond Pettibone, Christopher Wool, or even Barbara Kruger and Jenny Holzer. The fact that ordinary language is taken for granted as an art material is due in large part to the Fluxus precedent. In addition, there is the conspicuous role played by language in Conceptual art in the 1960s, a context in which language served as a primary, rather than extra or incidental, element of artistic works.[14]

Within the core of Visual and Concrete poetry in the 1960s a number of different nodes of activity define specific approaches with varying points of commonality in theoretical or stylistic terms. As a kind of "second generation" of visual poets, these writers each developed their work in accord with a particular, often highly nuanced or narrowly defined, aesthetic principle. Pierre Garnier, for example, who founded his "spatialist" movement in 1963, used the concept of "space" as a metaphysical as well as formal and semiotically charged idea. Insisting on the expressive and signifying power of the literal, physical space between letters, Garnier felt that the process of coming into form in poetics was a manifestation of a world being born. The spiritual, metaphysical charge which Garnier gave to the visual structure of poetic form resonates with many of the principles which the French conceptual artist Yves Klein was working into his New Realist examination of the metaphysical abstraction and power of the void and space in the same years. The notion of *espace* as an element of aesthetic practice can be readily traced to Mallarmé's poetics – the dimensionality and structural complexity of the full form of *Un Coup de Dés* serving as the original spatialist poem. In Garnier's poetry the Mallarméan concepts are reworked through a new artistic sensibility trying to come to terms with the "cosmic being in the age of space" – an aesthetic which required, in Garnier's mind, that the word function as a "free object" – a phrase which combines the image of an entity floating in a gravity-free environment with a high modernist concept of textual autonomy and self-definition (cf. Solt 1968: 32). The linguistic implications of a such a position are many, not the least of which is a conviction that language functions significantly as a textual practice without the need for reference, a fundamental tenet of the new critical sensibility which was dominant in the 1960s. Similar critical concepts were an aspect of the forms of structuralist linguistics formulated by Leonard Bloomfield and even the early work of Noam Chomsky – most likely still unfamiliar to writers in a European context even if the idea of a syntactically based, rather than semantically replete, linguistics was shared among them.

By contrast with the highly structured and structuralist premises of Garnier's poetry, almost at the other extreme of a poetic spectrum, is the work of Charles Olson, a poet whose attention to visual form as an integral feature of poetic meaning pushed the conventions of poetic representation into new terrain (cf. Davidson 1993). The geographical metaphors are apt here, since Olson's spatialized concept of language – which could not be farther from that of Garnier's metaphysical structuralism – forged relations between "fields" of the page and "fields" of meaning in semantic as well as referential terms. Olson's visual innovations are a distinct contribution to a tradition of sensitivity to the graphic quality of poetry on the page which can be found in other modern poets as diverse as Gertrude Stein, e.e. cummings, even William Butler Yeats, or earlier, William Morris and Emily Dickinson (cf. Howe 1985 and McGann 1993). But the writing of William Burroughs and Brion Gysin forged new links between literary innovation and Visual poetry through their use of cut-up techniques, while many poets of the 1950s and early 1960s – the English writer Bob Cobbing serves as a useful specific example here – discovered a formal value in the structuring capacity of the typewriter which had hitherto been largely ignored (or else effaced in the standardizing process of typesetting in preparation for publication). Typewriter poetry and typewriter art – whether produced within a literary context or a visual art context – flourished in the 1960s and early 1970s in works as diverse as those of Maurizio Nannucci, Carl Andre, Henri Chopin, Pierre Garnier, and Ana Hatherly – to name only a few of the most remarkable. There was impetus from within literary tradition for these experiments – but also, increasingly, as in the case of Andre and Nannucci, from visual or conceptual artists as well.

In an international perspective these decades virtually explode with experiments in Visual poetry: In Czechoslovakia Jiří Kolář's work drew its unique character from his attention to Kasimir Malevich and Victor Vasarely as influences, thus combining a suprematist formalism with an optical-kinetic contemporary sensibility; the German artist Dieter Roth, working from a graphic design background into books as an artistic form in the 1950s, made use of found and reprinted visual material as premise for exploring sequence and structure; Scottish artist Ian Hamilton Finlay's individual form of concretism extended into environmental works through the gradual transformation of his entire garden into a linguistic and poetically articulated space; and Kitasono Katue introduced Visual poetry into the already fertile environment of the Japanese avant-garde in 1957. There are literally dozens of other artists and poets whose Visual poetry in this period makes a significant and unique contribution.[15]

As mentioned above, at the same time as these various experimental activities were finding their own course, the two major developments within the realm of mainstream visual arts – Pop art and Conceptual art – would have an impact upon Visual poetry in stylistic as well as conceptual terms. Vastly different in their linguistic orientation – Pop making use of commercial, product-oriented language as well as the graphic style of advertising and publicity and Conceptual art using the most neutral, unmarked, and "immaterial" forms it could manage while still making the words appear on a page, wall, canvas, or other document – they both contrived to make language as such, language in itself, and language as visual, written form, into a primary art object. No longer serving merely as title, as signature or other supplementary element, nor as a formal (if significant) element of a collage, language was, from the early 1960s and the exhibition of works by Ed Ruscha, John Baldessari, Art & Language, Lawrence Weiner, Andy Warhol, Richard Hamilton and others, to make a claim as an art practice.

In a related but separate arena, Bern Porter, Emmett Williams, Ed Ruscha, and Tom Phillips each began to make use of artists' books as medium for the exploration of visual properties of found and created texts with Porter's found poetry beginning in the 1950s, and Ruscha, Williams, and Phillips a decade later. Phillips began his extended work, *A Humument*, in 1966. Its relation to Concrete and Visual poetry explains only part of its aesthetic grounding. Phillips's work, based on a book which he bought and then transformed, page by page, into an exhaustive investigation of the complexities of text/image relations and meaning in the book format is both an exemplary sample of Visual poetry and a marked transgression of the earlier limits of what would be defined under such a rubric. Phillips's graphic inventiveness in this piece is a manifestation of conceptual interrogations of book structure and the very notion of what constitutes "visuality" within a text is challenged by this work. With Phillips, as with Williams (whose playful book structure poems are virtuoso performances of sustained spatial, sequential, linguistic transformations), or even Carl Andre or Lawrence Weiner, the premises of the work cannot be fully fleshed out without reference to traditions of Conceptual art, the use of found and transformed texts, environmental and spatialized extensions of visual and verbal material into a wider field, and any of the many other strains of artistic activity which by the 1960s had dissolved the boundaries between disciplines which had rigidly distinguished high modern visuality from high modern literariness at mid-century. At this point the capacity to contain the discussion of Visual poetry within the framework of Concretism is hopelessly moot – experimental innovation had interbred so successfully with other artistic sources as to make its kinship with orthodox Concrete poetry a remote and diluted relation at best.

In the case of Pop and Conceptual art the language used is also remote from poetics, and a surprising amount of the Visual poetry of the 1980s and 1990s draws upon these sources as much as upon the traditions of literary or visual poetics whose premises they extend.

Before turning attention to recent works, however, it is useful to study the case of Canadian "concretism." Here the term must be applied loosely, rather than in the narrower sense defined earlier, as it has been used to identify the visually experimental texts of bill bissett (sic), the late bpNichol (sic), and Steve McCaffery.[16] Poetically self-conscious, theoretically sophisticated, but unorthodox and non-academic, these poets serve as an interesting study in the ways Visual poetry in these later decades takes advantage of a more eclectic background than that of pure Concretism, one which borrows from some of the same precedents – Anglo-American poetry, French poetry, and the early twentieth-century avant-garde – while adding in important new elements. In particular, the work of bpNichol and Steve McCaffery, the sole members of the Toronto Research Group (founded in 1973) is a highly focused and in some ways unique example of a new maturity for visual poetics (see Bayard 1989). Their poetry is distinguished by the fact that it is well informed by traditions of poetics – the mainstream of conventional and experimental modern work as well as many eclectic precedents in pattern poetry, Sound poetry, and Visual poetry. Like Dick Higgins, the American Fluxus artist, publisher, and writer, McCaffery and Nichol were able to find inspiration in the graphic and phonetic experiments of poets from the middle ages and Renaissance to the present while situating their own practice within the contemporary context of immediate precedents in the work of European, Brazilian, and American contemporaries (cf. Higgins 1987). Among the documents of their collaborative "research," McCaffery and Nichol include a section of notes titled "The Book as Machine." The very title displays their affinity with "The Book as Spiritual Instrument" aspect of Mallarmé's writing, a metaphysical poetics of book form, though McCaffery continues to empha-

size the importance of Walter Benjamin's non-mystical and highly critical
analysis of culture as a counterpoint. Thus it is not surprising to find that the
"machine" invokes contemporary linguistic considerations and the self-
conscious critical attention to processes of textual production characteristic of
new semiotic and post-structuralist criticism. In a section of this text subtitled
"Twenty-one Facts that Could Alter Your Life" they examined specific
instances of Visual or Concrete poetry according to the ways these individual
activities defined certain parameters for their understanding of – and coming
to terms with – conceptual premises for their continued innovations
(McCaffery & Nichol 1992). This kind of "taking stock" which weaves
throughout the published reports of the Toronto Research Group makes clear
the ways in which their attention to critical assessments was integral with
poetic practice. Though they are careful to state that theory always follows
practice, is secondary to it, they are simultaneously steeping themselves in a
critical discourse in which distinctions between theory and creative practice
were being rapidly dissolved. Nichol's reading of the studies made by
linguists Benjamin Whorf and Edward Sapir on the Hopi language, for
instance, served direct poetic functions, not merely critical ones. The primacy
of the theoretical text, whether poetic or discursive in nature – which is a
feature of the 1970s reception of the work of Jacques Derrida, Julia Kristeva,
and Roland Barthes, for example, all writers McCaffery and Nichol were
reading at the time – allows their own work to become a hybrid of
theory/practice in which poetics participates fully. The old model of artistic or
avant-garde manifesto as a first declaration of aesthetic principles, from which
poetic or artistic work would follow, which was still a feature of Concretism
in the work of Gomringer and Noigandres, is here displaced by a new
paradigm. Theoretical, polemical, and poetic work is often one and the same,
and the positions are continually mutating through the practice. But the
characteristic tone of the Toronto Research Group's work is its pataphysical
sensibility. In the late 1960s, for instance, Nichol and McCaffery became
fascinated with the capacity of the xerox machine – because it could and
always did serve to disintegrate a text/image, rather than mechanically
reproduce an original. An attitude, "against the logic of performativity" and
"pinpointing post-industrial aporias" is fundamental to all of their activities.[17]

The visual component of Nichol and McCaffery's work takes many forms
– some more overtly linked to concrete precedents, others to literary formats
being stretched and reworked to suit their purposes. bpNichol's 1974 *Love: A
Book of Remembrances* makes use of hand drawn images of letters and words,
sometimes of purely visual or pictorial elements, to push the linguistic features
of poetry towards an almost entirely visual mode. In a form they termed "post-
semiotic poetry" Nichol and McCaffery insisted on the semantic as well as

syntactic resonance of language, particularly its visual aspects, in a manner which would never have been conceivable within Gomringer's aesthetics. McCaffery's epic *Carnival* (a typewriter/wall work in two long parts) is anti-reductive, chaotically replete with proliferating meanings whose relation to form is unorthodox and unsystematizable. The visual forms are continually invented so that the normative rules of a syntactic analysis would have to be similarly reinvented at each panel if a consistent relation to rule-bounded language were to operate as the function of meaning production. That it does not – and virtually could not – is part of the visual effectiveness of the work. Another influence which asserted an important force was McCaffery and Nichol's exposure to folk, "primitive" and non-western poetics – in the anthropologically influenced poetic research of the kind most clearly exemplified in the work of Jerome Rothenberg. What they took from this work was an emphasis on phonetic properties, sound patterns, and rhythm – all of which motivated McCaffery (and the group The Four Horsemen) towards performance in addition to typographic or graphic experiments. Nonetheless, for both McCaffery and Nichol the structure of the page and even of the book as a form are conspicuous features of their published poetry.

In short then, these Toronto poets make Visual poetry a form of theoretically informed work whose research techniques combine a broader field of poetic sources with an intuitive but well-considered understanding of the ways attention to materiality in visual and verbal form could extend the possibilities of earlier Concretism. A critical distinction made by the writer Stephen Scobie between the idea of a "clean" and a "dirty" concretism works well to demarcate the clean, well-ordered, and more highly regulated work of the Swiss/German nexus of poets, or even that of the Noigandres group from the Toronto poets' hybrid eclecticism, with its synthetic capacity to absorb material from any of a wide variety of conceptual, critical, and linguistic sources.

What becomes abundantly clear in this new formulation is that poetics is informed by notions not articulated within Concretism – not available – and that not only linguistic theory, but the construction of poetics as a strategy of representation engaged with issues of culture, ideology, and politics is central to the conception of poetic practice from its very outset. If the Toronto Research Group serves well as a study in work which came into being in a poetic context, self-consciously aware of and also continually coming to terms with critical and poetic traditions, it provides a model for other forms of poetry of the 1970s and 1980s mainly by its eclecticism. Which is to say that if one were to begin, now, in the mid 1990s, to examine the field of Visual poetry and to try to account for its forms and variations in terms of a forward moving history of poetics, much of the current activities could not be explained. Just as the retrospective evaluation of the Toronto Group forms a far clearer picture of its aims and intentions than the forward moving chronological account provided in its working notes, so the process of evaluating contemporary visual poetics as if there were a coherent historical development of which it is some current final outcome is an unsustainable fiction. This becomes increasingly true in an age in which the sources of poetics and graphics are taken from mass media, a readily available shared field of reference and form, as often as from any well-charted or regulated discourse of poetics or fine arts. These fields have been similarly affected – it would be impossible to discuss contemporary art without referring to television, star system and celebrity politics, rock music, or other culture industry forms – thus further complicating the identity of a form like Visual poetry which further hybridizes the already appropriated materials of these realms of artistic activity.

If I were to consider my own work in regard to these issues, for instance, my connection to critical discourse and poetic/visual production has transformed dramatically over the last twenty years. Initially I became interested in schematizing relations between meaning and appearance on the page as a way to investigate and develop semantic values, as well as to insist on a kind of latent quality of signifying potential in format or arrangement within page structures. By 1976, when I printed my first elaborately typographic book, *Twenty-six '76*, my sense of language as a material form had expanded. I found it useful to mark "found" language by its material expression, to indicate its origin in a heterogeneous linguistic field. Intimate involvement with the process of production – making use of lead type in letterpress printing – forced the issue of engineering effect (linguistic emphasis or inflection) through visual means. I could not, in 1976, have cited a single theoretical or critical writer as a way to articulate what I was doing – I simply had not read any. When informed by a colleague at the West Coast Print Center that I was working in the tradition of Mallarmé, I had to admit that I had never heard of *Un Coup de Dés*, let alone examined the many arcane discussions of its typographic rendition. Concretism, like artists' books, constructivist design, and modern poetry were all forms about which I was woefully ignorant – though I had been exposed to Dada and Surrealism in the brief course of academic work required by my art school for a B.F.A. degree. The original inspiration for exploring the potential of language as a material form came from the experience of "holding language in my hands" – lines of letterpress type shaped in a composing stick whose weight and presence were as much physical as linguistic – and from looking at language in the world. This situation changed dramatically once I entered graduate school, at which point, beginning in 1980, I learned some theory/history and began to integrate elements of structuralist and feminist theory into my work. The particular form of typographic poetics which formed the center of my work from the late 1970s was dedicated to exploring the non-linear potential of print form and to the power of visual material form to proliferate meaning within a semantic field through the visual structure. But it was also bound up with issues of female identity, prose traditions, and the relations between fiction as a literary form and fiction as a cultural form – tabloids, pulp novels, and genre writing – all of which served as useful points of departure in conceptualizing my work. Though all of this work from the last two decades can now, in my own critical writing, be framed in terms which locate it within traditions and contemporary frameworks of Visual poetry and aesthetic innovation, it was originally conceived without that information and with a far more intuitive and unregulated sensibility. I think, in fact, this is more typical than not – and I would be surprised if most of the poets I will mention here in closing could do more than retrospectively situate themselves within critical or poetic traditions. Nor would I wish them to – I think that the old avant-garde model of the proscriptive manifesto, the laying out of aesthetic terms and the subsequent attempt to fulfill them through practice had its moment of usefulness and has been superseded by other models of creativity – just as boundaries between art and literature, art and non-art, media culture and fine art culture have also become dissolved to the point of questionable usefulness – or dubious stability.

Any attempt to describe the full range of Visual poetry in the current moment would be difficult – many of the practitioners of Concrete and Visual poetry from the 1950s onward continue to be productive, continuing certain aspects of their activity in modified form. But there are new trends as well, some already of longstanding in the practice of individual poets or as a general premise. For instance, Robert Grenier, a California based poet, has been making handwritten palimpsest works for more than a decade. His poems are manuscript originals which he overwrites in a large, loose printed hand so that a maze of spindly lines of text interweave with each other. Each is readable, legible, discernible, and yet the gestalt of the page as a whole is *textural* rather than *textual* in character. Grenier's language sensibility is highly vernacular, extending the poetics of the likes of Bob Brown, Robert Creeley, and the New York school into a contemporary formulation but giving it a distinct visual quality which calls acute attention to writing process in the visual appearance of the final inscription on the page.

At another extreme of technological production would be the holographic poems of Eduardo Kac, for whom the spatialized dynamics of the page are transcended through a medium which allows dimensionality to be factored into the linguistic production. Kac's explorations extend the use of the computer as a tool in poetic composition employed by Max Bense, among others, in the 1960s, while also engaging with the sort of visual manipulation of surface appearance which characterized the work of Raymond Hains, also in the 1960s. However, in Kac's works as in Hains', the distortions introduced into the final form of the language through light projection, surface manipulation, or computer processing are not additions or supplements to the text. Instead, they are intended to be integral to its linguistic function, to extend the definition of what comprises linguistic function to include the potential of material to signify. Crag Hill's "interpretations" of the visual forms of words also integrates such visual manipulations – integrating them with texts speculating on the nature of language as a perceived phenomenon.

But perhaps the most telling new trend is one which has been amplified by the availability of computer and xerox technology – the use of visual and verbal elements in fluid combination with each other. If much of Concrete and Visual poetry put the word into a formal relation with an icon or pictorial structure through format on the page, or, in the case of McCaffery/Nichol, pushed the capacity of traditionally non-verbal visual forms into syntactic or semantic relations, then current experimentation actually blends visual and verbal elements into what is an increasingly a synthetic unity. The work of Spencer Selby, for instance, or of Thomas Taylor, depends to a large extent on either xerox or scanner capabilities for reduction/enlargement and rephotographing of images in order to take materials from newspapers, existing books, text, manuscripts, printed forms, and reformulate them. The additional typographic sophistication provided in personal computers has made the possibility of writing directly through such means a more common practice. A poet like Pete Spence, who makes elegant abstract compositions of letters, signs, lines and geometric forms in diagrammatic linguistic algebra, could have achieved these effects in letterpress (they bear some relation to the *druksels* of H.N. Werkman produced in the 1920s) – but the manipulations of Karl Kempton or John Byrum would have been impossible without a computer on which to generate the specific effects which give their work its particular character and value. Layered, overprinted, stretched, screened – these are all effects which are specific to the graphic codes of electronic and photographic media. Electronic media extend the kind of appropriation and recombination techniques typical of collage practices into new realms of visual and graphic sophistication. The result has been an intensification of hybrid syntheses of visual and verbal means. Electronically scanned images can be combined with an almost infinite set of possible typographic options which are in turn manipulated as images in the electronic darkroom. The borders of production between visual and verbal modes have never been so permeable, and the results are even more conspicuous in the mass media than in the realms of literature and the fine arts.

This closing is woefully inadequate to indicate the range of work in Visual poetry which is currently being produced – or even to give a sense of the history of this complex and diverse field. What is evident is that the terms of poetic tradition or linguistic analysis adequate for a critical understanding of earlier work is inadequate to confront the synthetic sensibility of the present. Recent work poses profound questions about the identity of art and poetry as cultural practices and raises new questions about the processes of signification so essential to these projects as they are conceived in aesthetic terms. It also marks its distance from and relation to the traditions of Concrete and Visual poetry against which it gains at least part of its definition. There is no group with the self-conscious identity of Noigandres or the German Concrete movement currently articulating a theoretical premise for such innovations – but the practices which find vital inspiration from a synthesis of visual and verbal materials are clearly continuing to be reinvented in each successive generation. As this happens, the critical attention to the history of these individual movements, and to the even more specific character of an individual's own practices within them, will hopefully become increasingly nuanced and more sharply and clearly investigated so that both similarities and differences will be productively understood in critical, historical, and poetic terms.

Notes

1. The 1955 meeting between Décio Pignatari (a member of the Brazilian Noigandres group) and Eugen Gomringer in Ulm, Germany resulted in their announcement of the formation of an international group of Concrete poetry which would further explorations each had already initiated within their own context. While there are important points of commonality in the work of these two poets and the other writers who formed their immediate circles, there are also significant points of difference in the sources for their poetics and in the nature of their practices, as shall become clear.

2. See the catalogue *Poésure et Peintrie* (1993) for an exhaustive representation of twentieth-century activity, and also Bann (1967), Williams (1967), Solt (1968), and Cobbing & Mayer (1978). None of these, however, goes much past the mid-1970s, even the 1993 publication, in terms of assessing new trends or figures.

3. Since the Chinese language, in its written form, depends upon these visual relations of proximity, sequence, and so forth, it is often invoked as a model. This is the case throughout the tradition of Western poetics – finding its modern articulation in the oft-cited work of Ernest Fenollosa and its echos in Ezra Pound. Most such interpretations are ill-informed and rely on an impression of Chinese language rather than any actual understanding of its organization, much like the mythic concept of the hieroglyphic in Western thought.

4. See Compton (1978), Janecek (1984), *Poésure et Peintrie* (1993), and Drucker

(1994). For more recent examples, see *Avant-Garde*, 5/6, 1991, on experimental poetry in the U.S.S.R.

5. The term constructivism has a specific meaning within Russian and early Soviet art practices. It is particularly associated with the work of Rodchenko for whom it designated experimentation with formal means as an aspect of a revolutionary aesthetic. It should be distinguished from Malevich's suprematism (which is engaged with issues of representation, anti-mimesis, and metaphysics) and Vladimir Tatlin's productivism (in which innovative formal means are used in application to industrial production). In a non-Soviet and especially post World War II context, the term constructivism is associated with a depoliticized formal visual language in fine arts and design, especially in the Dutch and Swiss schools.

6. This seems paradoxical – and to some extent it is. But there are many odd mutations of early avant-garde activity in the 1920s and 30s through which politically or socially motivated forms become appropriated as stylistic or merely graphic devices.

7. Precisely what Gomringer was reading is unclear – Wittgenstein seems likely, but the work of Claude Shannon and even Abraham Moles in information science are contemporary with Gomringer's formulations; the relation between the ideas of Gottlob Frege and Gomringer are striking – especially Frege's distinction between the linguistic functions of "immanent sense" and that of "external reference." For a discussion of Frege within the context of Concretism more generally, see Caroline Bayard's excellent *The New Poetics in Canada and Quebec* (Bayard 1989).

8. Cf. Solt (1968: 12). See also Reis (in this volume).

9. It is interesting to consider what "reference" meant for Gomringer – especially within the context of formulations in structuralist linguistics from Ferdinand de Saussure through Leonard Bloomfield and even the early Noam Chomsky. Bloomfield's work in the 1940s was rigorously concerned with syntactic structures to the deliberate exclusion of semantic considerations – Bloomfield understood that semantics pointed outside the system of language, toward the world, reality, and the social conditions of language, all of which introduced complexities he felt were unnecessary for understanding the syntactic structure of meaning production. The opposition and separation of sense and reference as two independent linguistic functions thus had a basis in theoretical linguistics whether Gomringer was aware of this and making use of it or not. Needless to say, such linguistic positions are themselves open to debate.

10. Raoul Hausmann, Ilia Zdanevich, and Kurt Schwitters, for instance, and so forth. See Hultberg (1993; this reference thanks to Eric Vos. JD).

11. See David Seaman (1981) and Willard Bohn (in this volume) but more directly, the writings of Jean-Paul Curtay, Isidore Isou, and Maurice Lemaitre themselves.

12. Again there are early twentieth-century examples of such activity in the work of Dada and Futurist artists, but the scope of activity broadened considerably in the 1960s into a major movement and mainstream artistic phenomenon.

13. Cf. Mac Low (in this volume). The idea of systematic chance should be distinguished from the cut-up operations of Brion Gysin and William Burroughs,

for instance, whose methods and results were closer to those of the surrealists than those of Cage.

14. This primary character of language is a feature of many Fluxus pieces (see also Smith in this volume) – I am thinking of the George Brecht performance cards, or of Alison Knowles's book works, to name two among many examples, but for Fluxus the ultimate emphasis is on experience, while in Conceptual art the final emphasis comes to rest on idea. Thus for Fluxus artists the language is a means of providing instructions or frameworks, while for Conceptual artists language is to be, paradoxically, the "dematerialized" manifestation of an art idea.

15. See the catalogue of the Ruth and Marvin Sackner Archive of Visual and Concrete Poetry for a sense of the scope of this material – an as yet unwritten history.

16. Nichol died in 1988.

17. McCaffery, in conversation with the author, September, 1995.

Bibliography

Bann, Stephen (ed.)
    1967   *Concrete Poetry*. London, London Magazine Editions.
Bayard, Caroline
    1989   *The New Poetics in Canada and Quebec*. Toronto, University of Toronto Press.
Cobbing, Bob & Peter Mayer (eds.)
    1978   *Concerning Concrete Poetry*. London, The Writers' Forum.
Compton, Susan
    1978   *World Backwards*. London, British Museum Publications.
Davidson, Michael
    1993   "Le texte matérialisé dans la poésie anglo-américaine." In: *Poésure et Peintrie*, 219-228.
Drucker, Johanna
    1994   *The Visible Word: Experimental Typography and Modern Art Practice*. Chicago, University of Chicago Press.
Haftmann, Werner
    1961   *Painting in the 20th Century*. Vol 1. New York, Praeger.
Higgins, Dick (ed.)
    1987   *Pattern Poetry*. Albany, State University of New York Press.
Howe, Susan
    1985   *My Emily Dickinson*. Berkeley, North Atlantic Books.
Hultberg, Teddy (ed.)
    1993   *Literally Speaking. Sound Poetry and Text-Sound Composition*. Gøteborg, Bo Ejeby Ed.
Janecek, Gerald
    1993   *The Look of Russian Literature*. Princeton, Princeton UP.

McCaffery, Steve & bpNichol
    1992   *Rational Geomancy*. Toronto, Talonbooks.
McGann, Jerome
    1993   *Black Riders*. Princeton, Princeton UP.
Poésure et Peintrie.
    1993   Marseille, Musées de Marseille.
Seaman, David
    1981   *Concrete Poetry in France*. Ann Arbor, UMI.
Solt, Mary Ellen (ed.)
    1968   *Concrete Poetry: A World View*. Bloomington, Indiana UP.
Williams, Emmett (ed.)
    1967   *Anthology of Concrete Poetry*. New York, Something Else Press.

B.
EXPERIMENTATION IN ITS
HISTORICAL MOMENT

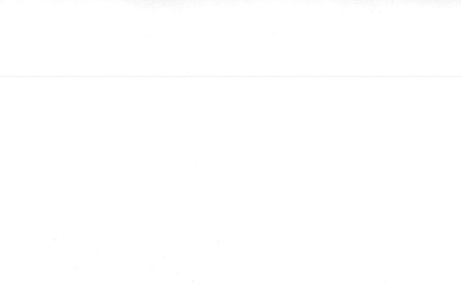

VOICES OF READING

Ana Hatherly

L'écrit, envol tacite d'abstraction, reprend ses droits
en face de la chute des sons nus
Stéphane Mallarmé, *Quant au livre*
(Mallarmé 1951: 385)

Writing is mute. The writer must dwell upon the silence of the written word, which is a visual representation of a meaning originally conveyed by sound. Writing obliterates sound.

Writing is mute speech, a materialization of the imaginary that requires a particular way of reading, a decoding appropriate to its own rules and communicative demands. Writer and reader must rely on the powers of imagination; in writing as in reading the symbolic function is at work. As many pedagogues found out long ago, to read is to make an appeal to the imaginary, for true reading starts when the actual presence of the text vanishes before the eyes, in the same way as the hand of the author disappears in the work.

Reading is a form of conquest: it strives for access into that realm of the invisible that we call "meaning," which constantly evades us and for that reason has to be constantly recreated. Writing is mute but reading calls for many voices.

In 1975, when I published *The Reinvention of Reading*,[1] I was deeply involved with the questions of writing and reading raised by contemporary and ancient Visual poetry, especially of the baroque age, which later became for me a main field of research and academic specialization. *The Reinvention of Reading* is an essay followed by 19 hand-written pattern poems, composed to illustrate the possibilities of Visual poetry as an encounter of text and image. They present a form of language design intended to emphasize the visual aspect of writing and require a new attitude toward the consideration of a poetic text. In this work, as in several others, I treated writing not so much as calligraphy but as a form of abstract, conceptual art. As I often said, "eu queria mostrar a escritura, não o escrito" – I wanted to show the writing not the written. I wanted to draw the attention to writing in order to appeal to a new form of reading. To achieve this I made texts practically or totally illegible so that they could no longer be read as pure linguistic objects. They were intended to be perceived as multilayered icons.

Ana Hatherly

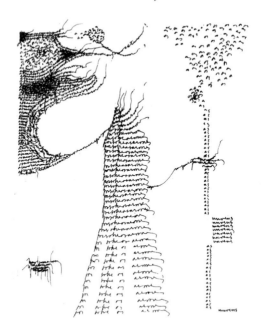

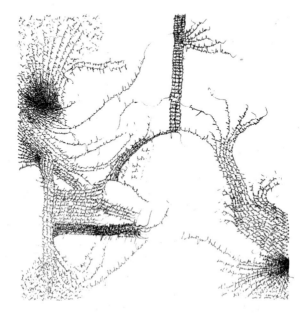

Ana Hatherly, two poems from "The Reinvention of Reading"

I was influenced by my study of Chinese calligraphy, which I described in *Mapas da Imaginação e da Memória*, but also by the New Criticism and the Oriental thought so prevalent in the 60s and 70s. Intimations of Eastern asceticism and Western skepticism are present in the demand for silence and essentiality expressed by many artists of that time. Concrete poetry, at its purest, is part of that.

In *The Reinvention of Reading*, I described creative writing as a "technology of fascination." As I explained, a poem – like a magical object and given the magical origin of writing – requires a creative reception, an inventive attitude towards the object and its meanings. In other words: it demands from the reader a "suspension of disbelief," a metareading. As in all forms of meaningful communication, one must read the text beneath the text: the reader must fill in the gaps, the blanks, the omissions, must see the invisible in the visible, hear the mute sound, receive the unsaid message, attain the meaning beyond meaning.

The poetics of writing, implying plural readings of the image, must always deal with the dialectics of visibility/invisibility, legibility/illegibility, and with questions related to communication through language, whatever its form. Expanding a conceptualization of the poem as a written thing, Concrete poetry and its various Experimentalist successors emphasized visual representation as – potentially – simultaneously synthetic and polysemic. The visual element of the poem (sometimes also the phonic element) became a decisive aspect of its structure, vitally partaking in the constellation of the intended meanings. When actually removing the poem from the page to present it as a three-dimensional object or as a performance, Experimentalism reinstated the poem as a tangible multi-dimensional object. This conceptualization of poetry was created centuries ago but had somehow been forgotten.

While emphasizing the visual nature of the text as a written message, Concrete poetry introduced other features that enriched the reading of a poem. Concrete poetry not only employs any of the elements of language, it is also open to any medium. Being a plural and *intermedia* form of expression, Concrete poetry is open to all kinds of experimentation. But to conceive the poem as a "magnetic field of possibilities" makes poetry a form of materialization of what Mallarmé (1951: 455) called "the prismatic division of the Idea," and this requires a new way of reading, a sort of Iconology of the Abstract, where the linguistic sign is only one among other sources of creative meaning.

Concrete and Experimental poets attempted to create a language fully deployed as a creative medium, going well beyond the Futuristic concept of *paroles en liberté*. Their particular reconsideration of the past and their incisive inscription in the present as a radical trend made history and still stand as a major step in creative evolution, representing an attempt towards a totalization of poetic expression.

As is well-known, the main object of all avant-garde movements of this century was to overthrow an established rule, a status quo considered oppressive or obsolete, in order to impose a new line of thought and action – ultimately, a new order. One of the most relevant effects of avant-garde movements of this century was their contribution to a new attitude towards the artistic object, in particular their new conceptualization of the function of beauty within the creative process. In fact, this often implied the negation or even the revilement of the concept of beauty as proposed by classical tradition, which, originally connected with harmony and spiritual aspiration, in the meantime had largely fallen in the hands of academism.

The process of disruption created by the avant-garde overthrow of established values contributed to a necessary change of attitude, and we now look at art with different eyes, we create in a different way, with different materials and different objectives. This new way of doing and reading art, among other things, enabled us to discover a new form of conciliating the past with the present.

Concretism, one of the most radical avant-garde trends of this century engaged in a critical reevaluation of the artistic object and its place in society, had a new way of looking at tradition. It was a forerunner of later neo-baroque and post-modern trends. Concrete poets were no antiquarians but neither did they shun the past. Their diachronic perspective, especially their concern with the tradition of Visual poetry, is documented in numerous anthologies with a historical scope, such as those by Robert Massin, Berjouhi Bowler, Milton Klonsky, Miguel d'Ors, Klaus Peter Dencker and many others. It also encouraged a number of research works, like Giovanni Pozzi's *La parola dipinta* (1981), my own *A Experiência do Prodígio* (1983), Dick Higgins's *Pattern Poetry: Guide to an Unknown Literature* (1987), Piotr Rypson's *Obraz stowa historia poezji wizualnej* (1989).

Notwithstanding their deep involvement with contemporary issues, concrete poets and Experimentalists in general were able to integrate aspects of old and even antique poetic experiences, European and non-European, in their innovative program and to generate a new synthesis. From this cross-fertilization of roots a new and multi-layered sapling emerged, whose purpose was to renovate artistic means and meanings and to design a new profile for the poet. No longer a romantic "legislator," the poet had to be(come) a socially responsible being engaged in all forms of artistic exploration, reinstating poetics at the center of creativity.

Combining a renovating intervention in the present with a revalidation of the past, the Portuguese EXPERIMENTALISTAS, as they called themselves, illustrate and represent this stance. The group POESIA EXPERIMENTAL (or PO.EX) was formed in the early 1960s by the first generation of Portuguese experimental poets – António Aragão, Salette Tavares, Melo e Castro, Ana Hatherly, José Alberto Marques. In its early days, and at the front of European Concrete poetry, the group quite closely adhered to the basic characteristics of the international Concrete poetry movement, represented by the Brazilian Noigandres group and its European counterparts. As its marginality became synonymous with clear-cut opposition to the establishment, both artistic and political, PO.EX exercised active rebellion.

When the Concrete poetry movement gushed out in the 60s, the Portuguese, living under a dictatorship almost half a century old, were undergoing a ruthless colonial war in Africa, which the younger generation rejected with disgust. So the EXPERIMENTALISTAS could not be just involved in their personal pursuits and the usual international avant-garde acts of artistic rebellion: they also had to face the particular situation of their country.

The leading poets of POESIA EXPERIMENTAL were definitely on the opposition side, and their work of the time proves it. In a country where censorship, repression, and the persecution of dissidents was a common prac-tice, they had to denounce that state of affairs. They had to place themselves well outside the official grounds, tearing the alienated and backward discourse of the ruling power to pieces. It was a daring form of radicalism to introduce, practice, and promote an overtly anti-nostalgic, anti-establishment interna-tional trend in a country with centuries of lyrical tradition, and it was under-stood as such by the established critics and even by many poets, who were not able to see the real scope of the movement right away.

With the 1974 Revolution, things changed. With the abolition of censor-ship, the release of political prisoners, and the end of the colonial war, ideas and ideologies began to circulate freely. When the Revolution broke out the whole country was suddenly engulfed by a wave of rejoicing, an explosion of collective euphoria quite unknown until then. There were moments of real communion of feeling and thought, and this privileged state of unanimity burst out in the open in a most creative way with the participation of artists, poets, musicians, everybody who felt in unison with the Revolution and the liberation of the people. As a slogan of the time stated, "poetry was really in the streets." Political posters, graffiti, and murals spread all over the country. Revolutionary speeches and songs proliferated. The voices of the Revolution filled the air.

Experimental poets were naturally part of it, and there are material vestiges of their participation, including my own film REVOLUÇÃO, which is a Visual poem that shows many of the political posters and graffiti that covered the walls of Lisbon at the time and also reproduces slogans, speeches, and songs everybody knew. Although everything presented in this film is real, the end result is not intended as documentary: it is a statement reflecting the spirit of the Revolution. The way the frames are shot and edited tries to convey the feeling of exhilaration and unrest, exaltation and disturbance caused by the events of that time. The images and the sounds comprise a mixture of revolutionary fervor and straightforward folklore, urban and rural, and through these the voice and perhaps the soul of the people. My perspective is that of

Ana Hatherly, from REVOLUÇÃO

the poet who, facing the real, sees hears, feels, thinks, and then recreates what he experienced.

As the revolutionary state of euphoria subsided, a period of unrest followed, until democracy was finally established in the country. With the social stability that ensued everyone could concentrate on their own work once again and contribute to the new cultural image that had to be created. New post-revolutionary concerns and forms of expression began to appear and to establish themselves.

Confirmed Experimentalists of the 1960s, together with the new generation that joined them in the 1970s and 1980s, felt free to pursue their own individual paths, but the earlier mystique of the movement was kept to a certain extent. Publications, collective exhibitions, performances and installations continued, nationally and internationally. While participating in all of those, my own project included research in Portuguese literature of the seventeenth and eighteenth centuries, started before the Revolution.

From the outset, Portuguese Experimentalists were interested not only in

Concrete poetry and experimental art, but also in Renaissance and Baroque traditions. Alongside avant-garde poets of the time, the first issue of POESIA EXPERIMENTAL, the magazine-manifesto of the group,[2] presented works by the German baroque bard Quirinus Kuhlmann and by Luís de Camões. Camões, the national epic poet of the sixteenth century, who was to become the "patron saint" of Melo e Castro and myself, both for his artistic stature and his overt criticism of the Portuguese establishment of his time. But this was not the only source of the Experimentalists's interest in past experiences. Several aspects of the baroque tradition, such as its performative sense of the poetic object and its ludic concept of creativity, were to become more and more important as the impact of strict Concrete poetry gradually faded out. The same happened in Brazil, especially in Minas Gerais, with Affonso Ávila as a leading figure. Visual imagery, so important for the baroque poets, their incredibly creative use of language, and above all their cult of pattern poetry played a decisive role in the reevaluation of the baroque style, which had been the avant-garde of its time and was, for that reason, also highly contested.

In Portugal, baroque literature had been considered a decadent form of art since neo-classical times; a point of view that persisted in the catalogue of clichés of the narrow-minded critics in Salazar's time and even after. This rejection by the establishment, together with a real interest in baroque poetry among Experimentalists like Melo e Castro and myself, stimulated our diligence in proving how valid baroque style still was in contemporary respects, and how well it corresponded to an essential trait in our idiosyncrasy. The implications of this anthropological stand were to be assumed by Melo e Castro (1976) in his book *Dialética das Vanguardas*, where he proposed an innovative reevaluation of baroque tradition.

After decades of study of baroque poetry, visual or otherwise, Portuguese or international, I came to the conclusion that one of its most important aspects lies in the special type of reading it requires. As I demonstrated elsewhere (Hatherly 1986), a full reading of a baroque poem can be a total experience in which all voices of meaning – the voices of reading – are to be taken into consideration and put to use. It really calls for a reinvention of reading, and in doing so it renovates our way of conceiving the artistic function of the poetic object. This verification gave me a particular insight into poetry making and above all into poetry reading. It lead me to realize that this new way of reading could and perhaps should be extended to all forms of creativity. Poetry, as a quintessential creative act, is an offering and has to be received, interpreted, and consumed as such. In the end, when *read*, the object produced creates its own reality.

Notes

1. An abstract of this essay, translated by Prof. William Watt, together with reproductions of some of the Visual poems included, was published in *Visible Language* XI, 3 (Summer 1977), 307-20.
2. For information on the history and developments of Portuguese Experimental poetry, see *PO. EX — Textos Teóricos e Documentos da Poesia Experimental Portuguesa* (Hatherly and Melo e Castro 1981).·

Bibliography

CLARO-ESCURO, Revista de Estudos Barrocos.
  1988-91   Lisboa, Quimera Editores. Nº 1, 1988; nº 2/3, 1989; nº 4/5, 1990; nº 6/7, 1991.
Hatherly, Ana
  1973   *Mapas da Imaginação e da Menória.* Lisboa, Moraes Editores.
  1975   *A Reinvenção da Leitura.* Lisboa, Futura.
  1983   *A Experiência do Prodígio.* Lisboa, Imprensa Nacional/Casa da Moeda.
  1986   "Reading Paths in Portuguese and Spanish Baroque Labyrinths." In: *Visible Language* XX/1, 52-64.
Hatherly, Ana and E.M. de Melo e Castro
  1981   *PO.EX. — Textos Teóricos e Documentos da Poesia Experimental Portuguesa.* Lisboa, Moraes Editores.
Higgins, Dick
  1987   *Pattern Poetry: Guide to an Unknown Literature.* Albany, State University of New York Press.
Mallarmé, Stéphane
  1951   *Oeuvres Complètes.* Paris, Gallimard (La Bibliothèque de la Pléiade).
Melo e Castro, E. M. de
  1976   *Dialética das Vanguardas.* Lisboa, Livros Horizonte.
Pozzi, Giovanni
  1981   *La parola dipinta.* Milano, Adelphi.
Rypson, Piotr
  1989   *Obraz stowa historia poezji wizualnej.* Warszawa, Akademia Ruchu.

THE MOREMARROW TRAJECTORY
OF OLIVERIO GIRONDO

Jorge Schwartz

Médulas, que han gloriosamente ardido,
Su forma dejarán, no su cuidado,
Serán ceniza, mas tendrán sentido,
Polvo serán, mas polvo enamorado.
Quevedo, "Sonetos a Lisi" no. XXXI

1. The City and the Countryside

Oliverio Girondo's critics agree unanimously when pointing out the clearly defined stages in his poetic evolution. These stages can be summed up into three large blocks and a parenthesis, which characterize the six books of poetry and a *plaquette* that make up the work of this Argentinean poet.

Girondo's trajectory began in the 1920s with *Veinte poemas para ser leídos en el tranvía* (1922) and *Calcomanías* (1925). These two foundational books, marking the inaugural style of the cosmopolitan vanguards of the group Martín Fierro, are internationalist in orientation and are structured around the traditional travel diary. The external world represented by the city takes hold of and dominates the poetic referent. What takes shape is a real celebration of the object, exalted in the spatial and temporal comings and goings of the tourist who takes delight in discovering a geographic route. In these first books, the word acts out its deictic function *par excellence*; in other words, it provides an indication of the surrounding space as support for a permanently ironized and caricatured urban referent.

This voyage of the look begins to recede from Girondo's work during the decade of the thirties, and it experiences an interiorized turn in the poetic prose of *Espantapájaros* (1932) and in *Interlunio* (1937). While the poet's first poetic production is accompanied by the diurnal and by a certain chromatic ecstasy, the second stage gives rise to a sensation of the lugubrious, grotesque, and deformed, which will become accentuated. The vibrant and many-colored caricatures of *Veinte Poemas* and *Calcomanías*, signed by Girondo himself, are now replaced by a somber scarecrow and by Lino Spilimbergo's illustrations which reveal a macabre despair of surrealist inspiration. Poetic prose is a distinctive trait of this stage, inherited from the poetic prose of *Veinte Poemas*.

The third moment consists of *Persuasión de los días* (1942) and *En la masmédula* (1954), whose common characteristics permit us to agglutinate them in a single block; this block appears interrupted by *Campo nuestro*, a poem published in 1946 in the form of a *plaquette*, which represents a real hiatus in Girondo's work. The ostensible nationalism of this poem transforms it into a homage to the Argentinean pampa (a kind of poetic version of *Don Segundo Sombra*) which shares no similarity with Girondo's work, either from the thematic or from the stylistic points of view, before or after it. As Adriana Rodríguez Pérsico affirms,

> La atmósfera eglógica, la apacibilidad del lenguaje, el tono religioso y el trasfondo de trascendencia hacen del texto una excrecencia en el corpus del editor.[1]

> [The eclogue-like atmosphere, the even-temperedness of language, the religious tone and the background of transcendence make this text an excrescence in the editorial body.]

Campo nuestro is a profoundly bucolic poem, which exalts the countryside in its traditional attributes. While doubt and existentialist questioning about being and nothingness are developed with more and more intensity starting with *Espantapájaros*, *Campo nuestro*, a highly referential poem, translates a universe of unequivocal certainty, untroubled by doubts or negations:

Este campo fue mar	[This field was sea
de sal y espuma.	of salt and foam.
Hoy oleaje de ovejas,	Today waves of sheep
voz de avena.	voice of oats.]
(Girondo 1968: 375)	

These verses and syntax are of a linearity foreign to the rest of Girondo's production. The still certainty of herds and wheat fields that abound in this poem are not only different but also oppose completely the loss of being announced at the beginning of the calligram which opens *Espantapájaros*:

Yo no sé nada	[I know nothing
Tú no sabes nada	You know nothing
Ud. no sabe nada	You [formal] know nothing
Él no sabe nada	He knows nothing
Ellos no saben nada	They know nothing
Ellas no saben nada	We know nothing]
Nosotros no sabemos nada.	
(Girondo 1968: 155)	

We could interpret *Campo nuestro* as a kind of autobiographical homage in the work of Girondo, who was a landowner and a member of the Argentinean oligarchy. A (typically) Argentinean voice defines Girondo's "rural stage" and coincides at this moment with the nationalist apogee of Perón's first presidency:[2]

> Fuiste viva presencia o fiel memoria
> desde mi más remota prehistoria
> Mucho antes de intimar con los palotes
> mi amistad te abraza en cada poste.
> (Girondo 1968: 379-380)

> [You were live presence or faithful memory
> since my most remote prehistory
> Long before intimating with drumsticks
> My friendship embraces you in every post.]

Passing from a reading of *Campo nuestro* to "La mezcla," inaugural poem of *En la masmédula*, the reader faces the slip towards the abyss created by its first verses:

> No sólo   [Not only
> el fofo fondo. . .   the spongy bottom...]
> (Girondo 1968: 403)

From the immovable certainty of the flat pampa we fall into the miasmic depths that will characterize *En la masmédula*: a trap, a slip that will bring us to recognize the turbulent waters of the last stages in Girondo's poetry.

2. The Moremarrow Trajectory

This last phase reveals one of the most extraordinary moments of revelation in contemporary poetry in the Spanish language. Girondo's precursors, Vallejo and Huidobro, each entered the history of the vanguard with a great work, a break with tradition (*Trilce*, 1922 and *Altazor*, 1931); by contrast, Girondo emerges from the cosmopolitan vanguards of the twenties in order to re-establish the "more medullar" vanguard of the fifties, initiated in 1942 with *Persuasión de los días*. If, as has been indicated, this tradition returns to Mariano Brull's *jitanjáforas*,[3] Girondo's poetry substitutes the nonsense of the Cuban's poetry – which is complacent and exhausts itself in mere speculative word games – with a determined and coherent meaning. Besides Brull, the cosmopolitan vanguard of Apollinaire and Cendrars leaves its marks on the total absence of punctuation which will characterize *En la masmédula*. The spatialization of the Mallarmesque background already made a timid appearance at the end of the poem "Croquis en la arena" of 1920 and re-emerges unexpectedly in the calligram of *Espantapájaros*, "silent homage to Apollinaire" (Molina 1968: 24). Spatialization is a process frequently used by Girondo, especially at the end of many poems of *En la masmédula*, or as a radical option, as in "Plexilio," where all the words in the poem are displaced in the open Mallarmesque constellation of the blank page. As I have demonstrated in a previous study (Schwartz 1993), the tuning in to European influences during the twenties and thirties is turned in the fifties from the traditional Buenos Aires/Paris axis towards a more Latin American direction: the Brazilian Concrete movement, officially founded in 1956 by Haroldo and Augusto de Campos and by Décio Pignatari. Girondo's tuning in to the Brazilian Concrete movement is not a case of influence, as usually happened with the mentioned *ancêtres* of the twenties, but of intertextuality, or, of precursors, as Borges would postulate. Girondo came into contact with the Brazilian Modernist vanguard rather late, through his personal contact with Oswald de Andrade, when he traveled through Brazil for six months in 1943, during his trip with Nora Lange. In turn, only in 1971 does Haroldo de Campos discover in a library in Austin, Texas, the second edition of 1956 of *En la masmédula* (Campos 1994: 152). The principles of Concrete poetry permit the re-reading of Girondo through a different prism. The gradual loss of a referent with the scope of reinforcing the poetic function, the *priem ostraniene* of Russian Formalism, which forces us to stop in front of the lexical strangeness of *En la masmédula*, the turn toward the materiality of language, and the employment of the graphic qualities of the page are some of the elements closest to the principles of Concrete composition. That which Delfina Muschietti (1988: 142) defines in Vallejo and Girondo as "actitud trituradora contra los códigos del lenguaje y la obsesión violenta por lo material" [the shredding attitude towards language and the violent obsession with the material], can be perfectly attributed to Concrete poetry. In contrast to the general group character of Noigandres, Girondo's trajectory has been that of a *poète maudit*: isolated, solitary, and misunderstood for decades[4] – but no less programmatic in regards to his poetic tasks. The major proof that Girondo was absolutely convinced of his poetic principles lies in the "work-in-progress" character of the several editions of *En la masmédula*. In the first edition of 1954 there are sixteen poems; in the edition of 1956 there are ten more poems, and in the *Obras Completas* of 1968, eleven more poems, totaling thus thirty-seven poems.

In a 1955 letter to Córdova Iturburu, Girondo affirms (cf. Schwartz 1987: 242):

> tengo la íntima y profunda convicción de que esos poemas – y los que incubo – son lo único válido que he escrito hasta ahora – lo demás son balbuceos de neófito.

> [I have the intimate and profound conviction that those poems – and those still incubating – are the only valid thing I have written until now – the rest are the stammerings of a neophyte.]

A few months later he reiterates this opinion to Carlos Ghiano (cf. ibid.: 245):

> . . . no sólo considero que *En la masmédula* es muchísimo superior a *Persuasión*, sino que es el único libro mío que realmente – y relativamente – me satisface.

> [. . . not only do I consider *En la masmédula* much superior to *Persuasión*, but it is my only book that actually – and relatively – satisfies me.]

In contrast to the Concretist project, which was sustained by various manifestos, Girondo's vanguardism did not rely on the pamphlet rhetoric which characterized him when he was a leader of the Martín Fierro group and when he signed the *Manifiesto Martín Fierro* of 1924. Another aspect that distinguishes *En la masmédula* from the Concretist movement is that, while the latter was a tributary of the Cubo-Futurist and Constructivist tradition that also characterized the Brazilian Modernism of the twenties, Girondo descends directly from a Surrealist tradition. Perhaps this is a reason that we do not encounter in Girondo's poetry the geometrism specific to Concrete poetry. It is not surprising that the generation of poets that gathered around him have been surrealist *avant la lettre*: Aldo Pellegrini, Olga Orozco, Enrique Molina.

3. Girondo, Neo-baroque poet?

Another aspect practically ignored by critics concerns the baroque characteristics of his poetry, traits which similarly relate him to the projects of Concrete poetry. Not only Lezama Lima, Alejo Carpentier, and Oswald de Andrade see in the Baroque an American sign,[5] but Girondo (1968: 146) casts an identical opinion in one of his "Membretes":

> El barroco necesitó cruzar el Atlántico en busca del trópico y de la selva para adquirir la ingenuidad candorosa y llena de fasto que ostenta en América.

[The Baroque needed to cross the Atlantic in search for the tropics and the jungle in order to acquire the candid and sumptuous naiveté which it displays in America.]

To see baroque nature as a sign emanated by the tropics not only relates Girondo to the American and Caribbean critical tradition of the Neo-baroque, but it also casts unsuspected light over his own work. Only Aldo Pellegrini (1964: 40) sensed a baroque trace in Girondo's work, but he did not expand upon this hunch: "Every poem has a theme which is developed according to a geometrically baroque construction." Pellegrini detects baroque thematics and syntaxes. But how can we define the "geometrically baroque construction" in Girondo's work? Similar to the way in which Deleuze (1988: 42) discovers the "baroque spirit" in Constructivism and in the Functionalism of Le Corbusier, the parallels between Girondo's poetry and that of Haroldo de Campos offer us tracks and possible solutions. On the one hand, the Concrete poet was the first Latin American critic to use the term and the concept of the Neo-baroque in 1955, anticipating Severo Sarduy's classical essay "El barroco y el neo-barroco" of 1972 by several years (cf. Sánchez Robayna 1985).[6] In a more recent article, Haroldo de Campos considers his 1952 text, "Teoria e prática do poema" a "manifesto of Neo-baroque poetics" (cf. Campos 1994: 140). On the other hand, we could affirm that there is a trajectory common to the two poetics which converge toward the Neo-baroque: in the same way that the baroque aesthetic that is initiated with *O âmago do ômega* (1955-1956) culminates with *Galáxias*, Girondo's baroque would culminate in 1954 with the first edition of *En la masmédula*.

But how are we to resolve the baroque antitheses between line and curve, between Constructivist principle and baroque volute, between lapidary conciseness and proliferating accumulation, between fragment and totality, silence and noise, emptiness and fullness? This apparent contradiction between an aesthetics of conciseness and of expansion was pointed out by the Spanish critic Andrés Sánchez Robayna (1985: 140) in the work of Haroldo de Campos: "Thus a kind of paradox is established, in effect, in the writings of Haroldo de Campos, between essentiality and concrete renouncing and the baroque device of *Galáxias*," arriving at the conclusion that "thus, there is no separation between the 'medullar' and the 'proliferating' poles as expressions of an apparent antithesis in the writings of Haroldo de Campos." We encounter these poles in a symbiotic relationship in Girondo's poetry. The innovative definition of the Baroque as exposed by Deleuze (who also relies on Sarduy) allows us to read Girondo's poetic production as a totality, not as differentiated blocks, as the majority of the critics have read it. If we lingered in front of Girondo's poetic production *in totum*, as if we were observing a landscape through its external movements, especially the lines of the horizon (an invitation to the "Croquis en la arena"), we would note an initial fold in the emergence of the first two books (*Veinte Poemas* and *Calcomanías*), which then unfolds in the poetic prose and vignettes of *Espantapájaros*, and which reaches a movement of maximum textual expansion interrupted by *Interlunio*, in order to culminate in the final fold of *Persuasion de los días* and *En la masmédula* – a flow of poems that fuse all possible semantic and syntactic contradictions. This Deleuzean vision of the Baroque, via Leibniz, permits us to overcome the universe of possible contradictions in Girondo's poetry, to understand the meaning of his phonetic and semantic agglutinations, such as the baroque proliferation at work especially in *En la masmédula*.

Yet, how can we reconcile this reading of Oliverio Girondo's poetry as a harmonious, uninterrupted series with the exceptional character of *Campo nuestro* of 1946? On December 10, 1950 Girondo published in the Buenos Aires daily, *La Nación*, the poem "Versos al campo," absent from *Obras Completas* for reasons beyond my understanding. Although it repeats the rural thematics of *Campo nuestro*, this poem is charged by a negativity which announces itself and is accumulated in the opening lines of the poem:

No es mar. No es tierra en pelo.	[It isn't sea. It isn't naked land
No es consistencia de cielo,	It isn't consistency of sky,
Ni horizonte altanero.	Nor proud horizon.]
(Schwartz 1987: 26)	

To the mythical and totalizing positivism of *Campo nuestro*, this poem opposes the rejection of natural elements, to culminate in an exacerbating nihilism:

Es nada. Es pura nada.	[It is nothing. Purely nothing.
Es la Nada ... que ladra.	It is Nothingness ... which barks.]
(ibid.)	

Nature no longer responds to the pacific and balanced bucolic of universal values, as in the poem published four years before. Instead of the earlier idyllic fusion, the subject is now split from the rustic object it describes: a fractured "I" which does not understand rural language:

Me están hablando los campos	[The fields are talking to me
Pero yo no los comprendo.	But I don't understand them.]
(ibid.: 28)	

The lyrical "I" of a swampy and dusty field is founded by the process of "nothingfication" of the "I" in the moment that it reiterates an isolated verse in the left margin of the page: "Yo nada" [I nothing]. In the face of negation and nonencounter, the solution is founding the "I" out of nothingness (Argentinean homage to *L'être et le néant* of Sartre?) The two poems complement each other in their antithetical visions of the countryside and cannot be read one without the other. The exaltation and the negation of the countryside are two sides of the same coin.

The Deleuzean perception of the work as a continuum, as a totality, coincides with Girondo's reflection (and with Borges's, that writing is a permanent process of rewriting the same one draft):

> Ambicionamos no plagiarnos ni a nosotros mismos, a ser siempre distintos, a renovarnos en cada poema, pero a medida que se acumulan y forman nuestra escueta o frondosa producción, *debemos reconocer que a lo largo de nuestra existencia hemos escrito un solo y único poema.* ("Membretes," Girondo 1968: 149, emphasis ours)

> [Our ambition is not to plagiarize, not even ourselves, to be always distinct, to renew ourselves with each poem, but as they [the poems] accumulate and make up our succinct or abundant production, *we must recognize that throughout our existence we have written only one poem.*]

Girondo's symphonic notion of poetic production supports our argument and allows us to discern the different parts of the poem as one unique corpus, which culminates in *En la masmédula*, convulsive universe of signifiers, a type of porous monad, a true poetic aleph, agglutinator of all signifiers.

In accordance with the most traditional principles of baroque composition, in *En la masmédula* we witness the decentering that causes the absence of a central nucleus in the poems. The exorbitantly grotesque and the permanent presence of the ludic in linguistic games (invention of words, contamination of signifiers, alliterations, paronomasia) are initiated with the fourth vignette of *Espantapájaros*:

> Abandoné las carambolas por el calambur, los madrigales por los mamboretás, los entreveros por los entretelones, las invertidos por los invertebrados. Dejé la sociabilidad a causa de los sociólogos, de los solistas, de los sodomitas, de los solitarios. No quise saber nada con los prostáticos. Preferí el sublimado a lo sublime. Lo edificante a lo edificado. Mi repulsión hacia los parentescos me hizo eludir los padrinazgos, los padrenuestros. Conjuré las conjuraciones más concomitantes con las conjugaciones conyugales. Fui célibe, con el mismo amor propio con que hubiese sido paraguas. A pesar de mis predilecciones, tuve que distanciarme de los contrabandistas y de los contrabajos; pero intimé en cambio, con la flagelación, con los flamencos (Girondo 1968: 163).

> [I abandoned chance for *calembours*, madrigals for mamboretás, confusions for interlinings, the inverted for the invertebrate. I left sociability because of sociolo-

gists, of soloists, of sodomites, of the solitary. I wanted nothing to do with prosta-
tics. I preferred the sublimated to the sublime. The edifying to the edified. My
repulsion towards the fatherly made me elude godfatherships and "Our Fathers." I
conjured the most concomitant conjurations with conjugal conjugations. I was
celibate, with the same self-love with which I would have been an umbrella. Despite
my predilections, I had to distance myself from contraband and from double basses;
but instead, I was intimate with the flagellation and with flamencos.]

On the other hand, "The Rebellion of Vocables" ("Rebelión de los vocablos")
of *Persuasión de los días*, is a privileged instance in the baroque predilection
for linguistic games, which will gain importance afterward in *En la masmédula*:

De pronto, sin motivo;	[Suddenly, without motive;
graznido, palaciego,	quack, palatial,
cejijunto, microbio,	frowned brow, microbe,
padrenuestro, dicterio;	Our Father, insult;
seguidos de: incoloro,	followed by: colorless,
bisiesto, tegumento,	leap, tegument,
ecuestre, Marco Polo,	equestrial, Marco Polo,
patizambo, complejo;	knock-kneed, complex;
en pos de: somormujo,	in pursuit of: grebe,
padrillo, reincidente,	stallion, relapsing,
herbívoro, profuso,	herbivorous, profuse,
ambidiestro, relieve;	ambidextrous, relief;
rodeados de: Afrodita,	surrounded by: Aphrodite,
núbil, huevo, ocarina,	nubile, egg, ocarina,
incruento, rechupete,	bloodless, splendid,
diametral, pelo fuente;	diametral, hair fountain;
en medio de pañales,	in the midst of diapers,
Flavio Lacio, penate,	Flavio Lacio, chambergods
toronjil, nigromante,	grapefruit, necromancer,
semibreve, sevicia;	semi-short, cruelty;
entre: cuervo, cornisa,	between: raven, cornice,
imberbe, garabato,	beardless, scribble,
parásito, almenado,	parasite, crenelated,
tarambana, equilátero;	scatterbrain, equilateral;
en torno de: nefando,	around: execrable,
hierofante, guayabo,	hierophant, guayabo,
esperpento, cofrade,	grotesque, member,
espiral, mendicante;	spiral, mendicant;
mientras llegan: incólume,	while there arrive: unharmed,
falaz, ritmo, pegote,	deceitful, rhythm, mess,
cliptondonte, resabio,	cliptodont, vicious,

fuego fatuo, archivado;
y se acercan: macabra,
cornamusa, heresiarca,
sabandija, señuelo,
artilugio, epiceno;
en el mismo momento
que castálico, envase,
llama sexo, estertóreo,
zodiacal, disparate;
junto a sierpe ... ¡no quiero!
Me resisto. Me niego.
Los que sigan viniendo
Han de quedarse adentro.
(Girondo 1968: 352-353)

vain fire, archived;
and there approach: macabre
bagpipe, heretic,
louse, bait,
artifice, epicene;
at the same moment
as Castalic, bottle
flame sex, death rattle,
zodiacal, nonsensical;
next to serpent. . . I don't want to!
I resist. I deny.
Those that keep coming
Must remain inside.]

This lexical explosion of signifiers that contaminate each other and accumulate through the forty-four verses of rigid heptasyllabic support reproduces the "uncontrolled proliferation of signifiers" and the "irrepressible metonimization" alluded to by Severo Sarduy in his definition of the Baroque and of the Neo-baroque (1972: 167-168). The artificiality of this process is designated by the "señuelo" ["bait" or "decoy"] cast by the poet and the "artilugio" ["contraption"]. The reference to "esperpento" with the implicit debts to Goya and to Valle-Inclán,[7] recuperates ugliness and deformation as principles of aesthetic composition, which appear in the first works and are accentuated in the last books.

A surprising example, revealing of the baroque thematics and tradition, appears in the poem "Tríptico II," in *Persuasión de los días*:

Ya estaba entre sus brazos
de soledad,
y frío,
acalladas las manos,
las venas detenidas,
sin un pliegue en los párpados,
en la frente,
en las sábanas,
más allá de la angustia,
desterrado del aire,
en soledad callada,
en vocación de polvo,
de humareda,
de olvido.
(Girondo 1968: 286)

[I was in her arms
of solitude
and cold,
hushed the hands,
the veins stayed,
without a fold on the lids,
on the forehead,
in the sheets,
beyond anguish,
exiled from air
in silenced solitude
in vocation of dust
of smoke,
of oblivion.]

The poem, fourteen lines long, could be interpreted as a vanguard poem, synthesized and reduced, the Horatian theme of *carpe diem* which Góngora immortalized in the sonnet whose last lines we remember now:

> en tierra, en humo, en polvo, en sombra, en nada.

> [into earth, smoke, dust, shadow, nothingness.]
> (Rivers 1988: 163)

The nihilism specific to baroque disenchantment culminates in this verse with the process of disintegration of matter, which in turn culminates in nothingness – key word that closes the poem. The lover's response by Quevedo emerges later in one of his poems to Lisi, whose last lines defends the idea of love that overcomes matter:

> Serán ceniza, mas tendrá sentido,
> Polvo serán, mas polvo enamorado.[8]

> [They will be ash, but it will have feelings;
> They will be dust, but dust which is in love]
> (Rivers 1988: 287)

Sor Juana Inés de la Cruz and Gregório de Matos have also worked this theme in memorable sonnets, always within the tradition of baroque poetry.[9]

Girondo renews the Renaissance tradition of unrequited love and of love's suffering by initiating his poem with the death with one of the lovers: "Ya estaba entre sus brazos / de soledad, / y frío. . . ." Girondo's ties to the baroque tradition emerge in the solution of the last verses, that echo the traditional themes of his precursors:

> en soledad callada,
> en vocación de polvo,
> de humareda,
> de olvido.

The intertextuality in Girondo's poem is of residual, fragmentary nature, inherent characteristic of modernity. The sonnet's fourteen verses appear camouflaged by the apparent irregularity of the free verse, which masks eleven perfect heptasyllabic verses:

Ya estaba entre sus brazos /
de soledad,
y frío, /
acalladas las manos, /
las venas detenidas, /
sin un pliegue en los párpados, /
en la frente,
en las sábanas, /
más allá de la angustia, /
desterrado del aire, /
en soledad callada, /
en vocación de polvo, /
de humareda,
de olvido. /

Baroque dissimulation is present in this artifice of vanguard reduction; yet, in contrast to his predecessors, Girondo transforms the dialectic of the lovers in order to suggest a love without tension, after death. Thus, the "frío" ("cold") and the "venas detenidas" ("stayed veins") no longer oppose the traditional fires and the flaming medullas of the Baroque. The ending doubtlessly is identified with Góngora's nihilism, on the basis of the inclusion of "polvo," ("dust") "humareda,"("smoke") and the substitution of "nada" ("nothing") by "olvido" ("oblivion"). However, the loneliness twice mentioned in the poem, is an existentialist and modernizing element of "Tríptico II," and Girondo's connotation of "soledad" ("solitude") differs completely from Góngora's "Soledades." These latter have their own theological and metaphysical meanings specific to the Renaissance and have little or nothing to do with the contemporary notion of "being and nothingness" of existentialist background. Girondo's nihilist trajectory, especially in *Persuasión de los días* and *En la masmédula*, exalts absence, silence, emptiness, nothingness. The "No" which opens *En la masmédula* and the word "silencio" ("silence") which closes the last poem ("Cansancio") render an unequivocally nihilist meaning to his last work.

4. Ostinato rigore

Within the tradition of Aristotle's "Poetics" and Poe's "Philosophy of Composition," we insist on a programmatic character as a conscious and rational principle of poetic creation. In this sense, criticism has practically ignored a key element in the composition of the poems in the last two books by Girondo: the extensive use of heptasyllabic verse that makes up the Alexandrine (two heptasyllabic hemistiches), a most traditional metric form, going back to the Middle Ages. Why does a poetry about the loss of self, about unleashed nihilism, opting for vanguard modes of composition like the total abolition of punctuation, choose such a conservative form in the tradition of Castilian poetry?[10] With extraordinary craft, Girondo manages to conceal the heptasyllable at all moments. A poetics of dissimulation is achieved through cutting of the verse, separation of words, truncated chains; a permanent *trompe l'oeil*.[11] The strength of the classical Alexandrine (represented by one of its heptasyllabic hemistiches), hidden to the visual perception of the page, is revealed with intensity by the rhythmic cadence of orality and by the inevitable syllabic scansion of the verse. The oral strength of the heptasyllable and the conviction of its being the best of his poetry perhaps convinced Girondo to record exclusively *En la masmédula* as an oral heritage, with the long-play recording of 1960. Perhaps the oral reading of *En la masmédula* in a grave voice, seemingly emerging from darkness, also hides the presence of the heptasyllable. The apparent free verse, the absence of rhyme, and the dispersion of words over the space of the page are combined in the cadence produced by the rhythm of classical poetry. Like the Pythagorean music of the spheres, the dissimulated chaos of the verbal galaxy of *En la masmédula* maintains its harmony thanks to the rhythm of the Alexandrine.

The camouflage of the heptasyllable is Girondo's most perfect way of achieving the co-existence of the classical with the avant-garde, of the Baroque with the Neo-baroque. This simulation already appears thematized in his first books. For instance, in "Café Concierto" (*Veinte poemas*, Girondo 1968: 55), "El telón, al cerrarse simula un telón entrabierto" ["The curtain on closing simulates a half-open curtain"]; in "Croquis en la arena" (*Veinte poemas*, ibid.: 56), "Bandadas de gaviotas, que fingen el vuelo destrozado de un pedazo blanco de papel" ["Flocks of gulls, that feign the torn flight of a white piece of paper"]; or, in *Calcomanías* (ibid.: 111) "Es tan real el paisaje que parece fingido" ["The landscape is so real it seems feigned"], we see how the representation appears exposed and denominated, with the purpose of demasking representation, calls attention to the mechanics of poetic construction, to break finally with the mimetic illusion.

In *En la masmédula*, these mechanisms are exacerbated, as a kind of surpassing of the Baroque. This is produced exactly by the pacific presence of the oxymoron and by the intense co-existence, never contradictory, of antitheses. In *Espantapájaros* Girondo affirms: "amé las contradicciones, las contrariedades, los contrasentidos" ["I loved contradictions, mishaps and absurdities"]. In *En la masmédula* it is no longer necessary to enunciate or describe the process, since this is realized by the intricate weaving of words. It is not by chance that the opening poem of *En la masmédula* is called precisely "La mezcla," ["The Mixture"], where we already see the fusion of opposite elements:

> la total mezcla plena
> pura impura mezcla (...)
> la mezcla
> sí
> la mezcla con que adherí mis puentes.
> (Girondo 1968: 403)

> [the total full mixing
> the pure impure mixing
> the mixing
> yes
> the mixing with which I tied my bridges.]

For instance, "sin no" ["without no"], final verse of "El puro no" (which also allows for the reading "sí no" ["yes no"]), re-establishes the equilibrium of the opposites of two grand universals of language: it does not deny them, it does not eliminate them. On the contrary, de-hierarchization prevails: "no démono no deo" ["no demon no God"]. In a similar vein, "levitabisma" ["levitabyss"] in "Topatumba" signals simultaneously opposite directions, while linguistic agglutination is the artifice used by Girondo to achieve the convergence of contradictory principles. In the verse "que nada toco/en todo" ['I touch nothing/in everything"] (Girondo 1968: 428) totality and absence do not appear as disjunctive principles. Eros and Thanatos confront each other and live pacifically in words like "sexotumba" ["sextomb"] or in the *trompe l'oeil* "hasta morirla" in which death allows for the simultaneous reading of love (as early as *Espantapájaros* Girondo would affirm: "¡Viva el esperma... aunque yo perezca!" ["Long live sperm... although I die!"]).

The constant confrontation and neutralization of opposite semantic fields has certain consequences. First, a suspension of time, which involves the abolition of history (Deleuze (1988: 49) mentions the possibility of "extending the Baroque beyond its historical limits"). The excess of prefixes and suffixes that spread through *En la masmédula*, with examples like "exóvulo" ["exo-vule"] and "poslodocosmos" ["postmudcosmos"] or in verses like "fugaces muertes sin memoria" ["fleeting deaths without memory"] or "sin lar sin can sin cala sin camastro sin coca sin historia," ["with no home, with no dog, with no penny, with no bed, with no coca, with no history"] recall a universe anterior and posterior to history.

The infinite, as a concept contrary to a normative idea of time, is insinuated fragmentarily by the possible permutation of words. Agglutination ("noctivozmusgo" ["nightvoicemusk"], "arpegialibaraña" ["arpegialibspider"], "reverberalíbido" ["reverberatelibido"] etc.) far from depleting itself in the game, is an attempt at utopic construction of a language which aspires to the infinite. The permutations "pezlampo – pezvel – pezgrifo" ["fishlamp – fishveil – fishtap"] (Girondo 1968: 410-411) or the Huidobran "enlucielabisma – descentratelura – venusafrodea" ["shinabyss – descenter-telluric – venus-aphrodite"] (ibid.: 421) are an essay to exhaust language in all of its semantic possibilities. The attempt at an infinite poem allows us to understand the character of poems apparently or intentionally left unfinished, with final verses like "recién entonces" ["recently then"] (ibid.: 413) or "y sin embargo" ["and nevertheless"] (ibid.: 416). The combinatory linguistic operation of *En la masmédula* surprises us because it has infinite semantic possibilities; "the Baroque invents the infinite work and the infinite operation," affirms Deleuze (1988: 50). Instead of culminating and exhausting itself in emptiness and in silence, as happens with Huidobro's *Altazor*, whose flight descends in a parachute and ends with the phonetic fragmentation and the abolition of the signified, *En la masmédula* is a vindication of the word and of the signified; like Girondo, "the Baroque Leibniz does not believe in the void" (ibid.: 52). Rather, Girondo reminds us of a medieval alchemist, who, with his "párpados videntes" ["visionary lids"] is searching for universal language. As in Mallarmé's *Le livre*, the combination of elements permits the agglutination of all signifieds and the surpassing of the Babelic curse.

Translated by Miruna Achim

Notes

1. Olga Orozco (1978: 242) also sees this poem as "un intervalo de apaciguamiento, de melancolía y tierna serenidad en Oliverio Girondo frente a la nada y lo abso-luto" ["an interval of appeasement, of melancholy, and tender serenity in Oliverio Girondo, in the face of nothingness and of the absolute"]. Graciela Montaldo (1993: 125) establishes a connection between *Interlunio* and *Campo nuestro*, by affirming: "son dos textos extraños entre sí pero que sin embargo funcionan en diálogo" ["these two texts are different from each other, but nonetheless, enter into dialogue"].
2. Girondo's nationalist preoccupations, motivated by the Second World War, are also reflected in a series of articles published beginning in 1937: "Nuestra actitud ante Europa," "El mal del siglo," and "Nuestra actitud ante el desastre," reprinted in my *Homenaje a Girondo* (Schwartz 1987).
3. Alfonso Reyes's "Las jitanjáforas" departs from a *jitanjáfora* by Mariano Brull to trace some characteristics of *jitanjáforas* in general: manifestations of

mythological energy, out of the reach of practical language and of grammatical regulations, they can be, on a technical level, mere oral signs, voices, onomatopoeia, glossolalias, nonsense, jokes against time and space, verbal inventions (Reyes 1962: 190-220).

4.   It is not surprising that he has been the translator of another *poète maudit*, Arthur Rimbaud, *Una temporada en el infierno*.

5.   See also José Lezama Lima (1988); Alejo Carpentier (1969). On the other hand, Oswald de Andrade (1978: 227) affirms in "Descoberta da África" and in the epigrammatic style of the "Manifiesto Antropófago:" "resta uma palavra sobre o Barroco. O estilo utópico. Nasceu com a América. Com a descoberta. Com a Utopia" ["one last word about the Baroque. The utopic style. It was born with America. With the Discovery. With Utopia"].

6.   In his article, Sarduy discusses contemporary "Neo-baroque" praxis in Cuban literature (exemplified by writers like himself, José Lezama Lima, Alejo Carpentier, Guillermo Cabrera Infante, and others) on the basis of a "formalist" analysis of the baroque, focusing in particular on mechanisms such as substitution, proliferation, condensation, parody, inter- and intratextuality, and eroticism.

7.   In *Luces de Bohemia*, one of Valle-Inclán's characters refers to "esperpento" as the grotesque deformation produced when the classical is reflected through a concave mirror (Valle-Inclán 1973: 132).

8.   In *Otras Inquisiciones* Borges (1974: 664) notes that "la memorable línea: Polvo serán, mas polvo enamorado es una recreación, o exaltación de una de Propercio (*Elegías*, I, 19): Ut meus oblito pulvis amore vacet" ["the memorable line: Polvo serán... is a re-creation, or exaltation of one by Propercio ..."].

9.   Sor Juana Inés de la Cruz's sonnet 145, *Sonetos Filosóficos-Morales* (1951: 277) reads: "es cadáver, es polvo, es sombra, es nada" ("it is corpse, it is dust, it is shadow, it is nothing"), while in "A Maria dos Povos, sua Futura Esposa," Gregório do Matos e Guerra (1976: 319) writes: "Em terra, em cinza, em pó, em sombra, em nada" ("into earth, into ashes, into dust, into shadow, into nothing").

10. We think that only Aldo Pellegrini (1964: 38) has paid due attention to this aspect of Girondo's poetry, although it went unnoticed afterwards: "The guidelines Girondo uses in his poetry are given by the almost permanent employment of the heptasyllabic meter. The heptasyllable forms, by duplication, the basic structure of the Alexandrine, the most solemn meter in Castillian poetry, and this solemnity is discovered in the ample and regular development of Girondo's cadences. With slight alterations, at times with typographical cuts (the heptasyllabic results from the union of two short verses which should be recited together), this meter runs almost through the entire text with its precise and uniform rhythm. Evidently, in this rhythmic tissue Girondo encountered the base for the change in tone in his poetry, as it is the dominant meter in *Persuasión de los días* and *En la masmédula*."

11. We encounter other examples, like "giro hondo," "impar ido," "mal digo," "pez hada," which can mean, respectively "deep spin" and "Girondo;" "gone uneven" and "unborn;" "bad I say" and "I curse;" "fish fairy" and "heavy," etc.

Bibliography

Andrade, Oswald de
  1978   *Do Pau-Brasil a Antropofagia e as Utopias*. Rio de Janeiro,
           Civilização Brasileira.
Borges, Jorge Luis
  1974   *Otras Inquisiciones. Obras Completas*. Buenos Aires, Emecé.
Carpentier, Alejo
  1960   "De lo real maravilloso americano." In: Carpentier, *Guerra del tiempo*,
           Santiago, Orbe, 7-22.
Campos, Haroldo de
  1994   "De la poesía concreta a *Galáxias* y *Finismundo*: cuarenta años de
           actividad poética en Brasil." In: Horácio Costa, ed., *Estudios
           Brasileños*, México, UNAM, 129-175.
Cruz, Sor Juana Inés de la
  1951   *Obras Completas*, vol 1. Ed. Alfonso Méndez Plancarte. México,
           Fondo de Cultura Económica.
Deleuze, Gilles
  1988   *El pliegue*. Buenos Aires, Paidós.
Girondo, Oliverio
  1960   *Oliverio Girondo por él mismo. En la masmédula*. Recorded by
           Arturo Cuadrado and Carlos A. Mazzani. Buenos Aires, AMB
           Discografía.
  1968   *Obras Completas*. Buenos Aires, Editorial Losada, S.A.
Lezama Lima, José
  1988   "La curiosidad barroca." In: Abel Prieto, ed., *Confluencias*, La Habana,
           Letras Cubanas, 229-246.
Matos e Guerra, Gregório de
  1976   *Poemas Escolhidos*. Ed. José Miguel Wisnik. São Paulo, Cultrix.
Molina, Enrique
  1968   "Hacia el fuego central o la poesía de Oliverio Girondo." In: Oliverio
           Girondo, *Obras Completas*, 7-40.
Montaldo, Graciela
  1993   *De pronto, el campo*. Rosario, Beatriz Viterbo.
Muschietti, Delfina
  1988   "El sujeto como cuerpo en dos poetas de vanguardia (César Vallejo,
           Oliverio Girondo)." In: *Filología* XXIII/1, 127-149.

Orozco, Olga
  1978   "Oliverio Girondo frente a la nada y lo absoluto." In: *Cuadernos Hispanoamericanos* vol. 335, 226-250.
Pellegrini, Aldo
  1964   "Mi visión personal de Oliverio Girondo." In: *Oliverio Girondo*, Buenos Aires, Ediciones Culturales Argentinas, 5-36.
Reyes, Alfonso
  1962   "Las jitanjáforas." In: *Obras Completas de Alfonso Reyes*, XIV, México, Letras mexicanas.
Rivers, Elías L.
  1988   *Renaissance and Baroque Poetry of Spain*. Prospect Heights, Illinois, Waveland Press, Inc.
Rodríguez Pérsico, Adriana
  1994   [Unpublished paper delivered at the Congress *Argentinidad y Oralidad*. University of Freiburg.]
Sánchez Robayna, Andrés
  1985   "Lectura de *Galáxias* de Haroldo de Campos." In: *Diario 16*, Madrid, 25 Aug.
Sarduy, Severo
  1972   "El barroco y el neo-barroco." In: César Fernández Moreno, ed., *America Latina en su literatura*, México, Unesco/Siglo Veintiuno, 167-184.
Schwartz, Jorge
  1987   *Homenaje a Girondo*. Buenos Aires, Corregidor.
  1993   "Continuidad de una tradición: Girondo y la Poesía Concreta." In: Schwartz, *Vanguardia y Cosmopolitismo en la Década del Veinte*, Rosario, Beatriz Viterbo, 233-267.
Valle-Inclán, Ramón del
  1973   *Luces de Bohemia*. Madrid, Espasa-Calpe, Serie Clásicos Castellanos.

SARDUY AND THE VISUAL TEXT

Roberto González Echevarría

Of the Latin American writers who emerged in the sixties, none was more radically and tenaciously experimental than Severo Sarduy. Within the international context to which they rightly belonged, Cortázar, García Márquez, Vargas Llosa, Fuentes, Donoso, Cabrera Infante and others were heirs to a modern tradition that I can sketch simply by mentioning a few names: James, Proust, Joyce, Kafka, Woolf, Dos Passos, Faulkner. The experiments of the Latin American novel of the sixties – which came to be known as the Boom – are predictable to some extent: stream of consciousness, disappearance of the omniscient author, unreliable narrators, fragmentation of the plot, extreme self-reflexiveness that shows the making of the text and its condition as artifact, intertextual games, collage, pastiche, sexually audacious themes, the incorporation of cinematic techniques, and so forth. It would be unfair not to recognize the refinement which Latin American writers added to all these devices, techniques and themes, and the indisputably original achievements made possible by the combination of several or all of these narrative methods in novels like *One Hundred Years of Solitude*, *Hopscotch*, *The Green House*, *The Obscene Bird of Night*, *Terra Nostra*, and *Three Trapped Tigers*. It is remarkable, perhaps instructive, that after so much debate over the so-called "novela del lenguaje" (novel of language) – many really political controversies – language has emerged unharmed and even more vigorous from so much experimentation. One can perhaps conclude that in the texts of the Boom, language was more an object of cult and celebration than of real questioning. In this Sarduy differs radically from the writers of the Boom, as he himself made clear in a notorious footnote in *Cobra*, which reads:

Tarado lector: si aún con estas pistas, groseras como postes no has comprendido que se trata de una metamorfosis del pintor del capítulo anterior … abandona esta novela y dedícate al templete o a leer las del Boom que son mucho más claras. (Sarduy 1972: 66)

Moronic reader: if even with these clues, thick as posts, you have not understood that we're dealing with a metamorphosis of the painter of the preceding chapter … abandon this novel and devote yourself to screwing or to reading the novels of the Boom, which are much easier. (Sarduy 1975: 42)

Despite their apparent irreverence when they were published, many, if not all, the important novels of the Boom were built upon the two most solid props of contemporary Latin American literary discourse: 1) the coherence of the self, even that of the author's, while engaged in a most anxious self-deconstruction; 2) and cultural identity, despite its being represented as shattered and in a state of flux. Artemio Cruz agonizes in the labyrinth of his solitude; Olivera suffers his Argentinean passion in the streets of Paris and Buenos Aires; the three trapped tigers explore their jiving in those of Havana. (I play here, of course, on the titles of three well-known essays that attempt to define Argentine, Mexican, and Cuban cultures: Octavio Paz's *El laberinto de la soledad*, Eduardo Mallea's *Historia de una pasión argentina*, and Jorge Mañach's *Indagación del choteo*.) In *From Cuba With A Song (De donde son los cantantes)*, that mock epic of the search for origins – and, to a certain extent, the repudiation of *Orígenes* – Sarduy lays bare the various narratives and stories that constitute the discourse of identity in the Cuban case. The novel takes apart and dramatizes that discourse's mechanisms of construction. For instance, the characters, who in previous fiction would have been endowed with a given gender, are now transvestites, and the zeal to ground Cuban identity in atavistic Spanish or African cultural retentions is shown to be a fetish to ward off the hegemony of a kitsch that has its source in popular culture, particularly that of mass-media. The characters move from one story to another, search for the self in a self-service restaurant (may I help myself to a little *dasein*?), worship a rotting image of Christ, and shake up the archive of Cuban commonplaces like an enormous maraca. The sound one hears is made up of echoes of Martí's poetry, commercial jingles, political speeches, and the daily prattle that constitutes the little edifying foundation of being. The characters are the discourse of identity caught in the process of being de-authorized.

Elsewhere (González Echevarría 1972, 1985, 1986), I traced Sarduy's sinuous itinerary after his lacerating exercise of cultural asceticism (better yet, with an eye for etymology, through the exercise of purging all cultural discourse) that is *From Cuba with a Song*. Since I believe that writers' itineraries tend to be manifold, divergent, parallel, asymptotic, conflicting, labyrinthine, and that, like everyone else, writers are inhabited by various selves – hypostasis and simulations, poses, and simulacra – this time I will follow another one of Sarduy's courses.

What distinguishes Sarduy from the writers of the Boom is his passion for painting and for painting's ties to writing – in other words, the scriptural in painting and the painterly in writing. I could begin with the following oversimplification: the paradoxes, deceptions, and perplexities of writing lead Sarduy to painting, to the fetish for the visual text. What better way of bringing about that forever thwarted wedding of signifier and signified than to turn them into one, just as husband and wife become one flesh in the Christian ritual? For Sarduy, this is not a matter of ekphrasis, of painting with words, but rather, of words that paint, words that are paintings.[1] This undoubtedly explains his obsession with action painting or with body art (tattoos, make-up, and other forms of corporeal painting), his frequent collaboration with painters and plastic artists like Martha Kuhn Weber and Alejandro, among many others, as well as his own work as a painter, to which he increasingly devoted his time towards the end of his life. Because the critic, or at least this critic, cannot respond to a graphic text with another graphic text, the dizzying circles of hermeneutics and even perhaps intoxications of heuristics become inescapable. Therefore, I will cast my own narrative over three visual texts of Sarduy, which I will examine in counterpoint with the other route, that traced by his major works. The texts are: "Espiral Negra" ("Black Spiral"), a poem from the booklet *Overdose*, published in Las Palmas in 1972; a picture of 1987, which Sarduy calls "Homage to Li Po" in an inscription to me written on a poster announcing the exhibit in which it was included, and, finally, a painting of 1992, titled "Self-portrait." My purpose is not only to observe the evolution of Sarduy with regards to the visual text, but also the insights that the latter generates when seen in relation to the novels that accompany it under Sarduy's signature. That "SS," Sarduy liked to call it, as in Steady State, but also "ése, ése," ("that one, that one"), as if spotting his fleeing, elusive "I."

"Black Spiral" (Ill. 1) is a text which aspires to evoke the sound of jazz, as well as to signify by means of its own shape. The poem, of which the part reproduced here is only the beginning, intends to make manifest the blacks' anger towards the slavery which uprooted them from their native land, as well as the transmutation of this anger into the musical fury of jazz. Jazz has spread to the entire world through all those bars, nightclubs, music halls, and cabarets, whose names are inscribed in the whorl printed on the page. The spiral swirls back upon a split center where points of departure (Congo, Costa de Oro) and points of arrival (Rio, Virginia) stand out. These names appear surrounded by the circling galaxy of names of places famous for their jazz. At the same time, "Black Spiral" refers to the letters printed on the blank page – a black spiral over a white background. What we see, however, is not only letters, but also names that float as in a cosmic void, a smoldering memory transforming itself into flaming form or frenzied sound.

"Black Spiral" is a poem strictly contemporaneous with *Cobra*, and barely two years earlier than *Barroco* (1974), books in which Sarduy advances versions of textuality derived from the Big Bang theory. The universe is in constant expansion because of the initial explosion of a star whose fragments are scattered through the universe, gradually distancing themselves from one

ESPIRAL NEGRA

a Piet Mondrian bailando

al woogie-boogie

al boogie-woogie

con elegguas   al Haig

a la Cigale

en los tobillos

cajas huesos boullas   al Cotton Club

con campanillas

bambú de las Antillas

frascos llenos de piedras   en las muñecas   al Chori otra vez

a Neuva Orleans

a La Habana

quijadas de caballo   al Tin Angel

a Congo Square   de la Costa de Oro   al Riverside

de Nigeria a Río   del Congo a Virginia

triángulo banjo cueros   del centro negro   al Saint Germain

de Río a Recife

del río   con cascabeles

con cajas de tabaco   al Tabou

al Eddie Condon   los reyes sometidos   con castillos de plumas

al Central Plaza   las mejillas tatuadas   con pulseras de oro   al Caméléon

inmóvil como un río   spiritual/spiral   al Half note

al Stuyvesant Casino

al Chori

al Jimmy Ryan's   wasn't dat a wide ribber   al Cafe Bohemia

flechas rojas, minúsculas   al Nick's

al Ember's

al Sociey

al Voyager's room

al Cafe Metropole

al Composers

al Savoy ballroom   al Birdland

al Apollo Theater   al Carnegie Hall

al Ecole Juillard

Ill. 1: Severo Sarduy, "Espiral Negra"

another, with a vague memory of the initial trauma and lost unity. The shape of "Black Spiral" reflects this dynamic structure, in its turn an allegory of the African Diaspora caused by the violence of slavery. *Overdose*, the title of the booklet that contains this poem, also refers to the shape of the spiral: the drug brings about an explosion of consciousness ("to blow the mind" one says in English), turning the self into a black hole around which spin scraps of meaning. The self is no more than the nebulous memory of a scattered unity. The names of the jazz emporia gyrate and are plunged into a gaping drain that suctions them towards nothingness and meaninglessness.

Sarduy wrote "Black Spiral" at a stopover in his itinerary strongly marked by Octavio Paz's theories about rotating signs and when the Mexican was writing poems like *Blanco*. This poem displays a typographical shape not unlike Sarduy's, and is very much derived from Mallarmé's "Un coup de dés." Of course, the thematics and politics of Sarduy's poem owe little to Paz, who, unlike Sarduy, is not heir to the African holocaust in America. Nonetheless, "Black Spiral" preserves a centered concept of language and its blank core can be seen as a representation of the *pneuma* of the spirit ("spirit/spiritual") which once endowed the now-orbiting signs with meaning. At the same time, the shape of the poem, like the theory of the Big Bang, retains a linear concept of language and of the process of representation. The text clings tenaciously to language as the representation of a being that is not pure materiality, but which, like the distant echo of the sea in a conch, was voice, cosmic hum, perhaps a wail. The case is instructive because this atavistic notion of the self will undermine Sarduy's most sustained efforts to reduce writing to mere materiality. The spiral shape, with its suggested reiterations, also announces returns, rebounds and recoils in Sarduy's route.

"Homage to Li Po" (cf. Color Plate 1, p. 10), a title I have somewhat arbitrarily chosen for this canvas by Sarduy, was included in an exhibition appropriately called "Écritures," in Paris, in the fall of 1987. Next to Sarduy's the works of Jean Cartor, Mehdi Qotbi, and Constantin Xenakis were also exhibited. I have called it thus because, when he dedicated the poster to me, Sarduy wrote: 'A Roberto, en el aire, este homenaje a Li Po' ('To Roberto, up in the air, this homage to Li Po' – he had just found out that I had become a pilot). Sarduy had experimented with this kind of texture from the beginning of the eighties. Paintings of his in this style coincide with *Maitreya* (1978), *Colibrí* (1983), and *Cocuyo* (1989), and reflect a sometime antithetical or dialectical relationship with these novels.

In contrast to "Black Spiral" the word has disappeared completely, as has the sensation of depth. There is no center, hole, or abyss to mark even the far-off perimeter of an absence. What appears now represented is (paradoxically) the rectangle of the page or of the frame and the proliferating, identical strokes, as identical as the hand is capable of drawing them. They appear compulsively repeated, as if to underline their sameness, not their difference. These strokes do not represent any voice; at most, only the sound of an insistent psalm. It would be difficult to imagine that these strokes represent, manifest, or act out the will of a creator. Yet, differences do exist. The interior and exterior frames are irregular, above all the interior which appears somewhat frayed. In the border of repeated signs there are differences of nuance, while in the ocher center there are stains, water marks where the thick pigment dried up more slowly.

If "Black Spiral" was an allegory of the disappearance of the self (only to restate the presence of its absence), here, the flat reiteration of strokes without referent does not even mark absence as a memory. The repetition appears to be rather an effort to fill up emptiness, to cover it with marks. Perhaps it is the trace of a laborious drill to pass the time. The whole thing could also be seen as a disciplined exercise of calligraphy in the futile pursuit of perfection. Here being would only leave traces in the minimal errors that betray a trembling of the artist's hand. Is the ocher center a void still to be filled? Can we imagine an interrupted process of becoming? Is the water stain the trace of an accident, of a tear in the smoothness of this seamless time invaded by strokes?

All these hypotheses do not mitigate the tendency of "Homage to Li Po" to elide all reference outside the one to its own support, to the scaffolding of its very possibility of existence. In "Black Spiral" there was a referent: the shape of the spiral itself. Besides, the loop of black letters over the page created a certain illusion of depth and even duration. In "Homage to Li Po" there are only two rectangles which, as I have already mentioned, evoke perhaps the page or the canvas itself – in other words, the material bearings of representation. Only by supposing the repetition of the rectangle within the rectangle as a process of abysmal composition can we sense, like in "Black Spiral," a certain temporality, submerged in an infinity without limits.

But there remain at least two other less apparent possibilities for reading this painting. One, already suggested, is that the inside rectangle represents an incompleteness. As the ocher of the center is also the background of the strokes, it would be possible to think of a void on its way to being filled up. This reading also opens up the possibility of a becoming, of a movement arrested before the canvas was completely covered by compulsive and more or less equal strokes. Of course, filling up the borders of the canvas would constitute the most complete obliteration of meaning, duration, and referentiality. The second reading is that the neat swarm of strokes represents the very weaving of the canvas or of the page, as seen through a powerful magnifying lens. In other words, if the referent of "Homage to Li Po" is the fabric upon which the painting is made, it would represent the most elemental, tangible, and humble bearing of representation. Every minimal stain would be a stitch in the elaboration of the fabric, of the structure that is the text. It is good to remember that the title of the exhibition that housed this painting: "Écritures." "Homage to Li Po" is a representation of writing, but of writing before writing, as something unconnected to language; previous or subsequent to it, but not concomitant with it.

Recourse to Li Po's style, or to that of certain Chinese poetry, calligraphy, and painting is so thorough in this painting by Sarduy that all effort toward originality and, therefore, toward identity appears to have been eliminated. One could recognize this canvas as a "Sarduy" only by observing many other identical or similar ones by him. This macro-repetition, not just of individual strokes but of entire canvases, would make manifest certain chromatic and structural preferences that could become a kind of signature. It would be possible then to notice, for instance, that "Homage to Li Po" is also an homage to some Western painters, like Rothko, to whom Sarduy was particularly devoted and about whom he wrote with an admiration bordering on reverence. The bright orange, like the insistent tonalities of red and the preference for simple shapes such as the square or the rectangle, remind one of Rothko. But the elision of the subject in "Homage to Li Po" is clear, even if we had to recognize that this homage contains perhaps another implicit one to Sarduy's Chinese ancestors. But the allusion is rather oblique, as oblique as those slanting and mocking eyes of Sarduy's that I can see right now giving me a playful look, watching (for) me from some Yoruba or Buddhist heaven.

"Self-portrait" (cf. Color Plate 2, p. 11) reflects an autobiographical tendency in Sarduy's work that is the opposite of the one just described, which is more concerned with eliding the subject. This is a path that deviates from the main course of his itinerary, becoming parallel to it at times, seemingly asymptotically, but then converges with it, turning into the main road. It is a tendency that becomes increasingly important late in Sarduy's life, when he had become well known and was provided with multiple images of his self. Around this time, among his intimate friends, Sarduy referred to himself, with false modesty and playful gender-crossing, as "Juana Pérez." For instance, "Have you seen the story on Juana Pérez in *Le Monde*?" The paradox could not be more evident at first glance: an author among whose favorite themes is the elision of the subject, with a Tel Quelean past stamped by structuralism and post-structuralism, turns around in order to look at himself. Of course, Roland Barthes, one of Sarduy's close friends and mentors had followed the same course. In any case, in *Maitreya* and in *Colibrí* there were already allusions in which the initiated could read summaries and reviews of Sarduy's life. For instance, in *Maitreya*, Luis Leng, the Chinese-Cuban cook, upon moving to Miami, states that "al triunfo de la revolución, y más por falta de materiales para tratar el carnero estofado de cinco maneras que por convicción o desaliento, habían emigrado" (Sarduy 1978: 114).[2] There is no question in my mind that Sarduy is saying here that he left Cuba, not because of his disappointment with the Revolution, but because he would not be allowed to practice his kind of highly formal art. In *Colibrí*, the exiled protagonist earns a living with a tiny box full of performing fleas dressed as mambo queens, a reduced and self-mocking model of Sarduy's own fiction. More directly, in essays like *La simulación* (1982) and *El Cristo de la rue Jacob* (1987), Sarduy includes vignettes from his own childhood and adolescence, while in the latter he retells his life in a narrative that follows all the scars and marks on his body. *Cocuyo* is a *Bildungsroman* that provides a portrait of the artist as a young man that is very clearly a version of Sarduy's own life. After years of reading Sarduy and a friendship that lasted a quarter of a century, I have just now come to realize that this novel plays out the dramatic core of Sarduy's work: the pains and fears associated with the difficult transition from adolescence to adulthood. Sarduy's characters never achieve this passage. *Cocuyo* plays out the terror and resentment towards the authority of adults who hold power and subject the protagonist to physical and, above all, moral violence. All of Sarduy's work appears as an all out effort not to modulate the voice of the master – not to be La Senecta, the Aged One – whose tone rings hollow, arbitrary, and threatening. *Cocuyo* is contemporary with "Self-portrait."

In "Self-portrait" Sarduy appears cornered, as if hiding or cowering in the upper left corner, whence he seems to witness the spectacle of his own being with eyes dilated by terror. "Self-portrait" emphasizes the insurmountable difficulties of painting oneself, of literally "making oneself up" and thereby, as various of his characters demonstrate, of transfiguring oneself violently. From the corner, this ogler, this peeping Tom, watches himself, a fleeting witness in disguise who almost leaves the painting (like that homonym of Velázquez that exits through the door in the background of "Las Meninas"). And what does this voyeur see? At first, one could say that he sees a bunch of doodles that align themselves without rhyme or reason, as in a drawing by a child. The on-looker is the child looking at his own painting. This watching child represents himself by means of a series of apparently non-referential, pre-linguistic strokes: fluid and sinuous lines that are arranged in parallel bundles of differing hues, fields of circular or ovoid figures which, like eyeballs, seem to be looking back at us while floating in some fluid. They are scribbles that appear to be writing, but are closer to doodles and drawings. But, drawings of what?

I think that looking closely one would notice that "Self-portrait" resembles an anatomical plate, like those in medical textbooks (one should not forget that Sarduy studied medicine and claimed – to me – to have won prizes in dissection). The parallel lines are like muscular fibers, and when the groups of parallel lines cross each other they resemble the representation of muscle-groups intersecting each other, as for instance, in the abdomen or the thigh. If we now look in the lower right hand corner we realize that the round shapes with a dot in the center – those little red bubbles – are like cells, and we can imagine the larger circles, not just as eyes, but as ganglia. Sarduy's "Self-portrait" makes literal the commonplace that a good portrait or self-portrait reveals the inside of a person. The painting is a most rending vision of being, of the self reduced to the most fundamental and material supports: the fibers and cells that make up the body.

The peeping Tom child, voyeur of himself, as well as those eye-like circles floating in the painting evoke the well-known theme of "the glance," a topic made popular by Lacanian psychoanalysis and present throughout Sarduy's work. Every glance, even or particularly a slanting or glancing one, is a projection of desire based on castration. The rent body is a ghastly representation of this in "Self-portrait," and the child's look, also directed at the spectator, not to mention the other wandering eyes, involve us in this economy of reflections and desires. The child's look at himself, however, is the most frightful element of the painting, for it creates a deadly form of self-containment that was absent in Sarduy's earlier work, as Oscar Montero (1988: 134-135) has shown in a masterly reading of them. The "prophylactic" eye Montero sees in *From Cuba with a Song*, linking it to the Cuban *azabaches* worn to protect one from the "evil eye," seems to have disappeared.

We have returned, as in the swirl of "Espiral negra," to the representation of being. In "Self-portrait" the literalization of the interior as a primitive form of somatic writing carries the problem of the visual text to its most tenacious impasse: it is not by chance that we come upon the body in the process of being dissected. As far back as the Bible, we find this same impasse throughout the Western tradition every time we confront the temptation of literalness: this is what lurks beneath writing reduced to its material shapes. The dilemma arises periodically in the tradition from Dante to Pound. Literalization kills: the letter itself cannot be but the dead letter. It is precisely for this reason that it is compelling and alluring. Literalization begins in fetishism and returns to it, and its extreme manifestation is idolatry. Consequently, Sarduy, like other modern writers, plays with the visual text, knocks his head against it, but at the same time he writes novels, not just visual texts. If the materiality of the text were the point of arrival of Sarduy's itinerary, we would not have *Maitreya* and *Colibrí*. Sarduy's work is the counterpoint between the fetish of somatic writing and another kind of writing which inevitably must invoke the spirit of the letter – or at least its fictions. This is one of the most productive contradictions in Sarduy: to have left us with texts anxious to see in his own body the very last cipher, and, at the same time, texts that endure beyond the extinction of all the fibers, cells, ganglia, and eyeballs of this mambo king whose spirit is reawakened with every reading, and whom I evoke and summon here.

Translated by Miruna Achim

Notes

1. The presence of painting in Sarduy's novels has been thoroughly studied by Justo and Leonor Ulloa (1985).
2. "Upon the triumph of the revolution, and more because of the lack of materials to make mutton stew in five ways than out of conviction or disappointment, the Chinaman and his pupil had emigrated..." (Sarduy 1987: 90).

Bibliography

González Echevarría, Roberto González
    1972   "In Search of the Lost Center." In: *Review 72* (Fall).
    1985   "Where the Singers Come From: Fragments." In: *The New England Review/Breadloaf Quarterly*, Special issue on The Caribbean, vol. 8, no. 4, 566-575.
    1986   *La ruta de Severo Sarduy*. Hanover, New Hampshire, Ediciones del Norte.
Montero, Oscar
    1988   *The Name Game: Writing/Fading Writer in De donde son los cantantes*. Chapel Hill, North Carolina Studies in the Romance Languages and Literatures.
Sarduy, Severo
    1972   *Cobra*. Buenos Aires, Editorial Sudamericana.
    1975   *Cobra*. New York, Dutton.
    1978   *Maitreya*. Barcelona, Seix Barral.
    1987   *Maitreya*. Hanover, Ediciones del Norte.
Ulloa, Justo and Leonor
    1985   "Severo Sarduy: pintura y literatura." In: *Hispamérica*, 14, no. 41, 85-94.

POETRY IN REVOLT:
Italian Avant-Garde Movements in the Sixties

John Picchione

In the context of the Italian poetic landscape, the 1960s doubtlessly represent a decisive break with traditional canons. Those years can in fact be identified with an aesthetics of transgression which revolts against both the linguistic code and the dominant literary models. On the one hand the major movement, the *Gruppo 63*, aims at destroying the conventional literary institutions without abandoning the linguistic medium; on the other, various groups – although their methodologies vary widely – share the desire to overcome the limits of poetry as a strictly verbal form of communication, transforming it through iconographic and figurative compositions of numerous kinds.

The publication of *I Novissimi* in 1961, including the work of Elio Pagliarani, Edoardo Sanguineti, Nanni Balestrini, Antonio Porta, Alfredo Giuliani, and edited by the latter, marks a turningpoint of Italian literary history in the latter half of the twentieth century.[1] This provocative and revolutionary anthology was to open the way to the formation of *Gruppo 63*, a movement which is synonymous with the new Italian avant-garde.

In general terms, the five poets reject the normal linguistic code because of its reification and commercialization, and because of the conservative ideological implications it conveyed. The alternative language was to be that of disorder, ambiguity, and estrangement. These poets thought that the deliberate construction of a language in crisis was the only way to engender a crisis in the usual representation of reality.

The almost blasphemous disorder of the *Novissimi* – their programmatic laceration and fragmentation of language on the syntactical, lexical, and prosodic levels – was a linguistic-ideological confrontation with closed and anti-critical contemporary language. The latter had become, the *Novissimi* declared, a degraded object too easily consumed and rigid with stereotypes. In its disorienting effects, the terroristic writing of the *Novissimi* refused to court the reader with seductive lyricism and aimed at thwarting habitual expectations. The new style fractured linear discourse, violating not only standard interpretative grammars but also worn-out conceptions of reality.

Poetry's function was to create a distance from the normality and automatism of everyday linguistic models by becoming the locus of a defying and anarchic linguistic construct. Poetry is conceived as a calculated linguistic madness, a "schizomorphous vision" as Giuliani (ed. 1965: 19) defines it, an ersatz schizophrenia that characterizes contemporary society. What matters is not what poetry says: it is the perturbing effects on the reader caused by the formal derangements that constitute new messages, new ways of establishing contact.

In Giuliani's case, poetry is totally guided by the desire to explore the inner movements of language. However, paradoxically, he soon realizes that the proliferation of images without beginning or end, the vertiginous verbal adventure, is a constant reminder of the impossibility of arresting the flux, of finding reassuring linguistic crystallizations. Language's vitality coincides with its own annihilation. The continuous movement from one image to another cannot but effect the dissolution of any possible unity. Poetry is torn between presence and absence, voice and silence, between the search for an authentic reality free from *a priori* schemes of perception and the insurmountable mediation of language. Closed in itself, in its tautological movements, language becomes intransitive and inevitably erases itself. There is no access to direct, primordial awareness. There is no escape from the prison-house of language.

In a collection such as *Povera Juliet e altre poesie*,[2] Giuliani (1965) experiments with poetry constructed as collages of everyday dialogues. These texts are held together only by the metrical and rhythmical order of the sequences, a delirious montage of heterogeneous linguistic scraps which on the one hand suggest that language is reduced to a nonreferential, material entity and, on the other, show the desire to reactivate its power to create new possible realities. Giuliani aims at reducing the linguistic sign to pure movement, to action, gestural invention – not the arbitrary entity that replaces or represents objective reality as a double, as a mirror. The aesthetic matrix of this operation includes the theater of Artaud, the Living Theater, if not Dadaistic experiments. However, Giuliani's obsessive search for the verbal sign in its pure state can also be interpreted as a poetic equivalent of avant-garde music as practiced, for instance, by Cage in his experiments with noises, environmental sounds, and sounds of nature.

Giuliani's poetry, with its dismembered sentences, isolated phonemes, amputated narrative sequences, shows a nonsensical flow which acts as a constant reminder that there is no possibility of intrinsic meaning. In a psychotic delirium, half-human creatures move in a labyrinth of linguistic signs which speak only of the death of all meaning. The being-toward-death of the sign corresponds to the being-toward-death of existence itself.

Another central figure of *Gruppo 63* is undoubtedly Edoardo Sanguineti. At the base of Sanguineti's theory of literature lies the postulate that literature is in its essence a metalinguistic production of ideologies. Convinced that a writer's form of language is his ideology, Sanguineti (1970: 133) argues that "the experience of words conditions – precedes – that of things." Transformation of reality (things) can occur solely through a transformation of ideology, which in turn can be transformed only through the demolition of conventional language.

Literature becomes a revolutionary act by contesting and destroying the ordered system of traditional language and by throwing into question the accepted vision of reality and opposing the dominant ideology. By experimenting with language in a critical fashion, neoavant-garde literature – the literature of "cruelty," as Sanguineti (ibid.: 135-135) defines it – "is not at the service of revolution, but 'is' the revolution at the level of words." The verbal revolution, in its contraposition to the linguistic code, attendant ideologies, and dominant literary models, represents an aesthetics of negation capable of providing a radical new perspective on the world in a struggle against the deceptive normality of contemporary reality. The new destructive form translates itself into a new content: the project of formal disorder denounces the false harmonies and reconciling modes of bourgeois writing, the function of which is to conceal alienation and social contradictions. Formal dissonance carries within itself a message of dialectical antithesis, the negation of the present system, and the desire for a new one. (There is no doubt that the aesthetic thought of the Frankfurt School, Adorno in particular, played an important role for the conception of these poetics.)

The linguistic disorder manifests itself in Sanguineti's poetry as a pathological language, as an objective representation of an historical and social alienation relived from the inside, on the page. For Sanguineti such a strategy stems from the urgency to plunge into the "Palus putredinis," into the historical, collective chaos of irrationality and alienation with the hope of coming out of it. Sanguineti's first collection, *Laborintus* (which actually dates back to 1954), is a modern epic of the alienated and neurotic state of mind represented by form itself, an abnormal, quasi-aphasic use of language.[3] *Laborintus* is constructed as a plurilinguistic text in which fragments of sentences, quotations from foreign languages (English, French, Greek, Latin), neologisms, scientific terms, and scraps of banal conversations are assembled in an anarchic, babelic montage that indiscriminately combines the language of erudition with that of the colloquial.

In Sanguineti's poetry the linguistic sign often undergoes the process of a radical de-semantization, thus effecting an irreconcilable split between signifiers and signifieds. The dismemberment of normal language is carried out not only on a syntagmatic level, but also within words, which are often shredded into phonemes or assembled on the page in a cluster of solitary and silent fragments. The reduction of language to a signification that constantly annihilates itself not only represents the insurmountable division between word and reality but declares the impotence of poetry and of all literature to make sense of the intricate manifestations of history and conscience. Sanguineti's aphasic gibberish communicates the impossibility of communication and denies literature any redeeming function. Poetry becomes a medium of derision and self-derision; it becomes a language of destruction and self-destruction. Sanguineti is inevitably confronted with an insurmountable paradox: as a bourgeois superstructure, poetry (and literature as a whole) must be sabotaged, but the task of sabotage is assigned to literature itself.

Antonio Porta also reaches radical moments of experimentation. In the early 60s he advances a conception of poetry as a discourse reduced to zero: the reduction of language to zero as negation of present reality and as tension awaiting new and liberating conditions of existence. A case in point is the experiment titled *Zero* (Porta 1963) in which the verbal signs, freed from syntactic constrictions and rhythmic recurrences, bring to life a montage of disconnected perceptions, a disquieting and crumbling world. This experiment aims at destroying the pseudo-rational order of daily communication and creates a poetic language that is comparable to the magmatic effects reached by Abstract Expressionism.

Balestrini takes the revolt of the *Novissimi* against the linguistic code and the traditional modes of writing to the extreme. In a world in which the capitalist structure has reduced language to commodity and exchange value, Balestrini finds it mystifying and self-defeating to search for any form of poetry as an authentic expression of the "I." His poetry instead can be defined as a series of Neo-Dadaist collages obtained by a cut-and-paste technique which assembles together the most disparate fragments of linguistic messages that seem to communicate the loss of all meaning. It must be said, however, that language becomes the subject of its own operation, and it takes on the task of recovering new possibilities of meaning. In pursuing this sort of phenomenological bracketing of subjectivity, Balestrini is one of the first in Italy to practice a form of electronic poetry obtained with the use of a computer. The texts "Tape Mark I" and "Mark II," which present a devastating vision of the first atomic bomb, are generated by an IBM computer program randomly selecting material from works by Lao-Tsu, Michihiko Hachiya, and Paul Goldwin.[4]

The groups which have pursued visual experimentation in poetry in the attempt to transcend the semantic confines of the linguistic sign have been particularly dynamic in the 60s and beyond. Their roots lie in the historical avant-gardes and in the works of previous experimental poets: Carlo Belloli, Emilio Villa, the Noigandres group, together with Gomringer, Max Bense, and others. At the same time, they take advantage of many new insights offered by the development of structural linguistics, the theory of information, and semiotics. Often classified as "visual writing," "new writing," or "verbal-visual poetry," this form of experimentation attracts a large number of groups whose work is centered around journals such as "Ana eccetera," "Techne," "Lotta poetica," "Ex," "Linea Sud." It is possible, however, to distinguish three main trends: concrete, symbiotic, and technological poetry.

Concrete poetry, represented by poets such as Arrigo Lora Totino, Mirella Bentivoglio, Adriano Spatola, explores the material base of language and the graphic possibilities it can produce. This poetry communicates its own formal structure, generally establishing an homological relation between form and content. "Concrete poetry," writes Lora Totino, "is an ideogram or a structured field of functions which relate to one another in all parts: graphic, spatial, oral, acoustic functions, as well as those pertaining to content."[5] In some cases, as in Spatola's series *Zeroglifici* (Spatola 1966), the word explodes, leaving behind only its own rabbles. Here, fragmented words, shattered syllables, and phonemes are not only charged with ideological overtones but emphasize the materiality of language. This metalinguistic operation on the one hand de-semanticizes the verbal sign and, on the other, semanticizes it at an iconographic level.

The merging of the territories of poetic writing and those pertaining to visual codes is also pursued with different materials and techniques by the poets who can be grouped in the area of symbiotic writing, in which various elements (phonetic, graphic, spatial, figurative, chromatic) interact, conditioning and modifying their ordinary meanings. The aim of poets such as Ugo Carrega and Vincenzo Accame is to go beyond the traditional boundaries of artistic communication, attempting a unified aesthetic act, embracing a form of "total poetry," a symbiosis of many different media. "Everything is language," claims Carrega; and Accame, in a theoretical statement, declares: "My work aims at producing an act of communication. Before being a word or a graphic entity, the mark which I impress on the paper is a 'sign' …without metaphoric or metaphysical mediation, readable for what it is, a visual objectification."[6]

The poets belonging to *Gruppo 70* (Lamberto Pignotti, Eugenio Miccini, Emilio Isgrò, Lucia Marcucci, Luciano Ori, Michele Perfetti) make extensive use of extralinguistic materials coming from images produced by the mass media (commercial photographs, advertisements, comic strips, photo romances and so on). Defined as technological poetry, this experimentation shifts poetic research from an exclusively verbal practice toward a general art of the sign. This poetry is the result of an encounter, a convergence of different codes of communication which, by interacting, offer new possibilities of signification. The intent, however, is political and ideological. The materials of mass communication are constantly de-contextualized and de-mystified through the use of desecrating and provocative collages. It is a sort of semiological warfare against the consumerist messages of our age. The aim of the technological poets is to return to the sender – the consumer society – its own products, shattered and shredded. "Pieces of our technological world," writes Pignotti (1968: 126), "are taken apart, classified, reassembled, inverted: it is essential to understand the mechanisms which regulate them... The result is comic-strip poetry, tabloid-poetry. Or, better said: counter comic-strip poetry, counter advertisement-poetry, counter tabloid-poetry. Forms and means of today's mass media are utilized and subverted at the same time...."

Two other poets of *Gruppo 70*, Miccini and Perfetti, claim that technological poetry is a "semiological transfiguration of all anthropological events of our times. It does not ignore its own civilization, it rejects it" (Miccini 1972: 3-4). Verbal and visual stereotypes are perceived as alienating and reified social products. Through techniques of irony, derangement and de-familiarization, these poets intend to practice an act of terrorism against the commercial exploitation of the various means of communication. The intent is to unmask the rhetorical mechanisms concealed behind words and images together with their emotional and subliminal effects. Poetry assumes the role of a political struggle which aims at developing a critical awareness capable of bringing about a cultural revolution charged with liberating effects.

Undoubtedly for all the groups and movements which have been discussed, the revolution of poetic forms carries with it the hope of a social and political revolution, the utopian dream of other possible worlds. As such, these movements share with the historical avant-gardes the social critique, the antagonistic-subversive thrust, and the visionary activism which express the aspiration of bringing about a new consciousness, a new behavior, a new and emancipated society.

Notes

1. All quotations are taken from the revised edition of *I Novissimi* (Giuliani ed. 1965); all translations from this and other volumes are mine.
2. Giuliani's poetic production of the 60s is also included in the collections *Chi l'avrebbe detto*. Turin: Einaudi, 1973, and *Versi e nonversi*. Milan: Feltrinelli, 1986.
3. The first edition of *Laborintus* came out in 1956 (Varese: Magenta); it was later reprinted in *Triperuno* (Milan: Feltrinelli, 1964) and in *Catamerone* (Milan: Feltrinelli, 1974).

4. The poems in question belong to the collection *Come si agisce*. Milan: Feltrinelli, 1963.
5. This statement is quoted from *Presenza Sud* 1, 1968, p. 45.
6. Both Carrega's and Accame's statements appear in Giannì (1986: 197).

Bibliography

Giannì, E.
1986   *Poiesis*. Arezzo, Istituto Statale d'Arte.
Giuliani, A.
1965   *Povera Juliet e altre poesie*. Milan, Feltrinelli.
Giuliani, A. (ed.)
1965   *I Novissimi: poesie per gli anni '60*. Turin, Einaudi (revised edition; first edition Milan, Rusconi e Paolazzi, 1961).
Miccini, E.
1972   *Poesia e/o poesia*. Brescia-Firenze, Sarmic.
Pignotti, L.
1968   *Istruzioni per l'uso degli ultimi modelli di poesia*. Milan, Lerici.
Porta, A.
1963   *Zero*. (Milan; revised edition in *I rapporti*. Milan, Feltrinelli, 1966).
Sanguineti, E.
1970   "La letteratura della crudeltà" [1967]. In: *Ideologia e linguaggio*, Milan, Feltrinelli.
Spatola, A.
1966   *Zeroglifici*. Bologna, Sanpietro; new edition *Zerogliphics*, Los Angeles, The Red Hill Press, 1977.

WHEN THE AVANT-GARDE REACHES ITS MASS:
The *Novissimi* and The Political Situation in Italy: 1977

William Anselmi

As the title of this paper suggests, there is something left unsaid about the Italian cultural milieu and the role of the avant-garde: a specific time frame and a convergence in a specific space of experimental practices which, simply put, have been removed from history.

When we consider critically the role of the Italian *Neoavanguardia* in the greater context of what constitutes the discourse about and of the avant-garde and experimentalism, we refer to a consolidation period of about eight years. We can start with the publication in 1961 of the anthology *I Novissimi* and end with the folding of the magazine *Quindici* because of political divergences among the members of the editorial board in 1969. Although somewhat arbitrary, this time span seems to prefigure the inevitable self-exhaustion of neoavant-garde praxis. Without having to resort to Paul Mann's *danse macabre* of *The Theory-Death of the Avant-Garde*, Edoardo Sanguineti's lucid analysis in *Ideologia e Linguaggio* clearly shows how the neoavant-garde works are destined to be fossilized in a museum space by entering into the framework of neocapitalistic markets, circulation and distribution labyrinths.

Yet, these privileged considerations act as a deterrent to critical-historical analysis. A neoavant-gardist movement is brought under scrutiny, its experimental practices evidenced, a time-frame set-up *et voilà*, the package is *ready made*, presentable for consumption. Besides a certain discourse of power and elitist presence of most of the participants of the magazine *Alfabeta*, during the late Seventies – the cultural/theoretical discursive continuation of the *Neoavanguardia* – it is not until the end of the Eighties with the publication of the anthology *Poesia della Contraddizione* (Poetry of Contradiction) and the appearance of the *Gruppo 93* that another discourse of and about experimental practices resurfaces. Somehow, a gap is created, but it is an invisible fracture, one that runs underneath the various cultural currents because of a contradictory malediction.

The time frame is the Seventies; in the public arena this period is best remembered for *Staying Alive* in Western Society. Although resistance to the hegemonic mandate on youth takes a nihilistic form such as the *Punk* movement in England – with the movie *The Great Rock & Roll Swindle* depicting its consumerist demise – in Italy the appearance of *il Movimento*, or "Movement '77" creates a counter-cultural praxis that invests mass consumption with an explosive effect. So much so that a strange political creature – an historical compromise of sorts between Italy's two major parties, the Christian Democrats and the Communist Party – tacitly eliminates any alternatives to itself in the sociopolitical arena. For this, there has to be a sacrificial victim in 1978 in the name of Aldo Moro, whom the Red Brigades immolate on the altar of avant-garde Marxist-Leninist revolutionary ideology. After his death a silence slowly permeates all counter-hegemonic practices, so that by the early Eighties the so-called emergency period is over. Yet, what remains is a schismatic reference to a dark period of the Italian political laboratory. On the one hand, a democracy under attack but still resistant, on the other an avant-garde death. In between these two analytical constructs – silence – a malediction. Running parallel to this space-time frame is the fall and subdued resurrection of the neoavant-garde.

The specific significance of Italian experimentalism – as exemplified by such *Novissimi* poets as Antonio Porta, Nanni Balestrini and Edoardo Sanguineti – was, basically, to attempt the de-alienation and de-reification of the human subject through language. Language is also the tool by which *Kapital* creates the illusion of a fruitful life world, investing it with altered conceptual frameworks borrowed from Romantic and post-Romantic discourses: creativity, the individual, life as *prêt-à-porter* art. In the Sixties, the *Novissimi*, in their textual practices and cultural interventions, initiated elitist antagonistic practices which by the mid-Seventies had become mass experimental practices within the *Movimento*. It is at this point that the avant-garde reached its critical mass, and it is precisely this period and this movement that has been removed and silenced in History.

Rather than a postmodern, posthistorical re-construct – putting a mask on a ghost – the attempt at work here is a critical analysis of how successful the transmission of experimental practices from an elite to the mass was. By doing so, it is hoped, certain considerations can be made about the role that avant-garde and/or neoavant-garde experimental practices have had, or still can have in this, our postmodern life-world.

How did the transmission occur? In the early Sixties, as already stated, the *Novissimi* had brought into the foray of Italian provincial/hermetic cultural discourses several critical practices through textual strategies and production, some of which can be characterized according to the following:

a) *de-automatization* – the detachment from an habitual vision of the state of things;

b) *consciousness-raising awareness* – of the subject as a reified object;

c) *de-alienation* – the re-integration of the self in its ludic and sensual aspect in the creative act;

d) *expression* – in the possibility that *parole* has to express a particular condition which does not adhere to the parameters imposed by the *loi-langue*; and finally

e) *poiesis* – giving, in the artistic doing, values and meaning to the world, of a subject re-integrated in his/her possible subjective totality.

This interpretation of what was implicated by the neoavant-garde praxis is imbued with a Nietzschean reading of reality, in that the subject becomes the self-sufficient creator of values understood to be necessary illusions, interchangeable and continuously renewable. Putting forward these categories, which underlined the experimental work, serves to demonstrate how some critics, such as Pasolini, failed to see the anarchic emancipatory potential which was present in the avant-garde materials. Having stopped to consider only the theatrical aspects, they forgot the necessity to represent or to attempt to represent the totality of being rather than the consideration of a schematic division between art and life, so easily identifiable as the bourgeoisie practice of false consciousness. So that in the end, the neoavant-garde is not only the manifestation of a presumed totality of a being recuperated from reification, but also an experimental praxis that found its natural ground in language, working in/through language to obtain immediate emancipatory results. Reality, then, is the final construct of language, through which identity is verified and affirmed. By altering the *modus operandi*, the fabric of reality is linguistically altered *ad infinitum* insofar as it deflates, de-structures, and de-contextualizes the way that *Kapital* works its way through language and being, as critics such as Ferruccio Rossi-Landi and Giorgio Ceserano have shown.

It is this background that should be seen as the one setting the stage for the mass participation of individuals in the Seventies that decried private space as a political space. In 1976 an exemplary text circulated within the movement, *Alice è il diavolo – sulla strada di Majakovskij: testi per una pratica di comunicazione sovversiva* (Alice is the devil – on the Mayakosvky trail: texts for the practice of subversive communication) by the *Collective A/traverso*. This book, the critical experience of a *radio libera* (independent radio) in Bologna, Radio Alice, served as a practical text of artistic emancipatory praxis.

Radio Alice was not an isolated case: the main frame, the illuminating scenery was all around. The walls of Italian cities had become the intersecting space of subject and object, of desire and praxis. Political/artistic graffiti had become the immediate expression of emancipatory practices. The vertical approach of liberation postulated in the works of the *Novissimi* – because of the hierarchization of intellectual work to which they had voluntarily fallen victim – had now become the horizontal landscape where students and workers met and exchanged knowledge and tools for radical change. *Indiani in città* (Indians in the city), by Egeria Di Nallo, is a key document in understanding the importance of the transmission from the high world of academia down to the low world of alienation, work and marginalization. In it a disappearing act is played out: historical documents now irretrievable are displayed, the very same that testify to an abundant production destroyed, burned, and willfully forgotten so as not to incur in the repressive actions of a belligerent but democratic state. For the Legge Reale (the *Reale* – real? royal? – law), a fascist remnant of Mussolini's legacy, was indiscriminately applied and anyone caught with "subversive" material could end up spending up to twelve years in prison. Contrast this with the polemic on *L'Espresso* between Umberto Eco and Julia Kristeva on the language of the movement: Futurist, Dadaist or Surrealist?[1]

Years later, it is still a mystery as to how an antagonistic generation could so easily be dismissed from history and with it, its cultural contribution, its counter-hegemonic practices. Immobilized between the spectacle, in the Debordian sense, of the armed struggle – the unfathomable *Partito Armato* (Armed Party) – and the democratic oppression – either with or against the state – all differences vanished. And a particular creative group from the area of the movement, the so-called *Metropolitan Indians* who testified to the diversity, solidity, and creativity of marginalized class melted into air.

A totality of beings in a body of silence

La scelta della voce (Choosing the voice) is the name of a section in Antonio Porta's work of poetry in 1980, *Passi Passaggi* (Steps Passages). It was a section commissioned and performed for theater, a visible way to break through the silence imposed by dominant social structures, so as to foreground the need for the Voice. Around the same time, Nanni Balestrini envisioned a performance of his work *Blackout* by singer Demetrio Stratos of the group *Area*, who had revolutionized the Italian music world and whose unsuccessful battle with leukemia cut the praxis short. In experimenting with his voice Demetrio Stratos was able to achieve sound poetry – the origins of which were to be found in futurists, dadaist and surrealists alike. His was an operation on language, words, and sound that best reflects the activity and the experimental practices that made the movement what it was: a reservoir of loose dogs – *cani sciolti* – and creative groups who did not differentiate the private from the political. It was a re-reading of the avant-garde and neoavant-garde experiences with the dominant desire of poiesis, of poetry for/in public under the guise of the collective rather than an individualistic reading; substituting *homo faber* with *homo ludens*.

Yet, another artist, singer-songwriter Claudio Lolli, best represents that historical moment when experimentalism reached its critical mass and became a collective/individual voice. At this intersection in time, the Italian music scene had arrived split in two worlds. In the old world, commercial discoish repetitions of the same; in the new, a proliferation of heterogeneous instances that had as praxis the totality of the individual, best expressed by the voice. The physical/spiritual antithetical division was resolved by the voice, simultaneously assailing the sky and giving the pleasure of the flesh, identity and desire. To become voice meant to convey the actor behind the words, the music that becomes other with respect to itself. In a still modern world, the dramatic and the comical would vie for it in a game of masks – the aspect of the single individual, in choosing a voice with respect to the chorus, the social, but also an imposed will of the collective vis-à-vis the individualistic. To become marginal as an actor meant to put oneself on the threshold of the passage, of becoming the presence, the word. It meant to leave oneself open, gesture, invitation – in other words, the utopian – of that which can be assimilated but cannot be reduced to a formula in being an individual. Possibly, the singer-songwriter circulated as a re-creation of one's embedding in the social, while the commercial singer entrusts itself to the object, the impersonal record, the same-as-self in a distorted reading of Benjamin's words.

Claudio Lolli then was the singer-songwriter of the Movement, as the subject through which a practical discourse can interject experimental praxis and mass distribution. The album *disoccupate le strade dai sogni* (Unoccupy the roads from dreams), which appeared at the apex of student and workers' counter-hegemonic praxis in 1977, presents a variety of antagonistic constructs/texts which find a unique voice. It becomes the exemplary text: the cover of the album itself is the framing, the title its consequence. The image is that of the song-writer dressed as a clown, holding a scythe (metonymic reminder of the icon of Communism as well as death, of harvest as well as violence). In the background skyscrapers crossed by a rainbow. The praxis of the song-writer is that of a ludic recuperation of the subject, not only through songs but also by the social space of the text, as emphasized in that period by the metropolitan Indians. The title lends itself to a double-entendre: un-occupy the streets from dreams/laid off the streets of dreams. Apocalyptic and joyful, the final tension of contradictory possibilities. Exempla:

a) Denunciation of his own work in *Autobiografia Industriale* (Industrial Autobiography), where a waltzy musical background is the host for an act of expiation; that is, on how one becomes a singer song-writer:

> Autobiografia industriale, viva le tette dell'industria culturale! Tette opulente e dissetanti, ma, tutto sommato un po' troppo 'pesanti'. Io a quel tempo stavo ancora aspettando Godot, cioè aspettavo la morte per poter dire 'rinascerò', fatto diverso, collegato d'amore alle masse << più cultura, più lotta di classe>> ma Godot non è mai arrivato .... Autobiografia industriale, come inserirsi nell'industria culturale, cioè: come possono gli intellettuali dare una mano per mantenere sempre gli stessi rapporti sociali. (Lolli 1977)[2]

b) Presentation of revolutionary praxis as opposed to utopian dreaming in *Attenzione* (Watch out):

> Attenzione che non ci ritroviamo tra le mani la paura immensa e vera, dentro il corpo, nella testa, tra le mani, la paura calda immensa e vera della rivoluzione. (Lolli 1977)[3]

c) Documentation of pre-revolutionary praxis and mass media consumption/ distortion of the same in *I Giornali di Marzo* (The Newspapers of March), a song that makes use of experimental techniques such as collage and composition. Lolli, in this song, used passages, except for the last two lines, from two Italian newspapers, *La Repubblica* (in the center-left political spectrum) and *Il Resto Del Carlino* (in the right-wing political spectrum). The relentless rhythm in words and music brings the listener/user towards the realization of a double isotopy: the reading of how facts are presented – the newspapers of March have spoken – coincides with the voice of those who have lived through them as a subject – the wind tickles those dreams stuck on the teeth's gate. But the relentless rhythm is possible only through the technique employed, the montage so dear to avant-garde praxis:

> I giornali di Marzo hanno spiegato, i giornali di Marzo hanno raccontato, èquello di ritrovare un accordo un colloquio (è sfuggito per miracolo al linciaggio) il più preoccupante per i medici è un carabiniere (ha inoltre fatto un esame esterno del cadavere) senza sapere dove andare, senza sapere che direzione prendere (inginocchiarsi, prendere la mira e sparare) solo la pasticceria memore della recente ferita è serrata (nel primissimo pomeriggio con il cielo ancora parzialmente sereno).... con i bottoni dorati e gli ottoni lucenti, fischiando la Marsigliese, mentre il vento fa il solletico ai sogni rimasti impigliati nel cancello dei denti. (Lolli 1977)[4]

This last example is a text that documents and chronicles the beginning of the end of the movement. It records the 11th and 12th of March uprisings of 1977. In Rome a peaceful protest march in memory of a young woman shot to death by the police was infiltrated by agent-provocateurs, and subsequently, the march degenerated into urban war. The revolt went on for two days, in Rome and in Bologna. About a year later, in May 1978, Aldo Moro's death brought the Movement to its knees, and finally, the ultimate act of contrition, to its disappearance from history. The newspapers chronicled its disappearance as a liberation from terrorism. Nanni Balestrini in his 1987 novel *Gli Invisibili* (The Invisible Ones) chronicled an alternate reading of the Movement. A Movement, in the end, of an unrealized alternative: one last great story before postmodernism gave us "words of love" in *La parola innamorata* ("Word in Love"), the significant closure to an unprecedented participation in experimentalism.

Notes

1. As reported in Castronovo and Tranfaglia (1976).
2. For this and the following passages from the album, I have provided a translation in English: "Industrial autobiography, hooray for cultural industry's tits! Opulent tits, thirst quenchers, but in the end too heavy. I was still waiting for Godot at that time, that is, I was still waiting for death in order to say 'I will be born again', a different fact, connected to the love for the masses 'more culture, more class struggle' but Godot never showed up .... Industrial autobiography, how to become part of the cultural industry, that is: how can intellectuals help to maintain the same social relations".
3. "Watch out that we don't find ourselves with our hands holding on to fear, immense, real fear, in the body, in the head, between our hands, the immense, warm fear of the revolution".
4. "The newspapers of March have explained, the newspapers of March have narrated, it is finding an agreement a dialogue (by a miracle he missed been lynched) more worrisome for the doctors is a paramilitary policeman (he also did the external examination of the corpse) without knowing where to go, without knowing what direction to take (get on your knees, aim, shoot) only the pastry-shop was closed down mindful of the previous wound (in the early afternoon with the sky still partially serene).... with golden buttons and shiny brass, whistling the Marseillaise, while the wind tickles the dreams stuck to the teeth's gate".

Bibliography

Balestrini, Nanni
	1980		*Blackout.* Milano, Feltrinelli.
	1987		*Gli Invisibili.* Milano, Bompiani.
Castronovo, V. and N. Tranfaglia
	1976		*La Stampa Italiana del Neocapitalismo* 5. Bari, La Terza.
Cavallo, F. and M. Lunetta
	1980		*Poesia Italiana della Contraddizione.* Roma, Newton Compton
			Editori.
Ceserano, G. and G. Collu
	1973		*Apocalisse e Rivoluzione.* Bari, Dedalo libri.
Collettivo A/traverso
	1976		*Alice è il diavolo - sulla strada di Majakovskij: testi per una pratica di
			comunicazione sovversiva.* Milano, L'Erba Voglio.
Di Nallo, Egeria
	1978		*Indiani in Città.* nuova universale cappelli.
Lolli, Claudio
	1977		*disoccupate le strade dai sogni.* Ultima spiaggia, GKAY 29713.
Pontiggia, G. and Enzo Di Mauro
	1978		*La parola innamorata.* Milano, Feltrinelli.
Mann, Paul
	1991		*The Theory-Death of the Avant-Garde.* Bloomington and Indianapolis,
			Indiana University Press.
Porta, Antonio
	1980		*Passi Passaggi.* Milano, Arnoldo Mondadori Editore.
Rossi-Landi, Ferruccio
	1983		*Language as Work and Trade.* Massachusetts, Bergin & Garvey
			Publishers.
Sanguineti, Edoardo
	1975		*Ideologia e Linguaggio.* Milano, Feltrinelli.

AVANT-GARDE AND TRADITION: A CRITIQUE

Lello Voce

What my Italian friends of *Baldus* (Biagio Cepollaro and Mariano Bàino) and I have already underlined in the past years is the exhaustion of the normative function of tradition at the moment when it crashed with postmodernism and with the postmodern period, in which the *pastiche* has given us one more chance (often badly used and transformed into an uncritical and magical-symbolistic jam-style), that has situated itself beyond the bipolarity avant-garde/tradition. What we have felt as the main problem wasn't trying to found again or reintroduce this or that neo- or ultra-neo-avant-garde, but trying to restore the basic, minimal conditions for whatever action was required to renew literary research: the possibility of critical recovering and reuse of different side materials, of obscured traditions driven back beyond the borders of the literary semio-sphere. We have turned our attention to macaronic poets, to minor and forgotten ones from the past and the present, and it has not been for the sake of the bizarre, the unusual, in search of up-to-date fashionable materials for always new mannerisms. On the contrary, it has been a try, felt as necessary and not postponable, to prospect the ruins, an attempt to construct a critical archeology that could replace the fuzzy postmodernist catalog of remains with a critical, useful cartography, committed to the recovering of any building materials necessary for the realization of a communicative project, which would be complex and absolutely contemporary.

Tradition works thanks to a *selection*, which as far as it is concerned aims toward a *preservation* and a subsequent *transmission*, which is supposed to be endless: the great poet, the one who founds a tradition, "eternalizes" himself. Now, if you carefully look at it, at least from a certain point of view, avant-garde seems to have been working following similar ways. It aims to occupy the center of the symbolic chess board and by removing at least in principle any aesthetic-cultural value (in a word: market value) from everything that isn't avant-garde, selects and does nothing but set up a norm again which aims to make itself absolute. To cut it short: it does nothing but found a new tradition. That is maybe more than the recognized aporia that leads avant-garde between the arms of the Museum: other alarming reflections can be identified. If tradition exorcises the future, the dynamism which is inborn in any system of representation and of expression, through the harmonic, stagnant, timeless immobility of what is once and once for all, the virus that produces *anxiety of influence*, avant-garde, on its side, doesn't treat the future any better, but excludes any Musilian "nostalgia of the future," deeply convinced as it is that it already *is* the future. It cohabits with an anguish for the getting over, a sort of "anxiety of tomorrow" and it doesn't conceive another avant-garde following itself, but it prophesies, at regular intervals, art's death: final solution of any contradiction between text and context, between art and life. In both the cases, the dialogue with history, with the complex and subtle globality, is replaced with an exclusive relationship, which is in some way also short-sighted, with a certain historical series, which is supposed to be unique, predictable, "direct to," since avant-garde and tradition are both the daughters of the same flabby, historicist belly. Neo-mythological or neo-orphic, or Neo-romantic arcadia and avant-garde, or neo-avant-garde arcadia are equivalent from this point of view, the two faces of the same medal, and they lose, just because they are "mannerist," their bet with contemporaneousness and with the future.

From all this comes another paradox: if avant-garde is a strategy aiming to conquer the whole symbolic stake, to occupy the center of the artistic semio-sphere, and if we accept the anachronism thanks to which it would be possible to define as "avant-garde" all those poetics and cultural strategies that have succeeded in it, then tradition would risk being nothing but *genealogy of avant-gardes*.

An avant-garde which is worthy of the name can't do without its own revolution. It needs what I would define as a contestual "crutch." An avant-garde is never only a matter of style, or of poetics. It is always that and something more, a stake bet on the extra-text. On the other hand, avant-garde needs for this extra-text to develop itself by moving in a progressive, linear way: this must happen so that it can recognize itself as advanced in relation to the extra-text. There is no avant-garde that can resist in the face of aleatory or circular dynamics... And I think there is no doubt that the social and historical dynamics of the globe – no matter if they were random, sussultatory, ambi-guously circular or catastrophic – have been throwing themselves heart and soul for at least a thirty-year period into giving the lie to any historicism. All that, incidentally, in total absence of any revolution and in a contemporary flourishing of anthropological mutations, more or less tele-radio-activated...

With the single exception of the scientific-technological field, in which the march goes straight on, one revolution after the other, with the contrary risk, which I would define as inflationary, or redundancy which turns into a background noise or a buzz... It has gone beyond its own end with the speed of light; it has lapped its "day after," it has gone beyond, towards the galaxy of the virtual life and death... and it gives no sign of being willing to stop.

So it is understandable that today, whenever one faces avant-garde literary products, their "crutch" is technological rather than socio-political. So it sometimes happens that the author lays the stress on the means, on the technological equipment rather than on the message, on the meaning, on communication. But the technological instrument itself is not enough for artistic production; it is only just an instrument whose necessity is decided by any single author and which is not sufficient to the aesthetic success of an art product. The peana to Internet and/or to new technologies demonstrate a worrying superficiality and roughness in the analysis of the context in which any aesthetic production locates itself. They don't ask themselves anything about the economic and financial interests and structures that underlie the mechanisms of production and use of these *media*, anything of what in the past one would call the "communications channel's property." They lock themselves in a dimension that I would call – from a cultural-political point of view – *before hacker.*

I think that the adhesion of some lines of Italian *Neo Avanguardia* and of some of the Sound, Visual, and Concrete European and international research to the coeval and present and future technological fashions is understandable in this ambit, but I also think that it can have sometimes based itself upon an idea of "progress" which is uncritical and devoid of any anthropological and political-philosophical considerations and that has ignored the warnings by Benjamin and Bloch about the "spatial and temporal inequalities," so hiding the porousness of the real landscape. Possibly, the new avant-garde will never escape the settling of the score with the problem of non-contemporaneousness of historical development and therefore with the guilty conscience of its being markedly eurocentric. To say it the way Bodei said it: "We all live in the same chronological time and on the surface of the same planet, but time and space are not homogeneous, equal for everyone. Different historical times condense and intertwine in the current year and we are lost, placed along different spatial and temporal axes, or, better, along inequalities which are both historical and geographical." Avant-garde, by believing in a linear and unique process of development, at the head of which it places itself, betrays the *multiversum* formed by the simultaneous presence of different *Jet-Zeit*. Its being on time, as a matter of fact even early, as to its own temporal series, is also its absolutely European and Western untimeliness and its being non-simultaneous as regards all the rest of the world.

Haroldo de Campos – semiologist and poet, writer and philologist, theorist of literature and translator – has shown a different way to escape the narrow passages of avant-garde/tradition bipolarity, framing a poetics that faces traditions (in particular the Romance one of the beginning), spraining and renewing them with excellent experimental acumen, thanks to a production in which the contributions from the work of troubadours and of Dante, of the baroque poetics and of the minor Romance authors mix with the most important acquisitions of literary research. Haroldo de Campos points out with great confidence the presence of tradition *inside* avant-garde. He underlines the fact that any experimentation can't do without a dimension which is both intertextual and historical, in which any new text is the further tessera of an endless dialogue with the past and the future. The purpose of this research is not so much the "being beyond," but instead the getting deeper and deeper inside the meaning and the roots of the literary event. It is a creative dynamics, which is able to renew word by word, verse by verse, the unavoidable necessity of a future which goes beyond any mannerist cul de sac... He demonstrates the evident need for the beginning of a debate that finally points out the whole richness of the contribution of the forgotten traditions inside experimental dynamics.

There is another, final problem... As I have already said, avant-garde is not only a matter of style. It is always this and something more than this. It needs that contextual and already-mentioned "crutch." That is to say, avant-garde doesn't affect only the text but the context all together. As Guido Guglielmi underlines in one of his recent essays, it is only the will and the "political purpose of the word" that make possible the discrimination between experimental language and postmodern language, which isn't less daring, but is techno-arcadic at the same time.

In a word, there's no avant-garde without its revolution. Now starting from, I would say, 1989, that is what has been in crisis: we lack an idea of revolution. The "end of Communism" (would it be true or supposed), far from being the end of any possibility of creating a "new world," anyway, for sure, marks the end of a revolutionary model – in substance the Soviet one of 1917 – and sets the necessity of planning a new one. This is certainly a titanic effort which isn't up to the men of letters, or at least not only up to them. Anyway, the thing is that till that moment, talking about avant-garde will be nothing but *poetese* ("poetish"), but reducing the problem to a mere matter of style, precisely to what it is not.

C.
EXPERIMENTATION IN
THE LANGUAGE ARTS

THE ENDLESS ENDS OF LANGUAGES OF POETRY
Between Experiments and Cognitive Quests

Wladimir Krysinski

1.0

I will begin by raising some semi-provocative and semi-naive questions. First: do we still need such terms as "the avant-garde"? Such categories as "transgression" and "rupture"? As "innovation" and as "the new"? Second: can we give an unequivocal meaning to the term "experimentation" and to the general category of "experimental poetry"? And third: how can one determine where artistic language stops? These questions give a direction to my critical purpose which may be summarized as follows: to review some significant moments and achievements of so-called experimental and/or avant-garde poetry in order both to relativize and to enhance the critical and historical validity of the above-mentioned terms. It is obvious that nowadays they either still guide critical reflections on poetry, art, and literature or have been simply rejected. I do not intend to indulge in a well-known postmodern dogma saying that the avant-garde is dead. Nor do I want to overemphasize the importance of the avant-garde and its supportive elements, that is to say, "transgression," "rupture," "new," or "innovation." I will rather attempt to review and to rethink a number of concrete creative facts and critical views.

The two following quotations will provide a good basis for achieving an approximate cognitive mapping of the various problems and phenomena linked to the emergence of Concrete, Visual, or Spatial poetry in the 60s. My first quotation is a "Concrete" poem and the second one is a critical comment. The Concrete poem is the famous *Pós-tudo* by Augusto de Campos (1994: 34-35; cf. ill.1). I translate it into colloquial language:

> I had to change everything
> I changed everything
> Now after everything
> Exeverything
> I change / am silent

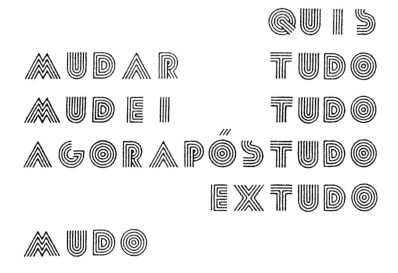

ill.1: Augusto de Campos, "Pós-tudo" (1984)

The critical comment comes from Richard Kostelanetz's *On Innovative Art(ist)s*. Kostelanetz (1992: 265) says: "There is no end in contemporary art, but only an endless stream of new beginnings."

The *Pós-tudo* poem may be considered an allegory of the discursive situation of modern and postmodern art in the broadest sense of the word. It encompasses literature, painting, music, poetry, theatre. *Pós-tudo* achieves an intellectual and poetic synthesis of the present, an epochal configuration of artistic discourses and, by the same token, of what I would call "poetic utterances and meta-utterances," that is to say, the totality of poetic discourses produced as an enormous series of intentionally lyrical, paralyrical, meta-poetic, Concrete, Visual, or Sound statements. However, *Pós-tudo* contains a meaningful ambiguity in the last line, in the very last word. In fact "mudo" means both "I am silent," "I am mute," and "I change." Then, in the spirit of allegory, we can interpret this poem as a sort of clinical statement, as medical diagnosis, and as a program, an expression of the idea that poetry continues notwithstanding the fact that we live in the "post-all" era. In a way, we may assume that Augusto de Campos's poem comes close to expressing what Kostelanetz says differently: "There is no end in contemporary art, but only an endless stream of new beginnings." To accept this assumption means still to believe in the functional validity of the avant-garde and of innovation. I feel that Haroldo de Campos would agree, although he claims that modern poetry is a poetry of post-utopia. But at the same time, as his book *Metalinguagem e outros metas* testifies, Haroldo gambles on the *obra de invenção*, the innovative work of literature or art (H. de Campos 1992: 12). And I would also agree with Kostelanetz, provided that we rethink the critical parameters of the avant-garde's persistency and validity.[1] In order to do so we should recall and review some literary and critical facts of an historical and synchronic sort. Since this is a different subject per se, I will provisionally tackle this question by posing problems while referring to some concrete aesthetic creative gestures.

2.0

In the 60s the avant-garde is not a forgotten or old-fashioned word. On the contrary, it triggers some specific problems linked to the recognition of the evolving dimension of modern art. Specifically, in literature, it results from the fact that both poetry and prose undergo discursive operations which confirm the avant-garde's functional purpose and meaning. The groups of *Noigandres* in Brazil, *I Novissimi* in Italy, *Tel Quel* and *Change* in France attempt to reinvent successfully the languages of poetry and prose. Their specific creative postulates stem from the intention both to extend the poetic process begun in Mallarmé's *Un coup de dés* and to achieve an "interformal" and interdiscursive poetry.

As avant-garde movements, they share some artistic and axiological presuppositions, and they act during a pretty long "inter-semiotic" moment, to recall Haroldo de Campos's (1986: 52) expression from his study "Europe Under the Sign of Devoration." They recognize the importance and the necessity of tradition which indicates a cognitive model of the artistic and ideological intelligibility of the world and language. In that sense the manifestoes "plano-pilôto para poesia concreta" (A. de Campos et al. 1987: 156-158 [1958]), the "Introduzione" by Alfredo Giuliani (1965 [1961]) to the Anthology of *I Novissimi, Poesie per gli anni '60*, "Programme" by Philippe Sollers (1971 [1967]), and "Déclaration du collectif Change à la Havane" (Faye 1974 [1968]) constitute new approaches to the avant-garde problem and to literary discourse. The model is not the "bombastic" futuristic avant-garde of assertive and ostentatious aggressiveness.[2] It rather relies on the cognitive and combinatory function of poetry and of literature understood *sensu stricto* as concomitant languages constantly undergoing functional changes in view of the text's cognitive, semantic, and semiotic events. And these semantic and semiotic events occur and emerge as meaningful forms and messages.

It is precisely in the 60s that the above-mentioned various groups redefine the new parameters for the avant-garde. The Brazilian Concretist poets call for the practice of concreteness understood as constellatory poetic discourse.

Their redefinition of the new cycle of poetry, which comes after the cycle of
verse viewed in terms of the unity of rhythm and form, stems from a cognitive
rereading and from a new understanding of such artistic phenomena as Mallarmé's spatiality, Joyce's organic interpenetration of time and space, Pound's
ideogrammatic method, cummings's atomization of words, Webern's, Boulez's and Stockhausen's dodecaphonic and concrete music.[3]

I Novissimi argue that the intelligibility of the world can be achieved only
through the creation of new artistic languages. As far as poetry is concerned it
has to be "contemporary." And its new languages must dialogue with the
media idioms of the technocratically-minded society. The critical perception
of the social world as schizomorphic and schizophrenic structures imposes
upon Pagliarani, Sanguineti, Giuliani, Balestrini, and Porta the necessity of
inventing new poetic forms.[4] These forms are variable, but they tend towards
the adequate and tensional expression of the overall alienation of the human
subject immersed in present-day industrial and in future post-industrial
society.

In 1967 P. Sollers publishes *Programme*, which is in fact the manifesto of
Tel Quel, première manière. For Sollers the new writing is "textual," and it
builds upon a selectively chosen tradition of "texts of rupture." Dante, Sade,
Lautréamont, Mallarmé, Artaud, Bataille are the most important representatives and models of the "textual writing." They have produced texts with a
strong coefficient of "theoretical and formal contestation" (Sollers 1971: 9).
Sollers establishes a functional and dialectical relationship between reading
and writing. The texts of rupture are not reducible to the classical and mimetic
concept of the written text with respect to the "textual writing." Sollers (ibid.:
11) says:

> what it writes is only a part of what it is. It turns the rupture into an intersection of
> the two networks (two irreconcilable statuses of language). By analogy with reading
> it relates to the openly stated act by which writing chooses its fields of reading
> (cutting [*découpage*], syntax, logic), the "surfaces" where it acts, its *glidings* on
> these fields, on theses surfaces.

In 1968 the group *Change* declares the following (cf. Faye 1974: 2):

> The world in which we live is the world of countless wickets where everything can
> be changed into something else by way of this very function of change: the function
> of language and of writing. Writing is precisely this immense network where the
> world's things and the human gestures circulate: our project consists in showing this
> change.

3.0

In the 60s the emergent idea and practice of experimentation or rather of experimentalism ("sperimentalismo") sheds new light on the problem of the avant-garde. To put it briefly: on the one hand, there is an affirmation of the fact that the avant-garde process is in a way finished and that the process of experimentation begins, marking a new beginning in the field of artistic creation. In 1963, Angelo Guglielmi argues that what he calls the "situation of avant-gardism" does not exist in Italian literature (Guglielmi 1976: 334). Guglielmi stresses the fact that "experimentalism is the style of modern culture." Whereas the revolt of the avant-garde artists was of a thematic and emotional nature, the new experimentalism is rather oriented towards form (ibid.: 332). For Guglielmi "from now on language as representation is a mad mechanism (*congegno matto*). Nevertheless recognizing reality is the purpose of writing" (ibid.: 331).

3.1

The relation between the problem of the avant-garde and the problem of experimentation can be seen in two ways, complementary or mutually exclusive. They stand to each other as reciprocal integration, functional inclusion, or as an exclusion and a new beginning. Thus, being an experimental poet or writer implies either being an avant-garde poet or not being an avant-garde poet. One may see here a new aporia of the avant-garde. And when we return to the declarations and practices of such writers as E. Sanguineti, N. Balestrini, A. Porta in Italy; P. Sollers, M. Pleynet, J. P. Faye, M. Roche, J. Roubaud in France; A. Hatherly and E. M. de Melo e Castro in Portugal; R. Kostelanetz, R. Federman, J. Barth, J. Ashbery in the United States; and Haroldo and Augusto de Campos, Décio Pignatari in Brazil,[5] we notice that either element may be stressed and put into relief. In any event we should point out that both terms are, if not necessary, at least functional, and their utilization still has quite a brilliant future as long as the new terms will not be invented. It seems to me that Jean-François Lyotard has rightly seen the problem of the avant-garde when he attributes to it the role of "rewriting modernity" (Lyotard 1988: 33-44). And the idea of rewriting modernity stems from the Freudian concept of *Durcharbeitung*. In that sense experimentalism could be considered a means and the avant-garde a context in terms of values. That is to say, in terms of Lyotard's understanding of modernity as being preceded by postmodernism and being rewritten as reconstruction and re-elaboration of tradition and of formal, thematic, and ideological material (ibid.: 35).

What is striking in the creative and theoretical activities of the above-mentioned groups is the rethinking and rewriting of Mallarmé's poetics. It occurs as an amplified interdiscursive and intertextual extension of

Mallarmé's intuitions and principles such as constellatory writing, expansion of the depersonalized poetic ego, expanding inscription of the effects that things produce and not the inscription of the thing itself.

4.0

We must recognize the fact that in the various areas of experimentalism, there occurs a continuous and remarkably coherent process of what I would call the self-fulfillment of poetry through Mallarmean operators, such as the "elocutory disappearance of the poet," the typographic and spatial organization of the text, the dialectical re- and counter-writing of prose and poetry. The experimental poets are numerous. Among the most remarkable are Helmut Heißenbüttel, Haroldo and Augusto de Campos, Décio Pignatari, and Jacques Roubaud.

In the volume *Mallarmé* published in 1980 by the Campos brothers and by Décio Pignatari, Haroldo de Campos quotes Hugh Kenner from his *The Poetry of Ezra Pound*. This quotation gives a good idea of the ways that the rewriting of Mallarmé passes into the Brazilian Concrete poetry. Says H. Kenner: "The fragmenting of the Aesthetic idea into allotropic images, as first theorized by Mallarmé, was a discovery whose importance for the artist corresponds to that of nuclear fission for the physicist" (cf. A. de Campos et al. 1980: 178). I would suggest that the "allotropic images" constitute a common denominator of the expandingly inventive Brazilian Concrete poetry.

5.0

Haroldo de Campos's poetic work is a continuous "obra de invenção" cogently engendered by various operators but basically by that of Mallarmé's poetic principles. Haroldo's work goes from *Xadrez de Estrelas* to *Galáxias*. In these works the experiments occur in the sense of testing material as potentially verbal and spatial, discontinous combinations of poetic discourse, of images, of metaphors, of rhythms, and of semantic icons. In that sense Haroldo's poem-anti-poem "Mallarmargem" (in A. de Campos et al. 1980: 17) expresses with typographic, graphic, and spatial relevance the meta-Mallarmean project of a concretizing rewriting of *Un coup de dés*. As Severo Sarduy (1986: 64) puts it in his essay "Towards Concreteness": "constant change, movement and permutation of phonemes, slippage and escape that is manifested above all when the text voluntarily limits its space, drawing a precise geometry on the page, a clear contour, hard edge, or formal enclosure whose drawing arrests the internal fervor of signs, the crackling of sounds, the constant noise of letters appearing mechanically at regular intervals like a telex, or changing, like the electronic screens at airports, until it forms, after multiple metamorphoses at the limit of meaning or legibility, a clear, obvious, immediately decipherable and effective message."

If the experiment is an act, an operation, or process designed to discover some unknown truth, principle, or effect, or to test an hypothesis, what happens in and through Haroldo de Campos's texts may be described as a constant widening of poetic space and discourse, understood as both verbally and spatially determined, and as a limitless operation. The ludic operator also plays an important role in this operation. It may be an aleatory expansion of a word, of an image, of a metaphor and of a quotation. As in the poem "Stone":

> stone
> this lady
> who
>
> sables!
>
> words
> words
> words
>
> I swirl the
> sky
> for a
> squirrel
>
> stone
> lady
> paper
>
> trompe
> l'oeil
>
> all
> paradise
> in para-
> ffin

(H. de Campos 1986: 73)

And in the "proem" and "poem" "Transient Servitude" ("Servidão de Passagem") the quotations of Hölderlin's and Heidegger's sentences as well as those of Feuerbach and Brecht underlie the specific development of the text by repetition and by permutation (cf. H. de Campos 1983: 57). The sentences in question are Hölderlin's "Und wozu Dichter in dürftiger Zeit?" ("And what is poetry for in a time of scarcity?"), Heidegger's "Poetry is the foundation of being through the word," Feuerbach's "Der Mensch ist was er isst" ("Man is what he eats"), and Brecht's "Erst kommt das Fressen denn kommt die Moral" ("First comes grub, then comes the moral").

I will quote a fragment of the poem (ibid.: 53; English translation by Edwin Morgan) in which the permutation of the key words from the above-quoted sentences is emphasized:

poesia em tempo de fome	poetry in time of hunger
fome em tempo de poesia	hunger in time of poetry
poesia em lugar do homem	poetry in place of humanity
pronome em lugar do nome	pronoun in place of noun
homem em lugar de poesia	humanity in place of poetry
nome em lugar do pronome	noun in place of pronoun
poesia de dar o nome	poetry of giving the name
nomear é dar o nome	naming is giving the noun
nomeio o nome	i name the noun
nomeio o homem	i name humanity
no meio a fome	in mid-naming is hunger
nomeio a fome	i name it hunger

As one can see, Haroldo de Campos wrote a "rapid" text, so to speak, based on a series of short sentences and on a combination of terms, on their permutative and repetitive appearance in the proem/poem. All the permuting terms converge towards an assumption that the pure poetry is a pure myth of poetry. The poem should be read according to the code defined by Haroldo de Campos himself (ibid.: 57) in the following terms: "A committed poetry, without giving up the devices and technical achievements of concrete poetry."

6.0

However, here a question arises: what is the language of poetry looked upon from the perspective of the Brazilian Concretists and some European poets who at the same time practice the so-called Spatial poetry and other sorts of poetry, such as visual, objective, mechanistic or permutational, phonic and phonetic? It is evident that the well-known Jakobsonean definition of the poetic function cannot help us understand the sense of the Concretist revolution that produces a completely new understanding of poetry. For Jakobson (1960: 358) the so-called "poetic function" "projects the principle of equivalence from the axis of selection into the axis of combination." This definition confines poetry to what the Brazilian Concretists call the cycle of verse. And Concrete poetry initiates a new cycle, that is, the cycle of poetry of meta- and of para-verse. By using these terms I am trying to suggest that, notwithstanding the programmatic declarations of the Brazilian Concretist poets, their poetry in particular poems does not necessarily escape from the principle of verse making, understood as a sequential continuum of words. In many Noigandres poems one has to recognize that such sequential continuums of words still are more or less functional. However, what is "meta" and "para" with respect to the verse stems from what I would call the "spatial and the iconic drive." The continuums of words are relegated to a relatively secondary role. The language of Concrete poetry is therefore a semiotic symbiosis of the verbal, the visual, the iconic, the phonetic and the vocal. The semiotic symbiosis resides in the fact that all these elements coincide in conveying the message. Through the form, the visualization of signs, the spatialization principle, Concrete poetry approaches the referential world of what is visible, audible, and oral.

7.0

We can admit with Mihai Nadin (1980: 258), who deals with the problem of defining Concrete poetry in his article "Sur le sens de la poésie concrète," that there may be two definitions of it, one negative and one positive. The negative definition underlines the fact that Concrete poetry "opposes itself to traditional poetry, to individualism, to the expression of personal feelings, to subjectivism, to mimetism, to representation and to estheticism." The positive definition says that Concrete poetry is a "form of poetic objectification, relevant because of its constructive aspect as well as its expansion towards the visual, the auditive, and the kinetic."

What seems to be problematic, however, about these definitions, is a really objective definition which would encompass all the signifying elements. While admitting the functional symbiosis of the elements enumerated by M. Nadin, one cannot forget that the concreteness of Concrete poetry cannot be unequivocallly defined. It sometimes requires recourse to the verbal and to explanation of the verbal by the iconic. I would therefore like to suggest that by its very structural, formal, semantic, and semiotic polyvalence Concrete poetry fulfills a meaningful individuation of the message. Not in the sense of a subjective commitment of the creative subject, but because the variety of modalities of combining the visual, the iconic, the verbal, and the vocal contributes to a very strong differentiation of what is conveyed in terms of signs and their interpretation.

8.0

If we try to define the language of Concrete poetry on the basis of pragmatic, semantic, and syntactic components, we should recognize the following: in the pragmatic dimension, the presence of the subject as an uttering instance is quite significantly relativized. The implication of the subject in its relationships to signs is rather limited to the manipulation of the verbal, the visual, and the vocal material, and it presupposes a choice in the ever-growing quantity of signs functioning in the social space. *Ars animae* becomes *ars combinatoria*. *Subjectus liricus* is transformed into *subjectus inventor*.

In the semantic dimension one perceives a series of raw entities taken from the environment. Objects, photos, various icons, advertisements, reproduced signs or words of previous social messages. And in the syntactic dimension one should tackle the various combinatory networks of heterodoxal signs. There is no absolute syntax in Concrete poetry. It exists rather as a prevailing principle of joining together the verbal, the visual and the vocal. The problem of semiosis in Concrete poetry is therefore pretty ambiguous. The poem functions as a set of signs and not as a continuum of words. As M. Nadin (1980: 258) remarks: "It is hardly possible to elaborate a theory which would account for the production of meaning in Concrete poetry."

9.0

Now, how can one identify the signs of transgression and the signs of experimentalism in Concrete poetry? Obviously the norms or structures transgressed are hardly identifiable. Concrete poetry is a mobile and constantly self-inventing artistic text which is metatextually and para-textually oriented. In that sense it constantly both establishes and breaks its norms. The same may be said about the experimental dimension of Concrete poetry. As experimental poetry it should be understood as a constant invention of form as a vehicle of message. In this sense it is an ambiguous operation which does not clearly fix its experimental finality. The opposite can be said about some particular enterprises of literary or metaliterary writings in modern poetry, for instance by Helmut Heißenbüttel, Jacques Roubaud, or Edoardo Sanguineti. They pursue a series of clearly-defined experiences.

I would just recall Heißenbüttel's statement about the scope of his experimental writing. In his "Frankfurt Lectures" Heißenbüttel (1977: 9-10) reminds us that "anti-grammatical, anti-syntactical transformation, and reproduction of language are effective principles in twentieth century literature…. Personally I regard the concept of experimental literature as a product of educational politics, a tactical resort, with no factual validity. Yet it can be used as a means of making oneself understood."

Heißenbüttel overcomes the autobiographical and lyrical material by using it not for self-expression, but to experiment with language. As Michael Hamburger (1977: 10) puts it:

> More and more, it is the verbal processes that count. These verbal processes, in turn, serve to reveal possibilities of meaning, possibilities of truth, inherent in language itself, rather than in the individual consciousness and sensibility that we expect to meet in the poems, short stories, novels and plays of writers less austerely, less rigorously experimental.

If we admit that Heißenbüttel's writing is a systematically-led experiment with language and with literature as a specific metalanguage,[6] we have to acknowledge that the constitution of the textual stage by Heißenbüttel draws directly upon the Wittgensteinean conception of language. In Heißenbüttel's works, this conception affects a rigorous demonstration of the "language game." While referring to the famous phrase of the *Tractatus Logico-Philosophicus*, "The limits of my language are the limits of my world," the author-performer-experimentator plays language in a multiplicity of perspectives: as a statement that is repetitive, permutational, citational, narratively and logically advancing, auto-reflexive, logical, para-logical, lexical, semantic, semiotic and literary. In announcing his performative and experimental project as follows: "To utter the utterable, to repeat the repeatable, to recapitulate the recapitulable is my theme," Heißenbüttel posits contradictory dialectical terms: "Nicht Rekapitulierbares" ("What is not recapitulable"). Theses terms lead to the spectacle of the "language game," with a character of a polydimensional happening where the One Man Show strives to assert itself as a fundamental operator of the indeterminacy of language, paradoxically and dialectically overdetermined by gaming activities such as poetry, novel, philosophy, politics, psychoanalysis, music, and theater. The spectacle of language presented by Heißenbüttel may have the possible effect of an anti-catharsis; it demythifies the metaphysics of a static logocentrism. Played language belongs to everyone and to no one. It does not reinforce the relationships between objects and language. It confirms the permanent state of tautological determination of man in the world:

> the shadow that I cast is the shadow that I cast
> the situation into which I have got is the situation into which I have got
> the situation in which I have got is yes and no
> situation my situation my special situation...
> (Heißenbüttel 1977: 30)

10.0

In light of these and previous considerations, how can we answer the initial series of provocative and semi-naive questions? The necessity of such terms as "avant-garde," "transgression," "innovation," "experimentalism," and "the new," turns out to be a conclusion of a possible global approach to and analysis of a multiplicity of phenomena subsumed under Concrete and experimental poetry. However, in order to mediate all these terms we have to reinvest them with new contents. Avant-garde does not extend the almost imperialist ambitions present in the so-called historical avant-gardes. They wanted to change the world and to eradicate literary tradition. The "post-historical" avant-gardes are rather the cognitive quests that interrogate the historicity of language. The signs of transgression are not easily visible. Concrete poetry does not transgress the traditional norms; it rather begins with some new but not rigid norms. The innovation is not globally affirmed as the religion of the avant-garde. It becomes much more punctual and cannot be measured in terms of an absolute novelty. If every poem is somewhat different, every poem is not absolutely new or innovative. As far as avant-garde and novelty are concerned, they must be understood at the level of one particular work which is a work of invention in terms of formal and linguistic structures. Such is the case of Carlo Emilio Gadda's work in Italy and of João Guimarães Rosa in Brazil.[7]

To experiment nowadays in the field of poetry implies therefore the awareness of the instability and historical character of language facing the poet who is no longer a free subjective individual, but rather an active participant in inventions.

Notes

1. The problem of the avant-garde as a still necessary concept or as a non-valid critical category seems to cross numerous writings. The "death of the avant-garde" is a critical commonplace of postmodern discourse or of any critical discourse which emphasizes the end of modernity or, at least, purports that specific features of the "modern" text such as transgression, negation, or novelty have lost most of their relevance. In one of the sub-chapters ("The Twilight of the Avant-Garde") of his book *Children of the Mire*, O. Paz writes the following: "Negation is no longer creative. I am not saying that we are living the end of art: we are living the end of *the idea of modern art*" (Paz 1974: 149). Theories proclaiming the death of the avant-garde seem to base their assumption on the strong ideological reduction of the avant-garde to one single pattern of creative or social behaviour, as was established by the so-called "historical avant-gardes." However, as P. Mann

suggests, the avant-garde is a concept without a clear delimitation of its content. It also is a phenomenon which is not singular. We "must distinguish among movements within a range of avant-garde" (Mann 1991: 8). In a debate with M. Pleynet (1974: 92), P. Sollers reminds us of the tactical value of the term. He submits that some 20th century avant-garde work has not been recuperated by the bourgeois class, notably Mayakovsky's. Above and beyond any unifying definition, one has to acknowledge that "the avant-garde" still has a strong attractive and functional validity as a denomination. Beyond the historical avant-gardes, the term retains its explicative and heuristic function in a considerable number of literary or artistic works (see critical analyses by Pignotti 1968, Russell 1981, Morawski 1989, Kostelanetz 1992). The same holds true for such groups as *Noigandres* in Brasil, *I Novissimi* and *Gruppo 63* in Italy, or *Tel Quel* and *Change* in France.

2. See my article "The Metatext of the Avant-Garde" (Krysinski 1994).

3. All these methods and proceedings underlie the artistic activities of the Brazilian Concretist poets. They may constitute a sort of metacommentary and a grid of reading for their innovative poetic idiom. As such they shed light on the cognitive function and the semiotic intelligibility of "Concrete poetry" as an intellectual and aesthetic project.

4. As Giuliani (1965: 9) puts it in his "Preface": "When emphasizing the common feature of *I Novissimi* through the notion of 'schizomorphic vision', I was fascinated by the obvious social and cultural implications of schizophrenia as a modality of existence, wherein subjectivity and objectivity of the world are simultaneously impossible."

5. These poets and writers have at least one thing in common: they assume that language is the fundamental material of "literature" or of "poetry"; therefore it must be posited, both formally and semantically, in an historical perspective. As a result, the textuality of prose and poetry involves changing perspectives *through* manipulating their linguistic structures. As such a process, textuality also implies a reflection of the historical situation of prose and poetry inasmuch as it deals with language as an historically given material used to convey the topical messages. Edoardo Sanguineti (1967: 84) clearly elaborates on this problem in an interview with Ferdinando Camon. He says: "What is above all fruitful in the avant-garde is the awareness, at least virtual, and historically concrete, of the historic nature of language."

6. The problem of experimental literature, poetry, theatre, music, and art is that it involves a considerable number of approaches to the act of experimenting. However, the experimenting process presupposes the overcoming or putting into brackets of the pre-experimental states of different arts. Concrete poetry for instance gives rise to new structuring of the "poetic" text; Heißenbüttel's texts act as a metalanguage of the language of literature; *I Novissimi* or *Tel Quel* recognize the fact that they go beyond a lyrical poetry as a definitely surpassed state of poetry, or beyond a realistic state of the novel. Heißenbüttel (1972: 131) underlines that according to M. Bense, whom he quotes from "Programmierung des Schönen" ("Programming the beauty"), "the aesthetic information can never deny its provisory character; it can only be represented through experiment." In

the horizon of doing ("im Horizont des Machens"), where civilization also lies, experiment and tendency ("Tendenz") are not only the purest categories of beauty, they also are the ones that least conceal its creative meaning. E. M. de Melo e Castro (1987: 82) defines experimental poetry in terms of "morphological radicalism, word as object, text as material, visualization, combinatory syntax , signifier/signified, another semantic." He observes: "With experimental poetry, an ethical position of rejection and research is proposed for the first time in Portugal... research is a means of destruction of the obsolete, a demystification of the lying, a methodological openness for the creative production."

7. As a critical category, the notion of "work of invention" refers to the properties of both form and message which can be attributed to some "significant" works. The "inventiveness" of a given work should be assessed from the viewpoint of its relativizing axiology. In the case of novel or poetry, works of invention can only be recognized as such after they have been compared and confronted with other works belonging to the same genre. Examples include *Laborintus* by E. Sanguineti, *Galáxias* by H. de Campos, *Violenza illustrata* by N. Balestrini or *Paradis* by P. Sollers.

Bibliography

Campos, A. de
1994   "Pós-tudo" [1984]. In: A. de Campos, *Despoesia*, São Paulo, Perspectiva, 34-35.
Campos, A. de, D. Pignatari, H. de Campos
1980   *Mallarmé*. São Paulo, Perspectiva.
1987   *Teoria da poesia concreta. Textos críticos e manifestos 1950-1960*. São Paulo, Brasiliense [3rd ed.].
Campos, H. de
1983   "Servidao de passagem." In: E. Brasil & W.J. Smith, eds., *Brazilian Poetry, 1950-1980*, Middletown, CT.: Wesleyan UP., 52-57.
1986   "The Rule of Anthropophagy: Europe under the Sign of Devoration." In: *Latin American Literary Review, Special Issue on Brazilian Literature*, vol. 27, nr. 14, 42-60.
1992   *Metalinguagem & outros metas*. São Paulo, Perspectiva.
Faye, J. P.
1974   "Déclaration du collectif *Change* à la Havane, 8 janvier 1968" [1968]. In: *Change, Première suite* 10/18, 2.
Giuliani, A.
1965   "Prefazione alla presente edizione" [1961]. In: *I Novissimi. Poesie per gli anni 60*, Torino, Einaudi, 15-32.

Guglielmi, A.
1976 "Avanguardia e sperimentalismo" [1963]. In: R. Barilli & Guglielmi, eds., *Gruppo 63, Critica e teoria*, Milano, Feltrinelli, 328-334.

Hamburger, M.
1977 "Introduction." In: Heißenbüttel 1977.

Heißenbuttel, H.
1972 "Keine Experimente? Anmerkungen zu einem Schlagwort." In: Heißenbüttel, *Zur Tradition der Moderne. Aufsatze und Anmerkungen 1964-1971*, Neuwied & Berlin, Luchterhand, 126-135.
1977 *Texts*. Sel. and transl. by M. Hamburger. London, Marion Boyars.

Jakobson, R.
1963 "Closing Statement: Linguistics and Poetics." In: T.A. Sebeok, ed., *Style in Language*, Cambridge, Mass., MIT Press, 339-377.

Kostelanetz, R.
1992 "The End of Art (1969)." In: Kostelanetz, *On Innovative Art(ist)s*, Jefferson, NC & London, Mc Farland & Company, 261-265.

Krysinski, W.
1994 "The Avant-Garde and its Metatexts." In: *Texte*, No. 15-16, 111-135.

Lyotard, J.-F.
1988 "Réécrire la modernité." In: Lyotard, *L'Inhumain, causeries sur le temps*, Paris, Galilée, 33-44.

Mann, P.
1991 *The Theory-Death of the Avant-Garde*. Bloomington & Indianapolis, Indiana UP.

Melo e Castro, E. M. de
1987 *As Vanguardas na Poesia Portuguesa do Século Vinte*. Lisboa, Biblioteca Breve.

Minarelli, E.
1993 *Poesie Doccaso*. Reggio, E. Edizioni Elytra.

Morawski, S.
1989 "On the Avant-Garde, Neo-avant-garde and the Case of Postmodernism." In: *Literary Studies in Poland* XXI, Wroclaw etc., Zaklad Narodowy im. Ossolinskich, 81-106.

Nadin, M.
1980 "Sur le sens de la poésie concrète." In: *Poétique* 42, 250-264.

Paz, O.
1974 *Children of the Mire. Modern Poetry from Romanticism to the Avant-Garde*. Cambridge & London, Harvard UP.

Pignotti, L.
1968 *Istruzioni per l'uso degli ultimi modelli di poesia*. Roma, Lerici.

Pleynet, M.
1974 *Pour quoi? Pour qui?* Grenoble, Presses Universitaires de Grenoble.

Russell, Ch., ed.
1981 *The Avant-Garde Today. An International Anthology* Urbana etc., University of Illinois Press.

Sanguineti, E.
    1967   "Pour une avant-garde révolutionaire." In: *Tel Quel*, No.29, 76-95.
Sarduy, S.
    1986   "Towards Concreteness." In: *Latin American Literary Review, Special Issue Brazilian Literature*, vol. 27, no. 14, 61-69.
Sollers, P.
    1971   "Programme" [1967]. In: Sollers, *L'écriture et l'expérience des limites*. Paris, Seuil, 8-13.

HAROLDO DE CAMPOS' LITERARY EXPERIMENTATION OF THE SECOND KIND

Walter Moser

0. Approach

How can we approach Haroldo's protean oral as well as written production in discourse? What kind of a critical attitude can we adopt that would be adequate to such a proliferating universe made of language which – in the best Romantic "Hyena" tradition[1] – already contains its own critical reflection?

The task seems all the more difficult since the limits of this essay do not allow the deployment of impressive documentation or for lengthy developments. I have therefore chosen, arbitrarily, to "carve out" just one single aspect or issue of Haroldo's universe: its specific experimental nature. Such a procedure, while it cannot do justice to the richness and abundance of my object, should at least have the advantage of treating one dimension of it with some rigor and in some detail.

As a reader of Haroldo's – as well as a listener to his oral performances[2] – my experience is paradoxical. I would like to start out with a sketchy description of this experience, then provide an hypothesis that I will develop at some length.

Haroldo's work has a built-in tendency not to bring about the end of language in a chronological sense (a final moment when language would cease to exist) but rather to carry language, while using it, to its own limits – and beyond. Haroldo has indeed developed a poetic practice – his Concrete poetry is a striking example – that carries poetry beyond the limits of language. His poetry tends to project language outside of itself while exploiting and experiencing its materiality. This praxis breaks language down into its minimal units – single words, letters floating in the white or black space of the page – and explores the interaction which takes them beyond the function of signifying units, or at least beyond their accepted ways of functioning.

Yet this minimalist use of language, which leads to an ascetic attitude towards language, is only one side of the coin. On the other side is the permanent feast which Haroldo gives rise to, the abundance of his production within various discourses and genres. In poetry take the word flow of *Galáxias*, for example, or the ever-expanding volume of his ongoing production as a translator, theorist, and critic. Here the reader finds himself on language's middle ground, participating in the pleasure, even in the sensual delight, of combining all its registers and using its full range. Instead of excluding or reducing, Haroldo accumulates all the resources of language in an affirmation, if not an apotheosis, of its possibilities.

These are, then, the elements of the paradox I experience as a reader and listener: I perceive in Haroldo's texts an ascetic of language, and, at the same time, an Epicurean of language at work.

1. Experimentation in fiction and in poetry

I used the phrases "to explore language" and also "to experience language." This brings me to the hypothesis I would like to formulate and to "verify" later on in this paper. It has to do with the relationship between experimentation and literature, or, in Haroldo's case more precisely, with the relationship between experimentation and poetry. I would say that his poetry is part of a lasting tradition that we might call "experimental literature." Yet, within this tradition, it represents a second kind of experimental literature. In the following pages, two types of literary experimentation will be distinguished, allowing us to subsequently focus on the second one.

1.1. Experimental literature of the first kind

In his 1975 book on *Experimentelle Literatur und konkrete Poesie*,[3] Harald Hartung reaches the conclusion that experimental literature is undergoing a process of aging and might soon come to an end. In this he follows a diagnosis already established by Adorno in his *Ästhetische Theorie*:

> Meist kristallisiert das Experiment, als Ausproben von Möglichkeiten, vorwiegend Typen und Gattungen und setzt leicht das konkrete Gebilde zum Schulfall herab: eines der Motive fürs Altern der neuen Kunst. (Adorno 1973: 62)

Hartung goes on to say that this decline of experimental literature is brought about by the loss of a theoretical component that has been replaced by mere play:

> ... die Theorie trat zurück zugunsten des Spiels. ... Womit deutlich wird, daß die konkrete Poesie ihre hohen Ansprüche hat fahren lassen und Spiel geworden ist, nur mehr Spiel und nichts sonst. (Hartung 1975: 97)

Briefly put, I think that this observation on the fall and decay of experimental literature, with the implicit prediction of its future disappearance, only concerns an experimental literature of the first kind. With his negative use of the word "play" – presumably opposed to "work" as a serious activity, for instance the "politische Arbeit" he ascribes to serious literary experimentation (Hartung 1975: 99) – Hartung gives us a good indication of what this "first kind" consists of. I shall call it, more appropriately, literary experimentation of the modern kind.

In an essay published in 1989, I explored the history of the interaction between "Experiment and Fiction." Before the division – which more or less persists in the same form today – between literature and science was established in terms of discursive and institutional orders at the end of the eighteenth century, there was a long period (roughly between 1600 and 1800) during which two significant features could be observed:

1. On the one hand, starting with Bacon, experimental philosophy put forward a concept of "experimentation" which was part of a general attitude towards the world to be known, more precisely part of a scientific method that could be called aggressive and interventionist. According to this concept, in order to know a natural object it was necessary to observe it under experimental conditions that would modify it following a preestablished experimental procedure. A good indication of the content of this concept and the scientific practice to which it gave rise is the fact that it was often metaphorically explained in juridical terms: in order to obtain Nature's testimony and therefore know its hidden truth, the scientist had to put it to the question (cf. Kargon 1971).

2. On the other hand, since the discursive system had not yet stabilized what later became the borderline between science, philosophy and literature, experiment and fiction could still overlap and give rise to hybrid forms such as fictional experimentation (a "thought experiment" with no empirical data, but carried out as if it were real, such as the discursive staging of Condillac's statue) and experimental fiction (a fictional text following an experimental plot: for example Marivaux's play *La Dispute*).

This concept of experimentation was an integral part of the project of modernity that implied the cognitive and eventually the technological conquest of nature by man, as well as the mastery and exploitation of its resources. In this ideological context, the scientific experiment had the status of an epistemic instrument designed to bring forth the truth of Nature's hidden laws. Its function was an instrumental one, for it was considered as an efficient means to produce decisive results that lie beyond its own limits. What counted was the result brought forth once the experiment had been carried out and completed.

This modern concept of experimentation has been transferred into the field of art, and more specifically of literature, in basically two different ways.[4] First, experimentation was seen as a method of writing. In other words, writing became an experiment with human as well as social realities. This kind of experimental literature was supposed to allow writers to compete with scientists in terms of seriousness and usefulness, and also in terms of the ethos of modernity that consisted in the impetus of changing the world and improving society. To give just two examples: Zola's *Roman expérimental* (1888), properly applied, was supposed to help to eradicate criminality; Brecht's idea of an experimental theater (developed in the thirties), in a quite different aesthetic setting, was equally aimed at "arriving at the better social condition" (Brecht 1967: 285-305). In both cases, literary experimentation was quite directly borrowed from the scientific field and became the expression of a social as well as a political commitment. Language was used as a means of representation and as an instrument to bring about changes outside of language. It was an experimentation in language about something language could represent: human psychology, social behavior (Zola), and the mechanics of society (Brecht).

Secondly, we can observe a different kind of literary experimentation when writers experiment in language with language. That is, the object put to the question in order to make it reveal its own truth and the rules which govern it, is language itself. The experimental inquiry carried out in literature is thus about language itself. In this case we can speak of an experimental self-referentiality of language in literature. This kind of experimental literature can still be aimed at producing a result; it is supposed to force language into saying its own truth, be it in terms of a general philosophy of language (such as the one proposed by Humboldt and developed later on by Sapir-Whorf), or in terms of political or ideological biases implied in specific, unreflected language uses. In the second case, the experiment uses techniques of fragmentation, distortion, transgression, and de-automatization to break down the stereotypes of linguistic usage that alienate human consciousness.

This different type of experimentation in literature can be observed from the historical avant-gardes to the Vienna Group,[5] at least up to the moment when Hartung observes the decline of experimental literature and announces its end. In drama, a good example of this literary experimentation focused on language itself would be Peter Handke's *Kaspar*, an experiment in the constitution and decontruction of the subject through language.

In my opinion, these two modes of literary experimentation still belong to the modern kind. In both cases language is used as an instrument to produce truth as the result of experimentation; in the first case it is the truth about an extra-linguistic reality (transitive experimentation), and in the second case about language itself (auto-reflective experimentation). This second mode is more difficult to deal with for the critic. It has a performative dimension (language is both the means and the objective, the doing and the saying) that makes it more complex than the purely instrumental use of language in the first mode. Yet, it still functions within a modern *Zweckrationalität* inasmuch as it is a strategy designed to use language in a way that lets us recognize how we are caught up in its never-innocent matter or in social usages that appear to be our only access to reality. Language, as the object of experimentation, is violently interrogated, coerced if necessary into saying or at least showing its own truth. And this truth always has an epistemic (our cognitive relationship to reality), political (the establishment of discursive rules of inclusion and exclusion), and ideological (the distortion of our access to reality and to society) component. Therefore, this experimental literary practice still has strong affinities with the practice of *Ideologiekritik*, supposedly performing in literature what *Ideologiekritik* does in philosophy: it breaks up ideologically rigid forms and usages of language and creates the possibility of emancipation by liberating the discursive subjects from the alienating forces of automatized discourses.[6]

In the perspective of a modern conceptual framework, as long as experimentation functions in this way, as long as it yields some kind of final truth, its workings are perceived as being serious. Consequently, it is justified by its results as a creative method, and can therefore be considered as a credit to (politically) committed writers. Since Hartung adopts the perspective of such a conceptuality, he can only notice the decline and end of experimental literature when this seriousness begins lacking, especially when it gives way to a more playful mode of experimentation.

Insofar as Concrete poetry still has a semantic content or can be translated into the propositional content of a critical discourse that makes its truth explicit, it belongs to this second type of modern experimentation in literature. However, it nevertheless has a built-in tendency to transgress these conditions by pushing language beyond its own limits, either by reducing it to its own materiality, by breaking it down into infrasemantic units (such as letters or sounds), by working exclusively with "spatiality" on the page,[7] or by "falling" into mere play.

If the experimental work reaches these limits and goes beyond, something quite serious happens: the political, and even revolutionary work that it is supposed to perform becomes uncontrollable. It can no longer be oriented since its semantic content – that which can be put into predication – has become undecidable or has melted away altogether. This is where the well-known dividing line between formalism and realism has been placed. This is also why, in the thirties, both the fascist and the communist regimes rejected formalist and, to an even greater degree, experimental art.

However, one can try to recuperate this radical form of experimentalism inherent to most Concrete poetry by ascribing a revolutionary function and value to the breaking down of language, to its reduction to the status of pure material. Chris Bezzel (1971: 35-36) puts it this way:

> revolutionär ist damit eine dichtung, die das medium sprache selbst verändert, umfunktioniert, die den hierarchischen sprachlichen charakter zerstört, die im neuartigen sprachspiel und durch das neuartige sprachspiel diejenige gesellschaftliche umwälzung vorwegnimmt, für die alle revolutionäre arbeiten. dichter unter diesem aspekt ist also der, der mit poetischen mitteln im medium der sprache die sprache selbst als ein menschliches zeichensystem für menschen revolutioniert. dichtung der revolution bedeutet revolution der dichtung.

The question of revolutionary radicalness in experimental literature brings us to a breaking point between an instrumental, representational attitude towards language (language can reach reality and change it) and an ontological attitude (language is the prime reality we live in) according to which experiment, in and with language, can itself be seen as a revolutionary act, as a radical questioning of means. While displacing the question of literary experimentation, these terms can still be situated in the modern tradition.

We might want not to limit ourselves to such terms when dealing with experimental literature and more precisely with Concrete poetry, for this could prevent us from formulating an altogether different mode of joining experiment with fiction.

But first I must admit that I am no longer using the terms "experiment" and "fiction," but "experiment" and "poetry." Somewhere in this discussion of experimental literature I have imperceptibly drifted from fiction and literature to poetry. This displacement entails certain issues that can not be overlooked if we are to take Concrete poetry seriously. The occidental poetic tradition carries within itself certain nearly archetypal desires – be they articulated nostalgically or as utopias – that we must rapidly identify here. In negative terms, they derive from a sort of post-lapsarian linguistic consciousness that, in a very global and imprecise formulation, defines our modern condition. In Saussurean terms, I could describe it as the reign of the "signe non-motivé" in natural languages, responsible for our modern efficiency and mastery as well as for our modern alienation as "dwellers in the house of language."

Justifying the hope of undoing this modern condition, poetry has thus become a discursive and cultural locus of refuge. I would like to identify five different configurations that have become modalities of entertaining this hope:

1. The orphic tradition, especially its ideal of an efficient poetic word whose utterance could change the world. This ideal has been articulated in magical or

theological terms, and in Romantic poetry it has been reactivated by an etymological link to the Greek word *poïein*, to make, to do.

2. The Cratylist tradition with its central myth of an essential continuity between word and thing, signifier and signified. It often adopts the form of an (exotic?) projection in time (Adamic, pre-Babelian language) or space (for instance the tradition of occidental fantasies about Chinese ideograms).[8]

3. The tradition of universal mathesis as a system of symbols whose manipulation would entail the manipulation of the world. It manifests itself in the idea of a rigorous symbolic logic, organizing symbols, signs, words, and letters in a mathematical order. The permutational mode of Concrete poetry has a strong link with this tradition.[9]

4. The (nostalgic) idea of the harmonious co-origination of speech, music and poetry.[10] Grown out of a culture centered on writing and printing, this idea has been identified – and at the same time discredited – as a form of phonocentrism and, one would have to add, of audiocentrism.

5. The fantasy of an autonomous and self-revealing language that would not be a transitive instrument in relation to the world but its tantamount, a counter-world. In his short text "Monolog" Novalis (1981: 672-673) has developed this idea in contrasting ways. He opposes two attitudes towards language. On the first hand, the human subject uses language to represent the world and to express a preestablished truth. Language is used instrumentally (its nuclear paradigmatic phrase is: "etwas sagen wollen," the will to say something). This attitude can be described in general terms as paradigmatic of a modern language practice. Secondly, the human subject accepts to be a mere instrument through which language, becoming a non-anthropomorphic agency, produces the ultimate truth. (The nuclear paradigmatic phrases are: "reden müssen" [the urge to speak] or "die Sprache reden lassen" [to let language speak].)

Now, where does this lead us to? I cannot possibly develop here all these traditions with their panoply of corresponding fantasies. I shall therefore make a conclusive statement that will stand as an hypothesis, trying subsequently to give it some argumentative strength: these traditions, constitutive in different ways and to various degrees of occidental poetic discourse, are active in Concrete poetry.

1. 2 Experimental literature of the second kind

In the mainstream of modern discursive tradition, these different archetypal desires represent either nostalgic undercurrents or outright marginal – and potentially disturbing – deformities that can be tolerated only as long as they stay within the realm of poetry, which is their "proper" discursive place. They have the potential, though, to carry the commonsensical notion of language to its limits, and beyond. This is the case in Concrete poetry, as I have already indicated at the beginning. Haroldo de Campos also realizes and explores this potential in his own Concrete poetry, where he can be considered an ascetic of language insofar as he concentrates in each Concrete poem on a minimalist program related to these archetypal desires.

This is where, I think, an experimental literature of the second kind emerges. I propose to approach it by means of a philological detour, that is, by looking closely into the use of certain key words, especially the family of words linked to the epithet "experimental": experiment, experimentation, experience. Consulting the *Oxford Dictionary of English*, one could affirm that this second kind of literary experimentation is simply the regression from a scientifically specialized meaning of the word "experiment" ("An action or operation undertaken in order to discover something unknown, to test a hypothesis, or establish or illustrate some known truth") to its more general and common language meaning ("The action of trying anything").[11]

The first meaning is entirely result-oriented and always implies a functional as well as an instrumental rationality. The second, more common meaning does not contain this teleological dimension; it focuses much more on the processive (*ODE*: "Of the nature of a process") aspect of an act, on an ongoing process, and therefore also on its inconclusiveness.

This first semantic component can further be illustrated by the German word-family that comprises the noun *Versuch* and the verb *versuchen*. *Versuch* designates a scientific experiment, yet it also simply means the action of trying out, *ausprobieren*, that is an inconclusive probing of something concrete.[12] Such an active yet tentative attitude is adopted towards language and stated like a credo in Haroldo's poem "Mínima Moralia": "Já fiz de tudo com as palavras" ["I've already done everything with words"] (Campos 1992b: 100). In order to describe his own practice of writing, he also mobilizes the Portuguese word *ensaio*, which links the verb expressing the inchoate action par excellence to the activity of writing and even to a specific genre:

> ... um livro ensaia o livro
> todo livro é um livro de ensaio de ensaios do livro por isso o fim –
> começo começa e fina recomeça ... [13]

> [A book practices a book
> every book is a book of practice of practices of a book and therefore the end –
> beginning begins and ends begins ...]

A second semantic component stems from this intransitive process. It concerns less directly the process itself than the relationship the human subject establishes to it: the human subject renounces its mastery over the process insofar as an aesthetic activity allows for such a behavior. It rather engages itself in the same way we engage in a gaming activity whose rules constitute our status and our function as players.[14] In Novalis' sense, then, we become the instruments of language[15] instead of using language as the instrument to realize our own objectives. We enter the *Sprachspiel* not just in Wittgenstein's logical and pragmatic sense, but also ontologically. The experiment, then, becomes playful in a radical way, not as a game we might play, even with very high stakes at risk. We rather accept to abandon our*selves* to play, somehow jumping over the shadow of the negative connotation a modern like Hartung attaches to this attitude.

A third semantic component can be activated if we focus on the experiential side of the word "experimental." Thus, poetry is experimental inasmuch as it makes us experience language, especially its material aspect. Such a poetry engages the body, our body, to experience the body of language. Here poetry recuperates the possibility of becoming an experience for sense perceptions. It is true that Concrete poetry privileges the visual perception and explores the spatiality essential to our culture of writing and printing. But this aspect of experimentation which somehow gives back language's body by reconnecting the "experiment" with the "experience," brings into play the whole potential of a material anthropology envisaged by the young Marx in his *Pariser Manuskripte* around 1844 and alluded to by Haroldo de Campos in his cycle of poems *A Educação dos Cinco Sentidos* (1992b: 91-106).[16]

Literary experimentation of the second kind can therefore be characterized by its processive, playful, and experiential aspects. Its processive nature affirms the very process of writing, as well as its performance (also when it is recited orally) and performative nature, insofar as it tends to contain an ongoing interplay between the level of poetic practice (its poetic doing, performing) and the level of poetic theory (what it says, states about poetry). Its playful nature can no longer be opposed to "serious work" or to political commitment. Rather, it implies a total engagement with language whereby the poetic subject, to a certain extent, gives up his or her modern agency and lets language have its turn and its way. Its experiential nature, finally, makes the poet accept a *corps-à-corps* with language. Not only must he or she accept the material side of language in its various aspects, but also valorize it, to derive what one could call a semiotic pleasure from the bodily perception of entering a universe of language considered as milieu rather than instrument.

I have repeatedly called the literary experimentation of the first kind a modern paradigm. Should, consequently, this second paradigm be labeled "postmodern"? Yes and no.

No, if this implies that the words "modern" and "postmodern" designate historical periods that would follow each other in a linear, chronological way (the modern exits ... enter postmodernism). This would be a caricature of modern history. More importantly, this would not correspond to the facts, because the two modes of experimental literature do overlap today, and they coexist in complex ways. For instance, in Concrete poetry we can find the modern ethos or impetus to demonstrate something about language or about society (in language), but also derive pleasure from manipulating materials of language in the space of writing and printing in a playful mode.

Yes, if "postmodern" points to a modernity weakened by the crisis of its internal dialectics, and which can no more keep all its "others" from reentering its own boundaries. Among these "others" of modernity I could cite the materiality of language, the hidden machinery of written culture (the medium of writing and printing), the bodily culture, the magics of language, and the efficiency of the image. All these "others" have either been forgotten, marginalized, repressed, or instrumentalized by modernity. In part, they belong to pre-modern paradigms, and have residually survived in the restricted discursive space of poetry as unfulfilled nostalgic or utopian desires produced by modernity as it became dominant and triumphant.

2. Haroldo de Campos' workings in language

I am not interested in simply putting a postmodern label on Haroldo's poetry and work. But I do not hesitate to affirm that his workings in language quite clearly belong to the literary experimentation of the second kind. His outright affirmation, in theory as well as in poetry, of experimenting/experiencing (with, in) language, and thus without the functional or ideological control and subordination of a modern master narrative, has earned him trouble with people in Brazil who have adopted such a narrative. If we accept for a moment the imprecision of labels, we can observe a persistent dichotomy in the Brazilian milieu of literary studies between formalists and semioticians on the one hand and representatives of a socio-historical approach to literature on the other. Haroldo's identification with the formalists is directly linked to his experimental workings in language, although it would be wrong to affirm that they make him an a-historical author and thinker, alien to social concerns. Rather, one should stress the fact that his way of participating in history and in raising social issues as a worker in language do not derive from any modern master narrative.

What I call his workings are comprised of an extremely vast array of linguistic production. It could be said that their coherence as a work lies in their common contribution to a literary experimentation of the second kind. I shall certainly not be able to analyze his whole work in order to support this thesis with convincing evidence. I can only sketch a few elements of such an undertaking. Let me, then, concentrate on the difference and the interplay between two very different types of production by Haroldo de Campos: his poetry on the one side and his literary criticism and theory on the other.

As I already mentioned at the beginning, there is a definite contradiction between the urge for a certain scarcity of material in certain poetic works, particularly in his Concrete poetry, and an urge for abundance in his critical and theoretical writings. From this I must evidently exclude *Galáxias*, an experimentation in language that follows an aesthetic principle of semiotic proliferation triggered by the body of words and sustained by chains of signifiers. Haroldo's Concrete poetry represents a surprising exercise in reducing the experimental elements to a minimum: few words, spatially organized on the empty page, in a permutational setting, and giving rise to pictorial structures.[17] In this vein, during the late fifties, Haroldo came very close to the limits of language; he approached a pure pictoriality of the poem, leaving behind the semantics of natural language. This can indeed be seen as an effective way of conceiving the end of language; one can consider it in Concrete poetry as a reduction of our writing/printing culture to its constitutive pictoriality. Another approach is indicated in everyday life, along the lines of an audio-visual culture that may be in the process of becoming the dominant feature of our cultural situation in general. Here the main issue in relation to language, briefly put, is the overflow of images produced and distributed by a powerful technology, and the difficulty for language to keep up with the quantity as well as the velocity of this flow, not to mention the impossibility of semanticizing it in slower, verbal discourse.

However, even in his most minimalist Concrete poems, Haroldo did not leave behind the semantic universe. This is to say that, even coming close to pure pictoriality, his poetic practice stayed within the limits of language, and contributed to the ongoing reflection – more and more urgent today – on the relationship between "Word and Image." Yet however close he came to this specific limit of language in poetry, he never ceased other discursive activities (theory, translation, criticism) situated on middle ground of discursive practice and which represent, as theoretical developments, an apotheosis of language, and as practices, a feast of language. This is why even the most abstract theoretical discourse by Haroldo never loses its bodily aspect, the perceptual pleasure of experiencing language. Maybe this last aspect is the innermost driving force of Haroldo's workings in language.

Considering Haroldo's critical and theoretical writings, we can recognize a strong and broad affirmation of a literary experimentation of the second kind. He brews a theoretical concoction that certainly does not correspond to modern standards of theoretical purity. But this "impurity" of his theorizing, in the sense of Guy Scarpetta's *L'Impureté* that one could read as a no-more-modern manifesto, must be seen in the polemical context of the Brazilian debate where Haroldo, for quite some time, has been holding a position designed to resist certain stereotypical modern stances while reusing, among others, modernist materials.

A good example among many is his *O seqüestro do barroco na formação da literatura brasileira* (1989), also his article "The Rule of Anthropophagy: Europe under the Sign of Devoration" (1986a, first published in Portuguese in 1981). In these writings we can observe a double strategy that leads to the constitution and affirmation of an experimental/experiential attitude towards language. In the effort to establish some kind of an alliance for a no-more-modern being in language, he simultaneously mobilizes contemporary "friendly" positions and past or ancient cultural paradigms. Among the second group we find the old tradition of written experimentation with language that goes back to the baroque period, the Middle Ages, and even to the Ancient Greeks.[18] We also find the very ancient tradition of what was initially a feature of popular culture and, through the writings of Mikhail Bakhtin, was theoretically introduced into the literary debate and adapted to high literature: the carnival and literary carnivalization. Finally we find the baroque tradition itself, especially in its rich and complex literary form. These three traditions are focused upon and reactivated by Haroldo. They have in common a conflictive relationship to modernity, because they all have, although in different ways, pre-modern roots. They were therefore suspect to modernity, treated accordingly through control and exclusion, by way of marginalization, axiological negation, and hierarchical domination. These traditions also share an affirmation of the material aspect of language and the interest and pleasure of manipulating it. These practices are reactivated by Haroldo, freed from their sequestration by modernity and theoretically put into power again. The forerunners are thus put into a position of becoming contemporaries, which is illustrated in the case of the baroque poet Gregório de Matos. Evidently, this is only made possible by a gesture which is historically bold if not outright a-historical.[19] The de-historicizing that undoubtedly takes place (it might have its own historical reasons) is in my opinion a strategic gesture directed against a certain modern master narrative. In this sense it is a postmodern gesture making it possible to reconnect present day culture with the "others" of modernity and to reactivate their cultural potential and energies.

In a second group of "friendly" positions, we find, among others, anthro-pophagism and deconstruction, a very heterogeneous pairing indeed. Yet, they have two things in common that are relevant to Haroldo's elaboration of a different experimental working in language: first, by working within a tradition while turning it against itself, they both represent strategies of critical devouring[20]; second, they both affirm, in their workings, the body of language. This last aspect is of course substantially epitomized by the anthropophagic metaphor used in the discourse on cultural processes.

Put together, all these cultural traditions and theoretical positions make a very heterogeneous theoretical brew indeed, on top of their being treated with no respect whatsoever in relation to their historical ordering. Haroldo has been criticized for this, and has been involved in an ongoing polemics. Yet in each one of these debates all of Haroldo's opponents operate in some way from within modernity; they all defend some kind of modern paradigm, be it nationalist discourse, the discourse of evolution and emancipation, historiographical discourse, or the discourse of the subordination of literature to some "noble" non-literary objective. The main issue, then, is how to overcome such positions without repeating them. We should therefore evaluate Haroldo's own position in strategic terms. In other words, we should consider less the purity of his theoretical position than its cultural and historical efficiency. The stakes are high: freeing language from its modern instrumentalization, reactivating the repressed or forgotten potential of different workings in language, and, especially, reconnecting both the body with language and ourselves with the body of language. Haroldo, for a long time already, and in many different fields of discursive as well as cultural practice, has worked in this direction, in and with language. His commitment is not a-political nor a-historical, but it is first and foremost a commitment with language: an experimental exploration of its possibilities and resources, without modern exclusions or reductions. I propose to call the general orientation of his endeavors an experimental literature of a second kind.

Notes

1. Cf. Haroldo de Campos' word play in his poem "Sinal de tráfego" (Campos 1992b: 143).
2. I am referring on the one hand to his own readings of Concrete poetry *viva voce*, and on the other to his own recordings of his *Galáxias* (Campos 1992a). There also exists a CD titled *Espaços Habitados*, proposing the recitation of fragments of *Galáxias* by Anna Maria Kieffer and Conrado Silva (1994).
3. Three years later Siegfried J. Schmidt (1978) edited documentation on *Das Experiment in Literatur und Kunst*. The general outlook is less pessimistic because the contributors are ready to consider a wider range of experimental forms and possibilities in art than Hartung.
4. Cf. Helmut Heißenbüttel's reflection on this transfer: "Was bedeutet eigentlich das Wort Experiment?" (Heißenbüttel 1963).
5. See for instance Rühm (ed. 1967).

6. Winfried Freund's theory of parody functions very much in the same way (Freund 1978).
7. Pierre Garnier has developed a version of Concrete poetry, called "spatialisme," that foregrounds this specific aspect (cf. Lengellé 1979).
8. It is interesting to observe that, by the detour of Ezra Pound and Ernest Fenollosa, Haroldo de Campos reactivates this "archetype" in view of his own poetic production. See the volume he has organized under the title *Ideograma. Lógica, Poesia, Linguagem* (Campos 1986b).
9. In his *Symbolismus und symbolische Logik. Die Idee der Ars Combinatoria in der Entwicklung der modernen Dichtung* John Neubauer (1978) offers a global presentation of this tradition. Its concrete appearance in baroque poetry has been well documented by Ana Hatherly (1983).
10. Put forward for instance by Jean-Jacques Rousseau in his *Essai sur l'origine des langues* (1970).
11. In Schmidt (1978: 14), Oldemeyer proposes to go back to pre-scientific experimental attitudes in order to understand certain artistic experiments.
12. Elsewhere (Moser 1985) I have shown how Robert Musil, by activating this family of words, and especially by diverting the scientific experiment into a processual writing, develops the poetics of an essayistic writing strategy which can also be linked to the genre of the essay.
13. Haroldo de Campos (1984: without pagination). In its 1976 edition (*Xadrez de Estrelas, percurso textual.* São Paulo: Editora Perspectiva, 1976), the full title was still *Livro de Ensaios Galáxias*, which became *Versuchsbuch / Galaxien* in its German translation.
14. At least this is how Hans Georg Gadamer (1965: 97-127) conceptualizes the notion of play (Spiel) in his *Truth and Method.*
15. Even in the sense of musical instruments.
16. As I already mentioned, Haroldo de Campos likes to recite his own Concrete poems and to give a vocal body to works the reader perceives as exclusively visual.
17. In this sense the early series "De O â Mago do ô Mega" (1955-56), "Fome de Forma/Forma de fome" (1958) are among the extremest examples (Campos 1992b: 43-50).
18. This tradition has been documented by Jeremy Adler and Ulrich Ernst in their interesting volume titled *Text als Figur. Visuelle Poesie von der Antike bis zur Moderne* (1987). A book published by a former student of Haroldo de Campos belongs in this same category: Maria dos Prazeres Gomes, *Outrora agora. Relações dialógicas na poesia portuguesa de invenção* (1993).
19. In the debate on Gregório de Matos' poetry, this is the line of attack and argumentation adopted by João Adolfo Hansen in his *A Sátira e o Engenho. Gregório de Matos e a Bahia do Século XVII* (1989), as well as in other writings.
20. In this sense, they are in line with the (ironical?) definition of postmodernism we find in Tabucchi's novel *Requiem* (1994: 112-113): "Pós-moderno? . . . é um sítio que rompeu com a tradição recuperando a tradição."

Bibliography

Adler, Jeremy and Ulrich Ernst
1987   *Text als Figur. Visuelle Poesie von der Antike bis zur Moderne.*
         Weinheim, Herzog August Bibliothek Wolfenbüttel.
Adorno, Theodor W.
1973   *Ästhetische Theorie.* Frankfurt am Main, Suhrkamp.
Bezzel, Chris
1971   "Konkrete Kunst und Gesellschaft." In: *Text und Kritik* 25, 35-36.
Brecht, Bertold
1967   "Über experimentelles Theater." In: Brecht, *Gesammelte Werke* 15,
         Frankfurt am Main, Suhrkamp, 285-305.
Campos, Haroldo de
1976   *A Operação do Texto.* São Paulo, Editora Perspectiva.
1984   *Galáxias.* São Paulo, Editora Ex Libris.
1986a   "The Rule of Anthropophagy: Europe under the Sign of Devoration."
         In: *Latin American Literary Review* 14. 27, 42-60.
1986b   *Ideograma. Lógica, Poesia,* Linguagem (edited by --). São Paulo,
         EDUSP. [1977]
1989   *O seqüestro do barroco na formação da literatura brasileira. O caso
         Gregório de Matos,* Salvador, Fundação Casa Jorge Amado.
1992a   *Isto não é um livro de viagem. 16 fragmentos de Galáxias.* Rio de
         Janeiro, Editora 34.
1992b   *Os melhores poemas de Haroldo de Campos.* Inês Oseki Dépré, ed. Rio
         de Janeiro, Global Editora.
1992c   *Metalinguagem & outras metas.* São Paulo, Editora Perspectiva.
Freund, Winfried
1981   *Die literarische Parodie.* Stuttgart, Metzler.
Gadamer, Hans-Georg
1965   *Wahrheit und Methode. Grundzüge einer philosophischen
         Hermeneutik* [2nd ed.]. Tübingen, J.C.B. Mohr.
Gomes, Maria dos Prazeres
1993   *Outrora agora. Relações dialógicas na poesia portuguesa de invenção.*
         São Paulo, Editora da PUC.
Hansen, João Adolfo
1989   *A Sátira e o engenho. Gregório de Matos e a Bahia do século XVII.* São
         Paulo, Companhia das Letras/Secretaria de Estado de Cultura.
Hardenberg, Friedrich von [Novalis]
1981   "Monolog." In: Novalis, *Schriften* II, Stuttgart, Kohlhammer, 672-673.
Hartung, Harald
1975   *Experimentelle Literatur und konkrete Poesie.* Göttingen,
         Vandenhoeck & Ruprecht.

Hatherly, Ana
    1983   *A Experiência do Prodígio. Bases teóricas e antologia de textos visuais portugueses dos séculos XVII et XVIII.* Lisboa, Imprensa Nacional/Casa da Moeda.
Heißenbüttel, Helmut
    1963   "Was bedeutet eigentlich das Wort Experiment?" *Magnum* 47, 8-10. Rpt. in: Thomas Kopfermann, ed. *Theoretische Positionen zur konkreten Poesie*, Tübingen, Niemeyer, 1974, 147-152.
Kargon, R.
    1971   "The Testimony of Nature. Boyle, Hooke and Experimental Philosophy." In: *Albion* 3, 72-80.
Kieffer, Anna Maria & Conrado Silva
    1994   *Espaços habitados.* São Paulo, Laboratório de Linguagens Sonoras PUC. [Fragments from *Galáxias*]
Lengellé, Martial
    1979   *Le spatialisme selon l'itinéraire de Pierre Garnier.* Paris, Éditions André Silvaire.
Moser, Walter
    1985   "La mise a l'essai des discours dans *L'Homme sans qualités.*" *Revue Canadienne de littérature comparée* 12. 1, 12-45.
    1989   "Experiment and Fiction." In: Frederick Amrine, ed. *Literature and Science as Modes of Expression*, Dordrecht, Kluwer Academic Publishers, 61-80.
Neubauer, John
    1978   *Symbolismus und symbolische Logik. Die Idee der Ars combinatoria in der Entwicklung der modernen Dichtung.* München, W. Fink Verlag.
Rousseau, Jean-Jacques
    1970   *Essai sur l'origine des langues.* Critical edition by Charles Porset. Bordeaux, Ducros.
Rühm, Gerhard, ed.
    1967   *Die Wiener Gruppe. Achleitner, Artmann, Bayer, Rühm, Wiener. Texte, Gemeinschaftsarbeiten, Aktionen.* Hamburg, Rowohlt.
Scarpetta, Guy
    1985   *L'Impureté.* Paris, Grasset.
Schmidt, Siegfried J., ed.
    1978   *Das Experiment in Literatur und Kunst.* München, W. Fink Verlag.
Tabucchi, Antonio
    1994   *Requiem.* Lisboa, Quetzal Editores.

GALÁXIAS [excerpts]

Haroldo de Campos

mais uma vez junto ao mar polifluxbórboro polivozbárbaro polúphloisbos
polyfizzyboisterous weitaufrauschend fluctissonante esse mar esse mar
esse mar esse martexto por quem os signos dobram marujando num estuário
de papel num mortuário num monstruário de papel múrmur-rúmor-remurmunhante
escribalbuciando você converte estes signos-sinos num dobre numa dobra
de finados enfim nada de papel estes signos você os ergue contra tuas
ruínas ou tuas ruínas contra estes signos balbucilente sololetreando a
sóbrio neste eldorido feldorado latinoamargo tua barrouca mortopopéia
ibericaña na primeira posição do amor ela ergue os joelhos quase êmbolos
castanho-lisos e um vagido sussubmisso começa a escorrer como saliva e
a mesma castanho-lisa mão retira agora uma lauda datiloscrita da máquina-
-de-escrever quando a saliva já remora na memória o seu ponto saturado
de perfume apenas a lembrança de um ter-sido que não foi ou foi não-sendo
ou sido é-se pois os signos dobram por este texto que subsume os contextos
e os produz como figuras de escrita uma polipalavra contendo todo o
rumor do mar uma palavra-búzio que homero soprou e que se deixa transoprar
através do sucessivo escarcéu de traduções encadeadas vogais vogando
contra o encapelo móvel das consoantes assim também viagem microviagem
num livro-de-viagens na segunda posição ela está boca-à-terra e um
fauno varicoso e senil a empala todocoberto de racimos de uva e revoado
por vespas raivecidas que prelibam o mel mascavo minado das regiões
escuras dizer que essas palavras convivem no mesmo mar de sargaços
memória é dizer que a linguagem é uma água de barrela uma borra de
baixela e que a tela se entretela à tela e tudo se entremela na mesma
charada charamela de charonhas carantonhas ou carantelas que trelam e
taramelam o pesardelo de um babuíno bêbedo e seus palradisos pastifíciosos
terrorescendo os festins floriletos pois a linguagem é resíduo
de drenagem é ressaca e é cloaca e nessa noite nócua é que está sua
mensagem nesse publiexposto putriexposto palincesto de todos os passíveis
excessos de linguagem abcesso obsesso e houve também a estória daquele
alemão que queria aprender o francês por um método rápido assimil de sua
invenção e que aprendia uma palavra por dia un mot par jour zept mots
jaque zemaine e ao cabo de um mês e ao fim de seis meses e ao fim e
ao cabo de um ano tinha já tudo sabido trezentas e sessenta e cinco
palavras sabidas tout reglé en ordre bien classé là voui là dans mon cul
la kultura aveva raggione quello tedesco e a civilização quero que se
danem e é sarro e barro e escarro e amaro isto que fermenta no mais
profundo fundo do pélago-linguagem onde o livro faz-se pois não se trata
aqui de um livro-rosa para almicândidas e demidonzelas ohfélias nem de
um best-seller fimfeliz para amadores d'amordorflor mas sim de um
nigrolivro um pesteseller um horrídeodigesto de leitura apfelstúrdia
para vagamundos e gatopingados e sesquipedantes e sestralunáticos
abstractores enfim quintessentes do elixir caximônico em cartapáceos
galáticos na terceira posição ela é signo e sino e por quem dobra

nudez o papel-carcassa fede-branco osso que supura esse esqueleto
verminoso onde ainda é vida a lepra rói uma quina do edifício na rua
23 e vê-se um sol murchado margarida-gigante despetalar restos de
plástico num vidro violentado como um olho em celofane sérum
o bicho-tênia recede nas cavernas do amarelo muco esgotescroto
quem move a mola do narrar quem dis para esse dis negpositivo da
fá intestino escritural bula tinteiro-tênia autossugante vermi
celo vermiculum celilúbrico mudez o papel-carcassa fedor-branco quem
solitudinário odisseu ouninguém nenhúrio ausculta um tirésias de
fezes vermicego verminíquo vermicoleando augúrios uma labirintestina
oudisséia perderás todos os companh tautofágica retornarás marmorto
fecalporto gondondoleando em nulaparte tudonada solilóquio a lunavoz
oudisseu nenhumnome et devant l'agression rétorquer a margarida
despetala violentada restos de plástico celofanam fanam celúltima
cena miss pussy biondinuda massageia um turfálico polifemo unicórneo
manilúvio newyorquino nesse cavernocálido umidoscuro rés do chão do
edifício leproso da rua 23 entra-se por uma porta em coração estames
de purpurina pistilos ou da rua 48 enjoy the ultimate in massage
new york grooviest men's club the gemini porta partida em coração
lovely masseuses sauna waterbeds circe ao cono esplêndido benecomata
oudisseu nenhumnome parou aqui este livro uma tautodisséia dizendo-se
parou aqui e passou além morto roxo exposto como um delfim
tot rot und offen à beira-vênus num nascimento de vênus aphródes
escumante e deixar que tudo se organize num azul sutilíssimo
tapeçaria vitrificada por onde raiam caules de luz amaranto
cúspides de glicínias desabrochando em reis góticos em naipes de
um tarot glacial irisados por fogos distantes tudo isso surdinando
em murmúrio de fonte o aquilo produzido no isto ou viceversa por
uma torção do tempo famosus ille fabulator que se faz memória
mementomomentomonumental matéria evêntica desventrada do tempo
da marsúpia vide espaço do tempo um livro também constrói o leitor
um livro de viagem em que o leitor seja a viagem um livro-areia
escorrendo entre os dedos e fazendo-se da figura desfeita onde
há pouco era o rugitar da areia constelada um livro perime o sujeito
e propõe o leitor como um ponto de fuga este livro-agora travessia
de significantes que cintilam como asas migratórias de novo a quina
pulverulenta do edifício da rua 23 de novo circe la masseuse
entre cortinas de mercúrio fluorescente e a cara glabra de um eunuco
ressupino metade-convertendo-se em focinho porcino beneconata circe
quem ouve a fábula exsurgindo entre safira e fezes quem a vê que
desponta sua réstea de rádium entre lixívia e sémen para um rebanho
de orelhas varicosas grandes ouvidos moucos orelhas de abano flácidas
bandeiras murchas que des contemporains ne savent pas lire ouver

(p. 242)

from: Haroldo de Campos, *Xadrez de estrelas. Percurso textual 1949-1974.*
São Paulo, Editora Perspectiva.

PALABRÁS: THE HAROLDIC EMBLEM

K. Alfons Knauth

The Brazilian Haroldo de Campos (b. 1929) is one of the major "operators" of word literature today. His work may be considered as the verbal constellation of both an expanding and circular universe, where the very new and the very old interact permanently and nearly indistinctly: "tudo riocorrente" ("everything riverrunrecurrent").[1] He thus becomes the modern archetype of an atavistic avant-gardist. As such, he combines the features of a dodecaglot translator, poet, philologist, critic, and multimedia performance artist, acting in the present, re-acting the past. Throughout his work in progress,[2] there is a constant concern with the materiality of language, with verbal world making and the processing of a Concrete, multilingual literature. Part of this process is its condensed representation in auto referential language emblems. The emblems are organized in a dynamic ensemble of shifting fields, constituting the poetological pattern of the "campos elísios" (*Teoria e prática do poema*, 1976a: 56). The "Elysian fields" are to be seen as self-reflecting constellations of Haroldo de Campos's *Xadrez de Estrelas*, the "celestial chessboard," which the poet himself seems to understand as the basic design of his work.[3]

Before reviewing the main emblems of Haroldo's poetry, we want to give it a critical label, blazoning its verbal art as a whole. "Palabrás" may be proposed as *the* Haroldic emblem, on the ground of the poet's multilingual "polipalavra"(1976a: 239),[4] his word-centered art, that has become a kind of a Brazilian institution. Thinking of national institutions like Petrobrás or Eletrobrás, Palabrás connotes even the engineering principle underlying the poetry of Haroldo de Campos. In fact, he imagines his verbal production as a "fábrica de letras" (1976a: 226), or sees himself in the line of Pindar, Arnaut Daniel, Dante, Pound, and Eliot as an archetypal word smith, "il miglior fabbro," forging like Vulcano his verbal arms for the worldlovewar with Venus: "Ele forja, vulcanamoroso, a vénussílaba para a verbogênese." ("He forges, following the loving Vulcano, the Venus syllable for the verbal genesis," 1976a: 58).

The arms are associated with the armorial items which the poet fabricates as heraldic blazons of poetry, reaching from the early *Ciropédia* – "O Príncipe recebe os seus brasões de Estado: Blau...As armas!"("The Prince receives his State blazons: Blue...To arms!," 1976a: 50) – to the avant-garde symbol of "a proa de brasões" ("the blazoned bow") in *A invincível armada* (1976a: 66).[5]

As there is an important component of collective production in Haroldo's poetics, one might apply the blazon of "Palabrás" to the whole group of Noigandres poets, particularly its central core including, besides Haroldo de Campos, his brother Augusto and Décio Pignatari. Their common enterprise of verbal world making on a multilingual and multimedia scale had a substantial share in the elaboration of contemporary Brazilian avant-garde literature and its world-wide diffusion.

1. The Verbarium

There are two kinds or codes of symbolizing language in Haroldo's poetry: the denotative and the connotative one. The denotative code means the direct de-nomination of language, including synonymous, paronymous, and polysemic variations of the basic symbol; the connotative code means its metaphorical or metonymical representation.

The denotative series of language emblems is built up around the central words of "fala"("speech") and "fábula" ("fable"). Especially in *Galáxias*, Haroldo develops the equivalence of both terms, on the ground of their etymological identity (from the Greek "mythos" to the Latin "fas"/"fabula" up to the Portuguese "fala"/"fábula"). The realistic stories as well as the fantastic ones are reduced to fabulous word stories. In love incidents or care accidents, in mythological fables, animal fables or fairy tales the represented world is essentially a verbal one. Just as Haroldo demonstrated the coincidence of "fá-bula" and "fala" in Guimarães Rosa's totemistic jaguar fable *Iauaretê* (1967: 51), Guimarães Rosa considered the *Galáxias* as a fabulous forest of verbal beasts: "Todos os iauaretês urram." ("All the jaguars are snarling," in: H. de Campos 1976a: 251). Octavio Paz has chosen the equivalence of "fábula" and "fala" in *Galáxias* as the emblematic device of this work: "Me gustaría escoger como divisa el final del primer fragmento: el vocablo es mi fábula..." ("I would like to choose as a device the end of the first fragment: the vocable is my fable," ibid.).

Besides the poetical and etymological synonymy of "fábula" and "fala," Haroldo emphasizes the polyvalence of both; the reduction of the two terms is followed by their expansion. The emblematic term for the plurality of poetic language is "multifarious." By the expression "poesia multifária" (*Ode em defesa da poesia*) the poet not only designates multiple speech, but also materializes it by suggesting its etymological origin ("multum fari"), thus the multilingual status of his language and of poetic language as such. The neologism "polipalavra" is an equivalent of "poesia multifária" in a parallel word series.

Complementary components of the "fala"-scale are the paronymous words "fa," "favila," and "fava" (1976a: 64, 200, 242). The last two terms signify – as in C.E. Gadda's *Primo libro delle favole* – the wit and humor of the linguistic fables, whereas the first term "fa" denotes their musical dimension. The fractional structure of the "fá...bula" emblem points out another feature of Haroldo's word art: its dissonance, disruption, and dispersion. The fragment "dis" itself occurs in the same context and reinforces the phenomenon. The fractional structure is also marked by the paronymous terms "falha" (1979: 95, 1976a: 226) or "farfalha" (1979: 95), the "fissures," "filings," and "failings" of the word smith, negating constantly the principle of ideal "fala." "Falha" and "farfalha" announce the very opposite of "fala," which happens to be the perfectly rhyming silence of "cala" ("keeping quiet," 1976a: 226).

The multilingual silence of Haroldo's "polipalavra" is articulated in other oxymora like "peixepalavra" ("fishspeech," 1976a: 241) or, in a strictly denotative way, in the couplings of "palavra silêncio," "escrito excrito," "texto extexto" ("silence word," "exwritten writings," "extexted text," 1976a: 229).

The denotative language emblems already carry quite often a connotative meaning, especially through paronomasia (like "falha") and word compounding (like "peixepalavra"). There is a continuous shifting between the two series.

Basically, the connotative language emblems don't need a material support in order to fulfill their symbolic function. Mainly they act on the ground of semantic analogy. The connotative emblems establish the auto reflexive imagery of language in an iconic space of interfering metaphorical fields. Haroldo de Campos draws most of his poetic symbols from traditional imagery, though transforming them thoroughly.

The iconic supplies come from inanimate matter (metals, stones), vegetal forms (flowers, trees), maritime and cosmic phenomena, the human body, artifacts (music instruments and the media), and the animal world. Thus the emblematic space of Haroldo's poetry is mainly formed by a kind of lapidarium, herbarium, aquarium, planetarium, sensorium, instrumentarium,[6] and bestiarium. To this "fictionary" may be added the verbarium, containing the denotative emblems of language.

The whole of the denotative and connotative emblems set up by the poet, together with the critic's analysis, can be seen as an overall emblematic structure, in which, roughly speaking, the denotative emblems represent the inscriptio or device, the connotative emblems the pictura or icon, and the critical explanation its "moral" subscriptio. This is a general design of Haroldo de Campos's much more labyrinthine "babelbarroco" (1976a: 211). The particular features will be presented in the following review of the emblematic fictionary. Its leading figure will be – besides the aspect of "multifário" – the double paradox of "dis negpositivo" (1976a: 242), which establishes a new aesthetic "oxymoral."

2. The Lapidarium

The quest for the precious philosophical stone is a central symbol of the alchemic Work in Progress. Haroldo de Campos puts this quest into the center of the penultimate piece of *Galáxias*, where the "lapidário" (1976a: 241) is ever to be searched and never to be reached, symbolizing the endless spiral of the writing and reading process and the impossibility of either getting hold of sense or fixing literary form.

Even the historical search for the American Eldorado, poetically recreated in Pietro Pietra's and Macunaíma's quest for the Muiraquitã, is seen as a failure. As in Lautréamont's *Chants de Maldoror* the Eldorado is distorted and becomes an "eldorido" ("dolorous Eldorado") and "feldorado" ("Galldorado," 1976a: 239), renewing one of the prototypes of oxymoron, the bittersweet image of "mel e fel" ("honey and gall"). The Eldorado, similar to *Macunaíma*'s Muiraquitã,[7] is the emblem not only of the individual work of art, but also of the Brazilian and Latin American literature as a whole: "neste eldorido feldorado latinoamargo tua barrouca mortopopéia ibericaña" ("in this eldolorous bitterlatinamerican galldorado your baroque ibericanned lethepopee," ibid.).

Haroldo's lapidarium contains a rich collection of precious stones, reaching from amethyst, diamond, obsidian, onyx , topaz, and sapphire to the baroque corals, pearls, conches, and murex shells. Each one symbolizes the paradise of perfect poetic form, the "palavra topázio" ("topaz word," 1979: 51), but at the same time its abysmal descent, its inaccessibility, loss or dissolution, or the copresence of its opposite: the literary work emerges "entre safira e fezes" ("between sapphire and feces," 1976a: 242). Even if the poet succeeded in creating a pure poem, he would not be understood by his public, like the classical fabulist in *Pullus ad margaritam*: "Margaritas ante porcos" ("casting pearls before swine," 1976a: 58).

Considering the fundamental failure of pure poetry and its symbolization by the lasting statue or the precious stone, the poet ridicules in the last fragment of *Galáxias* the idea and the icon of the literary monument: "mementomomentomonumental" (1976a: 242). He dissolves the classic and Parnassian principle of "Exegi monumentum aere perennius" ("I erected a monument outlasting iron") into the mere matter of sand, its instant appearance and disappearance: "um livro-areia escorrendo entre os dedos" ("a sand-book running through one's fingers," ibid.). The static emblem has been replaced by a dynamic one. The precious stone reduced to dust. The "lapidário" survives but in the minimal form of the support of writing, the "lápis" ("pencil," 1979: 45).

3. The Herbarium

Besides the precious stone, the flower has been one of the most conspicuous emblems of poetic beauty since antiquity. Its ephemeral condition has been compensated either by choosing evergreen plants like laurel to wreathe the poet's crown, or by eternalizing the flower mythologically in the Elysian fields beyond the Atlantic Ocean, in the gracious gardens of the Charites, or on the slopes of the poet's mountains, the "montes alegres" of Helicon and Parnassus.[8] Becoming words, the flowers survive in the wreaths of the Pindaric odes, where the poetic herald announces and crowns the triumph of the athletes of language – echoed by Haroldo: "Nos campos do equilíbrio elísios....ágil atleta alado" ("in the Elysian fields of equilibrium... agile winged athlete" (1976a: 56). Anthologies or florilegia help to perpetuate the rhetorical flowers.

By settling down in the gardens of Provençal poetry, the Noigandres group put the flower into its blazon: "ieu colore mon chan d'un aital flor don...l'olors d'enoi gandres" (Arnaut Daniel).[9] Baudelaire's *Fleurs du mal* gave it the modern "oxymoral" shade. Since the *Fleurs du mal* detected the neurosis of poetic roses, flower symbolism couldn't be merely enthusiastic any more. The perfume of verbal flowers wasn't yet sufficient to prevent the poet from ennui; he had to add the smell of the intestinal flora: "a flor é fezes" ("flower is feces," 1976a: 237).[10] The roses of poetic paradise died away – "Lostparadiso abrindo em rosas de necrose" ("Lostparadise opening in necrosing roses," 1976a: 50) – or turned into parodical prose – "uma rosa é uma rosa como uma prosa é uma prosa" ("a rose is a rose like a prose is a prose," 1976a: 238).

The flower, after having been eternalized by the everlasting spring of classical myth and poetry, has been temporized again. This temporality is materialized in the new word flower of "crisântempo" ("chrysantempus") and its laser apparition in the sky of São Paulo on the occasion of the 70th anniversary celebration of the *Folha de São Paulo*.[11] The laser modernizes the "escritura solar" of the "crisântemos" ("solar scripture of chrysanthemums") in *Signantia quasi coelum* (1979: 48) and strengthens the natural temporality of flower by its technical time lapse.

Besides its temporization, the flower has been popularized and tropicalized through Haroldo's "circuladô de fulô" (1976a: 213) and its setting to music by Caetano Veloso. The creation of this multilingual "patch of flowers" or "scat-

tering of flowers" (according to Caetano's authorized translation) is attributed
to the genius of the people, the Brazilian *sertanejo* singers, from whom
Haroldo borrowed the expression.[12] Through the new "polipalavra" of "circuladô de fulô" they became "inventalínguas" ("tongue-inventors").

Another way of creating new rhetorical flowers is the crossing of vegetal
elements with nonvegetal ones. The result is luxurious tropical tropes, such as
the "hailed babelic language bird tree" – "A Árvore Ave! para o babelidioma"
– the roots of which reach the bottom of the sea and are to be discovered by
the "Escafandrista às raízes" ("root diver," 1976a: 50).

Searching for the impossible "Flor. Última" ("Flower. Last one," ibid.), the
poet moves between the "jardins suspensos"("hanging gardens"), the different
levels of the "texto jardim" ("garden text," 1976a: 236). His real place is the
"entretexto" ("in-between text," ibid.). In his to and fro voyages between the
various fields of language, he turns out to be an "argonauta" (1976a: 51) or
"agronauta," as one might call him according to the amphibian Neptune who
sails and ploughs simultaneously on sea and on earth, followed by "Dom diniz
lavrador de suas lavras de espuma" ("Dom Diniz laboring his fields of foam,"
1976a: 42).[13]

4. The Aquarium

The poet's Aquarium offers an Odyssey to the searcher of nautical emblems.
In the long history of poetic navigation (see Knauth 1990 and 1986-87),
Haroldo de Campos occupies a particular avant-garde position by his utmost
density and variety, his original transformation of an abundant tradition. The
principle he realizes best is the endlessness of language. It is symbolized by
the "pélago-linguagem" ("pelagian tongue") and the "martexto" ("sea-text,"
1976a: 239) and by the infinite navigation through it, especially in *Galáxias*.
The book itself becomes a "livro viagem" ("traveling book"), which is materialized by the constant flow of speech, the continuous renewing and inventing
of words, as well as by the boundlessness of the individual fragments that
communicate between each other, and can be repeated, permuted, or
completed. The "multitudinous seas," "o mar multitudinário" (1976a: 203),
stimulate the inner- and interlingustic creativity. They are the ideal and real
spaces of multilingualism. The Me^h_ersprachigkeit ("polyglossy of the sea") is
realized either in a subliminal form (like "a um ponto euxino de beleza
abissal" (Portuguese/ancient Greek "at an Euxinian point/in a Black Sea of
abyssal beauty," 1976a: 65) or by the obvious mixing of languages (like "junto
ao mar polifluxbórboro polivozbárbaro polúphloisbos polifizzyboisterous
weitaufrauschend fluctissonante" ("next to the polyfluxrumbling polyvox-

barbarian polyphloisbos polyfizzyboisterous weitaufrauschend fluctissonante sea,"[14] 1976a: 239).

The crossing of languages, on the various levels of discourse and at different degrees, is perhaps the most efficient way of enlarging permanently the linguistic and literary horizon, of keeping alive the "idiomar" ("sea of language"[15]). In a global society, linked by the internet of "internauts" (cf. Petitjean 1995), multilingual literature can be one of the leading innovations of language and of culture as a whole, especially in relation with other arts and media. Haroldo de Campos is one of the most comprehensive and sophisticated agents of literary multilingualism.[16] He adapts Goethe's concept of *Weltliteratur* in the most concrete, the multilingual and multimedia way. Both phenomena are symbolized by the all-dissolving and fusing maritime imagery.

But the maritime trip not only offers a merry time. The monster of PARA-DOXYMORON demands sacrifice. The fear of failure, of FINISPOEMA, haunts the modern Ulysses. In front of his liquid green screen (*Finismundo*), navigating between the Scylla of redundancy and the Charybdis of entropy, he is afraid of getting submerged by the floods of information, or worse: of being dulled by the computerized hazard (*Finismundo*). Eventually, he becomes an anonymous "Oudisseu nenhumnome" ("nameless and none Ulysses"), whose subject is dissolved by a self-organizing language, the "tautodisséia dizendo-se" ("tautodyssey speaking itself," 1976a: 242).

Haroldo expresses the paradox of poetry in two basic ways. In a kind of Mallarméan sublimity he transforms the tragic "nau-frágio" ("ship-wreck") into the triumph of "victa...ficta alegria" ("the blitheness of defeated fiction," 1976a: 65, 68). Or he blends sublimity with triviality: the "multitudinous seas" are linked not only to heroic or erotic drownings but also lead to the banality of anal canals, the underground of the human body and the body social. The ABC of navigating in this "marmorto" ("dead sea") is drifting inside the poem: "nos canais competentes... nos anais recorrentes... os banais semo-ventes... os fecais incidentes... mar morto" ("in the competent channels and canals... in the anal recurrences... the self moving banalities... the fecal incidents...dead sea," 1976a: 201).

The reader plays an important part in Haroldo's logbook. He becomes a navigator himself – "um livro de viagem em que o leitor seja a viagem" – who commands the "travessia de significantes" ("the crossing of the sea of signs," 1976a: 242). Before Gabriele Contardi's *Navi di carta* (Paper ships, 1990), *Galáxias* is the first introduction into "hermenautics."

As a critic such as myself, the reader contributes to the rescue of the shipwrecked poet. He helps to cryptanalyze the blurred emblem of the sinking ship, "a proa de brasões extinta" ("the extinguished blazoned bow," 1976a: 66). Il est là pour redorer le blason.[17]

5. The Planetarium

Since Mallarmé the complementarity of maritime and stellar imagery has been almost compulsory in metalinguistic poetry: the sea and the sky reflect each other and poetry reflects itself in both. Basically, the planetarium is the most comprehensive poetic space, totalizing the maritime as well as the other emblematic fields. The overall concept of the verbal constellation and the titles of Haroldo's main collections of poems, *Xadrez de Estrelas*, including *Galáxias*, and *Signantia quasi Coelum* may testify to this priority. Nevertheless there is a material priority of maritime symbolism inside the stellar field. The title chosen by João Alexandre Barbosa for his introductory essay to *Signantia quasi coelum* may illustrate this interference: "Um cosmonauta do significante: Navegar é preciso" ("A semiotic cosmonaut: Navigation is a necessity").

I will only point out a few essentials of the "estelário"("stellarium," 1976a: 212). The central concept underlying the poetic constellations of Haroldo de Campos is a decentralizing one: the "de-constellation" ("desconstelização," 1967: 102). His planetarium is not a fixed space, but an expanding one. He first used the concept in his critical essay on "Bandeira, o Desconstelizador" (1967: 99-105), demonstrating the "desconstelização" of the romantic "star" Gonçalves Dias by the new paradigma of Concrete poetry, practiced by Manuel Bandeira.

As a poet, Haroldo de Campos used the concept almost in the same way, by de-constellating Mallarmé's *Un coup de dés* through the substitution of the white page by an inverted black page with its white word constellations (*O â mago do ô mega*, 1955-1956). Against this background, the neo-baroque oxymoron of "luz negra" (1979: 68) gains a new symbolic shade, including tropicalistic and Afro-Brazilian connotations.[18]

Another way of innovating in the field of Mallarméan constellations is the procedure of realizing the infinite complexity through minimalist forms, for instance word compoundings condensing contradictory ideas like chaos and order in "caleidocosmos" (1985: 72). On the other hand, *Galáxias* de-constellate Mallarmé by the very opposite means of extreme extension and mobility of poetic constellations, becoming a real perpetuum mobile.

An essential feature of this new type of verbal constellation is its multilingualism. The galaxy of universalistic literature cannot be but polyglot. Given the multiplicity of stars, the multiplicity of words necessarily tends to be multilingual. The Mallarméan pattern of primarily monolingual constellations has been radically reconsidered.[19]

However, the de-constellation not only applies to the works of other poets, but also to the poetry of one's own. Even in the very moment of de-constellating traditional patterns – such as the inversion of Dante's ascending dynamics in *Signantia* – the poet himself risks the "de-constelação" (1979: 108), the aesthetic "damnation" ("danação," 1979: 110). His real position is the in-between of Purgatory:

o purgatório é isso:	Purgatory is this:
entre/inter-	between/inter-
considere	consider
o que vai da palavra stella	the distance between the word stella
à palavra styx	and the word Styx.
(1985: 13)	

6. The Sensorium

The human body as the signifying microcosm of macrocosm – "o cisco do sol no olho" ("sun dust in the eye," 1985: 5) – is the center of the emblematic "sensório" ("sensorium," 1985: 30). In all, he/she symbolizes the concreteness and materiality of poetic language, which Haroldo has summed up in *A educação dos cinco sentidos*.

As the body speaks directly through the organs of speech and indirectly through the other parts, his/her poetic symbolism will be either of a more metonymical or a more metaphorical kind. There are frequent blendings between both sides or with other emblematic fields beyond the boundaries of the body.

The body as a whole symbolizes the literary text as well as the individual words, "os corpos verbais" (1976a: 234). Haroldo gives this topos a concrete physiognomy by putting the textual body into different situations, such as sexual or ritual action schemes. Under the impact of acupuncture in the "suplício chinês ("Chinese torture," 1976a: 235), the tissue becomes a texture of superficial "significantes" and invisible subcutaneous "significados" with unforseeable effects. Grounding on the graphic support of "pele-papel" ("skin-paper," 1976a: 240) and their obvious semantic similarity, the skin represents the paper that surrounds the poem's body. To this natural wrapping can be added an artificial one like the kimono symbolizing the Japanese vellum of a calligraphic book which turns out to be an oriental woman, "a mulher-livro" ("the woman book," 1976a: 240). The communication with this book is an erotic one, similar to that of the occidental poet with his Muse (see Musset or Valéry), but strongly marked by an oriental sensuality. The literary creation is seen as a sort of cuni-linguistics, an inter-lingual act on a cross-cultural scene. The result is an "incunábulo escrito em língua cunilingue" ("an incunabulum written in cunilingual language," 1976a: 240), or in "ludolabilibidolingual," a variety of the "ludilínguas" (1976a: 58) and the "labilingue" that Meisterludi taught his pupil poet in *Ciropédia*.

An additional component is the musical one. The tongue, the lips, the vocal cords, and the arteriae are each imagined as the poet's lyre: "labilira" ("labial lyre," 1976a: 51), "cítara da língua" ("lingual cithara," 1976a: 56), "violíngua" ("lingual violin," 1976a: 63), "a corda vocal" ("vocal cords," 1985: 14), "a harpa das artérias/Sangue lira" ("the harp of the arterias/sanguine lyre," 1976a: 60). All of them are concrete variations of the romantic lyre, the strings of which are made of the fibers of the poet's heart (Novalis, Lamartine, Hugo).[20]

There are poems, such as *Naja*, that are totally structured by corporal imagery. In the case of *Naja* ("snake") it is the vertebral column that forms the backbone of the text, in a partly calligrammatic design. Besides the vertical composition of the poem, the spine symbolizes the spelling of the poet's alphabet, "o alfabeto das vértebras" (1979: 73). The alphabet is essentially an erotic and a musical one. Along the central letter of lambda, representing the snake and the siren's tail, it runs through the scale of the siren sound, articulating itself in "SOL FÁ" syllables. This scene is imagined by a silen, the "finispoeta" of "silen cio" ("silen-ce"), who plays the flute ("flau/tassoando") on the vertebral column[21] of the "NINFA raquidiana" ("the rachidian nymph"), in the SOL minor key of "SOLidão" ("SOLitude"), his "palavrAMAR" ("loveseaword") not being answered.

The unwrapped body of the skeleton, the "cadavrescrito" ("text corpse," 1976a: 238) or the "papel-carcassa" ("carcass paper," 1976a: 242), is the most striking emblem of silence and the possible end of language. But although the language has been declared dead, "língua morta" (1976a: 228, 238), right from the beginning of the poem, it doesn't die, while speaking vividly of its death. The Memento mori paradoxically becomes the emblem of vitality; and paradoxically this vitality is guaranteed by the conviviality with the past, with "linguamortas" ("dead tongues," 1976a: 47) – an impressive Memento memoriae!

7. The Bestiarium

Haroldo's bestiarium is teeming with animals. Some of the most emblematic ones are: the cicada, the snake, the spider, the scorpion, and the bird. The only fable they are involved in is that of language. These animals are individual word animals – "ele compôs uma criatura sonora ÁUREAMUSARON-DINAALÚVIA" ("AUREATEMUSEALLUVIALSWALLOW," 1976a: 49) – and each one symbolizes the synonymy of "fábula" and "fala."

The cicada, being the most typical emblem of Mediterranean poetry since antiquity, belongs to the Provençal setting of the Noigandres group. Paraphrasing Arnaut Daniel's formula "lo son e.ls motz"("the sound and the words") Haroldo de Campos in his *Provença: Motz e.l.son* makes the "som de cigarra" ("the sound of the cicada") the very principle of sound-centered poetry.[22] He realizes some of its basic patterns like anaphoric repetition, inner- and intertextual permutation as well as paronomasia and polyptoton. The apparent monotony of the cicada's and the poet's song turns out to be a sophisticated synaesthesia of light and sound effects. There isn't any "Noisdanger" (Joyce) in Noigandres.[23]

The euphoria of this "flawless" poem "sem falha" is contradicted by the lyric "cigarras para a Morte" ("lethal cigarras") in *Orfeu e o discípulo* (1976a: 59) or the "cigarras cítaradolorosas" ("citharadolorous") of *Ciropédia* (1976a: 51). There the poet is conscious of the fact that the aesthetic ecstasy only lasts a summer's time, but he seems to be convinced that it is worthwhile nevertheless. As in Bashô's corresponding haiku (translated by Bandeira), the cicada becomes the emblem of the aesthetic oxymoral, with its juxtaposition of the extreme vitality of poetic language and its sudden end. The question is if, historically speaking too, la poésie ne chanta-t-elle qu'un été? And if the possible end of language is caused by the economical ant (cf. Knauth 1989).

The snake *ouroboros* could give an emblematic answer to these questions. Haroldo uses several times (especially 1976a: 236, 242) the mythical emblem of the self-devouring snake and gives it a special emphasis at the end of *Galáxias*. The traditional *ouroboros* undergoes a radical metamorphosis and becomes the "autossugante" ("selfsucking") tapeworm, living in the caverns of the intestinal labyrinth. Together with the "intestino escritural" ("the scriptural intestines"), the "bicho-tênia" ("the beast Taenia") symbolizes the circular and spiral structure, the endlessness of the book and the literary process. Besides the paradox of simultaneous ending and beginning – "dis/para" ("startstop") – the new *ouroboros* represents the general dispositive of "dis negpositivo," which is neither "either negative or positive," nor "negative as well as positive," nor "neither negative nor positive," but "sowohl als noch weder auch," "as well as nor neither too." In other words, it is the chaotic order of a constant "in between," the continuous movement, even "tatibitateando"[24] ("stutteringfumbling"), between words, texts, genres, author and reader, between language and silence, between the media.[25]

There is a shifting too between the emblematic areas: the writing "bicho-tênia" not only moves inside the intestines, but *is* the "intestino escritural," while the "intestino escritural," through the figures of synecdoche and paronomasia, becomes also a string instrument, the "vermi celo" ("worm cello"), which mac[a]ironically connotes the Italian or English "vermicelli" or the French "vermicelles;" eventually, the migration through the emblematic fields of endlessness – "Errant par les champs de la Gr$^{â}_{è}$ce"[26] – leads to the "labirintestina oudisséia" ("labyrintestinal Odyssey"), the dominating maritime symbolism of *Galáxias*.

Other animals of "entre-espaço" ("interspace," 1976a: 229) are the spider and the scorpion, collaborating in fragment 27 of *Galáxias* (1976a: 226). The spider, without speaking at all, spins the web of words, creating one of the most discreet patterns of silent language. On the other hand, the violent "escorpião de palavras" ("word scorpion") drives his sting like a stylet into his own body, in order to carve words out of silence. Similar to the scarabaeus, he turns the emblem of auto reflexive self-destruction and self-creation, the protagonist of the fable "entre nada e nada" ("between nothing and nothing"), between "texto" and "extexto" ("text and extext").

The silence, of course, has many meanings. It means either metaphysical, cosmic, historical, individual, or social silence, the paradoxical silence of the mass media, or the structural silence of poetic rhythms – "silêncio e som" ("silence and sound," *Bird song*, 1985: 49) – and of elliptic or allusive figures of discourse.

The silence caused by electronic mass media marks the end of the early poem *Thálassa thálassa...* Telephone replaces ornithopoetry – "os telefones serão pássaros de gargantas ocas" ("the phones will be birds with hollow throats"), and the civilized scorpion devours the nightingale's tongue, subordinates poetry to the Grand Ordinateur, the "encephalic electronics" ("Encéfalo Electrônico").

However the greatest risk of undesired silence seems to come from the individual fear of failure, of vain creative pain. It is symbolized by the icons of cage (*Claustrofobia*, 1976a: 57) or the butcher's shop (1976a: 230, 241), where the birds have lost their flying power, their feathers and wings having been stripped off or fallen off: "galinhas depenadas num açougue" ("plucked hens at the butcher's," 1976a: 230), "a primeira plúmula do livro viável... despluma e se cala" ("the first tiny feather of the viable book... plucked and silenced," 1976a: 229).

But the poet, being a "fênixbardo" ("Phenixbard," 1976a: 58), can be reborn after every breakdown. In spite of losing some feathers, the "Homem-pena... homopluma" ("the struggling bird man," 1976a: 235) takes wing again.[27] The survival of poetic language basically depends on its practice, the individual pen or pain. Looking at Haroldo's practice, the critic cannot but conclude: ESCREVER VALE A PENA! ("Writing is worth a pun").[28]

Notes

I would like to thank Dr. Walter Bachem for a linguistic revision of this study.

1. H. de Campos, *pánta rhei*, in *Heráclito revisitado* (1985: 73). The formula is a re-creation of Joyce's "riverrun" and its translation by Augusto de Campos: the crossing of the Portuguese/Italian "rio corrente" ("running river/brook"), the Italian "ri" and the Portuguese "ocorrente" ("re-occuring") combines para-doxically the ideas of perpetual progression and repetition. See my interpretation, agreed to by the poet, in Knauth (1991: 77).

2. Haroldo de Campos's work ranges from the neo-baroque Noigandres poems of the early fifties (*Thálassa, Ciropédia, As disciplinas*) and the Concrete poetry of the verbivocovisual and "revolutionary" Noigandres periods in the late fifties and the early sixties (*O â mago do ô mega, Fome de forma, Forma de fome, Lacunae*) up to the inner and intertextual space Odyssey of *Galáxias* in the sixtics and the early seventies (all of them collected in *Xadrez de estrelas. Percurso textual 1949-1974*, 1976) and finally the deconstellations of *Signantia quasi coelum* (1979), the syntactic mobiles of *A educação dos cinco sentidos* (1985) and the post-utopian *Finismundo* (1989-1990). It includes the literary re-creations ("transcriações") of Homer, Pindar, The Bible, Dante, Leopardi, Ungaretti, Li T'ai Po, Li Shang-Yin, Bashô, Buson, Goethe, Hölderlin, Schwitters, Mallarmé, Mayakovsky, Poe, Pound, Joyce, Góngora, Lezama Lima, and Octavio Paz. Furthermore, it includes the literary criticism and theory of *Teoria da poesia concreta* (together with Augusto de Campos and Décio Pignatari, 1965), *Metalinguagem* (1967), *A arte no horizonte do provável* (1969), *Morfologia do Macunaíma* (1973), *A operação do texto* (1976), *A ruptura dos gêneros na literatura latino-americana* (1977), *Deus e o Diabo no Fausto de Goethe* (1981), *O sequestro do barocco na formação da literatura brasileira: O caso Gregório de Matos* (1989), and countless articles in books and reviews dealing with avant-garde problems and covering a large part of classical and contemporary world literature.

3. 1994: 141. The "jogos onomásticos" ("puns with proper names" – the title of a collection of poems by Manuel Bandeira) are part of Haroldo de Campos's poetic code (see his *Teoria e prática do poema, Ode em defesa da poesia* and *Ideocable-gram*). For the general concept of emblematic field structures and its application to the particular emblems of the ship and the bee, see Knauth (1986, chapter "Das Bienenbildfeld") and (1986-1987).

4. "Palabrás" is a crossing of the Portuguese word "palavras" ("words") and the morphem "brás," an abbreviation of "Brasil," entering in word compounds like "Petrobrás," the Brazilian Petroleum Company; "polipalavra" means "multiple word."

5. There are certainly intertextual echoes of the poetic avant-garde navigations in Pessoa's "Brasão" (*Mensagem*), in Borges's manifesto of *Proa* 13 ("blasón de independencia"/"blazon of independence"), in Mallarmés *Salut* ("vous à l''avant," "you at the bow of the poet's ship"), and in Mário de Andrade's *Brasão*.

6. This emblematic section is treated here in combination with other emblems.

7. Relating to the literary symbolism of the precious stone Muiraquitã in Mário de Andrade's *Macunaíma* see H. de Campos (1973: 271 ff.).

8. "Monte alegre" ("The happy mountain") is the deliberately chosen address of the Noigandres poets in São Paulo. See H. de Campos (1985: 113).

9. "I color my song with a flower... smelling so well that it removes ennui." Haroldo de Campos himself refers to these words as "emblemas de búsqueda y de pesquisa poética" ("emblems of poetic search and research") for the Noigandres group (1994: 133).

10. A quasi-quotation from João Cabral de Melo Neto.

11. A photograph can be found on the title page of the *Folha de São Paulo* of 20 February 1991.

12. The Afro-Brazilian form "fulô" has already been used in the poetry of Jorge de Lima (*Novos poemas*, 1929, and *Poemas negros*, 1937).

13. See also Pessoa's poem "D. Dinis" (in: *Mensagem. Brasão*). Referring to the tradition of the sailing and ploughing Neptune see Knauth (1972).

14. The untranslated Greek, German, and Portuguese words are synonyms of the English/Portuguese "polifizzyboisterous."

15. The term stems from Andrés Sánchez Robayna (1979: 129) and corresponds to H. de Campos's "algaravia marítima" ("maritime gibberish," 1976a: 42) and "marlenguaje" ("sea of language," 1994: 138).

16. See my essay "Haroldo de Campos en el contexto de la poesía poliglota" (in *Homenaje a H. de Campos*, ed. Lisa Block de Behar, Montevideo, in print).

17. This idiomatic expression means literally "It's his [i.e. the critic's] task to polish up the blazon."

18. This trope has been chosen as a song title by Elizeth Cardoso and as the general title of a record commemorating the Brazilian centenary of the abolition of slavery in 1988 (Ariola Discos "Somlivre").

19. Eugen Gomringer's multilingual *konstellationen, constellations, constelaciones* (1953) worked in the same sense.

20. See also the neural and capillary music of Haroldo's poem "This planetary music for mortal ears" (*Dichtungsring* 17-18, 1989-1990).

21. A "transcriação" of Mayakovsky's Vertebral Flute.

22. See also Augusto de Campos's "transcriação" of e.e.cummings's "Grasshopper" (in: A. de Campos 1987: 38).

23. With the exception, of course, of poetic "bruitisme" ("noise art").

24. See Haroldo's "tatibitexto" (1976a: 195).

25. See Lisa Block de Behar's (1990) essays on intermediate aesthetics.
26. "Wandering through the fields of Grace/Greece" – a re-creation of the first verse of Ronsard's Pindaric "Ode à Michel de l'Hospital."
27. See also the ambiguous "revôo" ("taking wing again") of the poet in Haroldo's translation of Poe's "The Raven" (1976b: 30 ff.).
28. The literal translation is "Writing is worth the pain/the pen." The pun is based on the poet's use of "pena" in "Homem-pena" with the triple sense of the word, which can mean either "feather," "pen," or "pain."

Bibliography

Barbosa, João Alexandre
  1979   "Um cosmonauta do significante: Navegar é preciso." In: H. de Campos 1979, 11-24.
Block de Behar, Lisa
  1990   *Dos medios entre dos medios.* México, Siglo XXI.
Campos, Augusto de, Décio Pignatari, Haroldo de Campos
  1987   *Teoria da poesia concreta. Textos críticos e manifestos 1950-1960.* São Paulo, Editora Brasiliense. (First edition 1965).
Campos, Haroldo de
  1967   *Metalinguagem. Ensaios de teoria e crítica literária.* Petrópolis, Editora Vozes.
  1973   *Morfologia do Macunaíma.* São Paulo, Editora Perspectiva.
  1976a   *Xadrez de estrelas. Percurso textual 1949-1974.* São Paulo, Editora Perspectiva.
  1976b   *A operação do texto.* São Paulo, Editora Perspectiva.
  1979   *Signantia quais coelum. Signância quase céu.* São Paulo, Editora Perspectiva.
  1985   *A educação dos cinco sentidos. Poemas.* São Paulo, Editora Brasiliense.
  1994   "De la poesía concreta a Galáxias y Finismundo: cuarenta años de actividad poética en Brasil." In: Horácio Costa (ed.), *Estudios brasileños*, México, Facultad de Filosofía y Letras, UNAM, 129-175.
Knauth, K. Alfons
  1972   "Mythos, Magie und Hermetismus in Rimbauds Marine." In: *Poetica* 5, 348-373.
  1986   *Literaturlabor - La muse au point.* Rheinbach-Merzbach, CMZ.
  1986-87   "Ships & Chips." In: *Dichtungsring* 11-12, 88-159.
  1989   "Mutierende Tiere." In: *Dichtungsring* 16, 101-193.
  1990   "Das Schiff in der Tinte." In: *Dichtungsring* 19, 47-77.

1991   "poethik polyglott." In: *Dichtungsring* 20, 42-80.
Petitjean, Gérard
   1995   "Bienvenue dans le cybermonde." In: *Le Nouvel Observateur*
                16/2/1995, 42-43.
Sánchez Robayna, Andrés
   1979   "A micrologia da elusão." In: H. de Campos 1979, 127-141.
Sarduy, Severo
   1979   "Rumo a concretude." In: H. de Campos 1979, 117-125.

FROM HIEROGLYPHICS TO HYPERGRAPHICS

Willard Bohn

In order to enable language to recover its expressive power, the Lettrists argue that poetry has no need of words, which pose serious obstacles to direct communication. The trouble with words, the Lettrist Manifesto proclaims, is that they suffer from mechanization, fossilization, rigidity, and old age (Curtay 1974: 295-300). Instead of helping to express ourselves they dislocate our personal rhythm, bury our feelings, and smother any traces of inspiration. For above all, Isidore Isou insists, "le mot est le grand niveleur" ("the word is a great steamroller"). Words destroy not only the fanciful arabesques traced by the imagination but the capacity to express delicate nuances and to explore hidden domains ("*infraréalités*"). Isou is also bothered by the realization that aesthetics has been hopelessly contaminated by bourgeois ideology. Anyone who does not speak the language of the middle class is automatically disenfranchised. Among those who fall into this category are avant-garde artists and writers, minority voices, and dissidents of any stripe. For that matter, since power tends to be reserved for the wealthy and the elderly, young people and poor people stand little chance of influencing events. Since language is fully implicated in this situation, it represents yet another enemy. "*Toute victoire de la jeunesse*," the Lettrist Manifesto declares, "*a été une victoire contre les mots*" ("*Every victory by the younger generation has been a victory over words.*") As Roland Barthes (1957) has demonstrated, the bourgeoisie manages to disguise its favorite myths as facts by marginalizing any opposition and naturalizing its own ideology. The task of the avant-garde in general, Herbert Marcuse (1960: x) maintains, is to sabotage these efforts by rejecting their teleological and linguistic authority. The avant-garde strives "to break the power of facts over the word and to speak a language which is not the language of those who establish, enforce, and benefit from the facts." The simplest way to carry out this program, the Lettrists reason, is to break up the words themselves.

If linguistics stops at the sentence and Concrete poetry stops at the word, *Lettrisme* refuses to venture beyond the individual sign. By emphasizing the autonomy of the letter at the expense of the larger word, by reducing each letter to a phonetic or a visual counter, the Lettrists aim to destroy signification itself. Meaning is not only discredited, not only fragmented, but is completely effaced. To be sure, these remarks describe the progressive disintegration of the linguistic framework. What happens in practice is that meaning is displaced onto other, nonverbal structures that function as linguistic supports. Poetry stops being decoded on the left side of the brain, Jean-Paul Curtay (1983: 72) explains, and addresses more diffuse areas on the right side. In other words, as recent studies by Betty Edwards (1979) and others have shown, it approximates the condition of music and/or painting.

The Phonocentric Works

Like some of the Concrete poets, some of the Lettrists have concentrated on sound poetry, combining letters in various fashions according to their phonetic values. This genre possesses one undeniable advantage: like their visual counterparts, poems composed exclusively of phonemes are essentially unmediated and thus instantaneously accessible. While they must still be experienced line by line, word by word, they no longer have to be decoded. One of the attractions of sound poetry – or "text-sound art" as it is also known – is precisely the promise of universal intelligibility. In addition to the phonemes that we are accustomed to, many sound poems include growls, sighs, hiccups, kissing noises, belches, and the sound of snoring (see Curtay 1974: 42-43).

Maurice Lemaître even likes to design signs and letters of his own. Becoming something of an obsession, the construction of new alphabets and symbolic systems has preoccupied him from the beginning. At the same time, the Lettrists developed an intense interest in pictographic writing that continues to this day. Like the comic strip, which continues to fascinate them, the rebus has had considerable influence on their compositions. While some texts consist of words interspersed with pictures, others dispense with language altogether and consist entirely of pictograms.

A rapid review of the literature suggests that two kinds of rebus have vied with each other over the centuries. One gathers from this that the rebus harbors two distinct, but related, semiotic systems. On the one hand, the pictograms may represent a series of objects and/or operations that are somehow related to each other, most often by cause and effect. In other words, the rebus may be composed of a series of ideograms. On the other hand, the pictograms may refer to the *words* for the various objects and/or operations and be completely unrelated to each other. That is, the rebus may consist of a series of hieroglyphs. Since the visual signs simply stand for phonemes, in theory their pictorial value is minimal.

Although the ideographic and the hieroglyphic rebus both possess a long and varied history, the Lettrists have shown surprisingly little interest in the former. They have devoted far more attention to the hieroglyphic rebus, which appears to be easier to manipulate and which allows them to construct elaborate puzzles. Consider a composition by Albert Dupont (ill.1; Sackner 1986), from a series of drawings and mixed media entitled "Le Jardin des délices" ("The Garden of Delights"). While the text's appearance recalls the Futurists' experiments with *parole in libertà*, Dupont is not interested in rapid communi-

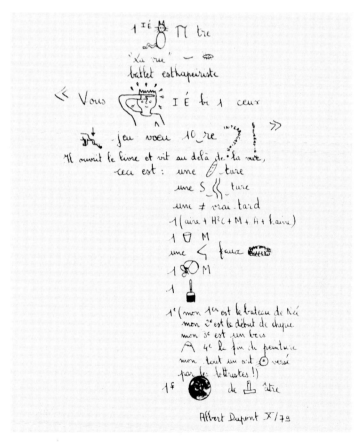

ill.1: Albert Dupont [from "Le Jardin des délices," 1979]

cation or instantaneous perception. To the contrary, he disrupts the reading process by forcing the hapless reader to pause at every turn. The visual signs are neither analogical nor isomorphic nor mimetic but rather serve as phonetic symbols. Instead of aiding the reader to grasp the verbal intricacies, they present a series of obstacles. Conceived as an "Aesthapeirist ballet" (< Gr. *apeiros*: "infinite"), Dupont's composition exemplifies the Lettrists' preoccupation with "Infinitesimal Aesthetics." As such it belongs to a long line of unperformable works that appeal primarily to the imagination. Since the ballet occupies a purely mental space, it is perhaps best described as an imaginary performance piece. As Isou declares in his "Introduction à une esthétique imaginaire," there is no need to manipulate physical elements to create a work of art. Despite its crude notation, therefore, Dupont's composition possesses tremendous aesthetic potential. It is up to us as imaginative readers and viewers to create the perfect virtual reality.

In a similar vein, Lemaître has coined the term "hypergraphics" (*hypergraphie*) to describe Lettrist experiments that transcend the limitations traditionally placed on writing. Since it superimposes graphic traces on virtually everything, hypergraphics may be seen to constitute a superior form of writing, a superwriting. To some observers, the Lettrists seem to want to dominate the world through their art. Others claim they are merely seeking to apprehend the world and to translate it into aesthetic terms. This viewpoint resembles that adopted by Lemaître (1954: 154), who defines hypergraphics as follows:

> Ensemble de notations capable de rendre, plus exactement que toutes les anciennes pratiques fragmentaires et partielles (alphabets phonétiques, algèbre, géométrie, peinture, musique, etc.) la réalité conquise par la connaissance.

> [A complex of signs capable of reproducing the experience of reality more precisely than all the former partial and fragmentary systems (phonetic alphabets, algebra, geometry, painting, music, etc.)]

The Iconic Works

Leaving the phonocentric works behind, the concept of hypergraphics expands at this juncture to embrace the notion of pure art. Like other visual poets, the Lettrists vary the size, shape, and distribution of the signs they employ to produce the graphic equivalent of drawing. Usurping the traditional prerogatives of painting, graphic conventions have been placed at the service of visual composition from the very beginning. Not surprisingly, the concept of visual poetry intersects with that of visual art. An inherently interdisciplinary movement, Lettrism juxtaposes not only letters and miscellaneous signs, but photographs and pictorial images in an attempt to transcend the limits of conventional representation. Stripped of their linguistic function, letters in particular are powerless to assert themselves, and the whole field of signs is reduced to the status of random marks on the page. The only recourse left to the spectator is to focus on their visual properties. Lacking verbal identity, letters function exclusively as pictorial signs, with the result that their significance derives according to the rules governing abstract art.

Unlike Concrete poetry, which is immediately recognizable, Lettrist compositions are harder to identify. Incredibly, there appear to be as many visual styles as there are members of the movement. The reason for this astonishing diversity, which contrasts with the relative uniformity of the isomorphic works, is readily apparent. Whereas the rules governing Concrete poetry are fairly restrictive, Lettrist regulations are remarkably permissive. Creators such as Micheline Hachette and Jacques Spacagna are free to do whatever they want, once the rebus has been left behind. For all intents and purposes there is no limit to their imagination. The only requirement is that their compositions must include visual signs. I use the term "creator" advisedly here because it is impossible to decide whether individuals at this end of the spectrum are poets or artists.

Although Hachette's "Van Gogh" (ill.2; Curtay 1983) is still dominated by the visual sign, it typifies the approach described above. In particular, it illustrates a central paradox shared by the remaining works I want to consider. While the composition consists entirely of graphic symbols, which are packed together like proverbial sardines, it is devoid of content. The density of the visual signs is not matched by a corresponding density of meaning. Now, in order to qualify as a sign, as Saussure (1967: 146-57) demonstrated long ago, a symbol must denote a specific concept. Closer examination reveals that the work is not composed of signs after all but of visual signifiers. The verbal signifieds, if there ever were any, have disappeared without a trace. To be sure, this does not mean the drawing has no meaning at all, merely that it has no linguistic significance. Since it has been erected on a verbal framework, which now lies in ruins, it represents what Barthes (1957: 222) calls a second-order semiotic system. Elsewhere (1964: 130-32) he distinguishes between two types of staggered system: connotative and metalinguistic. Like most forms of visual poetry, "Van Gogh" belongs to the first category. "Un système connoté," Barthes explains, "est un système dont le plan d'expression est constitué lui-même par un système de signification" ("A connotative system is a system whose plane of expression is constituted itself by a signifying system"). In this instance, it does not seem to matter that the primary system has been dismantled.

In contrast to denotative practice, Barthes adds, connotative signifiers are not only discontinuous but tend to be more scattered. As if to confirm this statement, Hachette strews the various symbols across the composition and isolates each one from its neighbors. The work itself looks something like a patchwork quilt. Arranged to form a rectangular pattern, it contains 130

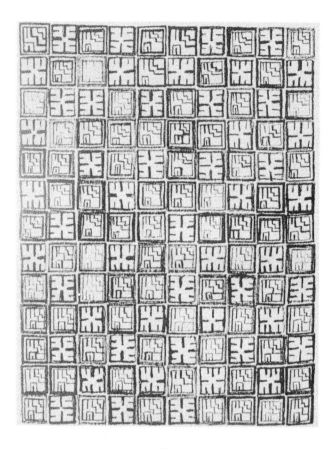

ill.2: Micheline Hachette, "Van Gogh" (1976)

identical squares each of which encloses a single symbol. The actual
characters, which recall Lemaître's "Mayan" hieroglyphs, are of three types.
A repetitive zig-zag motif characterizes the most common symbol which,
because it is widely distributed, provides a background for the other two. The
second character is divided into quarters, each of which is bisected by a
horizontal line. Rotated ninety degrees, it becomes a third symbol whose
quarters are bisected vertically. Interspersed with the zig-zag character, the
other two occupy alternate lines. Otherwise there is no discernible pattern to
the manner in which they are distributed. A fourth symbol turns up briefly in
the tenth line before disappearing forever.

   Again differing from denotative practice, Barthes notes, connotative
signifieds are simultaneously general, global, and diffuse. This observation is

supported by Hachette's composition, which addresses a single broad theme and manages to remain remarkably unfocused. The most that can be said is that it is concerned with graphic representation. Instead of imparting specific bits of information, the drawing strives to create a general impression. Although the title leads the viewer to believe it depicts Vincent van Gogh, no trace of the famous painter can be detected. In order to justify the title one is forced to resort to generalities. The search for a meaningful connection must be shifted to an abstract plane. At this level all that matters are the drawing's formal properties, which evoke similar qualities both in the painter and in his work. The fact that the composition is so forceful may refer to Van Gogh's temperament and to his characteristic style. That the drawing is so highly organized could allude to the painter's immense self-discipline and to its expression in his art. Furthermore, the individual symbols resemble the ideograms stamped on Japanese block prints, which greatly influenced Van Gogh and his colleagues. In any case, like his paintings' vibrant hues and energetic forms, they are certainly exotic. Finally, the drawing's pronounced tactile dimension reminds us that Van Gogh's works are heavily textured.

ill.3: Jacques Spacagna, "Voltagraphics-Hypergraphics" (1965)

In Jacques Spacagna's works, Curtay (1985) declares, cursive writing and organic patterning acquire unprecedented intensity and refinement. This is especially true of "Voltagraphics-Hypergraphics" (ill.3; Curtay 1985) which, like the preceding composition, is concerned with graphic representation. If Hachette's drawing is obsessively rectilinear, Spacagna prefers softer, rounder forms. While a few straight lines appear toward the bottom, they are drawn by hand rather than with a ruler. Despite the composition's commitment to abstraction, two of the shapes appear to be recognizable. Rightly or wrongly, the scene recalls certain landscapes by the German Expressionists. In the foreground, we seem to see one of Franz Marc's deer grazing peacefully in a meadow. Looming over the oblivious animal, a large mountain occupies the background. While most of it consists of bare rock, here and there traces of snow remain. Whereas the deer is depicted with a few rapid strokes, the mountain is drawn in meticulous detail. The fragility of the former contrasts markedly with the solidity of the latter, whose snow-capped peak is crowned with two heavy, dark lines. As before, the letters are densely squeezed together and give the composition an unusual texture. The symbols themselves, which at first look vaguely familiar, are unlike any we have ever seen before. Like Moses standing alone on Mt. Horeb, we struggle to comprehend the mysterious language that assails us.

By contrast, the language that appears in Alain Satié's "Prose" (ill.4; Curtay 1985) is secular rather than sacred. Although the characters express themselves in bizarre symbols, the experience they relate is strictly human. Trained as an industrial designer, Satié is a remarkable artist who possesses several distinctive styles. Like some of the Pop artists, especially Roy Lichtenstein, he draws much of his inspiration from comic strips. "There are certain things," Lichtenstein (1963) insists, "that are usable, forceful, and vital about commercial art." One of the things that clearly appeals to Satié is its clean, hard lines. Another is the tendency to concentrate on moments of maximum interest. Thus comic books tend to portray events that play an important role in the story. In addition they contain a high proportion of "action shots" – the more spectacular the better. Since each picture is worth a thousand words, the reader and the writer are both spared tedious descriptions.

The present story juxtaposes several events that are apparently widely separated in space and time. On the way to visit an isolated mountain castle, or perhaps a monastery, three women stop their car and get out to admire the marvelous view. While one of them points out something in the distance, another, who has presumably gone on ahead, suddenly recalls or imagines a very different scene. In the best Pop art tradition, Satié makes her a sexy young brunette (he also draws great blondes). At this juncture one can imagine several possible scenarios. Most likely, she is thinking of her fiancé, a pilot in

ill.4: Alain Satié, "Prose" (1971)

the airforce, who is off fighting a war somewhere. At this very moment, according to a peculiar comic strip convention, we see he has just bombed an oil refinery. Although the symbols enclosed in the "balloon" are impossible to read, there is no mistaking his sentiments. "Take that, you rotten scum!," he yells triumphantly as he heads back to his base. At the upper right, a female skier executes a difficult maneuver amid a flurry of snow. "I know I can win this race," she probably remarks to herself, "if I keep on skiing this well." How she is related to the rest of the composition is difficult to say. While the image could conceivably represent another thought or memory, it is totally inappropriate in the present context. The best explanation, it seems to me, is that the skier functions as a visual metaphor. Like the airplane surrounded by antiaircraft fire, she executes a sudden turn, accelerates, and dashes for home. In both cases, we get the feeling that victory is assured.

Like Satié, François Poyet also features nubile young women in his works. In many of his compositions, Curtay (1985) remarks, "highly complex signs in folds and spikes, sometimes fern-like, sometimes exotic bird-like, ...stroke or hug nude women engaged in meditation." This describes "Poiesis" (ill.5; Curtay 1985), for example, which depicts a nude female torso surrounded by a profusion of symbols. Whoever the woman is, she is deeply implicated in the signifying process. Although her body is arranged in a provocative pose, the title reveals she is not a real person but merely an abstraction. As the three automobiles alongside her proclaim – in a pun that works equally well in English – her body is a "véhicule sémantique." More precisely, it turns out to have both an erotic and an allegorical function. Lurking in the title, a second pun alludes to the creator of the composition. The woman embodies not only the creative act in general, it turns out, but the latter's personal theory of creativity. Her domain encompasses not only *poiesis* but *Poyet-sis*.

While Curtay believes the woman is meditating, closer examination reveals

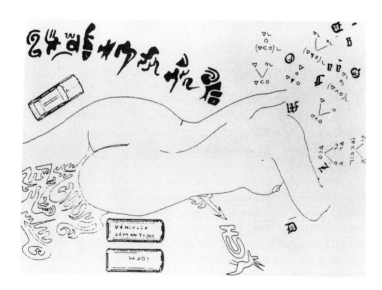

ill.5: François Poyet, "Poiesis" (1969)

she is reading a book. With a little effort one can make out the rectangular outline of the volume before her. The signs swirling about her head represent her thoughts as she mulls over some of the author's statements. The Gothic capitals testify to the volume's age and suggest she is engaged in the pursuit of knowledge. Resembling the notation employed in chemistry or symbolic logic, the triangular symbols indicate that her reasoning is methodical and precise. The bird-like symbols suspended above the woman seem to have no identifiable function. By contrast, the fern-like symbols beneath her are charged with erotic energy. Not only is one of them shaped and positioned like a phallus, but it points to another sign that appears to represent sexual intercourse. Unexpectedly, the seductive muse proves to be hermaphroditic. Theoretically at least she could copulate with herself. True creativity, Poyet seems to be saying, arises neither from the body nor from the mind but from their fruitful interaction. In order to create a valid work of art, thoughts and emotions must learn to make love.

Gérard-Philippe Broutin draws much of his inspiration from Egyptian and Native American systems of writing. In a fascinating work entitled "My Wrappings for Eternity" (ill.6; Curtay 1985), he constructs a double self-portrait which he covers with hieroglyphs, petroglyphs, and fragments of sentences. Although he superimposes a rectangular grid on the composition, like Hachette in "Van Gogh" (ill.2), it has little effect on the underlying images. Whereas each symbol occupies its own box in Hachette's drawing, Broutin's symbols often extend into neighboring squares. Like Native American rock carvings, furthermore, they frequently overlap. While the composition consists largely of pictograms, their relation to each other is open to conjecture. The most that can be said is that they tend to depict fruits, vegetables, and animals. Besides pumpkins, a bunch of grapes, and a pineapple the hieroglyphs portray several double-handled stirrup jars. Another object looks like a cross between an Egyptian *ankh* and an eggbeater. The petroglyphs are harder to identify but include pictures of turtles, snakes, fish, and birds.

If Broutin and his alter ego appear at first to be standing upright, the title seems to imply that they are reclining. Wrapped in linen bandages like a couple of mummies, they lie side by side beneath the lids of their twin sarcophagi inscribed with ancient hieratic signs. Still dressed in their mufflers and winter overcoats, they seem curiously alive, bearing mute testimony to the skill of the ancient Egyptian embalmers. To be sure, a number of questions remain to be answered. Why does Broutin choose to depict his own demise? Has he been smothered to death by the strange symbols, or are they purely decorative? What is the attraction of these markings in the first place? What could Broutin possibly have in common with an ancient Egyptian scribe or a Native American shaman? The answer to the last question, which provides a

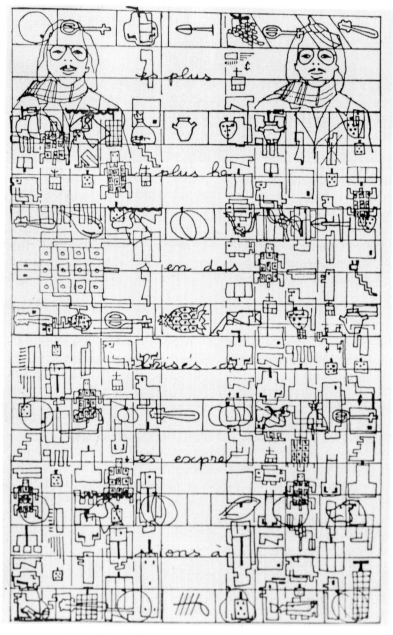

ill. 6: Gérard-Philippe Broutin, "My Wrappings for Eternity" (1971)

key to the others, is that they share a common preoccupation with signs. In life as in death, today as thousands of years ago, human existence is governed by symbolic relations. We are enmeshed in a network of signs from which we find it impossible to extricate ourselves.

Among other things, this explains why the portrait of the artist is so lifelike. Sooner or later it dawns on the viewer that the individual in the drawing is not dead after all. Broutin has simply transformed ancient Egyptian burial practice into a metaphor for the human condition. In reality, he has been gazing at us the whole time through a symbolic screen of his own devising. Once we grasp the drawing's basic premises, we can watch him watching us watch him watching us and so on ad infinitem. Perhaps this reciprocal *mise en abime* structure explains why Broutin chose to create a double portrait. At one level the symbolic screen represents the composition itself, which intervenes between us and Broutin. At another it signifies the work of art in general, which separates the author from the reader, the artist from the viewer, and the composer from the listener. At yet another level it represents the wall of signs that stands between us and everything else. Ultimately, the composition depicts not only a hieroglyphic world but itself in the act of depicting that world.

Like a great many visual poets, the Lettrists have repeatedly stressed writing's material aspect. By focusing on the individual sign, moreover, they have encouraged artists and writers to pay more attention to the signifying act. By demonstrating how meaning is generated, they have led them to re-examine how it is transferred from the creator to his or her audience. Above all, Lettrism has contributed a new awareness of the paradoxical nature of signification. On the one hand, signs perform a crucial function in enabling us to interpret (and to communicate) what we see and hear. Indeed, Wittgenstein (1958: 4-6) concludes that the ability to manipulate signs is synonymous with thinking itself. Without them neither the world nor our activities would have any significance. On the other hand, since signs are imposed from without, they inevitably obscure or distort what they purport to describe. "The mistake," W. J. T. Mitchell (1986: 92) observes, "is to think that we can know the truth about things by knowing the right names, signs, or representations of them." As Lettrism never tires of proclaiming, the modern crisis of the sign derives ultimately from its opacity. Since we can never divest ourselves of signs, we can never experience the world in its natural, unmediated state. Like Adam and Eve seeking one last glimpse of Paradise, we can only peer forlornly through the symbolic hedge that surrounds it.

Willard Bohn

Bibliography

Barthes, Roland
1957   *Mythologies.* Paris, Seuil.
1964   "Eléments de sémiologie." In: *Communications* 4/91, 135.
Curtay, Jean-Paul
1974   *La Poésie lettriste.* Paris, Seghers.
1983   "Lettrisme, Abstract Poetry, Mouth Symbols, and More..." In: *Dada/Surrealism* 12, 70-80.
1985   *Letterism and Hypergraphics: The Unknown Avant-Garde 1945-1985.* New York, Franklin Furnace.
Edwards, Betty
1979   *Drawing on the Right Side of the Brain.* Los Angeles, Tarcher.
Isou, Isidore
1956   "Introduction à une esthétique imaginaire." In: *Front de la Jeunesse* 7.
Lemaître, Maurice
1954   *Qu'est-ce que le lettrisme?* Paris, Fishbacher.
Lichtenstein, Roy
1975   "What is Pop Art?" In: *Art News.* Repr. in: Barbara Rose, ed., *Readings in American Art, 1900-1975*, New York, Praeger, 152-53.
Marcuse, Herbert
1960   *Reason and Revolution: Hegel and the Rise of Social Theory.* Boston, Beacon.
Mitchell, W. J. T.
1986   *Iconology: Image, Text, Ideology.* Chicago, Univ. of Chicago Press.
Sackner, Ruth & Marvin
1986   *The Ruth and Marvin Sackner Archive of Concrete and Visual Poetry.* Miami Beach [privately printed].
Saussure, Ferdinand de
1967   *Cours de linguistique générale.* Ed. Rudolf Engler. Wiesbaden, Harrassowitz. [1915]
Wittgenstein, Ludwig
1958   *The Blue and Brown Books.* New York, Harper.

FLUXUS, EXPERIMENTALISM, AND THE END OF LANGUAGE

Owen F. Smith

The following "study" is in the English natural language, is in common language. Or, it is *your* language in that it is a part, of the marks which you believe you "understand", "see the meaning of", "see the substance in".

...Consider the problem, question: Is there language (at some time and place), is there (ever) language? *If* the question can anywhere be asked, (the word) 'language' anywhere uscd, then there must be (some) language. *If it can even be asked* whether there is (ever) language, *then it is already answered affirmatively, then it is (already) assumed that there is (some) language*; no substantive information is given– the whole thing is empty; and thus the question can never be substantive, can only be vacuous. Suppose it is said 'There *is* language, all right – it is just not possible to substantively, non-vacuously ask whether there is'. If it is possible to say 'There is x', which is in effect 'Is there x? Yes', then it is possible to ask 'Is there x?'. Thus, if it is impossible to ask whether there is language, then it is impossible to say that there is language. But if it is said 'There *is* language, all right – it is just impossible to substantively, non-vacuously *say* that there is', then what does the first clause 'There *is* language' in the saying do? In other words, *if* there is language, it must be possible to substantively, non-vacuously ask whether there is. But since it cannot be possible, there can be no language.

The preceding is (not a conclusion but) an exhibit of ineluctable inferences. An exhibit which, remembering what was said first, *is the collapse of your language*. (Flynt 1964: 1)

I have quoted at length from Henry Flynt's "PRIMARY STUDY (1956-64) Version 7 (Winter 1963-64)" published in the Fluxus newspaper *cc VTRE* because it raises an aspect of the underlying language project of much Fluxus work. This is not to say that other writers and artists associated with Fluxus fully agreed with Flynt's statement, but rather that the questioning of language's fundamental existence and normative use was central to much exploration done in the context of Fluxus. The critical role played by Fluxus in reevaluating aspects of art, music, and performance in the early 1960s has gained increasing recognition; a similar important relationship between Fluxus and literature/language has often been overlooked. Fluxus and the artists who associated themselves at various times with this rubric had a significant role in the development of and explorations in literature in the late 1950s and early 1960s. The Fluxus project can be connected to four post-modern challenges to language: the enactment of a multiplicity of meaning systems (and states) and the apparent devaluation of specific meaning; a focus on the structure of discourse as opposed to its operative function; the loss of subjective definition in culture and discourse; the denial of historicity in social and linguistic change. This essay will specifically consider the first two of these aspects in depth because it is with regard to these two that Fluxus experimentalism and its intersections with language and art are most clearly evident.

It is important to qualify from the start what this essay is, and what it is not. This should not be seen as a discussion of the entirety of the directions and areas of language experimentalism in Fluxus. Nor should this be seen necessarily as a consideration of Fluxus exclusively. What I have attempted to do is to discuss some of the interstices of Fluxus, literature, and experimentalism as they are related to several artists, writers, and poets who were associated with Fluxus at various times. This consideration of some of the language-based concerns and issues that these individuals worked with or raised is not an attempt to locate Fluxus historically or define its project, rather it is an exploration of Fluxus works and ideas as related to language experimentalism. From the very beginning Fluxus refused to see the creative arena as clearly or rigidly segmented into various arts. This essay in looking at a variety of Fluxus experiments, some of which might not seem to be literary or poetic in nature, is a reflection of the Fluxus attitude which sees no validity in categorization. Thus, even though individual works may and do vary in degree of emphasis toward one art or another, they are also what Dick Higgins has called intermedial. For one of the most radical acts of Fluxus is to see all works as literary, musical, visual, and performative rather than just one form or another. This challenge to our traditional separation of media into types and/or genres was part of a process explored by Fluxus artists that was connected to a larger cultural shift: from a text based to a visual (field) oriented culture.

Fluxus's formation began around a concern, not for the specifics of language or literature per se, but for a lack of a means by which new and experimental work by a wide variety of artists, writers, and musicians could be published and widely distributed. The early lists of participants for planned Fluxus publications stress not a singularity of focus but a multiplicity of voices. The initial advertised list of contents for *Fluxus No. 1, U.S. Yearbox* (1962) included not only people who have come to be associated historically with Fluxus such as Dick Higgins, La Monte Young, Jackson Mac Low, Emmett Williams, and George Brecht, but also Diane Wakoski, Spencer Holst, Larry Poons, Claes Oldenburg, Simone Forti, Joseph Byrd, and many others. The birth of Fluxus was thus not connected to a specific view toward art or language, but a general concern for diversity and experimentalism in the arts. This kind of variety and support for experimentalism is evident in the pre- and proto-Fluxus performances and publications as well as in the later Fluxus-named activities. What all of these artists did share, those that would continue to be associated with Fluxus and those that would not, and what would become a point of emphasis in Fluxus itself, was an interest in change and an interest in collective or collaborative projects and actions. The *flux* and the *us* in Fluxus.

Language, Meaning and Indeterminacy

All activities and works produced by Fluxus can be said to be about language, especially the end of language as a proscriptive formula that restrictively shapes and dominates our cultural/world view. When Flynt questions language's ability to exist outside of itself, or as anything other than a tautology, he is laying bare one of the fundamental projects of Fluxus, that is, shifting our awareness of communicative structures from one of seeing them as natural (*not seeing* language), to seeing them as artificial constructs that often color and control everything we see and know. Fluxus not only acts in the gap between art and life, an aspect of Fluxus that many have commented on, but it also explores the gap between language and meaning. In "Shadow Piece II" (1964: n.p.) Chieko Shiomi gives the following instructions:

1. Project a shadow over other
      side of this card.
2. Observe the boundary between
      shadow and lighted part.
3. Become the boundary line.

In this formally simple but conceptually complex piece Shiomi sets into play a multiplicity of possibilities that extend the problem/questions raised by Flynt as well as create possible responses to it. For key to this piece by Shiomi as well as many other Fluxus "events" is both a shift in the nature of our perception, in this case from shadow to lighted part and back again, and a call for direct action by the viewer/reader, "become the boundary line." This work sets in motion a series of processes related to language and its functions and effects:

#1 It reevaluates language as static from the point of view of the reader – implicit in the role/place of the performer/reader is a proposition that meaning comes from a situational interaction not a static presence of an/the author and that there are no set boundaries between literature (the score/poem) and other art forms (its performance/realization);

#2 It questions and thereby criticizes linguistic processes – a focused awareness of the interconnected but shifting relation of the shadow and the thing that casts the shadow can be seen as analogous to the unfixed play between the sign and the signifier in language;

#3 It proposes that shaping awareness by the creation of boundaries is the principal function of language, not just transparent communication – a focus on the difference between the shadow and the light as a kind of presence and absence is parallel to linguistic shaped cognition which seeks boundaries in order to define and thus to exclude. Shiomi's "Shadow Piece II" exemplifies the wide range of potentials existent in many Fluxus events. A seemingly contradictory range from simplistic to complex, accepting to critical, humorous to serious, but in all of these possibilities what remains a nexus is the modeling of a potential new paradigm beyond the traditional confines of language.

One of the ideas that is centrally linked to Fluxus is that of indeterminacy, or its use in chance operations. Jackson Mac Low speaking about his own poetic work and the significance of chance operations stated that the intent was to let the meanings arise spontaneously and the materials of the work to a large extent speak for themselves (1980: 25). But he also remarked that such work is never fully egoless or meaningless:

> At first one thinks one can avoid the ego, make works that are egoless, by chance. This illusion passes after you work this way for a while. You realize that making a chance system is as egoic, in some ways, or even as emotional, as writing a poem spontaneously. But at the same time you realize that there *is* something more than just yourself doing it. & by interacting in that way with chance or the world or the environment or other people, one sees and *produces* possibilities that one's habitual associations… would have precluded. (Rothenberg, 1980: 52)

The general importance of indeterminacy is that it forms a significant basis for Fluxus's critique of the cultural status quo, with its over reliance on rationalism and egoism, as well as a means of creative production beyond such limitations. Almost all of the artists associated with Fluxus indicate a recognition of chance as an underlying factor for exploration in Fluxus-type work. It is this interest in randomness and chance that is also one of the most direct links to the past, most specifically to the ideas of Duchamp and Cage. Duchamp used chance as both a method of decision making and as an aspect of the process of making. Duchamp realized that chance is an operation of nature and as such impersonal. In addition to this Cage communicated through his works and in the class he taught at the New School for Social Research (that included several students who would later become involved in Fluxus such as Mac Low, Brecht, and Higgins) that art should harmonize with nature. The unifying force in nature, Cage believed, is one of process and change. Thus artists should utilize these operations of the natural world, particularly chance in the artistic process. These ideas about the importance of indeterminacy established for many Fluxus artists the significance of chance as a creative mechanism and as a philosophical concern. In his pamphlet *Chance Imagery* George Brecht (1966: 2) wrote:

> Chance in the arts provides a means for escaping the biases engraved in our personality by our culture and personal past history, that is, it is a means of attaining greater generality. The result is a method of approach with wide application.

The most direct connection between a use of indeterminacy and the other conceptual aspects of Fluxus is the emphasis of life over Literature and Art. Central to Fluxus is the idea that art is a part of nature and should therefore be founded on the universal processes of flux and change. The ultimate objective of this kind of thinking was to eliminate the idea that art possesses special qualities. It was held by many Fluxus artists that art should equal daily life and daily life should equal art, because it is within life that the things of greatest interest and fascination are to be found. Maciunas (1963: n.p.) stated that "Fluxus people must obtain their 'art' experiences from everyday experiences, eating, working, etc. – not concerts etc." Thus many Fluxus event pieces, such as those by Brecht, published in his "Water Yam," or by Mieko (Chieko) Shiomi published in her "Events and Games," are concerned with simple, almost mundane occurrences with very little evidence of expression of the individual as ego.

Indeterminacy was more than a method of artistic production: it created a basis for a kind of world view. The recognition of indeterminacy as a prevailing principle of nature, as well as a central aspect of a creative process, reinforced within the Fluxus attitude a perception that the world is based on ambiguities, ruptures, and incongruities. Following from this many Fluxus artists realized that deterministic processes, and key among these is written language, were not a reflection of reality but constructs reflective only of the "Western mind's" predilection towards structure and reason. The recognition and use of indeterminacy and a concomitant rejection of the ego-creator by Fluxus-related artists in the late 1950s and early 1960s initiated a fundamental challenge to literary expression. Not only was the personality of the author displaced from its front and center role, but the normative functions of language as a system of control, wherein power relations determine priority of meaning (the author's meaning dominates the reader's understanding), were partially or wholly abandoned. In this alteration one of the other important shifts came to the fore: a shift from the reader as passive receptor to the reader as active participant in the creation of meaning.

Performance and the Constitution of Meaning

In his *Exemplativist Manifesto* Dick Higgins describes the new more bi-directional relations as *post-cognitive* in that they require a greater degree of flexibility and openness that exists beyond the limitations of older cognitive/linguistic structures. The new art, such as that generated under the name Fluxus, in responding to such a new openness is no longer an end in itself or the sole expression of the unique artist but a presentation "of the entire range of possibilities of an aspect of reality" from which the audience interactively creates "a set of possibilities intended by the artist" (1975: n.p.). Brecht's "Drip Music," which is scored with the single word "Dripping," encompasses a range of possibilities from its staged performance at Fluxus performances (the main fluxversion of this piece consisted of a performer standing on a high ladder and pouring/dripping water from a pitcher into a vessel set at the base of the ladder) to any occurrence in which a dripping sound is heard. The open-ended nature of this piece allows for a viewer-related meaning (the viewer must create one, if there is to be one at all) and by extension a viewer-performed, life-integrated experience (it is performed whenever one hears dripping). Similar to "Drip Music," much Fluxus work is not only dependent on the specifics of its performance/presentation, but posits that the ultimate work exists only through the interaction with the reader/audience, and derives its meaning from this interaction, rather than receiving it from the author. In speaking about the relation of the reader/audience to the work Mac Low (1980: 27) stated:

> This [the replacement of the reader as the author in non-referential texts] is both true in reading and in being a member of the audience in performance works. Since there isn't any continuing meaning given by the author/composer, intended, in the work produced by more or less purely aleatoric means, then the meaning is something the reader or the audience member brings to the work. Each perceiver then becomes the center and the meanings are different for each person.

The fluidity of meaning and the increased significance of the reader/audience in Fluxus-type work does not abandon meaning, but it recognizes it as a situational construct rather than a fixed constant. Meaning becomes multiplied in its implications and varied in its possibilities, but the potentials for meaning are still scored or written by the author. Meaning is, as Higgins stated, not completely arbitrary but constructed from the set of possibilities intended by the author. Thus if we return again to Brecht's "Drip Music" the meaning and performance of the piece are open, but the possibilities of the work are directed by Brecht's given focus on "dripping." Jackson Mac Low's "Nuclei Method" of composition (Mac Low 1980: 18), in which words and phrases taken from chance-derived word lists function as interconnected "cores" of a poetic text, allows the poet to create fields of reference without abandoning aleatoric processes. The potential for meaning is created through this process but is not manipulated or imposed by it, for Mac Low (1980: 25) believes that meaning "appears during and, often with greater force, after the compositional phase." The "Nuclei Method" is in part a response to his understanding of the nature and force of language. Rather than try to force his meaning into the words he uses Mac Low (ibid.) sees his work as connected to a fundamental question about the relation between language and the creation of meaning: "If language (words) are capable – in fact, insist upon, organizing itself into meaning despite our interference, to what insights do these meanings lead us?" This interactive and interconnected way of creating a focus, without the author dominating the work, is found throughout Fluxus.

Explorations of the nature of meaning and how meanings are constructed and communicated are central to all Fluxus works. Such explorations, however, are part of the Fluxus paradigm shift which is concerned with a connotative mechanism of meaning rather than the more rigid and exacting denotative forms. For Fluxus, meaning is connected, as Mac Low suggests, with the world as it is for itself with all of its variances and ambiguities. In all Fluxus-type work the potential meanings are found both as an individual response (whether it be the viewer/reader's or the author's) and as an awareness of socially and culturally applied denotative meanings. Most art works traditionally function denotatively in that they are a mark or a sign of something, are a name or designation for something, or stand as a symbol for something. In all of these relations there is an intention, or at least belief, by both the artist/author and the viewer/reader, that there is a fixed connection between these elements through which meaning is communicated or given. Although Fluxus-type work might borrow these forms as a means to question them, more generally they make use of connotative processes to signify or suggest certain meanings, ideas, or forms that exist in addition to the primary of explicit meaning or to establish significance through association. To use a language-based metaphor traditional works are nouns, in that they have a singular presence, act or are acted upon, and have a dominant role in relation to the other elements, but Fluxus-type works are adjectives, in that they can exist only in a situational relationship to an other. Fluxus works do not inject other meaning and significance into the world, rather they function as a kind of plagiarism of prior denotative meanings as well as an exploration of the world as a text filled with connotative associations. George Maciunas's *Flux Paper Events* (1976) is not only explicitly a book, in that it is a bound series of pages with a title, author and publisher, but it is more importantly also a connotative cipher for a series of questions on the nature and function of the book. Rather than containing traditional text each page has been physically altered: one page is torn, one is cut, one has a cup stain ring, two are stapled together, and so on. This "book" is not intended to stand alone as an object but to act as reference to, and a critique of the established idea of a book's form (page + words = book), the notion of a book's contents (text + illustrations = contents), and the process of "reading" (meaningful text + literate reader → understanding). Thus in traditional Fluxus fashion a rather simple, even jokey idea communicated through simple means is connotatively a thoughtful and fundamental assault on the one of the intellectual underpinnings of our culture/civilization, the book. This process of questioning the physicality of the book was, for Maciunas, connected directly to the function of Fluxus as a publisher. Maciunas felt that all the Fluxus boxes, not just the ones that included text such as Brecht's "Water Yam" or Watts's "Events," were publications ("books"), albeit Concrete/Visual ones, and not just objects.

Emmett Williams's poem "SENSE SOUND" also functions similarly as a connotative reference to the nature of words. The poem, laid out in two columns headed by SENSE (in blue) in one column and **SOUND** (in red) in the other, shifts one letter at a time, with each replaced letter taking the color of the end word, from SENSE (SONCE, SOUSE, SOUNE) to **SOUND** and from **SOUND** (**SEUND, SENND, SENSD**) to SENSE. By addressing the issue of a text's materiality (the text as a thing and not just a sign for something else) Williams raises not only issues as to the relationship of the sign as a physical entity to its function as a signifier, but also creates a visual pun as to the connection between these two words and the cultural and social implications that they might have. A visual balance between the natural (sound) and the cultural (sense), this poem presents a series of questions about the word, the most basic, yet fundamental of which are: are they visual or textual?, and are they written or oral? In this poem Williams raises the two other major aspects of Fluxus's exploration and critique of language. What is the relationship between oral/performative language and written/read language?; What is the relationship between the materiality of written language (its concrete form) and its symbolic function?

The Fluxus Exploration of Language and Concretism

Much of the exploration of language and the critique of its normative functions by Fluxus-related artists revolves around the issue of concretism. Williams (1992: 60) has stressed that he is still a "poet," but one "who has found his expressive form in some untraditional ways of using language, of using it as raw material," and this idea can be extended to other Fluxus artists who explore language as well. From its earliest presentations Fluxus was linked to concretism, not only in poetry, but in all the arts. Many of the artists who were to become associated with Fluxus, such as Spoerri, Williams, Higgins, Mac Low, Maciunas, Wolf Vostell, La Monte Young, Nam June Paik, and others, were either aware of, or had worked with concretist experiments in language and sound by the late 1950s. For one of the first public presentations of Fluxus-type work in Europe, at Galerie Parnass in Wuppertal during 1962, Maciunas had written a statement titled NEO DADA IN MUSIC THEATRE, POETRY, ART (read by A. Caspari as "Neo-Dada in the United States") that specified the fundamental concern of such work with "concretism." In the English draft for the German translation, Maciunas (1962: 1) wrote that in "Neo-Dada" (i.e. Fluxus-type) work:

> Almost each category and each artist ... is bound within the concept of concretism ranging in intensity from pseudo concretism, surface concretism, structural concretism, method concretism (indeterminacy systems), to the extreme of concretism which is beyond the limits of art, and therefore sometimes referred to as anti-art, or art-nihilism.

The idea of concretism was, for Maciunas as well as many other artists associated with Fluxus, bound to/descriptive of their experimentalist approach. Concretism was "anti-art" in so far as it rejected the artificiality of art and literature and sought instead the reality of experience, not a reality that was abstracted or symbolized, but one that existed of and for its own sake. Thus concretism was bound to an interest in life/nature, not for what could be made from it or communicated through it as an extension of the artist's ego, but as Jackson Mac Low (1980: 25) has said:

> The whole point of chance operations is a non-willful kind of art – one where the materials (words, phrases, musical tones, performers, etc) speak for themselves to a large extent – & the meanings arise spontaneously in the minds of the perceivers – are not imposed by the artists.

Maciunas (1962: 1) had also commented on the connection between indeterminacy and concretism in his text NEO DADA IN MUSIC THEATRE, POETRY, ART:

> Further departure from artificial world of abstraction is affected by the concept of indeterminacy and improvisation. Since artificiality implies human pre-determination, contrivance, a truer concretist rejects predetermination of final form in order to perceive the reality of nature, the course of which, like that of man himself is largely indeterminate and unpredictable. Thus an indeterminate composition approaches greater concretism by allowing nature [to] complete its form in its own course.

In this text Maciunas also makes it clear that what is being explored, although related to Concrete poetry, a poetry which aims to break the traditional priority of the symbolism of the word by emphasizing its very physical materiality, goes beyond poetry to encompass more broadly most if not all communicative and creative approaches, in fact goes beyond art itself. Fluxus's emphasis on concretism not only concerned the work's material, beyond the individual's impositions, but often had multiple material forms, which reflects Fluxus's fundamental interest in and exploration of intermedia. A Fluxus text was thus simultaneously a physical mark (visual), a sound (aural and oral), and an action (duration and motion). Fluxus is filled with such intermedial, multi-dimensional, explorations: works that are objects and texts, Maciunas's "Your Name Spelled with Objects" or Tomas Schmit's "Poem" series from the early 1960s; works that are sounds and texts, Emmett Williams's "Litany and Response for Alison Knowles;" works that are performance scores and texts, Mac Low's "Letters for Iris – Numbers for Silence;" works that are objects, sounds, and scores or performances, Addi Koepcke's "Reading/Work Pieces" or Shiomi's "Spatial Poems."[1] It is clear from these few selected examples (of many that could have been used) that the text in Fluxus is no longer limited to words on a page and/or implications of such marks, but becomes a real object, connected to life, open ended and time based, that is also a means of creating potential foci for questioning, thinking, and exploration.

Associated with Fluxus's interest in concretism and language was a recognition that language, in addition to being a visual sign system, contained two other "physical" elements, sound and action, that were by nature not written but oral acts. In stressing the fundamental performative and oral nature of language Fluxus transfers the diacritical workings of language, the joining of disparate elements from within established meanings to create new meanings, from a fixed set of relationships (written) to a more fluid situational-based experience (oral). For this reason much of the Fluxus exploration of language is concerned with its performative nature. One of the main interests of many Fluxus artists was the nature of text as performance, or at least performative – both in the act of creation and in its subsequent re-production (what we might call a performance). By emphasizing the creation of the text through a structure, as Mac Low does, for example, with his Nuclei method, or through levels of existence, as Williams does with his exploration of the sound and visual qualities of words, the creation itself becomes a kind of performance. This performance then can result in a score which can in turn be used to create another work. The series of poems that Williams titled "Universal Poem" exemplifies this multi-level existence. They first existed as a "series of poems constructed by overlaying row after row of the twenty six letters of the alphabet, applied by rubber stamps" (Williams 1975: 397). This work, which itself has a very clear duration-based performative aspect, was later used as a kind of score for poetry actions in galleries, where he provided the stamps and ink pads and let the visitors construct mural-sized versions on the gallery wall. By interconnecting these aspects of creation and performance this work, and others like it, remains more fluid and thus more directly performative as well as concrete.

Not only does a recognition of the performative nature of language directly connect with the other facets of the Fluxus project, but it directly critiques the nature of language as enmeshed in power relationships. One example of this is that a number of Fluxus event scores are either written in the form of commands, such as Tomas Schmit's work that commands the participant to "GO HOME and wash your hands!, GO HOME and turn your head to the left!, GO HOME and open all of the windows of your apartment! STAY AT HOME and write a postcard to Fidel Castro!" (1978: n.p.), or are written to initiate action as commands do, such as Bob Watts's "casual events" (1964: n.p.):

drive car to filling station
inflate right front tire
continue to inflate until tire blows out
change tire*
drive home
*if car is a newer model drive home on blown out tire

Although such events can be discussed as they act to bring the spectator into the work, thereby breaking the fourth wall of the pieces and connecting them more directly with life, they also raise a question as to the nature and value of instructions and commands. One is instructed to carry out an act, as happens in many everyday situations, but the conflict between the form of such instructions (which seem reasonable) and the specific instructions (which seem unreasonable) brings into question commands and the value of following them. Fluxus thus uses the structures of language (reason) to critique reason (language). By using this form the event becomes either a self-cancelling act, the nature of the request overrides the command/instruction, or it leads one away from means-to-an-end thinking into an exploration of purposeless play.

Through their non-linearity, many Fluxus event scores emphasize that performance situations are transitive. In some instances this is related to the open-ended nature of the score: the performers need to go beyond interpretation to a level of creation. George Brecht's "two durations," for instance, is scored simply by two words, "red" and "green." The performer and/or viewer is given only minimal non-linear information that requires maximal interpretation and input on their part. In other cases, linear text/score structure is abandoned in order to extend the exploration of variation and chance within the performative situation. For instance, the score of Jackson Mac Low's "Letters for Iris – Numbers for Silence" consists of a number of cards on which are scattered letters and numbers; the letters are to indicate phonetic tones while the numbers indicate silences. This gives the performers some instructions on what to perform, but requires them to create the situation of the work. Describing the performative situation and instructions of some of his works Mac Low (1980: 21) stated:

> ... a situation is set up in which a group of people is given materials and a set of rules and procedures. Otherwise, they are free in many parameters when using these materials.
> ... although performers are not directly regulated by a central authority, eventually they are, since I as the composer am giving them the materials, procedures, rules, etc.... Nevertheless they're exercising their own initiative within the situation, the given materials being analogies of the real-life conditions provided by nature and society.

The aim of Fluxus to counter language/performative expectations is no where made more explicitly clear than in Emmett Williams's "Son of Man Trio." Williams (1992: 159) described the piece and its first performance in the following way:

> The first performance of this trio – for two people and a book – took place in Paris during July of 1963... Lette [Eisenhauer] was instructed to try and stop me from whatever I was going to do during the performance. The most convenient thing to do was read aloud from François Mauriac's Son of Man. (If Malevich's The Non-Objective World had been easier to reach in the performance area than Mauriac's book, then the piece would be known today as The Non-Objective World Trio.) Lette won the struggle. The great lengths she went to shut me up are well documented by the Zurich photographer Hans Emil Staub.

What the photographs show is that Williams (the reader) was interrupted by sounds being made, a roller being run across his mouth, things poked at his eyes, confetti thrown on him, tape put across his glasses and mouth, a bag chained over his head and shoulders, pages torn from the book, the book set on fire, and finally water poured over Williams and the book. The performance shifts from a vocal presentation of a text, where the text dominates, to a performance as non-text, in which the interruption of the text and its performance controls the action. Williams has stated that he feels that "the performer is refreshingly unaware of what his partner is up to, or going to do next. In a sense, I never know what the piece is about until it's all over – until I reflect upon what happened" (1975: 211). By emphasizing the unexpected in a performance and the context of its presentation rather than the text itself this work raises questions with regard to both the artificiality of the "independent" text and its traditional "reading." In Fluxus the approach to language is like a demonstration of scientific principle of the storage of energy and its transference from potential to kinetic. Many Fluxus works explore language as a kind of storage device, not of meaning, but of potential of action or sound. The works engage with language in an attempt to cause it to shift from its potential state (written) to a kinetic one (performance). This shift from thinking of language as static to engaging with language as action is directly connected to the Fluxus concern for play, not just as in humor, but the play within language, that is the operation of difference in the original Derridean sense.

The general focus of much of Fluxus, which explores the process of meaning making and highlights the continuous deconstruction of established meaning and the projection of new possibilities, is both a rejection of previously existing notions of language and an attempt to experiment with new ones. An exploration of difference in Fluxus does not offer an escape from the world but seeks to produce an endless play of quotidian effects. In this way the interest in the concrete in Fluxus is a dismissal of the romanticist vision of creativity and an art which seeks to escape into a world of its own creation. The Fluxus strategy, which seeks to affirm the play of difference in language, is not an attempt to create a new but different proscriptive language. It is instead a process that seeks to deflect language and its operations back to its starting point, the world itself with all of its vagueness, dislocations, and potentialities. Experimentalism in Fluxus thus seeks not to find a way of resolving contradictions, but rather to instigate the infinite play of imagination through language experimentalism as part of a desire to reflect the operations of life and reject the hierarchies of institutionalized culture and language. The Fluxus investigation of the concrete is a simple insistence on experience as an interaction between the subject (viewer) and the object (the performance, or work, or text) which seeks to minimize the potential closure of play. This emphasis on the concrete and the parallel absence of dominating abstract concepts or ideas in Fluxus is enacted as part of an attempt to extend the domain and the play of signification infinitely. The rejection of certain aspects of language in Fluxus, such as hierarchies, fixed meaning, and denotative forms, is related to an awareness of, and an emphasis on contextual experience and a recognition of language as an object (human made) and a mechanism (control system). The lesson of the play of language, as explored by Fluxus, is that the process of unending substitutions is an act of life, and the joy of such a recognition is that traditional systematics, such as written language, are no longer valid. Fluxus is not an end of all language, but an attempt to end the proscriptive, delimiting, and depersonalizing operations of language. Robert Filliou (1970: 79-80) wrote in his GOOD-FOR-NOTHING-GOOD-AT-EVERYTHING manifesto:

> I create because I know how.
> I know how good-for-nothing I am, that is.
> Art as communication is the contact between the good-for-nothing in one and the good-for-nothing in others.
> Art, as creation, is easy in the same sense as being god is easy. God is your perfect good-for-nothing.
> The world of creation being the good-for-nothing world, it belongs to anyone with creativeness, that is to say anyone claiming his natural birth gift: good-for-nothingness.

Note

1.   For illustrations of these works and more information on them, see Hendricks (1988).

Bibliography

Brecht, George
    1966   *Chance Imagery*. New York, Something Else Press.
Flynt, Henry
    1964   "PRIMARY STUDY (1956-64) Version 7 (Winter 1963-64)." In: *cc Valise e TRanglE*, No. 3, 1.
Filliou, Robert
    1970   *Teaching and Learning as Performance Arts*. Cologne, Verlag Gebr. Koenig.

Hendricks, Jon
   1988   *Fluxus Codex.* New York, Harry N. Abrams.
Higgins, Dick
   1976   *An Exemplativist Manifesto.* New York. Reprinted in: D. Higgins, *A Dialectic of Centuries. Notes towards a Theory of the New Arts*, New York & Barton, Printed Editions, 1978, 156-166.
Maciunas, George
   1962   *NEO DADA IN MUSIC THEATRE, POETRY, ART.* Stuttgart, Archiv Sohm, Staatsgallerie. A copy of this essay is reproduced in: C. Phillpot and J. Hendricks, *Fluxus*, New York, Museum of Modern Art, 1988.
   1963   Letter to Tomas Schmit, Gilbert and Lila Silverman Collection, New York and Detroit.
   1976   *Flux Paper Events.* Berlin, Edition Hundertmark.
Mac Low, Jackson
   1964   "Letters for Iris—Numbers for silence." In: *FLUXUS I .* New York, Fluxus.
   1980   "Interviews and correspondence: Jackson Mac Low and Gil Ott." In: *Paper Air* 2.3, 18-29.
   1986   *Representative Works: 1938-1985.* New York, Roof Books.
Rothenberg, Jerome
   1980   "Pre-Face." In: *Paper Air* 2.3, 51-54.
Schmit, Tomas
   1978   *tomas schmit, work 1962-1978.* Cologne, Kölnischer Kunstverein.
Shiomi, Mieko (Chieko)
   1964/65   *Events and Games.* New York, Fluxus.
Watts, Robert
   1964   *Events.* New York, Fluxus.
Williams, Emmett
   1967   *Anthology of Concrete Poetry.* (ed. by --) New York, Something Else Press.
   1975   *selected shorter poems 1950-1970.* New York, New Directions.
   1992   *MY LIFE IN FLUX AND VICE VERSA.* London, Thames and Hudson.

NONINTENTIONAL POETRY

Jackson Mac Low

I have been worrying the six questions in the Symphosophia questionnaire for over three months.[1] Unfortunately, though, I've had trouble answering all questionnaires at least since I first registered for the draft in early 1943, so the form itself presents an idiosyncratic difficulty. I finally decided to evade it. I will write primarily about my own work, the sense I give in the context of that work to the term "concrete poetry," and how I think my visual poetry may relate to others'.

In 1954, when I began producing most of my poetry that has been called "experimental" – some works written earlier (1938 to 1954) have been so characterized (see Mac Low 1986: 3-8 and 10-13) – I began using several "nonintentional" procedures in order to make works that "let language (at least, linguistic units and strings) speak for itself." Some were literally chance operations, involving dice, playing cards, random digits, etc. Examples appear in Mac Low (1986).

Others are nonintentional but in a sense deterministic. Among these were the "translation" of musical notation into words and vice versa, producing tonal music from verbal texts (employed since early 1955; see Mac Low 1986: 35-40), and two types of "reading-through text-selection procedures."

Acrostic text-selection methods (first devised and used in 1960) yield texts in which an index or seed word or string is spelled out by reading through a text and finding successive linguistic units that "spell out" the string by initial-letter acrostic, usually several times in succession.[2]

"Diastic" text-selection methods (developed in early 1963) give texts in which the selected strings spell out the seed with linguistic units in which the letters of the seed occupy corresponding places in the strings constituting the text.[3]

I have also made many works comprising (in text and/or realizations) units smaller than words: letters, phonemes, syllables, word fragments, etc. I began making works comprising such linguistic units in the late Fifties.

Beginning in early 1961 I have been making texts primarily meant as performance "scores," notably the Gathas (see Mac Low 1976: 234-247), verbal scores lettered on quadrille paper and first produced by chance operations, later more freely, and the Word Events (see Mac Low 1976: 134-135), realizations of two short instructional scores that ask their realizers to make an

204 *Jackson Mac Low*

improvised performance by spontaneously choosing among the phonemes of a specific name, word, or string and the words and syllables that may be produced by combining two or more of them.

That same year I began making Drawing-Asymmetries: visual and performance works that were made of words selected by nonintentional methods, first acrostic word-selection, later diastic, but placed on the pages by spontaneous choice and sometimes drawn or painted in ways that make them partially or wholly illegible.[4]

Somewhat later – in 1968 – I began my series of Vocabularies – drawings that are fields of words that are partial anagrams of a specific name (or of another kind of string) and that sometimes include musical notation, all usually placed on the pages spontaneously, following certain rules, but in one case with the help of random-digit chance operations. An atypical one, made on a typewriter, appears in Mac Low (1986: 279-81). Others have been reproduced in anthologies, critical books, and magazines.

My largest Vocabulary consisted of an installation occupying a whole room at the Queens, New York, performance space P.S. 1 in 1979. The installation included a 5,000-word list of words (with admissible suffixes) derivable from the name "Annie Brigitte Gilles Tardos," two wall-sized oil-paint stick drawings comprising sentences made up of groups of words drawn by chance operations from a large computer-produced list of 3,000 lines, each comprising one to ten randomly selected words from the original list, and designs composed of similar sentences printed on sheets of colored acetate that were placed over the windowpanes of this former schoolroom. See the complete description, reproductions of the window designs, and the 1980 poem "Antic Quatrains," derived from the same materials, in Mac Low (1986: 293-305).

All of these kinds of performance works may be (and the installation *could* be as long as it was exhibited) realized by performers who constantly choose from among a potentially infinite number of possibilities presented by the scores and instructions. Most of them, with the exception of the Word Events, can also be realized by vocalist-instrumentalists. Letter-to-pitch-class codes for "translating" the letters in these works into instrumental tones are included in their performance instructions.

These are among the works of mine often published and exhibited in Visual and Concrete poetry anthologies, shows, and archives and performed in Sound poetry festivals. They are both visual poems whose elements are words and letters and scores whose realizations are made up of the sounds corresponding to the various verbal-visual (and musical-notational) elements appearing in them. The fact that their realizations depend upon the performers' *choices* among the aural possibilities inherent in their elements does not make them less concrete than their visual scores.

The fact that the scores of such performance works have been produced by nonintentional methods and/or choice, but not intentional design, and that their realizations depend upon in-performance choices of the participants who are listening deeply and consciously relating with both the scores and all sounds audible in the performance space – both other performers' sounds and ambient ones – does not prevent them from being works of what is in my sense of the term "concrete poetry."

One other group of works should be mentioned here: a series of paintings and drawings in various media that I have been making since sometime in the Seventies. They began as celebrational presents for friends and comprised many repetitions of the appropriate greetings: e.g., repetitions of the phrase "Happy Birthday to X" would be written or hand-lettered over each other in every direction, usually in a variety of colors, so that eventually only parts of words that "stuck out" toward the margins could be read. Sometimes the letters of the repeated phrase would be dispersed over the surface many times.

Later these works were visual poems in which one phrase or a whole poem would be written over and over, usually in oil-paint stick on canvas or lithograph paper. A notable example of this is a painting now in the Ruth and Marvin Sackner Archive of Concrete and Visual Poetry in Miami Beach, which was commissioned by Dr. Sackner. He asked me to use Yogi Berra's saying, "It ain't over till it's over": I repeated the phrase over and over in oil-paint stick on lithograph paper, writing it in many different colors and directions (such works have no determinate orientation: any side may be the "top," although preferences for one or another may develop).

Since 1990, I've been making such works by writing a new poem as I made the painting, placing each new line on the canvas as I thought of it, so that it is handwritten or hand-lettered over the other lines. One of the first of these, a 48-by-36-inch painting (oil-paint stick on linen), entitled "100-line poem: for Gino Di Maggio," was shown in the "Ubi Fluxus ibi motus" pavilion of the 1990 Venice Biennale and is now in the collection of the Foundation Mudima, in Milan. "Wordpairs," a later painting of this kind (same dimensions and materials), comprises 120 two-word lines; it was exhibited at the Emily Harvey Gallery, New York, in 1990. This series is intermittently continuing.

These paintings and drawings differ from my other visual poems and scores (except for some of the Drawing-Asymmetries) in that the words in them are largely illegible. They begin as legible visual poems but as their making proceeds, they can no longer be read. They become paintings produced as described, but are they still visual *poems*? I'm inclined to think that they are. Just as many Zaum, Dada, and Merz poems, as well as some contemporary poems, are "unintelligible," but still poems, these are *illegible* poems.

I will end this survey of my "concrete" work by describing my recent book

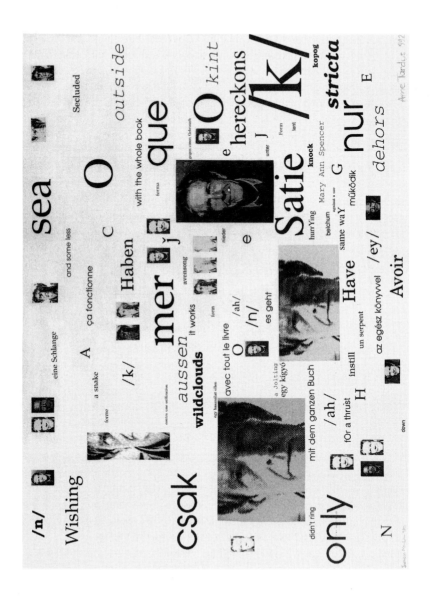

Anne Tardos and Jackson Mac Low,
1st Four-Language Word Event In Memoriam John Cage (1992)

of nonintentional poetry, *42 Merzgedichte in Memoriam Kurt Schwitters*, (Mac Low 1994). This is my first group of works written on the computer alone.[5]

Produced by impulse-chance selection of words, phrases, and sentences from certain books about Schwitters and his work and some reflections of my own, it uses several different type formats to indicate the voices of Schwitters, his friends, his enemies, critics, and myself. This poem and its sources became, in turn, source material for random-digit chance operations involving MS-Word's glossary function, through which I made "Merzgedichte 2-30." The last twelve were made by running earlier Merzgedichte through one or more of three different computer programs, DIASTEXT and DIASTEX4, Charles O. Hartman's computer-automations of two of my diastic text-selection procedures, and Hugh Kenner and Joseph O'Rourke's TRAVESTY. In the last group of them, words are fragmented and run together by TRAVESTY. They resemble Concrete poetry because of capitalizations within words and other features and are often used by my wife, Anne Tardos, and me as scores for Sound poetry performances. The book concludes with a verbal score, instructions, and ten pages of musical notation for performing the "22nd Merzgedicht."

38th Merzgedicht in Memoriam *Kurt Schwitters*

KAr
HülseTHes,
KArATe
BucTurAPsor
LIs lovewood revonTTed.

Ander,
IcTes.

Ang Iners con
LysAff brIne
Alsend brub HAgmes mencess kInces AumeIng
GerHe HITTHe IIsTers,
To AdversTATescIITTe
NAgen blensTure Aus enber,
HAnds,
PIcATIvewordemboldecIIff b slooTAnTer souPT frAmPII InTTer.

A major aim of all my texts and scores written by means of nonintentional methods, chance and deterministic, is to display language in its concreteness. (I realize that this is complicated, and to some, rendered "impure," by my sometimes admitting instrumental sounds "translating" the letters in them into tones.) To achieve concreteness in this sense I devised and used methods in which my choice figured minimally and various non-personal determinants were primary. Nearly all of them have a double existence as texts and performance scores, and the realizations of scores are usually indeterminate, in that the choices of performers among the scores' possibilities produce the realizations, usually spontaneously during performances.

In these texts and scores, both the lexical meanings, commonly shared connotations, sound, and appearance of each constituent word and string are concretely foregrounded, as against any meaning or planned design of my own. The procedures often yielded texts having similar general visual formats – members of each group of them have family resemblances. Sometimes certain meanings of my own come through by virtue of my choices of source texts, but the major effort is to let the words themselves speak.

To me all aspects of words are involved in most of my procedurally composed texts and are of equal interest and relevance: what they look like, how they sound, and what they commonly mean and connote. When, as often happened in the Fifties and Sixties, people spoke of my early nonintentional works as "abstract," I always countered with the assertion that they were not abstract but "concrete." This is the sense in which I have most frequently used the term "concrete," even after I began to become aware of the predominantly Visual poetry whose makers used that term differently.

Now what, aside from the illegibility of the recent paintings and some drawings, distinguishes most of my works from those of the artists who constitute the recognized Concrete poetry movement? Probably both how they were produced and how they look.

Most Concrete works are the result of verbal-visual planning and design, and their realizations are more often circumscribed (than are those of my works) by the poems themselves and by certain conventions of their aural realization, if not explicit rules. Often also, specific semantic "points" are made by their verbal-visual designs. Some Concrete poems are also visually mimetic, even representational.

What is most absent in all such Concrete poems and their aural realizations is nonintentionality and unpredictability. This is not universally true, of course, but it holds for much the greater number of Concrete poems produced by leading members of the international Concrete poetry and Sound poetry movements.

Also, I have not thought much about "the materiality of signifiers," which is of great concern to most Concrete poets. However, I believe that my independently formulated notions of "foregrounding language as such" and "letting words speak for themselves," at which I arrived independently around the time that the Noigandres group and European and expatriate American Concretists were becoming active, may not differ greatly from this idea.

Certainly, in making poems that are of a unique kind, similar at most only to certain earlier design poems, and then but remotely, they eminently foreground the visual materiality of signifiers. The designs of their Concrete poems are usually elegant in a way that my own visual poems are not (nor were they meant to be). Although much of my work is in other ways "Apollonian," theirs is immediately perceptible as such. Some of my visual poetry often appears more nearly "Dionysian." This is especially true of the Drawing-Asymmetries and paintings, as well as the drawings that preceded the latter.

However, all of my works made by nonintentional procedures, as well as many made in other ways, bring to the fore both the visual and the aural materiality of signifiers and of the graphemes and phonemes that constitute them. But the emphasis on materiality in both Concrete poetry (by members of the movement) and my own concrete poetry raises the question of meaning. To what extent is meaning ineluctably bound up with the materiality of signifiers?

In my work, I assume that every signifier carries with it at least its common lexical meanings (or structural meanings), as well as many commonly shared connotations. This is true even when I have not intended these meanings and connotations, since I have brought the signifiers into the works by means of nonintentional procedures. Also, because of the concatenations and configurations of the signifiers new meanings and connotations that I could not possibly predict are "enacted" by readers and auditors. The first of these kinds of meanings seems equally "concrete" with the signifiers' visual and aural aspects in that the most common usages are bound to them. Is materiality then a sine qua non of concreteness?

There is no question that the meanings of the words in most other artists' Concrete poems are both intended and integral with the forms of the poems. Are these "nonmaterial" aspects of the signifiers extraneous to the poems' concreteness – are they to be thought of as "epiphenomena" proceeding from or surrounding the material signifiers?

I realize that my use of the term "concrete" comprises both the material and the mental aspects of the signifiers. Is its usage among the Concrete poets very much different from my own? How and where does meaning figure in the poetics of Concretists?

New York: 18-21 September 1995

Notes

1. Cf. p. 367 ff. of this volume. [Editors' note]
2. For instance in the *Stanzas for Iris Lezak*, written in 1960 and the Numbered Asymmetries, written 1960-61 (Mac Low 1972 and 1980). For examples of both, including Asymmetries not in the earlier book, see Mac Low (1986: 71-127). Both groups may be performed; see Mac Low (1972: 411-20), (1980: xiii-xix and 252-55), and (1986: 79-85 and 106-17).
3. Notably, *The Pronouns – A Collection of 40 Dances – For the Dancers*, written 1964 (Mac Low 1979), *21 Matched Asymmetries*, written 1967 (Mac Low 1978), *The Virginia Woolf Poems*, written 1976-77 (Mac Low 1985a), and *Words nd Ends from Ez*, written 1981-83 (Mac Low 1989). The *Pronouns* poems may be read and/or realized by dancers or performance artists.
4. See the serigraph portfolio *Eight Drawing-Asymmetries*, drawn 1961 (Mac Low 1985b).
5. The first of these, which was written at the request of the editors of the *Kurt Schwitters Almanach 1987* (Cologne: Postskriptum Verlag), was originally entitled "Pieces o' Six – XXXIII" and appeared in the US first in *Sulfur* magazine and in my *Pieces o' Six* (Mac Low 1992).

Bibliography

Mac Low, Jackson

1972　　Stanzas for Iris Lezak. Barton VT, Something Else Press.

1978　　21 Matched Asymmetries. London, Aloes Books.

1979　　The Pronouns – A Collection of 40 Dances – For the Dancers. Barrytown N.Y., Station Hill Press.

1980　　Asymmetries 1-260. New York, Printed Editions.

1985a　　The Virginia Woolf Poems. Providence, Burning Deck.

1985b　　Eight Drawing-Asymmetries. Verona, Francesco Conz.

1986　　Representative Works: 1938-1985. New York, Roof Books.

1989　　Words nd Ends from Ez. Bolinas CA, Avenue B.

1992　　Pieces o' Six. Los Angeles, Sun & Moon.

1994　　42 Merzgedichte in Memoriam Kurt Schwitters. Barrytown NY, Station Hill Press.

A MINI-ANTHOLOGY ON THE STATE OF CONTEMPORARY POETRY
(With Special Reference to the USA)

Harry Polkinhorn, Compiler

1. Hyperotics: Towards A Theory of Experimental Poetry

Harry Polkinhorn

1.1

First, it is *towards* a theory; we shall never arrive. The "theory" marks a horizon, all too easily overlooked in the heat of the actual journey. What is important, as Olson knew, is the energy and direction of motion. Second, it is towards a *théory*, that is, some system of rules for explanation and prediction. We can only move towards such a state; otherwise we would immediately land in contradiction, because these rules by definition are to be distinguished from practice or experiment. By its nature, experimentation is process and therefore soaked through with curiosity, contingency, longing, materiality, the unknown and perhaps unknowable or non-theorizable. Ultimately, practice absorbs theory, the latter becoming a more limited form of the former.

Interestingly enough, the term "experimental" is taken from the sciences, and an early adaptation of it was made by the French novelist Zola. His so-called experimentalism was passed off as an ironic reflection upon the glaringly obvious social failures which science and technology as the rationale of industrialism had spawned. Zola attacked the "rotten ... lyricism" which had become the marking feature of Romanticism's flight from the more obvious ravages of the Industrial Revolution. Curiously, Zola assumes the persona of the objective, neutral observer, the prototype mask of the emergent scientist. As he succinctly puts it, "we are very much mistaken when we think that the characteristic of a good style is a sublime confusion with just a dash of madness added; in reality, the excellence of a style depends upon its logic and clearness" (*The Experimental Novel and Other Essays*. New York: Haskell House, 1964, p. 48). Zola's comments (recalling a neoclassical view of style) are not based on facile distinctions between sublime and vulgar, elevated and demotic, which come down from the Greeks, passing through the Renaissance doctrine of decorum (analyzed by Rosamund Tuve), into the nineteenth century. He seeks rather to undermine by donning the white lab apron of sanitized objectivity in order to smuggle a charge of subjectivity back into the formula. Zola thus *pretends* to look frankly to science as a curative balance. The specific discipline he cites is medicine, which provides him with appropriate metaphoric overtones of sickness and health in the realm of culture. He praises Claude Bernard's treatment of the experimental method in medicine and goes on to say that "experiment is but provoked observation. All experiment is based on doubt, for the experimentalist should have no pre-conceived idea, in the face of nature, and should always retain his liberty of thought" (p. 3). The semblance of this Cartesian flight from preconception as a dangerous dilutant of the truth grows out of the natural science methods which had their origins in the Latin Middle Ages. It was not until the En-lightenment had hypothetically purged the mind of superstitious adherence to religious and primitive complexes (read preconceptions) that this experi-mental method began to deliver dramatic results (Copernicus, Boyle, Priest-ley, Newton, Pasteur). Disinterested experimentalist objectivity, backed to the hilt by the official justifications provided by analytic philosophies (Locke, Bentham), continued to make ground right through the nineteenth century.

In his subtle mockery, Zola claims that "the experimental novel is a conse-quence of the scientific evolution of the century ... the literature of our scientific age," (p. 23) and he speaks of the "impersonal character of the method" (p. 43). Zola's "experimental novel" sought to generate character through a solid basis of all narrative data in concrete social situations. These situations, however, were drawn from the lower-class degradation spawned by the new manufacturing economy. A class situation was delineated; characters were "placed" in the social milieu much as a rat might be placed somewhere in a maze; the author/reader then "observed" the outcome (the all-seeing, removed eye), which was morally disastrous, as would be expected, since the preconceptions had entered through the process of selecting the situation. Contrary to the intrusion of an all-knowing narrator, in the experimental novel incursions of the ego were supposed to be held to a minimum. In this way Zola emulated the suppression of the subjective, taking as his model scientific empiricism; however, insofar as his works are in fact selective (structured on preconceptions), they derive value from the presence of this factor, which Zola reconstitutes in accordance with those changes in the social/economic structure he perceived as important: "It is the characteristic of the experimental method to depend only on itself ... It recognizes no authority but that of the facts, and it frees itself from personal authority" (p. 44).

How things have changed! Now experimentalism is identified with the rampant exploration of purely personal authority or "expression," the erosion of facts, imbrication of poetry with other forms of discourse both textual and non-textual, obsession with communications technology and mass media, and sublime (or ridiculous) confusion, with more than a dash of madness thrown in. But of course, as I have argued, Zola knew very well that experimentalism in literature could not be equated with the experimental method in medical science.

I offer these considerations as an arbitrary but fixed starting point, by means of which I propose to avoid the trap which the distinction between theory and practice has laid for me. I will assert, therefore, the arbitrary nature of the division between the cultural activities of theory and practice (this arbitrariness mirrors that of power distribution in society). The following set of linked questions lays out a trajectory which I hope to explore in the second part of this discussion.

Why were they separated? What is the quality of their antagonistic relations which has confused some of our best thinkers? Why is it almost always the case that those who say how things are (critics as theorists speaking in the abstract voice of Truth, beyond preconception) occupy university positions, whereas most of those who produce so-called experimental poetry do not and in fact have little or no social or cultural status? Why is there no identifiable movement of experimental poetry in the U.S.? Why, with very few exceptions, are there no established journals, reviews, or magazines dedicated to experimental poetry here? Why, with very few exceptions, are there no sound-poetry, video-poetry, or intermedia poetry festivals in this country, no tradition of formal or informal support for this cultural activity? Why do those people who think about these things at all ignorantly and narrowly identify poetic experimentation almost exclusively with one or two self-defined "movements" whose adherents have spent almost as much time proselytizing (under the guise of theorizing) as producing fresh work?

1.2

As the poets affiliated with these purposefully misleading labels will be the first to tell you, however disingenuously, there is no such thing as a given movement. Each poet is unique. By the same token, there is no such thing as experimental poetry, confessional poetry, working-class poetry, or any other kind (only critical formulations thereof). Yet, as we all know, this is being two-faced, because in another way of course there is.

Therefore, the argument is perhaps best understood as being conducted on two nested levels: 1) formal; and 2) concealed within the formal, another argument is being carried on covertly among the critics. There are big stakes to continuing these arguments. Among them are the chance to define cultural history, not to mention more mundane consequences such as tenured university positions with full health, vision, and dental coverage as well as the possibility of retiring without sliding into poverty. So assertions about what is and is not experimental poetry (or some other cultural form) will continue, and as usual the primary beneficiaries of these discussions will continue to be the arguers, not those about whose works the arguments are being conducted. Sometimes, of course, a poet is also a critic, or vice versa, but the really powerful critical voices are almost never primarily poets. These are social roles, and as such money and power (or their relative lack) saturate every aspect of their manifestation in our lives.

As well, one should mention that almost always the debate pretends to a kind of universality which in fact is indefensible even on the most elementary level. That is, not only are the avant-garde or experimental discoveries of a given country and time seen in a Hegelian/universal perspective of the end of history ("the death of literature;" "the *dernier cri* of poetic experimentation beyond which it is impossible for *anyone, anywhere in the world* to go and still be poetry," etc.), but even within that country the attempt is continuously, forcibly made to close off all future avenues of possible poetic development through a process of monumentalizing the discoveries of a few, thereby constantly marginalizing ongoing poetic production which would build on and extend into new arenas.

1.3

Having established this as a contingency context, I want to continue pointing towards my ideal because unreachable horizon for experimental poetry. "Hyperotics" suggests both parts of my theoretical orientation. "Hyper" connotes "over, above, beyond, exceeding, in great amount." "Erotics" pertains to sexual love, "the sum of all self-preservative, as opposed to self-destructive instincts or drives." On the formal level, experimental poetry is that moment of the material which manifests the urge to exceed either itself or its perceptions of its antecedents. It wants to go beyond, to surmount, to venture forth, to become lost again by leaving behind the conventional, the comfortable, the already understood, the traditional, the accepted. Although sometimes the case, this is not solely a retreat to pre-Freudian libido but includes going beyond its own achievements, continually redefining itself through staking out expanding, temporary boundaries beyond which to strive in subsequent incarnations. Sexual love goes backwards and forwards, backwards and forwards, until direction becomes irrelevant. The result? No formal definition of the object is possible. Eros of course is the deity who presides over just such energies. My argument, then, is that experimental poetry, insofar as it manifests this expansiveness, can be approached usefully with the classical model of sexual love, especially in its manic phase in which self and other are *con-fused (thrown together)*, in the interest of preservation of the self through a process of changing the self.

Some people, including some poets, of course, hate change. They would prefer poetry to stay the same from one generation to the next, just as they would prefer poets to repeat themselves. These consumers espouse "standards of value," which they call "quality." They like to measure everything against what they already know, and any deviations from this they usually reject as manifestations of lesser quality, invoking an unexpressed and ultimately inexpressible, elitist, and hierarchical standard which then saves them from the logical embarrassment of trying to defend their choices and manifold exclusions.

That's my sketchy move towards a theory. Experimental poetry has no essence but is structurally defined by its difference from the safe, the predictable, and the orderly. I have kept my comments brief because I have come to place less and less stock in theories as such. As mentioned above, they have their social/economic uses, to be sure, but as explanatory tools, they seem more and more inadequate to the increasing complexities of poetic experimentation.

When it comes to disporting in the vast fields of the experimental, I find that other forms of writing are much more sophisticated and satisfactory. In addition, I have deferred to the practice of the day in these matters by elaborating a theory without mentioning a single example. This was done partially out of irony. What is the relationship between assertion and example, the abstract and the concrete? There are not several poets whose work could have been brought, but *hundreds*, if not *thousands* of experimental poets active throughout the country. Anyone who has seen *Factsheet Five* or Len Fulton's *International Directory* or *Sound Choice* comes away bewildered and exhilarated by the intensity and variety of poetic explorations being carried on in this country, almost all of which is beneath notice by the academy, needless to say. Thus, through its irrepressible libidinal expansiveness, experimental poetry as we see it today highlights the fact that a responsible criticism has never been born.

2. On Experimental Poetry

Michael Basinski

My first thought on experimental poetry is that it is hardly experimental enough. There is far too little pushing and pulling and manipulating of literary boundaries in the realm of the poem. I think that this is the result of poetic careerism. Some of our best and potentially brightest poets are more concerned with prizes and photo sessions than poetic limits. Experimental poetry is left to poetically positive outsiders, radicals, and eccentrics, and to the poets from the working classes or from working-class backgrounds. Fortunately, at this time this is a fantastically rich loom of writers who are not rich or suburban in mentality. There are two veins of progressive marginal writing. There are those working with the visual and aural potential of poetry and those pushing the moral content of poetry – that is, those engaged in writing about the body (particularly anything that has to do with human sexuality). Interestingly, both of these forms of writing are locating their audiences in an increasingly growing non-literary community. That is to say, there are non-poets listening and reading poetry! True, it is a small audience but real, and it is now there as it has not been in the near past. Experimental poetry is therefore a populace event. People are interested in it! Experimental poetry has made the poem again an exciting experience. And it must continue to do so. It is something that titillates the senses (as well as the mind). A poetry slam is as experimental in presentation as a performance in a dark, obscure gallery. Experimental poetry's mission is to engage the ordinary (this means ordinary people and ordinary readers too!) and to make poetry alive again to those beyond the egg-head world of too much of modern poemitry.

3. Articulating Freedom: Three Brief Notes Regarding the Contemporary Underground/Otherstream

Jake Berry

3.1

By designating particular works as experimental we dismiss them as unproved, hypothetical, of questionable veracity. This is our means of allaying the unknown's imposition on our intellectual security. It is not until the work is analyzed, cataloged, and finally judged valid that it sheds its ignominy, obscured and burdened now by whatever aesthetic code may be in currency. Yet, what we are too apprehensive to witness directly is the very thing we profess to seek. We erect a shrine that obstructs the beneficence of the power toward which the original impulse arose. This is an ancient condition, mythically tragic. We are method's hostage. What we know of reality isn't in what our terminology proposes to address but only the terminology, as it is an aspect of nature itself.

3.2

A poem is not the telling of a thing, but the thing itself utilizing language, in whatever form (and however the definition of language might be extended), to transmigrate from one "place" to another. It trans-forms to awaken to itself in renewed aspect, and to awaken others to its experience. The poem and poet call one another to a common ground of being, where they constitute a single entity. To be more specific, a poet is an individual poetic entity biologically appearing. It speaks, it bodies forth being, participates in the theater of objects. What might be the essential nature of such a pan-substantial creature can only be discovered through direct confrontation and mutual dissolution within the shared domain, the antipersonal dynamic this union cultivates. We are speaking then of the phenomenology of the open field. Yet, we must speak in the negative only since any absolute assertion would only project an apparition onto the field. The actual projection is the whole field of poet/poem and all participants, indistinguishable any longer as individuals (and there is much that surely remains unknown, latent in the field). And further, the field itself, being open, is never subject to definition, but is realized through experience, through communion in the common nature its very appearance makes evident.

3.3

Finally, we should not concern ourselves with the establishment of movements or schools, by the name "experimental" or any other. There is nothing noble in relinquishing our presence here to the status of artifact, shelved, another moment documented and weighed against the rest, even if that moment is granted fundamental importance. It falls on us to strive for a cognizance liberated from static ideologies and subservience to the symbol. The histories must be ended and the museums closed (they both are, as we now have them, closed anyway). We must find value in the moment's appearing rather than the misapprehended corpse of its past. With that approach it is our responsibility to be and allow creations presence that have in their character no tolerance for the spirit of closure no more than any other organism can tolerate imprisonment. They are creatures without dimension, the living courses of liberation through the infinite.

4. The Postypographic Era

Fabio Doctorovich

The publishing industry has remained virtually unchanged since 1455 when Gutenberg first printed the Bible. Now, we are witnessing the most important technological transformation in literature since the invention of the printing press: the Gutenberg Galaxy is starting to disintegrate into a myriad of small postypographical nebulae: the McLuhan Entropic Galaxy. At this point, the printing press is being complemented – not YET substituted – by a number of other publishing technologies such as audio recordings (in the form of sound poetry and audio books), computer media (CD-ROMs, electronic networks, and computer art), videotaping, and others. On the other hand, old "literary" techniques, such as, for example, singing and acting, are being revamped by performance and sound poetry (both of them frequently using technological refinements as well).

Not only the publishing industry, but also the act of reading, unchanged for several centuries, is being altered. In the case of computer CD-ROMs, reading has become an active, participant-directed process rather than passive, author-directed: turning pages in a book has been transformed into following hypertext links. The rational-visual act of reading has become an experience of sight, sounds, and colors. In the case of performance poetry, reading (a lonely act with a slow asynchronous response by the readers) mutates into a collective experience (a social action in which the answer of the public is received in an immediate and synchronized manner). As would seem obvious, writing techniques are also being profoundly altered. The writer of the not-so-distant future will have to be a more complete and unspecialized artist who will need to blend his writing skills with oral and visual artistic abilities and even technological knowledge. This, together with a literature that allows an active participatory reading and even the introduction of modifications made by the reader in the work of art, will perhaps help to rehumanize literature and achieve the avant-garde's unfulfilled dream of merging art and life. Literature and literacy as we know them today are not going to perish; they will simply acquire new meanings and dimensions: those of the Postypographic Era.

ARTE Y VIDA
ARTEVIDA
ARIDA
ARDA
ADA
A

5. The Question of the Experimental

Jack Foley

> Beyond all else that can be said, I consider "Leaves of Grass" and its theory experimental – as, in the deepest sense, I consider our American republic itself to be, with its theory. (I think I have at least enough philosophy not to be to absolutely certain of anything, or any results.)
> – Walt Whitman, *A Backward Glance O'er Travel'd Roads*

> EXPERIMENT: Indo-European root, per = Venturing, testing the way, taking a chance; hence, valuing; then, buying and selling. Cf. Greek *peira/* Latin *peril*. Related to Germanic *fear, fearful, fearless, fearsome*. Latin *experimentum*, a trial.
> Transitive verb: "To have experience of; to experience; to feel, suffer": a now obsolete meaning from the O.E.D.

> PERIL: danger.

The question of the "experimental" is raised in every "period" of literature. The term itself may be used to suggest the dubious nature of an enterprise – merely experimental. Or it may suggest an undertaking of great value, even heroism. The *Oxford English Dictionary* offers various examples. From 1787: "The laudable spirit of experimenting." From 1857: "The more I experiment … the more unexpected puzzles and wonders I find." In our own time William Carlos Williams asserts, "I'll experiment till I die." In all these instances, *risk, danger* is a necessary element. To experiment is to take a chance, to venture something. Robert Creeley once asserted his faith in the essentially "experimental" nature of his friend Allen Ginsberg by saying, "I am sure that Allen Ginsberg, despite the persistent concern he has shown for the moral state of this country, would nonetheless yield all for that moment of consciousness that might transform him." Walt Whitman took "our American republic" itself to be an example of the experimental.

The impulse towards risk, danger, the experimental – which may merge with a poetics of *not knowing*, as it does in Jack Spicer, Diane di Prima, and Michael McClure, or with "negative capability," as it does in Keats and Larry Eigner – the impulse towards risk exists always. A question we may ask is: What form does that impulse take now? What does "the experimental" mean for us?

I think the answer must be related to the great revolution in communications which is currently puzzling all of us. For writers, writing itself is "experimental." Has writing reached the end of its life? Is it finally *irrelevant*? Or has it hoodwinked us all and undergone a powerful transformation to re-emerge as e-mail and computers, as software, CD ROM, as a hundred and one other things? Where is the "spirit" in all this?

At this point, it seems to me, to experiment is to remain in a powerful open-ness, a consciousness which will allow for the genuinely polysemous content of absolutely everything. In a famous passage questioning the concept of "essence," Ludwig Wittgenstein wrote, "As in spinning a thread, we twist fibre on fibre ... the strength of the thread does not reside in the fact that some one fibre runs through its whole length, but in the overlapping of many fibres." That strength, it seems to me, is our strength, whether we wish to call it "collage" or "multiculturalism" or "experimentation." In his poem, "Stanzas Composed in Turmoil," Michael McClure writes, "WE'RE IN DANGER OF THE LOSS OF OUR DEEP, OUR DEEP BEHAVIOR." The poem goes on, "THAT'S WHAT WE LOVE! / WE LOVE THIS DANGER! / WE ARE DEEP INSIDE ... NO FEAR! NO FEAR! HEY! NO FEAR!" McClure's impulse is that of the genuine experimentalist: to recognize danger but to face it not with "fear" but with the drivenness of "love."

> dancing on the beaches in the car roar,
> dancing on the beaches in the car roar,
> in the Acid Rain, in the Acid Rain. No fear!
> NO FEAR! NO FEAR! HEY! NO FEAR! NO FEAR! HEY!
> NO FEAR!

6. The Tools of Writing / The Ends of Literature

Karl Young

It can be argued that with the advent of personal computers, telecommu-nications devices, and other technological developments, the tools of writing are changing in such a way as to destroy or invalidate older methods, and that the nature of writing will change with the change in media. This is true for some writers and some types of writing, but it ignores or discounts an enormous number of others.

Aside from those who still use pencils, pens, and typewriters, there are other areas that seem important, though less obvious. To me, an important and highly innovative area of writing is "tagging," the graffiti writing of names and short phrases on buildings, signs, busses, etc. Tagging should be differentiated from "Painting," the art of painting full murals in public places without much resistance from police or other authorities, sometimes with explicit or tacit consent of property owners. Practiced primarily by young people in economically blighted urban areas, tagging ignores computer technology, art history, and traditional literature altogether. Its basic tools are paint spraying devices, the mechanized equivalent of the paint spraying techniques of the artists at Lascaux and other stone age sites. Its specifically literary content tends to be limited, often involving no more than the invention of a personal name for a tagger or group of taggers. Aesthetically, it runs the gamut from trivial decoration to some of the best calligraphic experimentation of this century. Often letter forms are so highly stylized that only fellow taggers, and perhaps associated gang members, can decipher them – a characteristic shared by some of the most highly prized Sino-Japanese and Islamic calligraphy. Although taggers must work quickly and spontaneously, improvising a great deal on the spot, they often spend a good deal of time planning their tags, going through many stages of sketching and testing in less hurried circumstances. Taggers run the risk of being killed or crippled by the stunts they perform, risk being beaten by police or security guards, risk imprisonment, and risk health and psychological problems that could come from the drugs some taggers use to fortify themselves. This brings the romance of danger into this art form. The mystique of danger often leads to an artistically false value being placed on the work, but it also leads to something more important, in fact to the heart of this kind of expression. For the most part, taggers live in dreary, bleak, and oppressive environments. On the simplest level, tagging is a way of marking turf, of saying "I'm here – you can't ignore me." On a more profound level, they are saying "No!" to the social, racial, and economic restraints that imprison them. They don't simply accept the trap in which they find themselves, but try to make something better out of it, to make it something that expresses their own sense of beauty in the face of all that makes their lives and the lives of those around them ugly. The ferocity of attempts to stop them by property owners and police proves that this is not simply a matter of aesthetics, but an expression of the will to change society. If a drab building or poster represents the control and power of outsiders, tagging represents a revolutionary impulse, a seizing of power by the disenfranchised.

Although some visual artists and art historians acknowledge tagging as an art form, this is usually done in a condescending or voyeuristic manner, stressing the stunts of the taggers or the seeming peculiarity of their lives, at best seeing tags as folk art to be exploited temporarily and left behind. The taggers don't recognize other art forms, nor do they see the attention they get from critics as being much different from the attention they get from sociologists and journalists: to them it is unimportant and irrelevant. Taggers live in ghettos and write for people in those ghettos. They don't write for people like those of us participating in this conference. For them, we are a different species.

Traditional calligraphy follows another line of development in writing at the present time. Neither computers nor tagging had rendered calligraphy obsolete, and there is no reason to suppose it will disappear in the foreseeable future. As a matter of fact, traditional calligraphy seems to be growing and encompassing more invention at the present time than it has during the last half century. Using pen nibs and brushes that are simple refinements of tools hundreds or thousands of years old, many contemporary calligraphers have moved into the area of full illumination of text, sometimes a complete synthesis of word and image. A few calligraphers have tried to work closely with poets, but for the most part, they just need texts to use and their contacts with poets don't go much beyond seeking permission to use texts. Poets for the most part see calligraphers as decorators, as people who falsify texts by putting too much stress on letter forms, which they often see as quaint or precious. Although traditional calligraphy is still going strong, it exists in a genteel and comfortable ghetto at least as obscure as that of the taggers.

Moving from these areas of writing into what we might call literature proper, we encounter a bewildering maze of ghettos. Although there is some interaction between them, they tend to be exclusive and closed. Members of each ghetto tend to see themselves as the chosen people, to whom ultimate truth has been revealed. They tend to see people in other ghettos as unclean or lost in ignorance or simply irrelevant. Although people in many ghettos form alliances with those in other ghettos, they are often so dedicated to their ghetto or configuration of ghettos that they can't see their turf as a ghetto at all, but as the center of the world. Ghetto clusters can be complex. The cluster of ghettos often labeled "experimental writing" includes many sub-ghettos, as well as a large number of people (perhaps the majority) who don't belong to any specific sub-ghetto but remain unaffiliated inside the larger ghetto cluster.

Perhaps this sort of ghetto formation is essential to artists: something that helps concentrate energy and attention so that the enormous number of options available to artists doesn't become overwhelming or debilitating. Perhaps they offer enough camaraderie, status, and security to help keep members going. If this is so, we could see literature as something that is losing any cohesion or unity at present. This could be seen as a real advance for artists, something that frees them from obligation to theories or modes of expression that no longer apply to their practice. It could stimulate new forms of creation and give rise to new forms of analysis free from the critical demands of irrelevant canons. Perhaps most important of all, this could encourage more cooperation and mutual aid within small groups, bringing about a re-socialization of art. If this is the case, perhaps these small groups could be seen as operating a tribes instead of ghettos.

The problem with that, for the moment at least, is that each tribe or ghetto still carries the desire for authority, for dominance, for canonicity, for proving the tribe or ghetto any given person is in as the only one that matters and the one to which all others owe obeisance. As much as this may bring psychological benefits to individuals in small groups, it also cuts them off from a lot, not only from sources of new ideas but also from virtually any audience outside a particular tribe or ghetto.

At this point, it may be useful to look back at the concept of literature on a level as simplistic as that on which I mentioned tagging and traditional calligraphy as examples of writing. As a high school English teacher might put it, the purpose of literature is communication. That may be too simple a concept for many theoreticians, but it seems particularly useful at the moment. If we see tribes or ghettos as the major units of artistic production at present and for the foreseeable future, nothing would be healthier than an emphasis on communication between people working in different modes. This needn't mean adulterating or diluting anyone's work to make it more easily comprehensible. Just the opposite would seem more likely: the desire to communicate could take more of a "Come see what we're doing; don't be shy – bring what you're working on, too" attitude, and less one of "Here is absolute art: see, tremble, and submit."

You can read the phrase "the end of literature" in two ways: either as "the finishing of literature" or as "the purpose of literature." If we go with the second one, the best purpose of literature would seem to be to bring together the disparate groups of practitioners and to aid communication between them. No goal would be worthier at the present time, when so much is going on in so many divergent directions.

POLIPOESIA

Enzo Minarelli

Vocalism in literature represents a productive area of research both for the pre- and the post-Gutenberg era. A flexible instrument, especially because of its diachronic quality, vocalism is able to manipulate both the *ludo-creative* ("lullabies," amorous *stornellos*, the rhythm of the gondolier, etc.) and the *ludo-ideological* aspects of literature (Negro spirituals, folklore from the Po Valley, Eastern folk traditions, etc.). Huizinga's reading of poiesis as a playful function justifies our emphasis on the playful aspect, though it is especially Caillois who, eloquently defining *ludus* as regulated play and *paidia* as spontaneous play, gives two precious keys for interpreting the fundamental structure of vocalism (cf. *Il gioco* 1979).

The history of sound poetry, which is nothing but the synchronic course of vocalism, has sometimes chosen to emphasize *ratio* (Marinetti, Depero, Artaud, Dufrène, Garnier, Heidsieck, Rühm, Nannucci, Kostelanetz, Hanson, Santos, etc.), other times to emphasize emotions (Russolo, Krucenych, Ball, Tzara, Schwitters, Petrolini, Totò, Isou, Chopin, Higgins, Spatola, etc.). As McLuhan (1967) would say, both possibilities – inasmuch as they concern *voice*, phonetic, and later sonorous writing, as in the so-called myth of Cadmus – are *warm* means of communication and therefore full of theatrical energy. On the other end, a writing anchored to typography, to the steadiness of the page, the linearity of the verse, is but a *cold* means of communication. Confusing the two levels of operation is counterproductive though unfortunately not uncommon in recent times. Confusing the levels results in aporias, dead ends, and is inefficient both to linear and sound poetry. It would be useless to revive ancient practices of enchantment and ignore the great past that has been their prototype.

Beyond the unproductive comparison between sound and linear poetry, between their different though quite obvious ideological implications – beyond the problem of a differentiated audience – we must recognize that vocalism is a powerful proposition. During the past decade, this power has been channeled in a *rumorismo significante*, a theory that wished to destroy the body of the word, not so much because of a mania for destruction, but because it had well-defined goals that wanted to revive what was being perceived as stale, inefficient, and inadequate to the task.

At the beginning of the Nineties, the word came back in its double aspect of sound and sign and was proposed to be the interlocutor of the sound poet. What Stanislawski used to ask his students is again in vogue: "repeat in fifty different ways the word *tonight*." The word is compressed between rhythms-tones-phonemes-onomatopoeia-disharmonies-neologisms-timbre-heights-waves-significances (software) and samples-synthesizers-computers-DAT-microphones-recordings-mixer (hardware), with irremediable *logico-operative* or *logico-aesthetic* gaps, if it is legitimate to speak about aesthetics applied to the sound poem – and the canons or classifications through which we are filtering it demonstrate that in fact it is a legitimate consideration.

If the sound poem has often been a cerebral exercise, quite boring and unpleasant or oppressed by technical matters, it will now have the time and the facility to show itself as able to become an event, indeed in the way that Rilke (1937) meant the work of art, "a very intimate confession that becomes manifest with the pretext of an experience, of an event." Within an always more electrified context, where the iteration is an inalienable *Diktat*, even the sound poet can produce his *Erlebnis*, his own vision of the world, and a reason for existing. Repetition itself becomes the best arm of combat since "subjectivity may be assumed, paradoxically, only through repetition" (Baudrillard 1974). Bense (1974) too, speaking about repetition, emphasized the "frequencies of determined textual events" in order to underline their obvious importance.

We said that sound poetry is a warm means of communication and, therefore, that the hybrid between different media is necessary; however, "the encounter between two media is a moment of truth and of revelation from which a new form is born" (McLuhan 1967). At this point then, sound poetry opens up to *Polipoesia*, an efficient mixture of languages belonging to different media, where sound poetry continues to be, *conditio sine qua non*, the instrument of guidance, *primus inter pares*, the element that gives homogeneity and unity to all different medial components involved.

Polipoesia transforms in reality that synaesthetic dream Bakhtin (1988) defined so well when, speaking about European formalists, he stated that "the main goal of art is to understand visual, sound, and tactile qualities."

In 1987 in Valencia the *Manifesto of Polipoesia* appeared for the first time in the extensive catalogue *Tramesa de art en favor de la creativitat*, stating:

1)   Only the development of new technologies will mark the progress of sound poetry: electronic media and computers are and will be the true protagonists.

2)   The object language must be investigated in all its smallest and most extensive segments. The word, basic instrument of sonorous experimentation, takes the connotations of multi-word, penetrated all the way in and re-stitched on the outside. The word must be able to free its polyvalent sonorities.

3)   Sound elaboration admits no limits, it must be pushed beyond the sole of the pure *rumorismo*, of a significant *rumorismo*: the sonorous ambiguity, both vocal and linguistic, has a meaning if it fully exploits the instrumental apparatus of the mouth.

4)   Rescuing the sensitivity of time (the minute, the second) beyond the canons of harmony and disharmony, since only editing is the correct parameter of synthesis and balance.

5)   Language is rhythm; tonal values are real units of signification: first the rational act, then the emotional one.

6)   *Polipoesia* is conceived and made actual in the live show. It trusts sound poetry as the prima donna or point of departure in order to build a relationship with: musicality (accompaniment, rhythmical line), mime, gesture, dance (interpretation, extension, integration of the sound poem), image (televisional, color transparency, as association, explanation, redundancy, alternative), light, space, costumes, objects.

We might say that the theoretical approach to totality began with Lévi-Strauss (1974) as he wrote: "the primitive thought, that is the oral thought, is totalizing." Oral communication therefore should already be sufficient to guarantee totality, fully aware that "the entire body is working," according to what the Englishman Orderic Vitalis affirmed in the distant Middle Ages, and referring to the oral act. Barthes (1982) instead is rather inclined to support Lévi-Strauss, "the poetic word can never be false because it is a totality; it shines with an infinite freedom," and repeats what Kristeva (1980) has already said: "it is only in poetic language that totality is realized."

If you honestly wish to face the question of poetic totality, preliminary citations are important but not sufficient. They are limited because they are too impregnated with oral qualities we would have called vocal, without opening on the media's territory which, instead, is necessary in order to verify, at least, the poetic word outside of its cybernetic context of daily communication. From this perspective, even the otherwise formidable theory formulated by Walter Gropius seems to be lacking something. In his Manifesto from 1923 he trusted the Bauhaus not only with attending to the creation of a live art, but also the task of establishing harmony between the different varieties of art and all the artisan and artistic disciplines that are functional to a concept of construction.

Bakhtin (1988) gave, at different times, a valid, credible, and practicable theoretical formulation concerning totality, to which we will now refer. As we said above, we depart from the idea that "the main goal of art is to understand visual, sound, and tactile qualities," and that "we call the technical moment of art, all that is absolutely indispensable for the creation of the work of art in a well-defined linguistic or scientific naturalistic status," in order to reach the conclusion that "first of all, we must understand the aesthetic object synthetically and in its totality, and we must understand form and content in their essential and necessary reciprocal relationship." This last statement has a vague phenomenological resonance, at least in a strict Anceschian understanding.

Adriano Spatola (1978) abundantly uses the term totality in his *Toward Total Poetry*, consciously written under the influence of Anceschi's phenomenological theories, especially when he borrows from Viggo Brondai a concept of structure "not as a combination of elements, but as a whole formed by joint phenomena, whereby one phenomenon depends on the other through the established relationship." Spatola's book remains, in a way, unsurpassed, and it represents an undisputed achievement of poetic experimentation. Perhaps the only disputable point would be the so often acclaimed *totality*.

Let's see why: as a premise we must distinguish the *mixed media* from the *intermedia* that Higgins (1978) operates; in the mixed media, the media involved are always perfectly recognizable since they are always separated as in the opera or in a song. In the *intermedia* products, instead, "there is a conceptual *fusion*" (italics mine). The concept of fusion directly recalls a sometimes forgotten statement by Mallarmé who considered it, though limited in the visual field, well represented in the "institution of an exact relationship between images from which might derive a third possibility of *fusion*" (cf. Marinetti 1968; italics mine). This perspective would be accepted by the poets from the Cabaret Voltaire who claimed a fusion between spoken poetry, music, and theater, accepting the sound poem as focal point of these events typically *intermedia*. And again, Maurice Lemaître stated that the goal of *lettrisme* was to "fuse compositions able to integrate music, poetry, theater, and other disciplines" (cf. Foster 1983).

Already in the Sixties De Vree (1968) had also spoken of "*Poëzie in fusie*" ("poetry in fusion") with concrete, visual, and phonic elements in a state envisaged as "fusioneel," though he did not precise how deeply and in which way this fusion was to take place. Besides the obvious intuitions based on Futurism and simultaneity (and it is not a coincidence that the name of Barzun recurs indeed in a verse of the *Pisan Cantos*: "Monsieur Barzun had, indubitably, an idea, about anno"), Ezra Pound was a valid antecedent as he wrote in "Hugh Selwyn Mauberly" a quite illuminating stanza concerning this topic:

Poetry, her border of ideas,
The edge, uncertain, but a means of blending
With other strata
Where the lower and higher have ending.
(Pound 1977)

Even the *Vorticismo*, based on the vortex, was inclined to the exploration of psychical complexity in the poetic image and the implicated effects of simultaneity. Besides, in 1951 Northrop Frye in *The Archetypes of Literature* wrote "literature seems to be intermediate between music and painting: its words form rhythms which approach a musical sequence of sounds at one of its boundaries, and form patterns which approach the hieroglyphic or pictorial image at the other. The attempts to get as near to these boundaries as possible, form the main body of what is called experimental writing" (cf. Kostelanetz 1985).

Artaud, at a conference at the Sorbonne on December 10, 1931, speaking of possible openings a language of the senses must have, said

> such a language must be able to develop all the intellectual consequences on all levels and in all possible directions. Only this way one may substitute a poetry of language with a poetry of space, assuming all those aspects deriving from means applicable on a stage: music, dance, plastic, pantomime, mimic, gesture, intonations, architecture, illumination and choreography. Each of these means has its own intrinsic poetry and, at the same time, a sort of ironic poetry deriving from the way in which poetry *fuses* with the other means of expression. (Artaud 1978)

Dick Higgins, strong theoretician, launches his "Intermedia Manifesto," and borrows from S.T. Coleridge's writings the word *intermedia*: "art is an intermedia quality between the thought and the thing, union and reconciliation of all that is nature with what is exclusively human" (cf. Coleridge 1973). Charged with the implications of these words, it goes beyond them and asserts that "happening developed as an *intermedium*, it is not governed by rules," or, and this is the question most interesting to us, "sound poetry has music penetrating to the very core of the poem's being" (Higgins 1978). Such a claim does not displace much the level of discourse and leaves us with the impression of an observation rather than of a real theory. Among others, it is John Cage (1981) who gives us this impression when he writes that poetry is such "because it allows musical elements (time and sound) to introduce themselves in the world of words." Sometimes it seems that the concept of *intermedia* is applied only in a limited way to visual poetry, "the visual element (painting) is fused conceptually with the words." And anyway, Higgins (1978) is aware of this restriction when he wishes that sound poets still face, or better, explore, the true ground of *intermedia*, and come into closer relationship with "linguistic analysis," "sculpture," and "the environment." Spatola (1978) keeps on this wave length and, in some crucial passages of his book, in strict "total" terms, he trusts a vague and too generalized statement: "the new poetry seeks to become a total medium, to include theater, photography, music, painting, typographical art, cinematographical techniques and any other aspect of culture..." When he actually does theorize totality, he recalls Luciano Nanni's arguments: "since it is a totality instituted by fruition, such totality will be but a synergetic occurrence..." Again, we are sent back to the idea of a language cocktail, a mixture of languages, and a gestalt aspect of contextual leveling of elements. We forget, on the other end, as we have seen, the hierarchical aspect of *Polipoesia*, which is the net predominance of sound poetry on the other components of the final product, its inalienable role as guide, as lighthouse.

Sound poetry keeps its own structural characteristic, despite the continuous dialogue or the contribution of other media, since the strong framework of voice and experimentation with voice support similar entries. What Jakobson (1974) used to define as *dominating* within the structure of a poetic text, we apply to *Polipoesia*, which is entirely organized starting from the *dominating* sound poetry. Sound poetry guarantees the operation *in toto*, gives structural cohesion, and especially and most importantly, it hierarchizes all elements, becoming itself a measure governing, determining, and transforming others.

Sound poetry is substantially vocalism, an ideal status from the operative perspective, rich in intrinsic elements – consider rhythm, tonal differences, significations – allowing longed-for openings, which are, in a certain way, necessary because, if one wants the work of *Polipoesia* to be complete, one must take for granted that sound poetry is the protagonist and accept that the lot of the deuteragonists must have its own role. We have tried, at different times, to document how such integration takes place, taking a certain distance from an instinctive procedure, which would not be strictly based on a mathematical concept, as Max Bill's famous statement reminds us, though no doubt oriented toward, or better supported by, a precise reasoning. We are aware that we have reached the central point of creation, the nucleus which obviously involves also intuition, which is that irrational side one may qualify with difficulty, that *quid* which triggers some creative mechanisms. Such processes, strictly intuitive or deductive in proportion to the basic material already known, develop through rational channels purposely predisposed; the creativity, we shall say in synthesis, runs on reason's legs, in order to invent an anomalous oxymoron, a rational creativity. In "Poema," our oldest sound poem (1977/85), the choice of the word *poema* belongs to the rational sphere (first of all since it contains the phonemes *e-m* corresponding to the initials of our first and last name, and then because of the semantic value, the incipit *po*, the ending *ma*,) while choosing the phoneme *a* as the final phoneme and sonorous metonymy of sexual intercourse to unwind, for example, the orgasm, is a typically creative choice. Creative is also the triple successive repetition of the word *poema* as sonorous mimesis of a projectile, while the times of execution and the period of these sections are rational. Until now the poem has been a sound poem, but it inexorably becomes *Polipoesia* when, during the performance, for example, of the *poem-projectile*, the hand mimes pulling the trigger of a gun. To complete the picture, both the video-image that creatively interprets in a visual manner, for example, the orgasm, and the fixed image of a slide, which is there to strengthen the effect, in a static way, of some semantic passage of the sound text, are considered rational.

Polipoesia departs from a *sound-idea* to arrive at a *sound-action*, in order to understand the necessary passage in the event, starting from a strong theoretical assumption that inexorably guides and determines it. From this perspective, our definition of *Polipoesia* has little or nothing to do with the formulations based on an instinctive approach, as we have already said and as we now repeat. For example, Beuys (who believes that performing can only clarify the possible problems of performance since, if it weren't so and all was clear from the beginning, the performance would not have any significance) would not agree with our belief that a sound poetry directed toward the audience without an adequate theoretical support inevitably fails, as would any approach that is the result of sheer improvisation. Here we can feel perhaps in a decisive manner the difference between art performance and *Polipoesia*, though both have great expectations from the audience. And, in this regard, Philip Glass is right when he asserts that "we depend on the audience to complete the work" (Glass & Wilson 1976), because the spectator-listener has to move his own intellective being to compare himself with all that he is supposed to receive.

Translated by Francesca Seaman

Bibliography

Artaud, A.
1978   *Il teatro e il suo doppio*. Torino, Einaudi.
Bakhtin, M.
1988   *Estetica della creazione verbale*. Torino, Einaudi.
Barthes, R.
1982   *Il grado zero della scrittura*. Torino, Einaudi.
Baudrillard, J.
1974   *Per una critica dell'economia politica del segno*. Milano, Mazzotta.
Bense, M.
1974   *Estetica*. Milano, Bompiani.
Cage, J.
1981   *Silenzio*. Milano, Feltrinelli.

Coleridge, S.T.
1973   *Poesie e prose.* Milano, Mondadori.
Foster, S.C.
1983   *Lettrisme.* Iowa City, UIMA.
Glass, Ph. & R. Wilson
1976   *Einstein on the Beach.* [Venezia, Il teatro alla Biennale 76/Biennale di
         Venezia.]
Higgins, D.
1978   *A Dialectic of Centuries.* New York, Printed Editions.
Il gioco nella cultura moderne.
1979   Cosenza, Lerici.
Kostelanetz, R.
1985   *The Old Poetries and the New.* Ann Arbor, UMP.
Kristeva, J.
1980   *Materia e senso.* Torino, Einaudi.
Lévi-Strauss, C.
1974   *Il pensiero selvaggio.* Milano, Mondadori.
Marinetti, F.T.
1968   *Teoria e invenzione futurista.* Milano, Mondadori.
McLuhan, M.
1979   *Gli strumenti del comunicare.* Milano, Garzanti.
Pound, E.
1977   *Opere scelte.* Milano, Mondadori.
Rilke, R.M.
1937   *Lettres à un jeune poète.* Paris, Bernard Grasset.
Spatola, A.
1978   *Verso la poesia totale.* Torino, Paravia.
Tramese de art en favor de la creativitat.
1987   Valencia, Ajoutament de Valencia.
Vree, Paul de
1968   *Poëzie in fusie. Visueel, konkreet, fonetisch.* Lier, De Bladen voor de
         Poëzie.

VISUAL POETRY, VERBO-VISUAL WRITING

Lamberto Pignotti

Visual poetry, verbo-visual writing: it seems that today we should try to locate, in both a diachronic and a synchronic frame, the dynamic generally triggered by art pieces referring simultaneously to *writing* and to *visual art*. By which aesthetic views are they anchored? Toward which direction would they like to open up?

Here is their background. In little amounts: the Sixties, years of extroverted and ideologized art; the Seventies, years of auto-reflexive and intransitive art; the Eighties, years of eclectic and pluri-dimensional art; the Nineties, years of art in the remaking. Moreover, we know that we have seen everything, that we have read everything, that we have lived everything.

From this perspective we may locate the battleground of the present aesthetic operations. Here is placed – and has been placed since the beginning of the Sixties – that area, or genre as we would prefer to say today, of research in aesthetics which, conjugating writing and art, word and image, discourse and icon, language and representation, has in fact been variously called "Visual poetry," "new writing," "verbo-visual writing," etc. From the beginning, these experiences received their vitality from a meditation on the relationship between word and image as a sort of autonomous language – not a *sum* of languages – and from the intuition that such language was susceptible to the opening of new aesthetic values, even in the face of new technological media that were forming.

Visual poetry/verbo-visual writing has been the single artistic genre that did not succumb to fashion over the more than thirty-year journey of its existence. On the contrary, this *genre* has controlled fashion and has used it according to its own linguistic, aesthetic, and ideological goals. This has been possible especially since it knew how to create a pertinent relationship with new media (their modalities and their languages) and with new questions posed to society, culture, and art. The immediate employment of two codes – the visual and the verbal – and the potential use of other codes (as that of touch, taste, and smell) have favorably influenced the possibilities of visual poetry facing new media. Visual poetry has confronted the media one at a time or all at once, using old but always efficient theories formulated by Umberto Eco, in apocalyptic or integrated ways.

A perplexity may arise: perhaps, the inhibited flexibility of the employment of the code and its extreme availability to new media are reducing the ideological charge of a new artistic genre that is mostly recognized in the emblematic act of the one who sends back the merchandise to the sender. Such a perplexity is understandable, especially at a time like this when experiences of this kind are used experimentally and dangerously to enlarge the range of action of one's own language on one side, while on the other they appear in increasingly prestigious national and international exhibits.

To the lack of faith in literary discourse and in pictorial representation – in the official version offered by the respective institutions – in an aesthetic context in rapid transition where the mass media undergo transformation into new media any second, the artist reacts in multiple ways and offers very different answers to questions often not yet formulated. Aware that the logo-centric culture of the West has privileged the universe of the word over that of the image, trying constantly to reinvigorate the margin between two kinds of expressions, the verbo-visual artist spoils such a separation, but especially – as Vittorio Fagone (1988) has remarked – combines once again the strategies belonging to the two universes in a new mode. This new model reacts to the means of important communication systems; it takes advantage of the double use of word and image, typical of mass communication, in order to reinvigorate their critical and significative efficiency.

More precisely, Fagone (1988: 367) emphasizes that

> Visual poetry was not to be conceived in the elegant but inefficient positions of an experimentation and of a new avant-garde. I believe it should be specified that in the program of Visual poetry, which is to propose oneself as manifesto, as urban mirror, as explicit and reinvigorated signal of critical communication, the fundamental project of all modern art is still alive: a code of comprehension and of communication more directly referred to the space constitution art, a skill of imme-diate efficiency.

As we have previously remarked, the artist who places himself between the instruments of verbal communication and those of visual communication, or employs them in conjunction, may be understood as someone who, devoted to aesthetic bigamy (*bi-graphy*), loves poetry as much as painting or, vice versa, as someone who dislikes both to the point of dismissing them.

Then, both in retrospection and in anticipation, there is an aesthetic polygamy, a *pluri-graphy*, a *synesthetic writing*. From the beginning the artists supporting visual poetry have emphasized not only a poetry to be seen, but also a tension between the verbal and the visual message that was intended factually or virtually to involve all senses in the process of receiving a message. If such a preoccupation seemed premature and almost inconceivable thirty years ago (when, during the debates, the audience could still ask the authors to read one of their visual poems), today it appears as the responsibility and urgency of both practical and aesthetic communication. Usual and emerging mass media can no longer survive using just linguistic grammars and visual conventions. Generally they grope to find their way hoping that, sooner or later, they will recognize more reliable instruments of orientation in order to communicate in syntony with the interlinguistic and multimedial scenery characterizing present day society, with great joy and profit, of course, for those who exploit mass media and new media for their not so innocent little games.

It is obvious, then, why today visual poetry is considered both as a developing artistic current and as an aesthetic experience imitating the classics. (It appears in important national and international exhibits, as well as in encyclopedias, in academic anthologies, dissertations, columns of illustrated magazines, television programs, etc.).

Moreover, the verbo-visual experience is also an activity-in-planning, theoretical and ritual. There is no visual poet who is not also, at times at least, a critic and a promoter of debates or exhibits.

Visual poetry, considered as aesthetic activity, is not distinguishable from the artist's biography. The work of art itself is nothing but a moment, though certainly a special moment, of the artist's life. The artist's presence wishes to deny any distinction between art and life. As I have already had the occasion to argue in my last two essays (Pignotti 1990 and 1993), visual poetry is becoming a singular gesture, just like a lighthouse at the crossroads of different linguistic and identifying universes, or like a device reactivating the senses (presently underutilized and often removed) and the reconstruction, through the senses, of an always open aesthetic identity or of a different aesthetic identity, a never-concluded project.

From this perspective, it is possible to live on art – not only metaphorically – to nourish oneself with poetry, to dilate taste and involve all senses, not only sight and hearing. Certainly we were looking at a "synesthetic" involvement some centuries ago, for example in the spectacular dinner parties of the Florentine companies of the Paiuolo and of the Cazzuola, in which artists like Andrea del Sarto, Domenico Puligo and Giovan Francesco Rustici took part in the theatrical productions and stagings, as Vasari (1971 [1550]) tells us in the biography of Rustici in the book *Vite*.

Similar "artists' dinners" do not have an identifiable contiguity and, much less, a documented tradition. In order to find once again a "gastronomic line of art" one needs to arrive at the avant-gardes of our century, to the *Cucina Futurista* of the Thirties, to the *Taverna Santopalato* in Turin, to Marinetti's "pranzo estivo di pittura-scultura" ("Summer lunch of painting/sculpture"), to

Fillia's "pranzo tattile" ("tactile lunch"), to Diulgheroff's "pollo d'acciaio" ("steel chicken"), to Luciano Folgore's "antipasto folgorante" ("dazzling hors-d'oeuvre"), to Prampolini's "paradosso primaverile" ("Spring paradox"), etc.

From the beginning of the Sixties, artistic avant-gardes have also recalled the *gastronomic sense of art*, though only in a generally allusive way, and certainly not considering it edible. Surely, some works of the American Pop Art – the pot roasts, French fries, Oldenburg's ice creams, Warhol's Campbell soups, Rosenquist's fruit salad, etc. – did not mean to solicit appetite but rather to generate a sort of *dis-gusto* for all food of mass consumption. In the same way, the works of the peer European artists, like Jiří Kolář's apples wrapped in printed paper, Piero Gilardi's peaches in plastic sponge, Piero Manzoni's varnished roses, Daniel Spoerri's breakfasts glued to the tray, etc., were not meant to induce gluttony.

Not even the successive aesthetic experiences – from the group Fluxus to *Arte povera* to Conceptualism – intend to solicit an appetite with their works. Wolf Vostell's pile of bread loafs, Merz's igloo and Pistoletto's table both variously decorated with fruits, Diter Rot's page of cheese, Claudio Parmigiani's book of apricot, are all works that play around objects of alimentation though they renegade food in order to propose themselves as elements of an intersign and plurisensorial language detached from the word.

The role of food can be quite different in the context of a happening or of a performance. The spectacular element, the finality of involvement, the more or less emphasized playful intentionality, the sometimes hedonistic imprint, may still confer to food, beyond its effective possibility of taste, a significance basically inclined to rejoin the meaning of the artists' dinner parties of a few centuries ago. To these, ideally, are connected my performances *alimentari* which, in different ways, would like the "taste" of food to coincide with that of "art." The truth is that when we taste something good and when we admire a beautiful painting we have the same satisfied expression on our face; and I am simply paraphrasing Wittgenstein. From the *Chewing Poems* and the *Ostie* signed at the beginning of the Sixties to the more recent *Sweet Poems*, I seek, with great pleasure, an extravagant, unconventional, different, new "dolce stil novo."

Translated by Francesca Seaman

Bibliography

Fagone, Vittorio
1988   *Poesia Visiva 1963-1988 – 5 Maestri.* Verona, Henry Veyrier Ed./
        Galleria d'Arte Moderna.
Pignotti, Lamberto
1990   *Sine aesthetica, sinestetica.* Roma, Empiria.
1993   *I sensi delle arti. Sinestesia e interazioni estetiche.* Bari, Dedalo.
Vasari, Giorgio
1971   *Le vite dei piú eccellenti pittori, scultori e architetti.* Milano, Rizzoli.
        [Firenze 1550, 2nd ed. 1568]

THE CRYPTIC EYE

E. M. de Melo e Castro

The cryptic eye is an approach to infopoetry.

Infopoetry is made with the use of the computer, thus adding the virtual reality of the poetic images to the virtual, de-materialized substance of the synthetic imagery and writing produced by the computer.

Infopoetry is metavirtual, bringing with it the difficult reading of the non-obvious.

But in a society of literates such as ours, can we say we see the letters?

And. if so, do we see the meanings? And if we do see the meanings, do we see the letters?

Because if we do not see the letters, can we say we are literates?

Or are we, instead, letter haters?

Or, instead, are we letter eaters feeding ourselves with a substance that we do not see?

And what about the colors and shades?

Gray, the shade of gray, is as far as we humanly can see the synthesis of all colors. White being white, the full radiance of light. But gray is also the color of the stuff our brain is made of. Gray is the visual limit of our perception of speed as Paul Virilio recently pointed out.

Gray is gray. Gray is human, and when we say that we understand what we write and read, what do we really mean? Gray is the answer because to understand is no more than to repeat in a different way what we think we are understanding. To understand is to simulate. Simulation is the matter of poetry. Infopoetry being the simulation of the simulated is therefore gray as the gray is gray.

But we have the seven colors of the rainbow and in our computer a few thousands of different synthetic colors to play with. Colors that we can use freely to simulate that we understand each other when we speak and write. This simulation is therefore an exercise in trans-semiotics because the signs we use go from one place to another place with the speed of light, from one language to another language, and in between we are trying to grab these movements with the neuron cells of our brain.

Brain and eye; mind and hand; mind and computer are thus becoming one and the same thing: the cybernetics of our misunderstanding.

A counter-semiotics will be necessary to establish new and unexpected relations between the tools and the means we use to communicate: the words and the colors.

In "The Cryptic Eye" I'm bringing face to face nine Portuguese and nine English words that are connected only by similarities in phonetics or spelling. For the moment, the meanings are left alone.

I'm doing this with the explicit purpose of increasing the entropy and maybe take a further step towards the poetics of turbulence. These words are put together in pairs, as follows:

RAIN	FOG	WAR
RUA	FOGO	MAR
SEA	HOUSE	IN
SIM	ASA	NÃO
ICE	EYE	MIND
AÇO	MÃE	MÃO

[rua = street / fogo = fire / mar = sea / sim = yes / asa = wing / não = no / aço = steel / mãe = mother / mão = hand]

The order of these nine pairs is not important.

The conventional poetic images that result from putting together these words in English and Portuguese are far from important. What I want to show is the semiotic travel of the images from one language to the other, pointing to a new type of visual poem: a poem that is in itself a cryptogram, thus presenting a difficulty of reading.

Lacan once said that "a cryptogram only reaches its full dimension when it is in an unknown language." On the contrary, I think that a cryptogram only reaches its full dimension when it is in a language we know very well, which means that its cryptic quality is very high, the difficulty of reading or the unreadability being a poetic achievement.

The infopoems of the series "The Cryptic Eye" try to develop these principles, being exercises in various shades of gray and color as well as trans- and counter-semiotically written poems.

The question they ask is therefore the question of readability and ultimately of our capacity to read using our eyes or, as we say in Portuguese, *a capacidade de leitura.*

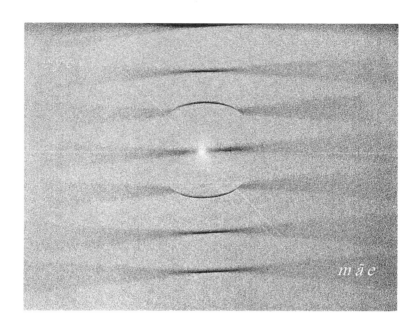

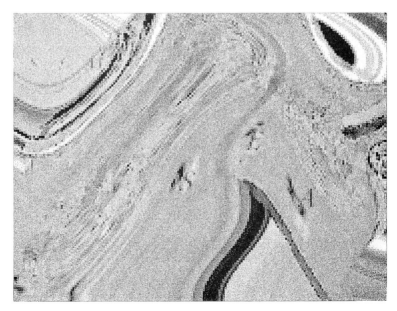

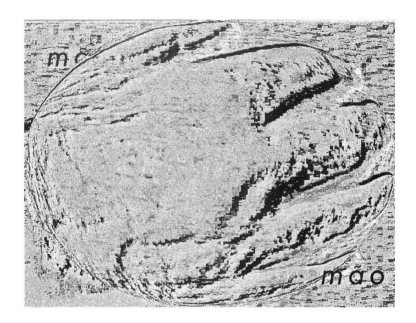

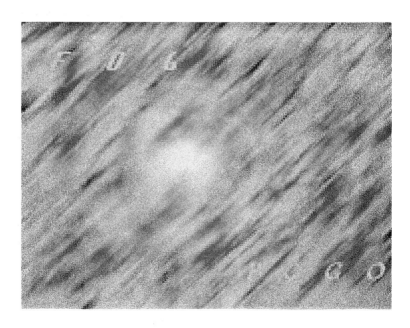

KEY CONCEPTS OF HOLOPOETRY

Eduardo Kac

Experimental poetry followed many directions in several countries in the twentieth century. Each new direction attempted to address the historical, cultural, and often political needs of its own time. Between 1978 and 1982 I worked with countless experimental poetic styles, trying to develop my own direction. I explored traditional versification, recitation, body-based performance, visual poetry, graffiti, collage, typography, color, object-poems, sound, and a number of other possibilities. As a result of this relentless experimentation, I felt on the one hand that the printed page imprisoned the word within its two-dimensional surface, thus creating specific limits to poetic expression. On the other hand, I realized that the construction of solid three-dimensional objects gave the word a permanence and a physical presence that contradicted the dynamics of language. I was looking for a poetic language that would be malleable, fluid, and elastic. It was clear that I had to work with a new medium, beyond the page and the object a new medium that would still allow for the private experience of reading a poem. My conclusion was that the solution might lie somewhere between the two-dimensional surface and the three-dimensional volume in thin air. I envisioned in my mind's eye a poetic form that would exist beyond the page without being embodied in tangible objects. A poetic form that would be flexible, buoyant, and oscillatory as the thought process itself, and that could give new communicative power to the word. As I projected with great enthusiasm in my mind's eye what such a poetry would be like, I also thought that this dream was unachievable since it founded the principles of this new syntax in new media that, at least for me, at the moment did not exist yet. My goals seemed, at first, anything but within reach.

Holography was in my mind. I had read about it, but could not quite visualize what a hologram was like until I saw one. The experience of seeing a hologram for the first time early in 1983 was intense. I immediately recognized in this new medium the immaterial and kinetic solution to the poetic problem I had developed. I spent the next couple of years making the first holopoems and developing the theory of holopoetry. This work resulted in the world's first exhibition of holopoems, in 1985, at the Museum of Image and Sound, in São Paulo. From the start the breaking down of the immaterial space of holography, as well as the development of turbulent and non-linear temporal systems, have been the basis of my holographic syntax.

My objective has always been not to use holography for its obvious three-dimensional qualities. I asked myself: what would be the difference between a sculpture of letters and a hologram of this sculpture? The difference was not significant. I immediately realized that holography was much more complex than the touted illusion of three-dimensional space. This new medium has an incredible power not only to create an immaterial visual poetic experience, but to manipulate temporal systems, and to store information in ways that can be carefully controlled to generate fascinating new perceptual experiences. That is what I was after, and that is what I have been exploring since then.

I must make it clear that I do not consider holographic poems those holograms that record or reproduce verbal material already successfully realized in other form or media. It is important to explore the unique qualities of the holographic medium itself and to develop a truly genuine holographic writing.

In order to clarify some of the unique aspects of my holopoetry, and also to help delineate some of the new compositional elements I have developed since 1983, I will discuss in what follows some of the key concepts of holopoetry. This will also work as a glossary of sorts, which can be used as a reference in the reading of my other texts as well as in the discussion of the holopoems themselves.

Animation

Animation in holopoetry refers to the fact that the words employed in a piece are set in motion. This is usually produced on a computer and then transferred to the hologram, although purely holographic animations are also used occasionally. Computer animations are created specially for the syntax of the holopoem. This involves a complex pre-visualization experience. Computer animations that are created for video or film do not work well in a hologram. This is due to the differences between the monoscopic surface of screen-based animations and the stereoscopic space of the hologram. A holographic animation must be created taking into account the stereoscopic perception of the viewer.

Behavior

In visual poems created for print, letters and words can be said to have a specific position on the page. These letters and words are arranged into a unified visual composition. In holopoetry, letters and words cannot be said to have a specific position or composition. Instead, they exhibit a particular kind of behavior. Something happens to letters and words as they are read by the viewer. Active behavior replaces static structure.

Binocular Reading

I call binocular reading the process according to which some holopoems present different letters and words to each eye simultaneously. This feature is unique to holopoetry, and transforms the reading process in an intense experience. Normally, when looking at objects around us, we perceive two different points of view of the very same object. Binocular reading takes place when we read one word or letter with the left eye and at the same time a completely different word or letter with the right eye. Many holopoems – for example, *Amalgam* – rely on this principle for their syntactic and semantic efficiency.

Amalgam (1990)

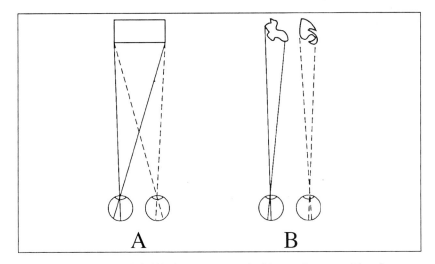

The diagram on the left (A) shows two eyes looking at the same object from two different points of view. This is how we usually see the three-dimensional world around us. The diagram on the right (B) illustrates a new situation in which each eye is made to see a completely different image. When this happens, the two images do not fuse into a coherent three-dimensional whole. In holopoetry, when this situation is created, it is called binocular reading, because each eye reads a completely different letter or word.

Color

In holopoetry color is not fixed. It is relative. One viewer can see a letter in one color and immediately see it change into another. Two readers looking at the same word could see it in different colors simultaneously. While many holographers are disturbed by this uncontrollable behavior, I find it perfectly appropriate to stress the ungraspable nature of meaning. The oscillatory nature of color in my holopoems moves away from traditional symbolism and from the use of color as a structuring visual element. The chromatic system of each holopoem is created within certain parameters, which I specify. The creation of viewing zones and the behavior of color in a holopoem are intrinsically related, since form and relative position of viewing zones affect the diffraction of light.

Quando?, When? (1987/88)

Digital Holopoems

Computer holopoems, or digital holopoems, are holopoems created from digital data, instead of physical letters made of metal, wood, and other materials. My first digital holopoem (*Quando?, When?*) was created between 1987 and 1988. Since 1989, all of my holopoems have been created with computers. If a holopoem is not made with the aid of a computer, I call it "optical holopoem."

Dicontinuous Space

Discontinuous space is created in a holopoem when the homogeneity of the three-dimensional volumetric space of the hologram is broken down into discrete spaces that may or may not overlap in space, or time.

Discontinuous Syntax

The holopoem organized in a discontinuous space takes advantage of the logic and topology of this new poetic space. It presents the verbal material with a syntax of actual, perceptually real leaps and oscillations.

Empty Space

Quite literally, in holopoetry "empty space" refers to the fact that the poem is read in an immaterial and empty space, visually located between the recording medium (holographic film) and the viewer and not on the surface of the page.

This implies that holopoetry does not operate within the logic of traditional visual poetry inherited from Mallarmé, according to which the white on the page represents silence and the black type represents sound. Holopoetry undermines the subjugation of written language to phonetic systems and affirms the verbal experience based on the possible appearance or disappearance of graphemes within empty spaces. The white on the page which represented silence is removed and what remains is empty space, an absence of (printing) support which has no primary symbolic value. The vacuous gaps between words and letters do not represent positively absence of sound, because the photonic inscriptions don't stand essentially for its presence. We are in the domain of spatiotemporal writing, four-dimensional writing, if we wish, where spatial gaps do not point to anything except for the potential presence of graphemes. The voids are not to be seen, unlike the white on the page. They are a quite literal interplay of absence and presence.

Fluid Sign
A fluid sign is essentially a verbal sign that changes its overall visual configuration in time, therefore escaping the constancy of meaning a printed sign would have. Fluid signs are time-reversible, which means that the transformations can flow from pole to pole as the beholder wishes, and they can also become smaller compositional units in much larger texts, where each fluid sign will be connected to other fluid signs through discontinuous syntaxes.

Souvenir D'Andromeda (1990)

Fluid signs can also operate metamorphoses between a word and an abstract shape, or between a word and a scene or object. When this happens, both poles reciprocally alter each other's meanings. A transfiguration takes place and it produces in between meanings that are dynamic and as important in holopoetry as the meanings produced momentarily at the poles. Fluid signs create a new kind of verbal unit, in which a sign is not either one thing or another thing. A fluid sign is perceptually relative. For two or more viewers reading together from distinct perspectives it can be different things at one time; for a non-stationary reader it can reverse itself and change uninterruptedly between as many poles as featured in the text. The holopoem *Souvenir D'Andromeda* is an example of this.

Holopoem

A holographic poem, or holopoem, is a poem conceived, made, and displayed holographically. This means, first of all, that such a poem is organized in an immaterial three-dimensional space, with complex non-linear temporal characteristics, and that even as the reader or viewer observes it, it changes and gives rise to new meanings. Thus as the viewer reads the poem he or she constantly modifies the text. As distinguished from traditional visual poetry, it seeks to express *dynamically* the discontinuity of thought; in other words, the perception of a holopoem takes place neither linearly nor simultaneously but rather through fragments seen at random by the observer, depending on the observer's position relative to the poem. Perception in space of colors, volumes, degrees of transparency, changes in form, relative positions of letters and words, animation, and the appearance and disappearance of forms is inseparable from the syntactic and semantic perception of the text.

Holopoetry

Holopoetry is the word I coined in 1983 to name the new poetics I then introduced. By virtue of necessity, holopoetry can only be fully experienced via the creation of experimental works with the medium of holography. Today holopoems are stored on film. In the future, however, digital holopoems will be stored optically on discs. The exact storage media will change. That is not what defines a holopoem. Holopoetry is defined by unstable spaces, immateriality, four-dimensionality, interactivity, movement, relative perception, and related concepts.

Hyperpoem

A hyperpoem is a digital interactive poem based on a system (hypertext) that branches out as the reader makes choices along the way. Hyperpoems promote a disengagement of the textual distribution characteristic of print. The node and not the syllable from which links irradiate is the new unit of measurement. The writer now defines the work as crisscrossing axes of combination. The reader has to make selections in a way that is similar, albeit not identical, to the writer's creative process. The reader is now presented not with one narrowed-down selection of words in strings or in graphic layouts, but with an electronic field that is a complex network with no final form. In each node the poet will deploy text or add sound and moving images to it. In the future, when holography becomes digital, holographic hyperpoems will become possible.

Immateriality

In holopoetry, immateriality refers to the fact that the verbal material is organized in a space made of diffracted light, and not on any tangible or concrete form, such as the printed page. This new space, defined by photons, has no mass or tangible expression.

Interactivity

A holopoem is interactive in the sense that the natural movement of the viewer in front of the holopoem is enough to change what he or she reads. Every new movement reveals new reading possibilities, including the appearance or disappearance of verbal forms. In the future, when digital holograms become scriptable, it will even be possible to modify or add to the elements in the holographic text.

Non-linearity

Holopoems are not organized with a beginning, middle, and end, as a poem in verse commonly is. Neither are holopoems printed on a page, with its suggested reading from left to right and top to bottom, or its opposite, the simultaneous ideogram. Discontinuous holopoems are read in leaps. Sequential holopoems are based on the principle of temporal reversal.

Parallax

An apparent change in the direction of an object, caused by a change in observational position that provides a new line of sight. Many holopoems explore parallax semantically. For example: in *Omen*, the word "eyes" spins inside a cloud of smoke. As the viewer moves from left to right and vice versa, the word appears and disappears, suggesting multiple readings.

Perceptual Syntax

If visual poetry developed a visual syntax based on the rejection of traditional syntax and on the elaborate visual treatment of words on the page, holopoetry develops a perceptual syntax based on the rejection of the static syntax of print and on the development of complex and dynamic spatiotemporal verbal systems. A holopoem calls for non-linear perceptual responses to the words, which are experienced in time – and not for the simultaneity of gestalts.

Pseudoscopy

Holo/Olho (1983)

The opposite of "orthoscopy," or the correct optical representation of a holographic image. Under certain conditions, a hologram can be made to reverse its image in space and time. A concave object is perceived as a convex pseudoscopic image. An object that rotates to the right is seen rotating to the left. Objects that appear in front of other objects are seen behind these objects in the pseudoscopic image. Objects that are seen behind the holographic plate float freely in pseudoscopic space in front of the plate. This feature is unique to holography and has been explored in holopoetry since the beginning. The first holopoem, Holo/Olho, from 1983, is based on this principle, and so is Chaos, and Wordsl 2.

Semantic Interpolation

In certain works, as the viewer moves relative to the holopoem, he or she perceives that each graphic line that renders the visual configuration of each letter starts to actually move in three-dimensional space. The viewer then perceives that as the lines and points undergo an actual topological transformation, they slowly start to reconfigure a different letter. In Astray in Deimos, what was read as an adjective is becoming a noun, for example. I call this semantic interpolation. If the viewer happens to move in the opposite direction, the noun is transformed into the adjective. The shifting of grammatical forms occurs not through syntactical dislocations in a stanza, but through a typographic metamorphosis that takes place outside syntax. The meanings of in-between configurations cannot be substituted by a verbal description, or by a synonym. Neither can it be replaced by a specific word, as gray suggests a specific intermediary position or a meaning between black and white. In holopoetry transient clusters of letters or ephemeral shapes that lie between a word and an image aim to dynamically stretch the poetic imagi-

Chaos
(1986)

Astray in Deimos
(1992)

nation and suggest meanings, ideas and feelings that are not possible to convey by traditional means.

Textual Instability
By textual instability I mean precisely that condition according to which a holographic text does not preserve a single visual structure in time as it is read by the viewer, producing different and transitory verbal configurations in response to the beholder's perceptual exploration.

Time-reversibility
Time-reversibility takes place in holopoems, such as *Zephyr*, which are made so as to be read from any temporal pole with equal semantic efficiency. This means, for example, that if one starts reading an animated holopoem from right to left (or top to bottom, or back to front), this holopoem can also be read from left to right (or bottom to top, or front to back). The time vector of the piece is reversible.

Transitional Discontinuity
In most holopoems, discontinuity is explored via leaps and gaps between the verbal material. In some cases, as in *Shema*, letters are embedded in color fields that operate verbal discontinuity via visual transitions of colors. I call this "transitional discontinuity."

Shema (1989)

Viewing Zone(s)
A viewing zone is a non-physical zone, located in front of the hologram, through which the reader can actually see the words in the poem. When I create a holopoem, it is part of my writing process to decide how wide, tall, and deep the viewing zones will be. I also decide the shape and relative position of these viewing zones. I can decide how many there will be and what

gaps there might be between them. I can combine multiple viewing zones and edit them in many ways. I can decide on a number of viewing-zone parameters, which I use to create the unique quality of each work. The reader never sees a visual representation of these viewing zones. They are invisible. Viewing zones can be rendered sequentially and discontinuously, which helps create the space and the syntax of each holopoem.

References

Kac, Eduardo
    1995   *Holopoetry: Essays, Manifestoes, Critical and Theoretical Writings; 1983-1995.* Lexington, New Media Editions.
Write to: University of Kentucky, New Media Area, 207 Fine Arts Bldg., Lexington, KY40506-0022, USA. The material published in the book is partially available on the Internet at:
    http://www.uky.edu/FineArts/Art/kac/kachome.html
This page also includes links to screen images of Kac's holopoems, his hyper- and VRML poems (available for downloading), and related (critical) materials.

INTERSIGN POETRY:
Visual and Sound Poetics in the Technologizing of Culture

Philadelpho Menezes

In order to discuss trends in Experimental, Concrete, and Visual poetry during the last four decades, we need, first of all, to establish a basic agreement about the meaning of those terms. I think it is correct to use "experimental poetry" as a generic term which embodies every kind of non-versified and non-declamatory poetics not linked to the rhetoric and stylistic configuration of traditional writing. In this way, every aesthetic which appeared in our century (Futurism, Dada, Surrealism, Cubo-futurism, phonetic poetry, Lettrism, Concretism, electronic poetry, Sound poetry, Visual poetry, and so on) is but a variety of aspects of the same poetics of experimentation, a poetics which emerges as an effect of the crisis of *écriture* and stretched out as a mark of the *intersemiosis* of the whole century.

But in what sense can "experimental poetry" be understood after the over-coming of the spirits of avant-garde and its poetics of revolution through the changing of the aesthetic sign? What does experimental poetry mean in a cultural period in which every activity of daily routine seems to deal with the newness of technologies and in which we all must experience the prospect of permanent change?

It is clear that "experimental" here doesn't carry the sense of *traditional experiments* as literary theory has been trying to establish. According to this point of view, every writer employs the techniques of experimentation in his particular process of creation in order to elaborate a special style which allows him to distinguish himself from his masters. The search for a specific style can be justifiable only in a culture of traditional writing where esteem for the masters has importance in a conception of the indisputable superiority of the past and the perpetual decadence of the present. Since Futurism, "experimental" has come to mean exactly the opposite: the crisis of past and the constant invention of the future from the reinvention of the present.

I adopt the term "experiment" to designate not the particular process of writing, but the poem as a complex of codes, signs, and techniques directed to a reception modified by the intersemiosis of contemporary mass culture. In the field of experimental poetics, to consider the private universe of the author does not matter. We must consider the social system of communication established between author, work of art, and consumers. In this way, it is possible to understand the importance of the new possibilities of form and techniques of work opened up by the old avant-gardes.

It is also important to rethink the role of reception as a fundamental element for the existence of a work of art. The poem-reception relation may be explained by the utopia of non-style and by the recipes for creation of poems that we can find from Futurism to the Concrete and Visual poetry of the 60s. These recipes functioned as an formula that could be used impersonally, by everybody, even though they didn't hinder many poets from fixing a distinctive *style* among the general rules of avant-garde poetics.

Nevertheless, experimental poetry cannot explain too much unless it is divided into two phases, as seems to occur in every art of our century. In the first half of the twentieth century, avant-garde poetry explored material and formal concerns; that is, it explored the material feature of signs as well as their organization inside the poem. It is well known that there was not a simple intention to innovate just for the sake of innovating. The main attempt was to provoke a rupture with the traditional rhetoric of poetry by inserting the materiality of the sign into the work of art as an index of daily life. Introducing a sign of daily life was an attempt to reconcile art and life in a utopian project of revolution of sensibility and mind.

On the other hand, materiality and organization allowed poets to create new forms of relation between signifieds and signifiers, new potentialities for the semantic level of communication. The last three decades have brought a general crisis of utopian·projects, together with a failure of avant-garde intentions, and new perspectives for artistic language have been offered with the non-materiality of technological signs. The immaterial sign of the new technologies begins by questioning and giving up formal and material experiment, inasmuch as it cancels the corporeal sign and its indexical relation with physical life.

What is the immediate effect of this overview, presented above, in experimental poetry? It seems to me that poets have found two outlets. One is a trend among those who are linked to historical fashions of experimental poetry: the option is to seize upon the verbal constructions which can offer them a paradigm of security among the instability of new features of technological signs. Nevertheless, this cannot prevent them from experimenting with the new technologies, notwithstanding the old manner of their application of media. This trend is commonly seen in Visual poetry.

The other tendency is to adopt non-materiality as an axis for contemporary communication. Counterbalancing that peculiar condition, poets put themselves at stake in the unique material sign of poem. This leads to an enigmatic postulation where the poet works like a technologized *musarum sacerdos*. The poem emerges as immaterial and intangible, a kind of secret and lost language linked to Epiphany. The mystical approach towards technology can be observed from McLuhan's theory of a Pentecostal reintegration of the world to Paul Zumthor's search for the oral essence of mankind; from Hugo Ball's phonetic poems to Pierre Garnier's concept of a primordial *souffle*, and to recent Sound and performance poetry. They emphasize the characteristic feature of post-avant-garde art, which seems to be marked by a search for a revival of the sublime and an apathy of reception, a corollary of the emptying of the potentiality for transgression caused by daily life's routine of technical innovation.

Besides, I must observe that the two trends above described, each in its own way, are able to dialogue with the advent of a culture of new technologies. They differ radically from the nostalgic attitude which sees in new technologies the end of civilization, a rupture with the order of traditional humanism, and the coming of apocalypse. What I want to point out is that the poetics of technologies, undoubtedly an emblem of the poetry of this end of century, has not yet been explored as it could be: the new kind of expression that the discourse of image, sound, and word can produce. New dimensions and rhythms and even new conceptions of reality, suggested by the techno- logical media, might not require the revival of verbal discourse, as occurs predominantly in Visual poetry, or the revival of a mystical mode of Sound poetry.

In my practice as a poet, I have been trying to investigate especially the new forms that technological media suggest for organizing visual and sound signs in space and time. But I try to escape from the specific problems of form to head for a semantic field where the complex relation between reality and thought for aesthetic signs is imposed. In 1985 in São Paulo I organized a polemical exhibition, called "Intersign Poetry," in which I proposed that after decades of experiments with sound and image effects, experimental poetry must address itself also to the new meanings that new forms can produce. Such poetry must begin with the opened possibilities of organization of the form in new syntaxes required by technology, if one works with technical media, or suggested by technology, if one works on paper or with traditional means.

Linguistic and semiotic theories support the idea that our thought is conditioned by the form and the organization of the signs in a discourse. And these theories argue that language is fascist, as Roland Barthes said, because it imposes a procedure of thinking and guides us to a certain concept of reality which reinforces the system of language. We can escape from this vicious circle only if we are able to perceive the fragility of the links between signs and thought, language and reality. Poetry is the chief guide for this practice because it exposes the sign as a touchable event that makes signs as real as the material world, in spite of the fact that signs are a creation of thought. An expressive language based on new ways of combining different kinds of signs gives rise to another form of rationality and another conception of reality, but this is possible only if this language constitutes itself at a complex semantic level of interpretation-varied degrees of signification. Experimental poetry of the last four decades (especially Concrete, Visual, and Sound poetry) faced the fact that transgression and strangeness have become meaningless in a society saturated by daily technical changes. It also confronted the end of a utopian perspective which nourished the sense of revolution of the historical avant-gardes and put in its place the realm of technological features as a way to bring poetry perpetually up to date (as if it also renewed the poet physically).

Experimental poetry today, what I conceive as Intersign poetry, must confront the realm of visual and sound effects and must try to find ways to organize signs, in order to fill the technological products of poetry with the richness of ambiguity and complexity that signs contain when they are worked as ambivalent phenomena aimed at interpretation.

If the first technological phase was marked by the idea of *against interpretation*, experimental poetry today, which includes a second technological phase, must work on behalf of *reading visual and sound effects*. It would keep the spirit of experimentation, then nourished by an opened utopia, a *pluritopia* which expresses a permanent sense of reinvention and variation (or transformation) of the world.

Philadelpho Menezes, *neureka!* (undated)

D.
CONCRETE AND NEO-CONCRETE POETRY

CONCRETE POETRY:
CRITICAL PERSPECTIVES FROM THE 90S

Claus Clüver

In 1959 I came across a magazine from Argentina in which I found a text that irritated and disturbed me. It was supposedly art, a poem, and yet all it said was "ping pong" in several repetitions arranged on the space of the page in a peculiar manner. I did not know what to make of it. Yet I also never forgot it, nor did I forget the name of the "poet" – Eugen Gomringer.

ping pong
   ping pong ping
   pong ping pong
      ping pong

ill.1: Eugen Gomringer, "ping pong" (1953)

A decade later, at Indiana University in Bloomington, I saw an announcement of a poetry reading by two young Brazilian visitors and decided to attend; the event was to have a profound effect on my life. I went home and spent a long time trying to reconstruct on the typewriter a poem by Décio Pignatari that Haroldo de Campos had explained to us, and soon after I wrote an extensive *explication de texte* of Augusto de Campos's poem "terremoto."[1] I had finally also begun to learn how to play Gomringer's "ping pong," and I was ready to teach others.

The brothers de Campos had been invited to Bloomington by Mary Ellen Solt, whom I thus met because of them, and I began to use her anthology as a textbook in my course on literature and other arts. Students responded so enthusiastically to these texts and to Mary Ellen's visit to my class that they proposed to mount an exhibition, under the tutelage of Mary Ellen, Tom Ockerse, and myself. In retrospect the 1970 "expose: concrete poetry" and the month of events surrounding it, with the participation of Emmett Williams, davi det hompson, Vagn Steen, and Iannis Xenakis, is somewhat of a landmark in the history of Concrete poetry. The logo for the exhibition was Ockerse's version of Aram Saroyan's one-letter poem:

ill. 2: Aram Saroyan / Tom Ockerse [untitled] (1970)

Mary Ellen Solt joined our faculty soon after to help teach our courses in interarts studies, and the course on Concrete poetry she created is still being offered regularly at IU (see also SOLT in this volume). She brought to our campus other "experimental" and "avant-garde" poets represented in her anthology – among them Gomringer, Ernst Jandl, Kriwet, Jonathan Williams, and Aram Saroyan. The enthusiasm created among our students twenty-five years ago will still flare up today, in part still as the result of an encounter with the (for them) unknown, although many forms of textmaking that impressed us then as innovative have since become very familiar, not the least through their application to publicity and television texts.

It was only during my first research trip to Brazil in 1974, where I spent the summer interviewing the Noigandres poets and the painters and musicians close to them, that I became fully aware of the importance of Max Bill with regard to many facets of the movement known as "Concrete Poetry."[2] Since his first retrospective in São Paulo, in 1950, the "konkrete Kunst" advocated by Bill had left a strong impression on a number of younger visual artists in Latin America. Several of them went to study at the Hochschule für Gestaltung at Ulm, Bill's influential effort to re-establish the Bauhaus tradition in post-war Germany. It was their presence that took Décio Pignatari to Ulm in 1955, where he met Bill's secretary, Eugen Gomringer. The result of that meeting was the first trans-Atlantic baptism ever of an international literary movement, and the choice of the label "Concrete Poetry" was in part determined by Bill's example. One of the teachers at Ulm was Max Bense, who was to become closely associated with the Brazilians, notably Haroldo de Campos and the composer and conductor Júlio Medaglia, one of the first to explore the sound potential of the new poetry in multivocal recitations. (See also DRUCKER and WALTHER-BENSE in this volume.)

On both sides of the Atlantic the Concrete Poetry movement was driven by the desire to "make it new," to become "inventors" in the Poundian scheme, motivated by the sense that a new poetry for the new age required a "rupture" with the prevailing poetic practice. Pioneering into uncharted territory as the new avant-garde, the young poets welcomed like-minded efforts by others as confirmation of the validity of their own. The circulation of small and often precariously produced magazines by local groups led to contacts with other individuals and groups, both within the same national and linguistic boundaries and beyond. The movement originated in the early and mid fifties spontaneously and separately in several locations, and its history, which still waits to be written, was in the beginning more a history of mutual discovery than that of a poetic project spreading by inspiration and example – although that, too, was soon to happen. It was from the outset a relatively far-flung international movement, a fact that was reflected in the anthologies of Concrete poetry that began to appear in the mid-1960s. But, as we shall see in a moment with a brief glance at the Brazilian situation, it also had its individual and distinctly different fates and fortunes in different countries, cultures, or language areas.

While participants in the movement promoted the work of like-minded poets, they also frequently looked for support to artists working with a similar agenda in other media. That in itself was certainly nothing new in 20th-century Europe or in Brazil, which had seen writers, visual artists, and the composer Heitor Villa-Lobos join forces in the "Semana de Arte Moderna" of 1922. But it was a very natural move for poets interested in exploring the visual and spatial properties of the written text and simultaneously the sound potential of their poetry, for which the visual text was frequently intended to function as a score (not unlike the graphic scores of some of the new music). The reduction of Concrete poetry to a project in visual poetry has always been a harmful stumbling block to its understanding and appreciation both as a movement and as a genre. Texts from Augusto de Campos's *poetamenos* series, which was inspired by the concept of Klangfarbenmelodie, received an oral performance in 1954 with the help of young musicians, and again a year later, side by side with compositions by Anton von Webern and others. I have demonstrated elsewhere how the poet transformed the opening measures of Webern's Quartet op. 22 (1930) into the polychromatic poem "lygia fingers" from that series.[3]

The "Exposição Nacional de Arte Concreta" that opened in December, 1956, in São Paulo and moved a month later to Rio de Janeiro may have been the first exhibition ever where poster-poems, paintings, and sculptures were displayed side by side. An issue of the periodical *ad: arquitetura e decoração* served as the exhibit's catalogue, with a cover based on a Concrete painting by Hermelindo Fiaminghi and essays on Concrete art and poetry inside. The visual artists exhibiting with the Concrete poets had just recently formed groups whose names, "Ruptura" ('rupture'; São Paulo) and "Frente" ('front'; Rio de Janeiro), clearly announced their vanguard posture, justified by the fact that non-figurative constructivist art had not made its appearance in South America until the mid forties, at about the same time that the music of Anton von Webern and Schoenberg's twelve-tone serialism had begun to be known. But Nazism's persecution of "degenerate art" and the general discontinuities caused by World War II had also kept young artists in Germany ignorant about such music and such art in the early post-war period. Learning about the Bauhaus was for many simultaneously the discovery of the past and the confrontation with something new.

A similar experience of gaining access to something new which at the same time meant revising the past involved, at mid-century, even the master text to which many Concrete poets, and certainly both Gomringer and the Brazilian Noigandres group, referred as their chief inspiration and justification: Mallarmé's *Un coup de dés*. It was not until fifty years after its original publication that this text became accessible through the efforts of such critics as Robert Greer Cohn and thereby changed its status from aberration to crowning achievement within an already canonical œuvre. Gertrude Stein's *Tender Buttons* and Kurt Schwitters's *Sonate in Urlauten* and even the calligrammes of Apollinaire and a good many of e. e. cummings's poems had to wait until the next decade or longer until they found adequate critics. Where the young poets accompanied their creative work with manifestoes and critical and theoretical statements, as did the Brazilians, they made it clear that "making it new" meant continuing the work of earlier avant-gardes. It meant identifying those features in the production of the previous generation that pointed forward to what they conceived to be the future of poetry. In the process of exploring the work of those who were their models and sources of inspiration they thus created for themselves an ancestry and a tradition; however, until the very end of the decade it reached no further back than French Symbolism.

It is useful to dwell a bit longer on the Brazilian situation. The inclusion of poster-poems by the Noigandres poets and by Ferreira Gullar and Wlademir Dias-Pino in the "National Exhibition of Concrete Art" attracted a lot of attention in the national press, much of it polemical, and the poets were invited to collaborate with the Sunday supplement of the newspaper *Jornal do Brasil*. For over a year they had a national forum where they could not only present their own poetic project but also place their work in an international context of avant-garde literature, music, and visual art to which they introduced the Brazilian public for that purpose, in collaboration with like-minded critics. The results of their ongoing research into the work of precursors as well as the discovery of poetic projects elsewhere that were similar to their own, and even their encounters with new tendencies in aesthetics or with new sciences such as cybernetics, information theory, and semiotics that they found to solidify the theoretical base of Concrete poetry, were immediately communicated to the readers of the *Jornal do Brasil*. This often required the translation of texts as yet unknown in the country. It was this multiple role of poet, theorist, critic, translator, and *magister nationis* assumed by these young poets (Décio Pignatari was 30 in 1957, Haroldo and Augusto de Campos 28 and 26, respectively) that gave them such a high profile at the time and made "Concrete Poetry" a household word in intellectual circles, albeit often ridiculed. Presenting it as the direct though transformative development of the most innovative tendencies of the past and as corresponding to the avant-garde movements in contemporary arts and sciences, they insisted on the newness and forward-directedness of their poetic project. The summation of their program published in 1958 was tellingly titled "pilot plan." Even when they learned about the ancient form of the *carmen figuratum* and some of its successor forms from Charles Boultenhouse's article of 1959, they received the information with guarded interest: they were excited about seeing their ancestry extended into classical antiquity and rejoiced in the apparent parallel between the "Egg" of Simias of Rhodes and Augusto de Campos's "ovo novelo," but they also feared that this might arm their detractors with ammunition against their own claim of being innovators (see Pignatari 1960).

    While many individuals and groups published manifestoes and a number of poets also produced an extensive body of critical and theoretical work, it is probably correct to say that nobody developed such a coherent theory of Concrete poetry as did the founders of the Noigandres group in publications between 1955 and 1958; it culminated in their "Pilot Plan," to which they added in 1961, as a "post-scriptum," Mayakovsky's statement "Without revolutionary form there is no revolutionary art." Included in their portfolio of poster-poems published as *Noigandres* 4 (the only issue of their magazine that bore the title "poesia concreta"), the "Pilot Plan" was the condensed *summa* of their poetry and poetic as it had developed during the previous five years; crystallizing the ideas they held at that particular moment, it reflects what they would later call the "heroic phase" of Concrete poetry *à la* Noigandres. Here are the "Plan's" most salient points: It posited the end of linear-temporal verse and the arrival of spatio-temporal structures employing a spatial or visual syntax by means of a juxtaposition of elements, as in the ideogram. Defining Concrete poetry as "tension of word-things in space-time" it emphasized parallels to the "intervention" of time in Concrete art and of space in Webern's compositions and contemporary music, including *musique concrète* and electronic music. Conceived as an ideogram, the Concrete poem was seen as "an object in and of itself" that communicates its own structure and not a message about extra-poetic reality; it was not to be a means of expression, least of all of the subjectivity of its maker. Without giving up the "virtualities" of the word, or verbal semantics, the Concrete ideogram was presented as partaking of the advantages of non-verbal communication, both as sound and as visual *gestalt*; but the communication was to be one of form, not of messages. The Concrete poem would minimalize its verbal material to maximize its effect. It would rely on the structural principle of a spatio-temporal isomorphism and was shown to have developed from a prevalence of "organic form and the phenomenology of composition" (in imitation of natural appearance) to a "more advanced stage" in which "geometric form and the mathematics of composition" predominate, within a "pure structural movement." The task was "to create precise problems and solve them in terms of sensible language." The result of this process, the "poem-product," was offered as a *Gebrauchsgegenstand*, a(n aesthetically) "useful object" – a term echoing Max Bill and as such also employed by Gomringer.

This final stage, so close to the theories of Bill's Concrete art and to aspects of serialism in musical composition, is exemplified by the two poems by Haroldo de Campos that were included in *Noigandres* 4, "branco" and "mais e menos" ("more and less" / "plus and minus"), which is even more abstract

```
mais     mais

menos    mais    e    menos

         mais    ou    menos    sem    mais

                  nem    menos    nem    mais

                         nem    menos    menos
```

ill. 3: Haroldo de Campos, "mais e menos" (1957)

and self-referential than "branco" and appears to require that the reader construct its meaning by recognizing or re-solving the "problem" set up and solved in the text's quasi-mathematical structure.

When structural precision is of the essence, the apparent violation of its principle of construction in a slight dislocation caused by a typesetting error can make a poem almost unintelligible, as in the *Artes Hispánicas* version of Haroldo's "nascemorre" of 1958 (ill. 4a), another highly self-referential text:

```
            se
            nasce
            morre nasce
            morre nasce morre
                        renasce remorre renasce
                                remorre renasce
                                        remorre
                                        re


            re
            desnasce
     desmorre desnasce
desmorre desnasce desmorre
            nascemorrenasce
            morrenasce
            morre
            se
```

ill. 4a: Haroldo de Campos, "nascemorre" (1958)
[Artes Hispánicas 3/4 (1968), 103]

The original (correctly reproduced in ill. 4b) has all e's vertically aligned (except in the last triangular stanza in which all words are run together), so that the final e's of the third stanza form a continuation of the e column of nasce/morre/nasce in stanza 1 (not perfectly maintained in the *Artes Hispánicas* version); in stanza 2, the re of remorre on the right is echoed vertically in the closing re, which then reappears at the opening of stanza 3. While se and re bracket stanzas 1 and 2 and, in reverse order, stanzas 3 and 4, the hinge between stanzas 1 and 2 is formed by the vertically aligned re's of mo**rre** and **re**nasce: that formal and functional feature, essential for an understanding of the poem's structural semantics, has been obliterated in the *Artes Hispánicas* version by imperfect alignment. The inevitability of the cycle of birth/death/rebirth claimed by the verbal semantics is enacted by the spatio-temporal aspects of the text's visual design; any obvious sign of arbitrariness undermines the correspondence of verbal statement and visual structure.

```
                    se
                    nasce
                    morre nasce
                    morre nasce morre
                              renasce remorre renasce
                                      remorre renasce
                                              remorre
              re                                re
              desnasce
        desmorre desnasce
desmorre desnasce desmorre
                    nascemorrenasce
                    morrenasce
                    morre
                    se
```

ill. 4b: Haroldo de Campos, "nascemorre" [Williams ed. 1967, unpaged]

All three poems are quite clearly also minimal but striking sound structures, and "branco" has indeed been realized as a score for several voices which, in repeated passings through the text, sound out its possibilities for the separate or simultaneous sonorization of its horizontal, vertical, and diagonal lines of structure: a clear indication that the programmatic spatialization of the verbal

branco   branco   branco   branco

vermelho

estanco   vermelho

        espelho   vermelho

        estanco   branco

ill. 5: Haroldo de Campos, "branco" (1957)

text involved both its visual and its aural aspects. "Nascemorre" has been set to music by Gilberto Mendes.

The insistence on a "mathematics of composition" was enough to cause a rift with the collaborators in Rio de Janeiro, leading to the formation of "Neo-Concretism."[4] But as soon as that advanced principle of composition was enunciated it was also abandoned, and the actual advancement in the work of the Noigandres poets led in different directions. The anthology *do verso à poesia concreta* published in 1962 as *Noigandres 5* contains almost all the texts produced by the group that conform to the "Pilot Plan," and the collection of theoretical and critical essays and manifestoes published in 1965 as *Teoria da Poesia Concreta* spans about the same time as the poems in the anthology, 1950-1960, and concludes, somewhat out of chronological order, with the "plano-piloto."[5] What these poets began to produce in the early sixties, still under the label "poesia concreta," explored possibilities of text-making not yet foreseen in their previous program while disregarding some of its strictures, though it remained consistent with a number of its fundamental principles and assumptions. Reference returned, though less with an interest in iconic representation than in political and social engagement. The new forms of textmaking involved the short-lived project of designing a semiotic poetry (Décio Pignatari and Luiz Ângelo Pinto) and the production of "collage-poems" formed of preexistent images (e.g., Augusto de Campos's wordless "ôlho por ôlho," one of his "popcretos"). Haroldo developed a Concrete prose covering many pages (see his *Galáxias*), but he also allowed verse back in, and even the lyric "I" (cf. Clüver 1982: 144).

The first international anthologies, from Gomringer's *Kleine Anthologie konkreter Poesie* (1960) to Stephen Bann's *concrete poetry: an international anthology* (1967), which includes texts by five German-language poets, seven Brazilians, one Mexican, one Frenchman, and eight poets writing in English, are all composed of poems compatible with the main tenets of the "Pilot Plan" minus the mathematical principle. However, they vary in the degree in which they foreground formal properties at the expense of referentiality, and they certainly betray a considerable range of differing sensibilities at work. In his introduction, Stephen Bann has appropriate observations about differences between the Brazilians and the German-language poets dominated by the work of Gomringer, and in a more extended context these definitely need pursuing; here, I will only point to a broader distinction made by Bann between Concrete poems that are "intuitive and expressionist in character" and others that are "entirely rational and constructivist" – possibilities he saw best exemplified, respectively, by the texts of Pierre Garnier and Mathias Goeritz in his anthology. Though he felt fully justified in including both, he noted that "they demonstrate the difficulty of assigning a precise limit to the field of Concrete

Poetry once the periphery of small groups and well-defined traditions has been left behind" (Bann 1967: 19). In 1967, Bann is quite aware of the existence of a range of other potential candidates for inclusion, and he treats Concrete poetry as a genre, though difficult to define, and opts essentially for a purist decision.

That is not in keeping with the claims and hopes of the poets who headed the movement and whose goal to "make it new" embraced all of poetry. Mary Ellen Solt quotes a statement made by Eugen Gomringer in 1967, translated by Bann: "Today I am anxious in case Concrete Poetry is accepted purely as a separate genus of poetry. For me it is important, perhaps the most important aspect of the poetry of our time, and it should not develop into a form of poetry set apart from the main tradition..." (qtd. Solt 1970: 10). It may have been such considerations that made Solt opt for a far more catholic stance in compiling her Concrete poetry anthology, first published in 1968,[6] shortly after the *Anthology of Concrete Poetry* edited by Emmett Williams for Dick Higgins's Something Else Press, which is equally magnanimous in its inclusions and offers a welcome complement to hers. But a number of the texts included in either are hardly covered by the theoretical statements and manifestoes reproduced in the Solt anthology, unless one retreats to a phrase like the one in Öyvind Fahlström's "Manifesto for Concrete Poetry" of 1953: "there is no reason why poetry couldn't be experienced and created on the basis of language as concrete material" and who therefore admonishes the poet to "SQUEEZE the language material" in the same way Pierre Schaeffer has treated his sound material in his musique concrète (Solt 1970: 75, 78).

Our "expose: concrete poetry" in Bloomington was equally comprehensive without quarreling about the label, but the exhibition which opened shortly thereafter in Amsterdam only affirmed two other labels, "sound texts" and "visual texts," while it prefixed "concrete poetry" with a question mark. And it appears that some of its events were disturbed by the polemical intervention of a mostly Italian group that propagated its project of "poesia visiva" as a committed or engaged or participatory visual poetry as opposed to the perceived formalism of Concrete poetry. Subsequently, the label "Concrete" was more and more frequently replaced by "visual," at the same time that the material collected and displayed as "visual poetry" included fewer and fewer examples of the kinds of texts found in the Solt and Williams anthologies. A relatively early example is the *antologia da poesia visual européia* of 1977, edited by Josep Figueres and Manuel de Seabra in Lisbon, in which texts composed purely of verbal material comprise little more than one tenth of the whole. E. M. de Melo e Castro, who had published 25 Concrete poems as *Ideogramas* in 1962, edited in 1973 an *Antologia da Poesia Concreta em Portugal*, with José Alberto Marques; but the label chosen by him and a group of other Portuguese poets for the publication of their work in 1964 and again in 1966 was *Poesia Experimental*, and that label reappeared in 1981 in the subtitle of the volume in which Ana Hatherly and Melo e Castro combined theoretical texts produced over nearly twenty years.[7] It thus appears only appropriate that the combination "Experimental, Visual, & Concrete Poetry" formed the title of the 1995 "Symphosophia" at Yale University and has also been used elsewhere[8]; but it is not without problems.

Apart from the general doubt about the label "experimental" that Gertrude Stein once raised in a statement to Thornton Wilder when she insisted that what a writer publishes should be finished work whereas experiments belong into the wastebasket,[9] the triad suggests a hierarchy of categories, with "Concrete Poetry" forming part of "Visual Poetry" which is in turn a sub-category of "Experimental Poetry." Depending on the definitions attached to the labels, such a notion might be highly misleading. We have already seen that the reduction of Concrete poetry to its purely visual aspects is diminishing and falsifying, even though a number of Concrete poets have primarily or even exclusively explored the visual possibilities of written verbal material. As a phenomenon originating in the fifties, Concrete poetry can be, and certainly has been, seen as part of an "experimental" literature that Harald Hartung has traced back, at least in German literature, to Naturalism and the work of Arno Holz, in *Experimentelle Literatur und konkrete Poesie* (1975). "Visual poetry," however, unless we were to limit the term by fiat to a very specific kind of visual poetry or a particular period or movement, covers a much larger ground and is not necessarily experimental at all. It needs to be seen in the general context of word and image studies. In post-war Germany that may have been done first in 1960 by Franz Mon, collaborating with Walter Höllerer and Manfred de la Motte, in the beautiful volume *movens: Dokumente und Analysen zur Dichtung bildenden Kunst Musik Architektur.* Three years later Dietrich Mahlow designed a large exhibition which was shown in Amsterdam and Baden-Baden: *Schrift und Bild* covered a wide array of possibilities concerning writing and its image, including Western Renaissance and Islamic and Far-Eastern calligraphy but also Futurist and Dadaist texts, a number of Concrete poems, writing in paintings, writerly paintings from the earlier part of this century and from the present, and many other ways of interaction between word and image.[10] Quite obviously, many of these texts can hardly be considered "poems" at all unless one wants to stretch the label into meaninglessness[11]; but as the perspectives opened up by this exhibition and similar enterprises began to change our sense of past traditions they also began to qualify our conceptions about the newness of the new poetry and the depth of its rupture with the past.

The spread and diversification of the new visual poetry since the late 1950s has been accompanied by an increasing awareness of a wealth of older materials in many visual-verbal genres, some of which reach back into classical antiquity and have parallels in many non-Western cultures. But research into this more extensive realm of visual poetry is still sporadic and uncoordinated instead of being pursued systematically. The 70s saw the publication of a few volumes gathering relevant materials, such as Klaus Peter Dencker's *Text-Bilder: Visuelle Poesie international, von der Antike bis zur Gegenwart* (1972), Milton Klonsky's *Speaking Pictures* (1975), and Jérome Peignot's *Du calligramme* (1978).[12] Dick Higgins spent years gathering the materials published in his *Pattern Poetry* of 1987. But the international conference organized in the same year by Ulrich Ernst and Jeremy Adler at Wolffenbüttel was quite possibly the first of its kind. It was accompanied by an exhibition with a lavish catalogue, *Text als Figur*, but demonstrated, perhaps more than anything else, how much work is still to be done and how the relative isolation in which such work has so far been carried out has impeded the development of a coherent discourse among researchers with shared interests but specializing in different periods and cultures.

Nevertheless, we are gradually discovering the existence of a rich tradition, the history of which remains to be written – Ulrich Ernst's monumental history of the figured poem from its origins in antiquity to the end of the middle ages, *Carmen Figuratum*, published in 1991 in the new series "pictura et poesis," is a significant contribution. The shift of these kinds of texts from the marginal status they had been assigned for so long in Western culture is undoubtedly a direct result of the centrality of word and image phenonema in the present; in turn, our awareness of these traditions and the wealth and diversity of such materials inevitably changes our reading of the events in visual poetry since mid-century. We cannot but relate the newer texts to an ancestry unknown to their creators, which does not, however, result in shrugging them off as nothing new, as Décio Pignatari feared in 1960. On the contrary, the comparison gives them a sharper profile.

Dick Higgins may have a good point in refusing to carry the term "pattern poetry" into the twentieth century because the patterns of the new poetry have been differently conceived and received than most patterns in earlier texts, and because the "new poets" (Mallarmé, Futurists, Dadaists, and others) were generally unaware of the older traditions which had "gradually disappeared in the eighteenth and nineteenth centuries" (Higgins 1987: 17). We have already seen that information gaps caused by ideological suppression, war, geographic distance, and simple neglect by the mainstream culture gave poets involved in the Concrete poetry movement a sense of venturing into a poetic *terra incognita* that appears ungrounded, though understandable, in view of our much fuller knowledge of the wealth of activities by those "new poets" earlier in this century. But there seems to be a general critical agreement that for a number of years beginning in the 1950s there was a movement involving individuals who subscribed to very similar aesthetic ideas and objectives and produced a body of texts that can meaningfully be subsumed under the collective label "Concrete Poetry," and that the appearance of this movement did indeed constitute a new event in post-war Europe, the Americas, and also Japan. The announcement of "the death of concrete poetry" in 1970 by *Stereo Headphones* (see Vos 1992: 1) may have been somewhat premature, because it appears that the movement was still spreading into new linguistic, cultural, and political territories, and it is not yet clear whether the spread involved more than the repetition of already proven patterns in new languages[13]; but the repeated use of the term "post-Concrete" in the early 1980s, as in Christina Weiss's study *Seh-Texte: Zur Erweiterung des Text-Begriffs in konkreten und nach-konkreten visuellen Texten* (cf. also Schmidt 1982), made it clear that Concrete poetry was being seen as a historical phenomenon that had ceased as a movement, even though its legacy was very much alive. It was still possible to write Concrete poems, of course, but that meant writing in an available genre. Some of the major poets, such as the ever fascinating Heinz Gappmayr, continued to work along the lines they had chosen. Others, like Gomringer, appeared to consider their task done; as early as 1973, Gomringer referred to Concrete poetry as "ein abgeschlossenes kapitel der internationalen nach-kriegsliteratur." Still others, and certainly the Brazilians, have for a long time now produced texts that violate many of the tenets of Concrete manifestos like the "Pilot Plan," though the poets seem to have continued their adherence to its underlying motivations.

If we can now look back on Concrete poetry as a historical genre, we are still faced with a number of questions. From this distance, the poems no longer seem to have anything "experimental" about them, even if their status in the canon is somewhat uncertain. But we need to re-determine the justification of the poets' claim to being "innovators," to decide in what sense, if any, the movement can be seen to have "made it new." In response to an imposed question, "From Imagism to Concrete Poetry: Breakthrough or Blind Alley?," I observed in 1980 that the sense of rupture with the "mainstream" that derived from following non-canonical avant-garde models dissipated to the extent that new critical assessments were moving these very models from the margins into a reconceived mainstream; such reassessments were in turn prompted by contemporary developments in poetic production. With our increased familiarity with the production of the first half of the century we are now even more likely to construct continuities and to connect a good portion of the Concrete project with major facets of the Modernist aesthetic. In a number of ways one can consider "classical" Concrete poetry the final phase – or, if you want, the culmination – of earlier avant-garde tendencies, remembering that we have become used to thinking of avant-gardism itself as one of the "faces of modernity" (Calinescu 1987). But the very label "post-Concrete" indicates that the enterprise had an effect on subsequent production, and scholars have begun to investigate continuities and discontinuities that lead to a number of post-modernist genres and practices; in the case of Brazil, "the [several] concretisms" he distinguishes in the fifties and sixties have been constructed by a young critic, Philadelpho Menezes, as the first phase of the new "poesia visual" (Menezes 1991).

The tendency of equating Concrete with visual poetry, pernicious when it occurs in widely used literary glossaries and dictionaries, needs to be redirected: with the exception of those instances where the written notation is no more than the score for sonorization, Concrete poems can be considered as a distinct genre of visual poetry. And while it may be useful and necessary to sort out its relations to other contemporary genres of visual poetry, our increasing familiarity with much older traditions of pattern poetry and other types of visual texts will keep us re-evaluating our views of Concrete poetry in this respect.

But even the predominantly or exclusively visual Concrete poems appear to have more in common with Concrete sound poems than with most pre- or post-Concrete visual poems. Are there more useful categories that might direct our critical approach? Dick Higgins (1966) has introduced – or revived from Coleridge, as he claims – the term "intermedia," which I once found appealing in our context but have begun to question: the media of the classical Concrete poem are not different from those of traditional poetry, i.e. the printed page (or more rarely, as in the work of Carlfriedrich Claus and in many texts by Ana Hatherly, the inscribed page) and often the human voice. But Concrete poems draw on the codes of different sign systems, and I therefore like the term "textos intercódigos" – which might be translated as "intersemiotic texts."[14] Roland Greene (1992: 9) has used a statement by Max Bense to insert Concrete poetry in a much larger "trans-historical phenomenon in Western poetic writing" for which Bense uses the label "material poetry":

> Everything concrete is nothing but itself. To be understood concretely a word must be taken at its word. All art is concrete which uses its material functionally and not symbolically.[15]

This perspective provides a proper frame for the view of Concrete poetry as predominantly metapoetic and metalinguistic, as proposed among others by Christina Weiss (1984: 301), who begins the summary of her notes on the "Spracharbeit konkreter Texte" as follows: "Thematizing language as language means: concentration on the materials of language, on linguistic signs and the rules that govern them, their semantic dimension and their perceptual qualities" (my trans.). And she adds an important observation: "Semantics can also be 'thematized' by a refusal of legibility." Connecting the Concrete poem with traditions of intersemiotic texts in which their materiality and their metapoetic and metalinguistic functions are given particular emphasis appears to be at this time the most appropriate approach to analyzing and assessing the particularity, status, and effect of the Concrete project. Just as the creative and critical work of these poets has affected our construction of earlier literary history, the patterns of continuity, divergency, and contrast we are beginning to define in comparing Concrete and post-Concrete textmaking will influence the way we shape and reshape the image we form of their achievement. As I indicate elsewhere in this volume (p. 409-410), we may in the process have to begin to pay much more attention to regional and cultural differences.

The perspective I endorse may also affect our answer to the question, "How do I know a Concrete poem when I see one?" It is the question of defining the genre, of deciding on the criteria that might be employed in constructing it. Such decisions would determine, among other things, which texts I would include in an anthology of international Concrete poetry if I wanted to produce one today. (Mine would not be as purist as Stephen Bann's but probably not as generous as Mary Ellen Solt's.) I will not spell out my criteria here; the point is that some such decision is presupposed when we ask other questions which, in the perspective of the 90s, we may find more interesting because they emphasize the role of the reader, such as, "What makes me read this text as a Concrete Poem?" or, "What do I do when I read it as a Concrete Poem?" or "Can I read this as a Concrete Poem?"

I have sometimes asked that last question about particularly striking advertising logos, whose main function is, of course, to serve "as recognition symbols" and thus surely not as poems, as Marjorie Perloff has reminded us (1991: 119). Therefore the question is particularly relevant with regard to a logo that was designed as a Concrete Poem – or vice versa: Augusto's "Código" (see SAPER in this volume), which also serves as logo and title of a literary magazine, just as the one-letter Saroyan poem served as the logo for our exhibition. The minimal material of some Concrete ideograms or constellations, to use the terms employed by the Brazilians and Gomringer, respectively, lend these texts the quality of "signs" in the sense of traffic signs – which was indeed a part of Gomringer's program: instant recognizability. Does that diminish the poem's worth? Marjorie Perloff wonders "whether the conflation of Concrete poetry and advertising isn't a kind of dead end for the former" (1991: 119), and she further asks whether a text like Gomringer's "silencio" "can continue to hold our attention" (ibid.: 116). These are questions with which it is useful to conclude, and they are not easy to answer but seem crucial in assessing the status and achievement of Concrete poetry. Josef Albers, another producer of (relatively) minimal texts, once defined "the measure of art" as "the ratio of effort and effect." That is one of the standards that seems applicable here. "Silencio" is an effective icon, although how long it holds the reader's attention as such may depend on what she brings to it. Like all Concrete poems, "silencio" is also and perhaps primarily a metatext. What may be implied in exploring the metatextual aspects of the poem is suggested by the "Variations on a Poem by Gomringer" proposed long ago by Christian Wagenknecht. Exploring them can easily take up an hour of class time – as can the discussion of Aram Saroyan's [m]. Such a simple little text can raise enormous questions. Among the many lessons I have learned, and my students continue to learn, from Concrete poems is an understanding of the signifying potential of all the material aspects of the text. They have even taught me to become a much better reader of advertising logos.

Indiana University, Bloomington

Notes

1. Cf. Clüver (1978) for a later version of the essay; further revised and expanded, it is scheduled to appear in Portuguese in Clüver (1997). See Color Plate 3, p. 14 of this volume, for a reproduction of the poem.
2. On a trip to German-speaking Europe later that year to visit Gomringer and several others associated with the Concrete Poetry movement I unfortunately missed Max Bill, who afterwards told me in a letter that he had already composed the kind of poems later to be called "Concrete" in the 1940s. I never got to see those poems or to meet him, and I never will, for he died in 1994.

    At the advice of Max Bense and Elisabeth Walther I also went to see Hanns Sohm, who had built up an impressive collection of Fluxus materials and visual poetry, a collection now housed in the Staatsgalerie Stuttgart. This is apparently the largest collection of relevant materials in Germany, with the collections of Max Bense and Elisabeth Walther and that of Eugen Gomringer of similar importance in matters Concrete. In the US, the major collection is the Ruth and Marvin Sackner Archive of Concrete and Visual Poetry in Miami Beach, Florida. The former Jean Brown collection, now housed in The Getty Center for the History of Arts and the Humanities in Santa Monica, California, covers mainly Fluxus and Intermedia art in general, but also includes Concrete and visual poetry.
3. Cf. Clüver (1981). See Color Plate 4, p. 15 of this volume.
4. Cf. Menezes (1991/1995) for a brief introduction to the divergent positions.
5. The second edition (1975) was amplified by only two texts, in spite of a

considerable production of critical writings since 1960. The third edition (1987) is identical to the second.

6. As no. 3/4 of the periodical *Artes Hispánicas / Hispanic Arts*, which was discontinued after that issue. Reprinted in 1970 with a different cover and slight changes in the color design as *Concrete Poetry: A World View* by Indiana University Press (cf. Solt 1970).

7. This is also the label used in 1975 by Fernando Millán and Jesús García Sánchez for their anthology *La escritura en libertad: Antología de poesía experimental*.

8. Cf. the titles of the 1989 exhibition at the Università di Bologna: "Concreta, Visual, Experimental: Poesia Portuguesa 1959-1989" and, imposing a different hierarchy, César Espinoza, ed., *Corrosive Signs: Essays on experimental poetry (visual, concrete, alternative)*, 1980.

9. Raymond Federman expressed a similar opinion (cf. Federman 1982, 379).

10. In 1987 Mahlow gave us another present with his exhibit in the Gutenberg Museum Mainz, " – auf ein Wort! Aspekte visueller Poesie und visueller Musik," along with a rich catalogue.

11. Christina Weiss has proposed to designate texts mixing media and visual and verbal codes generally as "Seh-Texte" (which could be rendered as "visual texts" as long as it is clear that "text" here stands for the verbal element of the mix, in a much narrower application of the term than has become customary among many semioticians); Weiss insists on the "necessity of a strict separation between Concrete poetry and visual poetry" since, in contrast to the general designation "Seh-Text," concretization refers to "procedures of a specific treatment of language" (1984: 302-03; my trans.).

12. Higgins (1987: 15, 241, 249) lists two anthologies published in 1970 that I have not seen: one compiled by Robert Massin ("expanded from an earlier French edition"), the other by Berjouhi Barsamian Bowler.

13. The first anthology of Polish Concrete poetry appeared in 1978, edited by Stanisław Dróżdż, and contains poems written between 1967 and 1977. We are also becoming aware of a substantial production of Concrete poems in the Soviet Union, but often without learning when they were composed. Nearly a third of the texts collected in Guillermo Deisler's and Jörg Kowalski's anthology *wortBILD: Visuelle Poesie in der DDR* (1990), almost all of them previously unpublished, fall into the Concrete category and were thus unlikely to be printed in the German Democratic Republic; the compilers did not include details about the dates of composition.

14. Charles Perrone (1992: 48, note 21) has reminded us in his brief survey of Brazilian Concrete poetry that the subtitle of the first two numbers of the arts magazine *Qorpo Estranho* (1976) was "criação intersemiótica" – a label he used for his own study.

15. Bense (1965) quoted in English in *Concerning Concrete Poetry*, ed. Bob Cobbing and Peter Mayer (London: Writers Forum, 1978), p. 13 (Greene 1992: 9, note 1).

Bibliography

ad: arquitetura e decoração
1956   no. 20 (November/December). São Paulo.
Adler, Jeremy & Ulrich Ernst, Hrsgg.
1988   *Text als Figur: Visuelle Poesie von der Antike bis zur Moderne*
            (2nd, rev. ed.). Wolfenbüttel, Herzog August Bibliothek / Weinheim,
            VCH. [1987]
Aguiar, Fernando & Gabriel Rui Silva, orgs.
1989   *Concreta. Experimental. Visual: Poesia Portuguesa 1959-1989.*
            Exhibition catalogue, Università di Bologna, Facoltà di Scienze
            Politiche, Palazzo Hercolani, 10-17 April 1989. Lisbon, Instituto de
            Cultura e Língua Portuguesa.
Albers, Josef
1968   ["Was ist Kunst?"] In: Eugen Gomringer, *Josef Albers: Das Werk des
            Bauhausmeisters als Beitrag zur visuellen Gestaltung im 20.
            Jahrhundert*, Starnberg, Josef Keller Verlag, [7]. English: "What Is
            Art?" In: *Art and the Craftsman: The Best of the Yale Literary Review,
            1836-1961*, ed. Joseph Harned and Neil Goodwin, New Haven, CT,
            Yale Literary Magazine / Carbondale, Southern Illinois UP, 1961, 275.
Bann, Stephen, ed.
1967   *concrete poetry: an international anthology.* London, London
            Magazine Editions.
Boultenhouse, Charles
1959   "Poems in the Shape of Things. A Survey: 300 B.C. to A.D. 1958." In:
            Art News Annual, vol. 28, 64-83, 178.
Bowler, Berjouhi Barsamian, ed.
1970   *The Word as Image.* London, Studio Vista.
Calinescu, Matei
1987   *Five Faces of Modernity: Modernism, Avant-Garde, Decadence,
            Kitsch, Postmodernism.* Durham, NC, Duke UP.
Campos, Augusto de, Décio Pignatari & Haroldo de Campos
1958   "plano-piloto para poesia concreta." In: *Noigandres* 4 (São Paulo).
            Rpt. in: A. de Campos, D. Pignatari & H. de Campos 1987, 156-58.
            English: "Pilot Plan for Concrete Poetry." Trans. by the authors. In:
            Solt ed. 1970, 71-72.
1987   *Teoria da Poesia Concreta: Textos Críticos e Manifestos 1950-1960.*
            3rd ed. São Paulo, Brasiliense. [1st ed. 1965 (São Paulo, Edições
            Invenção). 2nd ed. enl. 1975 (São Paulo, Livraria Duas Cidades). 3rd
            ed. unchanged.]
Campos, Augusto de, Décio Pignatari, Haroldo de Campos, José Lino Grünewald &
Ronaldo Azeredo
1962   *Antologia: Do Verso à Poesia Concreta 1949-1962. Noigandres* 5. São
            Paulo, Massao Ohno.

Campos, Haroldo de
1958   "nascemorre." Rpt. in: A. de Campos, D. Pignatari & H. de Campos
        1987, 62. Also in Williams ed. 1967 (np). Incorrect version in Solt ed
        1970, 103.
Clüver, Claus
1978   "Augusto de Campos' 'terremoto': Cosmology as Ideogram." In:
        Contemporary Poetry, vol. 3, no. 1, 39-55.
1981   "Klangfarbenmelodie in Polychromatic Poems: A. von Webern and A.
        de Campos." In: *Comparative Literature Studies*, 18/3, 386-398.
1982   "Reflections on Verbivocovisual Ideograms." In: *Poetics Today*, vol. 3,
        no. 3, 137-148.
1987   "From Imagism to Concrete Poetry: Breakthrough or Blind Alley?"
        [1980] In: Rudolf Haas, Hrsg., *Amerikanische Lyrik: Perspektiven und
        Interpretationen*, Berlin, Erich Schmidt, 113-30.
1997   *Signos Intercódigos: Ensaios sobre Poesia Concreta e Outros Textos
        Verbivocovisuais*. Trans. Magnolia Rejane dos Santos. Foreword
        Haroldo de Campos. São Paulo, Perspectiva. [In press.]
Crommelin, Liesbeth, ed.
1970   *klankteksten / ? konkrete poëzie / visuele teksten*. Exhibition catalogue.
        Amsterdam, Stedelijk Museum.
Deisler, Guillermo & Jörg Kowalski, Hrsgg.
1990   *wortBILD: Visuelle Poesie in der DDR*. Leipzig, Mitteldeutscher
        Verlag.
Dencker, Klaus Peter, Hrsg.
1972   *Text-Bilder: Visuelle Poesie international. Von der Antike bis zur
        Gegenwart*. Köln, Verlag M. DuMont Schauberg.
Dróżdż, Stanisław, ed.
1978   *poezja konkretna: wybór tekstów polskich oraz dokumentacja z lat
        1967-1977*. Exhibition catalogue [?]. Wroclaw, Socjalistiyczny
        zwiazek studentów polskich akademicki ośrodek teatralny kalambur.
Ernst, Ulrich
1991   *Carmen figuratum. Geschichte des Figurengedichts von den antiken
        Ursprüngen bis zum Ausgang des Mittelalters*. Pictura et Poesis 1.
        Köln, Weimar / Wien, Böhlau.
Espinoza, César, ed.
1980   *Corrosive Signs: Essays on experimental poetry (visual, concrete,
        alternative)*. Washington, Maisonneuve Press.
Federman, Raymond
1982   "Surfiction – Four Propositions in Form of a Manifesto." In: Richard
        Kostelanetz, ed., *The Avant-Garde Tradition in Literature*, Buffalo,
        Prometheus Books, 378-384.
Figueres, Josep M. & Manuel de Seabra, eds.
1977   *antologia da poesia visual européia*. Lisboa, Editorial Futura.

Gomringer, Eugen
1973   "nachwort: am ende der konkreten poesie?" In: *eugen gomringer 1970-
          1972*. Planegg & München: edition UND [unpaged].
Gomringer, Eugen, Hrsg.
1960   "kleine anthologie konkreter Poesie." In: *Spirale* (Bern), nr. 8, 37-44.
Greene, Roland
1992   "The Concrete Historical." In: Greene, ed., *Material Poetry of the
          Renaissance / The Renaissance of Material Poetry. Harvard Library
          Bulletin* NS vol. 3, no. 2, (Summer), 9-18.
Hartung, Harald
1975   *Experimentelle Literatur und konkrete Poesie*. Göttingen,
          Vandenhoeck & Ruprecht.
Hatherly, Ana & E.M. de Melo e Castro, eds.
1981   *Po.Ex. - Textos teóricos e documentos da poesia experimental
          portuguesa*. Lisboa, Moraes Editores.
Higgins, Dick
1966   "Intermedia." *Something Else Newsletter*, vol. 1, no. 1, New York etc.,
          Something Else Press. Rpt. in: Higgins, *Horizons: The Poetics and
          Theory of the Intermedia*, Carbondale & Edwardsville, Southern
          Illinois UP, 1984, 18-23.
Higgins, Dick, ed.
1987   *Pattern Poetry: Guide to an Unknown Literature*. Albany/NY, State
          University of New York Press.
Klonsky, Milton,ed.
1975   *Speaking Pictures*. New York, Harmony Books.
Mahlow, Dietrich, Hrsg.
1963   *Schrift und Bild / Schrift en beeld / Art and Writing / L'art et l'écriture*.
          Katalogbuch. Frankfurt/M, Typos Verlag.
1987   *– auf ein Wort! Aspekte visueller Poesie und visueller Musik*.
          Exhibition catalogue Gutenberg-Museum (Mainz). Mainz, Ed. Braus.
Marques, José Alberto & E.M. de Melo e Castro, eds.
1973   *Antologia da Poesia Concreta em Portugal*. Lisboa, Assírio & Alvim.
Massin, [Robert], ed.
1970   *Letter and Image*. New York, Van Nostrand Reinhold.
Menezes, Philadelpho
1991   *Poética e visualidade: Uma trajetória da poesia brasileira
          contemporânea*. Campinas, SP, Ed. da UNICAMP. English: *Poetics
          and Visuality: A Trajectory of Contemporary Brazilian Poetry*, trans.
          Harry Polkinhorn, San Diego/CA, San Diego State UP, 1995.
Millán, Fernando & Jesús García Sánchez, eds.
1975   *La escritura en libertad: Antología de poesía experimental*. Madrid,
          Alianza.
Mon, Franz, Walter Höllerer & Manfred de la Motte, Hrsgg.
1960   *movens: Dokumente und Analysen zur Dichtung, bildenden Kunst,
          Musik, Architektur*. Wiesbaden, Limes Verlag.

noigandres 4: *poesia concreta*
1958   São Paulo.
Peignot, Jérome
1978   *Du calligramme*. Paris, Chêne.
Perloff, Marjorie
1991   *Radical Artifice: Writing Poetry in the Age of Media*. Chicago &
           London, University of Chicago Press.
Perrone, Charles A.
1992   "The Imperative of Invention: Brazilian Concrete Poetry and
           Intersemiotic Creation." In: Roland Greene, ed., *Material Poetry of the
           Renaissance / The Renaissance of Material Poetry*. *Harvard Library
           Bulletin* NS vol. 3, no. 2 (Summer), 44-53.
Pignatari, Décio
1960   "Ovo novo no velho." In: *Correio Paulistano*, 8 May 1960, page
           "Invenção." Rpt. in: A. de Campos, D. Pignatari & H. de Campos
           1987, 130-37.
Schmidt, Siegfried J.
1982   "Perspectives on the Development of Post-Concrete Poetry." In:
           Poetics Today, vol.3, no. 3, 101-136.
Solt, Mary Ellen, ed.
1968   *A World Look at Concrete Poetry*. Topical issue. *Artes Hispánicas /
           Hispanic Arts*, vol. 1, nos. 3-4.
1970   *Concrete Poetry: A World View*. Bloomington, Indiana UP.
Vos, Eric
1992   *Concrete Poetry as a Test Case for a Nominalistic Semiotics of Verbal
           Art*. Diss. University of Amsterdam.
Wagenknecht, Christian
1971   "Variationen über ein Thema von Gomringer." In: *Text + Kritik*, Heft
           25, 14-16.
Weiss, Christina
1984   *Seh-Texte: Zur Erweiterung des Text-Begriffs in konkreten und nach-
           konkreten visuellen Texten*. Zirndorf, Verlag für moderne Kunst.
Williams, Emmett, ed.
1967   *An Anthology of Concrete Poetry*. New York etc., Something Else
           Press.

CONCRETE POETRY: A GENERIC PERSPECTIVE

Pedro Reis

1. Introduction

The question I shall approach here concerns the generic status of Concrete poetry. This question covers the phenomenon in a global dimension, since the label "Concrete poetry" applies to an international set of poems. Consequently, the problems posed by Concretism from a generic perspective are not linked to any specific nationality or language but rather to a poetic production whose transnationality reveals a dominant configuration: the use of language in a reduced form which, according to at least some poets of this tendency, allows Concrete poetry to communicate with an objectivity similar to that of a scientific formula. Furthermore, it reflects other uses of language, such as the world of advertising and mass media, that are likewise forms of expression and communication based on international codes.

The generic perspective has been somewhat neglected as a methodological possibility of situating Concrete poetry in the literary field. This is largely due to the fact that this textual practice is based either on non-compliance with the canons or on miscegenation. Besides the lack of respect displayed by Concrete poets for the borders imposed by generic categories, the critics' reluctance to approach Concrete practice from the generic point of view can be explained by a once dominant epistemological perspective regarding genre theory – a perspective that considered texts as "belonging" to pre-existing categories. Concrete poetry brought unrecognizable elements to the poetic domain and thus created an irreducible incompatibility between the existing categories and its innovative practice. Hence, literary criticism's most conservative sectors have been hesitant to concede to it the status of an autonomous poetic genre. The situation has been further confused by the existence of different labels, such as "Concrete poetry," "Visual poetry," and "Experimental poetry," to designate similar productions whose specificity and interrelations have always appeared to be rather vague.

2. A break with the dominant culture

Concrete poetry arose as a poetic form that did not need, or intend to be in conformity with, the reigning precepts. It constituted a programmatic break with the recognized and established models of the dominant culture. Melo e Castro

(1965: 34) claimed that Concrete poetry was taking a stand against the closed generic classifications of the time, which reflected the accepted artistic and literary production and thus could not be adequate for an art that emerged precisely with the objective of challenging the established canons.

The Concrete poem was innovative: consequently, most critics and the general public did not possess the cultural competence needed to understand it. Because of its lack of conformity with fixed forms, preselected themes, or laws of style, Concrete poetry's qualification as poetry has often been questioned. That was indeed an intended response: as Claus Clüver (1987a: 115) has observed, "[Concrete poetry] places in doubt the 'literary' status of the text and challenges the reader's expectations concerning the nature and function of a poem." It is characteristic of Concrete poetry that it represents a permanent process of creating new expressive structures including the assimilation of new objects, sometimes even objects conventionally considered anti-poetic.

The radical nature of this new poetry can be gauged by the polemics it engendered, with critics accusing it of being neither poetry nor art and denying it access to the usual means of literary canonization: major publishing houses, the reviewing media, the classroom, and the awards.[1]

3. Historic continuity and artistic contiguity

At the same time that it claimed to perform a rupture with conventional poetry, Concrete poetry also presented itself as continuing and further developing a certain recent tradition, evoking Mallarmé's "subdivisions prismatiques de l'Idée," Pound's ideogrammic method, Joyce's "verbivocovisuality," and cummings's verbal mimicry and atomism, which converge in a new concept of poetic composition. It may appear paradoxical that a movement that claimed to break with contemporary poetic production and assumed an avant-garde stance in the cultural contexts where it emerged simultaneously placed itself in an artistic tradition. Yet that is what many of these poets did, as Clüver (1981: 386) has observed with regard to the members of the Brazilian Noigandres group[2] who "placed themselves firmly within the tradition of what they considered as the major achievements of the preceding generation – not only in literature, but also in music and the visual arts. Thus, besides Mallarmé, Apollinaire, Pound, cummings, and Joyce they constantly refer to Malevich and Mondrian, to Eisenstein, and to Schoenberg and Anton von Webern." Clüver also pointed out that the literary texts invoked were at that time generally considered marginal and not mainstream – which may resolve the paradox.

This sense of a historic continuity with the previous literary avant-garde was matched by an interartistic contiguity. Besides literary models, the poets also claimed plastic, musical, and cinematographic antecedents. Angel Crespo and Pilar Gómez Bedate (1963: 103) even claimed that the most striking parallels could be found in music:

> La abolición de la frase musical discursiva, que realizó Webern, y su sustitución por sonidos, aislados unos de otros pero con capacidad de producir una emoción estética por mera yuxtaposición, corresponde precisamente a la abolición de la frase sintáctica y la sustitución de los nexos gramaticales por los espacios en blanco encargados de unir o separar las palavras mediante un silencio que debe llenar la intuición del lector por si misma.

> [Webern's abolition of the discursive musical sentence and its replacement by sounds separated from each other but able to produce an aesthetic emotion just by juxtaposition, corresponds precisely to the abolition of the syntactic sentence and the replacement of the grammatical connections by the white spaces which would join or separate the words through the silence that should fulfil the reader's intuition. (My translation)]

The fact that it was possible to discover a dominant configuration within the modernist striving to "make it new" allowed Haroldo de Campos (1957, rpt. 1987: 108) to say that "Mallarmé, Mondrian e Webern pertencem a uma única família de inventores de formas" ("Mallarmé, Mondrian, and Webern belong to a same family of inventors of forms"; my translation), which suggests that Haroldo placed these artists among the "founding fathers" (David Fishelov's term) of the tradition programmatically continued by the Concrete poets. Like other poets, Haroldo emphasized the interrelation of the concretist project with experimental tendencies in other arts. Besides sharing the distinction of being "inventors," the composers, plastic artists, architects, and film makers held up as models or like-minded creators were considered to share in an affinity of foregrounded concepts and ideals such as functionality, geometricity, simultaneity, automatism, objectivity, and rationality, and the goal of constructing objects.

The participation of Concrete poetry in other artistic domains is indicated by the materials it uses as well as by the ways poems have been displayed. For instance, during the *Exposição Nacional de Arte Concreta* which opened in São Paulo's Museum of Modern Art in December, 1956, poster-poems by the Noigandres poets and two poets from Rio de Janeiro were hung on the walls in the same manner in which the Concrete paintings and graphic art were exhibited. A portfolio of poster-poems also made up the entire no. 4 of *noigandres* magazine in 1958; altogether, this is a rather common format of printing Concrete poems. The sound dimension of these poems has inspired multi-vocal concert-like recitals, revealing their affinity to music. According to Décio Pignatari (1957, rpt. 1987: 69-70), Augusto de Campos's multicolored "poetamenos" poems (1955 [1953]), which were based on Anton Webern's use of *Klangfarbenmelodie*, were presented in the Arena Theatre of São Paulo by the musical group *Ars Nova* in February, 1955, with the up to six colors of the poems performed by as many voices.[3]

Cassiano Ricardo (1965: 344-345) argued that the spatiality or visuality of the new poem indicates the adaptation of poetry to modern society, a civilization of the image, served by powerful audiovisual media, which have caused a natural change in the dominant language: there has been a shift from a culture of verbal language to a culture of audio-visual-kinetic language. Concrete poetry would then be the only poetic form to keep up with this change by using several materials and means of diffusion uncommon to conventional poetic practice.

As a result, Concrete poetry did not belong to any established literary genre and was often refused the status of a literary genre, which in the more conservative quarters gave rise to the idea that it was something non-poetic or even anti-poetic – or that it meant the end of poetry altogether. Defending their project against such views, the promoters of Concrete poetry were mainly occupied with confirming its poeticity and did not sufficiently concern themselves with clarifying its generic status – nor were they obliged to do so. But critics have also neglected the generic perspective on Concrete poetry, which I attribute to the indefinition and sense of incompatibility I have just sketched.

4. Concrete poetry: a literary phenomenon

In spite of their alleged disdain for the matter of which they sometimes tried to convince us (see H. de Campos 1960, rpt. 1987: 153), the Brazilian promoters of Concrete poetry made strong efforts to defend its literary and poetic status. They did this by the designation they chose – going so far as to reject the label "Concretism" (see A. de Campos 1965) – as well as by inserting their project into a poetic tradition that at first reached back to the turn of the century and was later extended through millennia, evoking a "paideuma" of authors from the Greek Simmias of Rhodes (ca. 300 B.C.) to Mallarmé and Pound.[4] The label "Concrete poetry" is a part of the "généricité autoriale" (see Schaeffer 1989) or of the paratextual set (see Genette 1982), which have essentially a pragmatic function, serving to direct the reading or attempting to legitimate the status of the author's practice at the same time as trying to assure a certain stability by evoking a previous literary tradition.

This suggests that the label must be related to a mode of organizing the literary field. Usually, that mode has been periodology rather than genealogy. This is easily confirmed by looking at the number of critics who have referred to concrete poetry as a movement. To cite but a few: M. L. Rosenthal (1967:

195) reported that "the international Concretist movement has come into wider recognition," Jon M. Tolman (1982: 149) maintained that "concrete poetry developed into the first truly classical movement of modern times," while the Brazilian critic Walmir Ayala held that Concretism was the most controversial and sensational movement of Brazilian poetry (cf. Franchetti 1992: 22), and the Portuguese critic and poet António Aragão (1963: 103) pointed to older experiments and several influences that helped shape the Concretist movement. By inserting the phenomenon into historical continuity and reflecting upon its participation in the social dynamics, Aragão obviously approached it from a temporal point of view; he insisted that new trends wear out in time and will give place to something new and original. His reference to the transitory aspects of innovation is rather similar to the way in which Tzvetan Todorov (1978: 48) and Jean Molino (1993: 12) have considered literary genres: not as stagnant categories but subject to change, in an ever-continuing process of newer forms of a genre replacing older ones.

The view of Concrete poetry as a movement can indeed be considered as valid. Concrete poetry does present features very similar to those used to classify other literary phenomena as movements: the existence of an artistic homogeneity determined by a collective consciousness and a theoretical agreement on the meanings and objectives of artistic production, the voluntary adherence to certain aesthetic values, the promulgation and defense of these values in programmatic manifestos, specific modes of production derived from the theoretical positions, the existence of groups of writers with their own vehicles for diffusing their ideas and texts (exhibitions, magazines, etc.), and more. However, this view focuses more on the contextual, historical, and sometimes even anecdotal facts and less on the nature of the texts produced. In other words, the periodological perspective pays more attention to the poets than to the poems.

But Concrete poetry intended to achieve a profound innovation, a break with the traditional modes of producing poems, proposing an enlargement of the poetic field. It is a project that struggles to revitalize language: it refuses discursive syntax and escapes from the logical-discursive articulation of syntactic normativity by having recourse to a spatial syntax, in which space functions as a relational element of structure. It constitutes, therefore, a break with habitual, temporal, and linear chrono-syntax which, less codified, opposes the atrophy of language that has resulted from its common use by maximizing material verbal functionality, appealing to non-verbal communication, integrating several semiotic experiments, and creating an aesthetic motivation that is predominantly syncretic. The result is a poetry that strives to achieve a maximum expressive efficiency in using a minimum of elements. Hence, this poetry is characterized by the use of language in a reduced, condensed, and autonomous form, so that the poem becomes impersonal, without any trace of the author's presence in the text. This industrial poem/object projects itself, not as interpreting exterior objects and/or more or less subjective sensations, but as communicating its own materiality, the concretion of its own structure.

Thus, it seems to me that, faced with a project that intended to bring about a revolution of poetic language, our attention should be drawn to the analysis of the poems' features through which these aesthetic ideals were to be achieved. A reflection on the generic specificity of the poems, on their interrelations with others in the literary domain and with other products of other domains, will lead to a fuller recognition of Concrete poetry. There is a need to be much more attentive to the work Concrete poets have left us, which remains up to date in the context of ongoing discussions about the limits of poetic experimentation and the possibility of new foundations for literary production.

5. Concrete poetry: a literary genre?

The proposition I am presenting will confirm the complementarity expressed by Claus Clüver (1987b: 2) in his reference to "the international discussion about the genre and the movement" labeled Concrete poetry, and it will offer new ways of satisfying the need stated by Eric Vos (1987: 559) in his observation that "all of us – literary historians and others – who are interested in concrete poetry sooner or later have to face the problem of identifying, characterizing, or defining this genre."

If, with Vos, we consider Concrete poetry as a genre, the label will designate both a literary production and its classification. But that does not relieve us of the need of defining the genre, i.e., of determining the boundaries that separate it from other forms of poetry. I have mentioned the scarcity of remarks by the poets themselves about the specific generic status of their work. Haroldo de Campos (1957, rpt. 1987: 100) cited Apollinaire's reference to his own work as "the new genre of visual poems" but simultaneously pointed out that "the 'calligram' of Apollinaire loses itself in the pictogram." The Brazilians have always attempted to separate their experiments from Apollinaire's calligram, insisting that the Concrete poem is of another kind because it completely rejects not only traditional verse but discursive syntax itself; besides, it is not figurative. That is one of the reasons why the Noigandres poets preferred to call their poems "ideograms." If the calligram was accepted by them as a "new genre" but different from the ideogram, then the latter must also be seen as a new genre, although both were related to each other as Visual poems. The Brazilians obviously saw no need to elaborate the generic distinctions further. A similar indefinition arises in Augusto de

Campos's remark that, although the configurations of *Un coup de dés* and Pound's *Cantos* are diverse, "the two poems belong structurally to the same genre" ("pertencem os dois poemas estruturalmente a um mesmo gênero"; 1956, rpt. 1987: 29). Augusto does not tell what genre that might be. The differences between the two works are enormous, which makes it difficult to accept that both "belong" to one and the same genre.

The difficulty is compounded by the habit of thinking of relations between text and genre in terms of "belonging." It would be more defensible to consider that in a certain perspective it is possible to detect some affinities between characteristic features in the two works so that some readers would make them participate in the same genre, if we discuss the generic status of a work as a question of "participation" instead of belonging, as Jacques Derrida (1980: 212) suggested when he maintained that "every text participates in one or several genres, there is not genreless text, there is always a genre and genres, yet such participation never amounts to belonging."[5] Considering that it is the reader's task to relate individual texts to established categories, this perspective introduces a relativism and a flexibility that allow one to deal openly and positively with hybrid texts.

I have already provided an extensive list of features and programmatic objectives of Concrete poetry, all of them under the heading of innovation; however, the list excluded the intertextual and intersemiotic relations of Concrete poetry, both to previously classified practices and to concomitant practices in other areas, which made us lose sight of the possibility that this production may have been related to larger categories.

We shall therefore have to continue discussing the generic status of Concrete poetry, an enterprise that still makes eminent sense today, because genre remains a determining concept for literary organization, both for theoretical and pragmatic reasons.

6. Concrete poetry as an intermedium
An important step in the direction just indicated was taken by Dick Higgins in his essay "Intermedia," first published as a *Something Else Newsletter* in 1966 (cf. Higgins 1984: 18-23). Higgins uses this term "to define works which fall conceptually between media that are already known" (ibid.: 23). In his poster-essay *Some Poetry Intermedia* (Higgins 1976), Visual and Concrete poetry are characterized as such intermedial forms.

Intermedia differ from mixed media, because they represent a conceptual fusion of elements. Thus, opera, for example, is a mixed medium "since the spectator can readily perceive the separation of the musical from the visual aspects of the work, and these two from the literary aspect" (Higgins 1976). According to Higgins (ibid.), "intermedia are therefore forms, with no quality judgement of the kind good or bad attached to them, and while they may be characteristic of one or another movement they can never in themselves constitute an art movement. It is therefore nonsense to speak of the 'concrete poetry movement'."

Visual/Concrete poetry is thus one of the intermedia that take root in poetry, with "video poetry," "object poetry," "postal poetry," "concept poetry," "sound poetry," and "action poetry." Neither a movement nor a genre itself, Concrete poetry, according to Higgins, is one of the several manifestations of this genre of "poetry intermedia."

In spite of Higgins having introduced the term "intermedia," a broader definition of the concept, given by Richard Kostelanetz, might confirm the adequacy of considering Concrete poetry as an intermedium. Kostelanetz (1982: 19) says:

> *Intermedia* is an encompassing term referring to the new art forms which were invented by marrying the materials and concepts of one traditional genre with another (or others), or by integrating art itself with something previously considered nonartistic.

In fact, everything I have just said to characterize Concrete poetry, its heuristic tendency, its participation in the poetic field integrating materials, techniques and concepts from other arts, as well as from other activities previously considered non-artistic, everything is included in this definition of intermedia.

The notion of intermedia should, then, be understood in a broad sense, as proposed by Kostelanetz, and should not be erroneously understood as a form that refers only to a product that lies conceptually between two predetermined domains. This restricted understanding of intermedia gave rise to opinions that contest Concrete poetry as an intermedium, such as Emmett Williams who used the word in a different sense, arguing that "the makers of the new poetry in the early fifties were not specifically seeking the intermedium between poetry and painting" (1967: vi). Thus, intermedia is a concept that may help to clarify the generic status of Concrete poetry, but only if it is used in a broader sense, since Concrete poetry is, in fact, characterized by the interaction of several codes, although often only the verbal and visual ones are mentioned. When Higgins places Concrete poetry between poetry and visual art, he conforms to this almost constant reference to the interpenetration of the linguistic and the pictorial. But semiotic interpenetration in Concrete poetry may be seen as a more complex production, in which the articulation of meanings is made by the interaction of several components. Consequently, it is important to point out its generalized semiotic nature.

In fact, as an intersemiotic practice, Concrete poetry is also made up of materials, techniques, and concepts from other artistic domains beyond painting, such as music, cinema, sculpture, architecture, and even other activities such as advertising, typography, or journalism, or some other scientific areas.

This complex net of hybrid elements present in Concrete poems confirms the extent of their intersemiotic nature. This can be demonstrated, for example, by Augusto de Campos's poem, "lygia fingers" (cf. Color Plate 4, p. 15). This is one of the six color poems of "poetamenos" published originally in no. 2 of *noigandres* magazine in February, 1955. The use of color and the spatial arrangement of the verbal material lead us to see these texts as visual images. In fact, at first glance it might appear as if the structural strategy used in this poem had been derived from pictorial models, beyond the obvious literary ones. As Clüver has pointed out (1981: 394), the poem has an emphatically lyric atmosphere as the expression of a personal love experience associated with women named Lygia and Solange. But it was, in fact, a musical model that provided the major impulse for the structure of the poem as revealed in a programmatic statement (A. de Campos 1955) introducing the texts:

or aspiring to the hope of a
          KLANGFARBENMELODIE
          (tonecolormelody)
          melody of timbres
                         with words
as in WEBERN:
          a melody continuously switching from one instrument to another, constantly changing its colour:
          instruments: phrase / word / syllable /letter(s), whose timbres are defined by a graphic-phonetic or 'ideogrammic' theme.

Therefore, it was a *Klangfarbenmelodie*, as in Webern, that Augusto de Campos had in mind and tried to achieve.

Thus, "lygia fingers" has simultaneously musical and visual elements, so that it is indeed a fine specimen of Concrete poetry revealing the participation of elements and concepts from other domains confirming it as a diversified intersemiotic practice. This fact leads me to exclude the possibility of considering it as a "mésogenre," an intermediate genre that emerges from the confrontation of two or more "microgenres" (Molino 1993: 8). So, it is an exclusively literary concept which reflects generic changes within the literary tradition as is the case of the "poème en prose." But the hybrid character of Concrete poetry crosses the borders of the literary field, so that considering it as a "mésogenre" would not encompass the full range of its intersemiotic nature.

7. The role of the reader

As we have seen, there is an undeniable advantage to considering the relation of texts to genres in terms of participation. This participation does not result from any ontological or essentialist determination, but is established mainly in the moment(s) of reception by the diversity of readers who establish a relation between a text and a genre or different genres, depending on their (in)formation and reading experiences.

In fact, Concrete poets have always insisted that the text present itself to the reader as an open work, as a product of invention that requires the reader's cooperation in the creation of poetic meanings. Poetic concretism stresses the polysemics or "totossemia" (Pignatari 1974) of the text. It relies on the reader's creative intervention, as Emmett Williams announced in 1967 when he characterized Concrete poetry as "a poetry far beyond paraphrase, a poetry that often asked to be completed or activated by the reader" (vi; cf. also Melo e Castro 1965: 97). Eric Vos (1987: 578) stated that "it is the reader's task to act upon" the procedures used in concrete poetry, and Claus Clüver (1987a: 114) observed that "the reader may become the participant in a challenging game for which the rules have been set by the poet but which the reader may play with better and even unexpected results." The idea that Concrete poetry demands the participation of the reader in the production of poetic plurisignificance has also been voiced by Ana Hatherly (1975, rpt. 1981: 143).

It cannot surprise, therefore, that in his earliest manifesto, "vom vers zur konstellation" (1954), Eugen Gomringer called for a "new reader" who would enter into a dialectical relation with the poet (Gomringer called his poems "constellations"):

> die konstellation wird vom dichter gesetzt. er bestimmt den spielraum, das kräftefeld und deutet seine möglichkeiten an. der leser, der neue leser, nimmt den spielsinn auf und mit sich. (1969: 281)

> [The constellation is instituted by the poet. He determines the play-area and indicates its possibilities. The reader, the new reader, grasps the sense of the play and carries it on. (Translated by Claus Clüver; cf. Mike Weaver's translation, rpt. in Solt ed. 1970: 67)]

Similarly, Mary Ellen Solt (1970: 64) spoke of "the new poet-reader" who understands that he is supposed to help create the poem and accepts the challenge. Jon Tolman (1982: 159) pointed out that the absence of the author from the text stresses the necessity that the text is to be realized by the reader. This "new reader" must not only face the demands of his new role, but also an engagement with texts marked by innovation and defamiliarization. Not the least among the difficulties is posed by the spatial syntax of the Concrete poem, one of its most striking features. In discussing the advantages gained by replacing traditional syntax with a spatial syntax Rosmarie Waldrop (1982: 322) has emphasized the reader's role:

> The advantage is precisely that its complexity is potential. It needs the reader to activate it. The absence of context and the non-linear combination leave words in their full lexical meaning, with none of its possibilities ruled out. The reader is free to construct his own contexts. He is given a stimulus rather than a closed product: he has to become a co-producer of the work. This is even more the case when a strewing effect lets one take the words in many different sequences. A great number of interpretations is possible. But beyond a purely linguistic one there is no way of claiming that one reading is right to the exclusion of all the others.

We may deduce from all of these statements that there is a need for innovation also on the side of reception. This innovation, the heuristic sense of the production, which gave rise to new poets and a new poetry, dialectically demanded a new reader.

Melo e Castro (1965: 98) even went so far as to claim that the concern of the Concrete poet was less the significance of his poems for his contemporaries than the cultivation, in the public mind, of the habit of participation in the act of poetic creation. The perspective of participation thus turns out to be also valid regarding the relation of the reader to the text: he participates in making the text meaningful. We can hold that the author's participation is greater because, besides contributing to the text as its author, he is also its first reader;[6] but clearly the different readers participate, and are expected to participate, in the making of textual significance. Similarly, one might argue that the participation of Concrete poetry in literature is greater than in other domains, because of its label, the literary traditions that uphold it, and its producers' status as poets; but it also participates in other fields, using their materials and concepts. So, in my opinion, the label "poetry" is to this production as the name of the author is to the text: the text does not belong to the author, rather, he participates in it, as do many poet-readers. Similarly, the Concrete poem does not belong to literature, rather, it participates in it, as it also participates in several other domains.

Concrete poetry has thus profoundly affected the roles played by authors and readers, which implies a change of attitude on the part of both poets and readers in an atmosphere of freedom, flexibility, relativism, and consequently and above all, responsibility. One of the earliest Brazilian manifestos, Augusto de Campos's "poesia concreta" published in the catalogue of the *Exposição Nacional de Arte Concreta* (1956),[7] opened with the line "a poesia concreta começa por assumir uma responsabilidade total perante a linguagem"

("Concrete poetry begins by assuming total responsibility before language";
rpt. 1987: 50). This claim referred to the poetry and the poet but, as we have
seen, it includes the reader as well, whose responsibility as co-creator is all the
greater because he has to deal with an object that is independent of its author.
In the same way that Concrete poetry represents an attenuation of the
boundaries separating poetry and other arts and activities, it represents an
attenuation of the boundaries separating author and reader.

This emphasis on the co-creative role of the reader, quite new in the fifties,
has since become a commonplace in critical theory. Next to the "généricité
autoriale" Jean-Marie Schaeffer (1989) has placed the "généricité lectoriale"
which depends on the reader's (in)formation and the time and place of reception. This includes the possibility that in different times and places readers will
make a text participate in (a) different genre(s). But different conclusions
reached because of a change in readers' architextual perceptions do not
contradict previous interpretations. Instead, they reveal that a change of perspective changes the participant relation between products and categories,
texts and genres; that is, they reveal the plurality of generic logics and the
consequent variability of the generic attribution. Genre attribution is part of
the process of assigning meanings to texts, and here as in the overall process
of text creation and interpretation we find a collusion of author and reader. In
fact, the author participates in the "généricité lectoriale" as his text's first reader, and the reader participates in the "généricité autoriale" as co-constructor
of the work. The "new reader" of Concrete poetry has indeed become, at least
in the eyes of contemporary theorists, the ordinary reader of today.

8. Conclusion

I have argued that generic attribution is related to perspective and that a
change of perspective proves the existence of a plurality of generic logics,
which implies the variability of generic identity at each moment of reception.

At the same time, the change in the paradigm that has occurred in the way
we conceive of the relation of text and genre – the change from belonging to
participation – may have brought about a more positive, affirmative, mode of
reflecting upon Concrete poetry, a theoretical position that corresponds to the
thought of the theorists of Concrete poetry themselves, who abandoned their
presentation of it as antidiscursive, antimetaphorical, and so forth, that is, in
negative terms, in order to adopt a more positive, affirmative attitude, insisting
on its status as a singular poetic mode that has the right to its own existence.

Finally, I think that in this perspective the classification of Concrete poetry
as a kind of intermedia poetry is a useful step because this concept includes a
broader heuristic sense of new poetic forms, forms that result from the fusion
of elements from various artistic domains or from the interpenetration of art

with something previously considered non artistic. Our fresh look at Concrete poetry from this perspective has enabled us to understand more clearly its role in preparing the way for the appearance of the "new reader" in critical discourse, and its insistence on the production of "open" texts. Concrete poetry anticipates the insight, now prevalent in poetic hermeneutics, that there are multiple possibilities of interpretive projections for different readers in different times and places.

Notes

I would like to express my gratitude to Prof. Claus Clüver for his well-considered critical comments on earlier versions of this paper as well as for his much needed corrections of my English.

1. In Portugal, the literary criticism of the time alluded to the scant sales of Concrete poetry. Little divulged, published in small editions by the authors themselves or small publishing houses, Concrete poetry never reached the mass market. In fact, since it did not look like poetry, the public kept away from it, being unfamiliar with poetry in the making, a poetry not already made.

2. The group was originally composed of Décio Pignatari and the brothers Augusto and Haroldo de Campos, who were later joined by Ronaldo Azeredo and José Lino Grünewald.

3. The same group presented another recital, with new poems, on 3 June 1957 in the Teatro Brasileiro de Comédia, with a score for verbalization by Willys de Castro, conducted by Diogo Pacheco (Pignatari 1957, rpt. 1987: 70n).

4. The work of Simmias of Rhodes and other early authors was not known to the Brazilians or the Europeans when they started the Concrete project. The Brazilian theorists have always been concerned with establishing a connection between Mallarmé and Pound. H. de Campos (1957, rpt. 1987: 99), for instance, argued that from the lexical point of view Mallarmé's poetry is at the opposite pole from Pound's, but from the structural perspective it is the immediate predecessor of Pound's experiments. (A. de Campos [1956, rpt. 1987: 23] associated the notion of structure with the arrangement of the elements in a functional typography; typographically, *Un coup de dés* and the *Cantos* are very different.) There was obviously an effort made to associate Mallarmé and Pound so that they could be presented as two important landmarks in the tradition being constructed by the Brazilians; the notion that it was an effort is supported by the fact that Pound himself did not include Mallarmé in his own "paideuma" of authors.

5. This opinion is also shared, for example, by Vincent Leitch (1992: 83) who states that "there is always genre but more than one, which is a methodological permutation of the claim that language is characterized by intertextuality and heteroglossia." To Leitch genres are socio-historical discursive constructions,

open to the genealogical production and paying attention to the literary conventions and cultural practices, as well as to institutional and ideological matters.
6. We could present additional arguments to demonstrate the greater participation of the author in the construction of a poem's meanings, although these may be more debatable. Among these are the facts that, if we look at the subject empirically, the name of the author links a text more to one person than to (an)other(s) and that the author obviously knows better than anybody else the elements of his own life that may help clarify some poetic intentions. This kind of biographical textual analysis, long considered questionable, has recently made a considerable come-back.
7. The periodical *ad – arquitetura e decoraçao* allowed its no. 20 (Nov./Dec. 1956) to serve as the exhibition's catalogue. After the exhibition had moved to Rio de Janeiro in 1957, Augusto's text was reprinted in the Sunday Supplement of the *Jornal do Brasil* (Rio de Janeiro), 5 Dec. 1957.

Bibliography

Aragão, António
  1963   "A Arte como 'campo de possibilidades'." In: *Jornal de Letras e Artes,*
            7/8/1963. Rpt. in Hatherly and Melo e Castro, eds., 1981, 102-105.
Campos, Augusto de, Décio Pignatari & Haroldo de Campos
  1987   *Teoria da Poesia Concreta.* São Paulo, Editora Brasiliense, 3rd ed.
  [1965]
Campos, Augusto de
  1955   "poetamenos." In: *noigandres,* no. 2.
  1956   "Pontos - Periferia - Poesia Concreta." In: *Suplemento Dominical do
            Jornal do Brasil,* 11/11/1956. Rpt. in A. de Campos et al., 1987, 23-31.
  1965   "Concreto e Ismo." In: *Revista de Cultura Brasileña,* no. 11, 395-398.
Campos, Haroldo de
  1957   "Aspectos da Poesia Concreta." In: *Diálogo,* no. 7. Rpt. in A. de
            Campos et al., 1987, 99-110.
  1960   "Contexto de uma Vanguarda." Rpt. in A. de Campos et al., 1987, 152-
            158.
Clüver, Claus
  1981   "Klangfarbenmelodie in Polychromatic Poems: A. von Webern and A.
            de Campos." In: *Comparative Literature Studies,* no.18, 386-398.
  1987a   "From Imagism to Concrete Poetry: Breakthrough or Blind Alley?" In:
            Rudolf Haas, ed., *Amerikanische Lyrik: Perspectiven und
            Interpretationen,* Berlin, Erich Schmidt Verlag, 113-130.
  1987b   "Iconicity and Isomorphism in Brazilian Concrete Poems." In: Jeremy
            Adler and Ulrich Ernst, eds., *Proceedings of the Conference on
            Visuelle Poesie im historischen Wandel - Changing Forms of Visual
            Poetry,* Wolfenbüttel, Herzog August Bibliothek, 1-20.

Crespo, Angel & Pilar Gómez Bedate
1963   "Situacion de la Poesia Concreta." In: *Revista de Cultura Brasileña*, no. 5, 89-130.
Derrida, Jacques
1980   "The law of genre." In: *Glyph*, no. 7, 202-232.
Fishelov, David
1991   "Genre theory and family resemblance - revisited." In: *Poetics*, vol. 20, 123-138.
Franchetti, Paulo
1992   *Alguns aspectos da teoria da poesia concreta*. Campinas, Editora da Unicamp.
Genette, Gérard
1982   *Palimpsestes*. Paris, Éditions du Seuil.
Gomringer, Eugen
1969   *worte sind schatten: die konstellationen 1951-1968*. Reinbek bei Hamburg, Rowohlt.
Hatherly, Ana
1975   "A reinvenção da leitura." Rpt. in Hatherly and Melo e Castro, eds., 1981, 138-152.
Hatherly, Ana & E. M. de Melo e Castro, eds.
1981   *Po.Ex - Textos teóricos e documentos da poesia experimental portuguesa*. Lisboa, Moraes Editores.
Higgins, Dick
1966   "Intermedia." *Something Else Newsletter*, vol. 1, no. 1. New York, Something Else Press. Rpt. in Higgins 1984, 18-23.
1976   *Some Poetry Intermedia*. New York, Unpublished Editions. Rpt. in Richard Kostelanetz, ed., *The Avant-Garde Tradition in Literature*, New York, Prometheus Books, 414-415.
1984   *Horizons. The Poetics and Theory of the Intermedia*. Carbondale & Edwardsville, Southern Illinois UP.
Kostelanetz, Richard
1982   "The ABC of Contemporary Reading." In: *Poetics Today*, vol. 3, no.3, 5-46.
Leitch, Vincent
1992   "(De)Coding (Generic) Discourse." In: *Genre*, no. 24, 83-98.
Melo e Castro, E. M. de
1965   *A Proposição* 2.01. Lisboa, Editora Ulisseia.
Molino, Jean
1993   "Les genres littéraires." In: *Poétique*, no. 93, 3-28.
Pignatari, Décio
1957   "Poesia Concreta: Pequena Marcação Histórico-Formal." In: *ad - arquitetura e decoração*, no. 2, ano IV. Rpt. in A. de Campos et al.,1987, 66-73.
1974   *Semiótica e Literatura*. São Paulo, Perspectiva.

Ricardo, Cassiano
    1965   "Vanguardia & Autonomismo." In: *Revista de Cultura Brasileña*, no.
                11, 340-348.
Rosenthal, M. L.
    1967   *The New Poets - American and British Poetry since World War II*. New
                York, Oxford University Press.
Schaeffer, Jean-Marie
    1989   *Qu'est-ce qu'un genre littéraire?* Paris, Éditions du Seuil.
Solt, Mary Ellen
    1970   "A World Look at Concrete Poetry." In: Solt, ed., 6-66.
Solt, Mary Ellen, ed.
    1970   *Concrete Poetry: A World View*, Bloomington & London, Indiana UP.
Todorov, Tzvetan
    1978   *Os Géneros do Discurso*. Lisboa, Edições 70.
Tolman, Jon M.
    1982   "The Context of a Vanguard: Toward a Definition of Concrete Poetry."
                In: *Poetics Today*, vol. 3, no. 3, 149-166.
Vos, Eric
    1987   "The Visual Turn in Poetry: Nominalistic Contributions to Literary
                Semiotics, exemplified by the case of Concrete Poetry." In: *New
                Literary History*, vol. 18, no.3, 559-591.
Waldrop, Rosmarie
    1982   "A Basis of Concrete Poetry." In: Richard Kostelanetz, ed., *The Avant-
                Garde Tradition in Literature*, New York, Prometheus Books, 315-
                323.
Williams, Emmett, ed.
    1967   *An Anthology of Concrete Poetry*. New York, Something Else Press.

CONSTRUCTIVIST POEMS

Pierre Garnier

The landscape: a region that evokes a general impression. Limited, unifying. Constructivist landscape: the organizing view creates the impression of a landscape, actually shapes it. Formative elements of the landscape could be: the mountain – thus the pyramid; a fir tree – a conic shape; the moon – a circle.
Geometry is a landscape that I can designate at will, interpret in my own words. Circle above line: sunrise or soccer match; triangle: fir, mountain, wave, bird. There is much freedom in naming and creating impressions; the simpler the shape, the greater the possibility to baptize and poeticize.

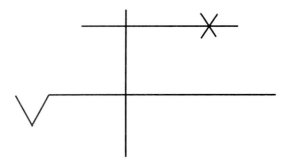

I could name this figure Star and Dust, or Light and Sea, pointing the spectator's mind to the relationships it can realize. I can read the following – Cathar – graffiti as crucifixion, resurrection, birth, or proclamation.

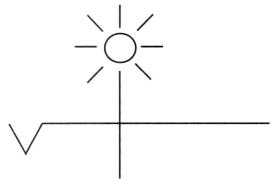

The simplest construction mentally evokes poetic creation: to see spaces and fields, to draw lines, to color, to animate; addressed by the text proposal the spectator performs the modeling. (Question, whether this is still constructivism?)

I have searched for these constructivist landscapes from a very early time – Art, Poetry grew too ponderous for me since the 1960s, even Paul Klee, even René Char. In my native region, the Picardie, I faced a constructivist landscape since childhood. In the wide plains of the Santerre the rising or setting sun is merely a circle above a line; the fields seem drawn with a ruler; the poplars stand upright in fixed distances as similar straight shapes; the geometrical structure is hardly interrupted by the rain-flattened hills, no more than by the people. Just a few lines create the landscape beneath the superior skies.

It is no hospitably open landscape – one must live with it, analyze and re-establish it, one must rouse it. *That* is the power of words: the Picardian landscape could be the great stage for a theatre of words, or the field from which poetic events germinate.

Words are *components of* the constructivist landscape. They determine the poetic course evoked in the reader's/spectator's mind. If I place the word WIND beneath a square, one sees the origin of the wind in the square; if I place it beneath a rectangle; one sees the wind blowing. The constructivist lyrical landscape is a starry sky, in which one must recognize and read the constellations.

With Concrete poetry, we have succeeded in making a poem from just a few words that remain in oscillation because of the arising relationships. Here, the togetherness (or opposition) of image and word, the image-word constellation, kindles the poetic spark.

Translated by Eric Vos

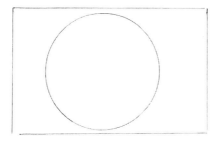

SCHWEIGEN

DER SCHREI

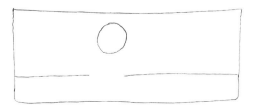

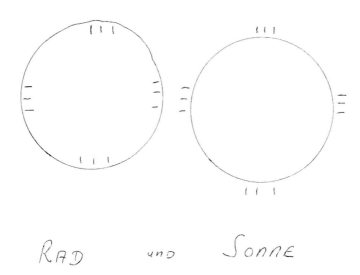

RAD und SONNE

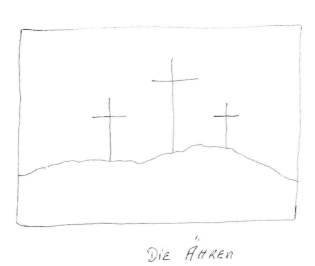

DIE ÄHREN

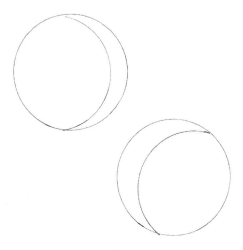

PER AMICA SILENTIA LUNAE

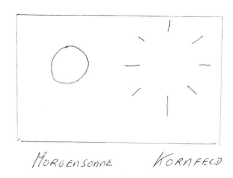

MORGENSONNE   KORNFELD

PIERRE GARNIER. 1992

UNDER CANCELLATION:
THE FUTURE ~~TONE~~ OF VISUAL POETRY

Craig Saper

My story begins in 1986 when I first saw an image on the cover of a Brazilian journal titled *Código*, one of many journals in my list of references for semiotics and code systems. *Código* was a journal about something called "Concrete poetry." In its concreteness, the image mocked a literary tradition that privileged long poems, that open poignant windows on the world, over this image-poem's all-at-once development that played on the code of the poem. What follows is a narrative of my journey from formalism and structuralism to conceptualism and post-neo-isms, from the histories of modernism and the international Concrete poetry movement to mail art networks and assemblings. My circling round a single logo for nearly a decade has led me not only to a series of de-codings and re-codings but also to humble resignations in the gaze of the code that writes my journey.

circle 1: received codes
Codigo, a poem by Augusto de Campos, captures a moment in the history of modernist poetics, following through on the *poetamenos* series that Campos

Augusto de Campos, "Codigo"

initiated in the 1950s. It looks like a series of concentric circles. Some of the circles are incomplete, some resemble stylized letters of the alphabet – a C, a G, an O, a D, an I – and the overall pattern makes the individual parts appear, at first glance, to be one single image. Because of the moiré effect of visual vibration created by the concentric circles, it is difficult at first to see which circles are complete and which are not; it simply looks like a logo. In fact, it is the logo for the journal of the same name, *Código*, that during its twelve issues, from the mid-1970s until the early 1980s, was the main inventive forum for semiotic poetry in Brazil; however, it is more than a logo for the journal. (Since the poem does not include an accent mark, it is referred to here as *Codigo*, in distinction to the journal's title.)

The poem's visual aesthetics stress the clean corporate lines of mass production, although always with the "I" of the poet already embedded in the codes. At the center of the poem is the English word "I," suggesting what our eyes see and look like in our coded world. This eye-like logo is a kind of emblem of semiotic poetry and subjects. The Portuguese word *digo* ("I say") is preceded by "co-" in the poem; thus: I co-say. All expressions in the mass mediated world appear only as part of the circles of codes, in which the co-signature provides a logo for both readers and poet. The reader has a chance to sign the poem. As Walter Benjamin argues, the significance of mass media images has less to do with some internal structure than with how these images make and meet their audience. They meet viewers half way, allowing for the possibility that readers become writers. To co-sign, readers need to understand how to write or perform this poem, presenting a painfully obvious difficulty.

The poem makes use of verbivocovisual relationships: the rhymes, portmanteau words, embedded words, etc. appear because of a visual layout that stresses these linguistic relationships. From these poetic tensions, semantic relationships appear as well; for example, we see embedded in this circular logic the words *código*, the Portuguese word for "code," as in zip code, and the English word "God," appearing toward the center of this image of logocentrism (we had already encountered the English "I" and the Portuguese "digo"). From these words, the reader immediately begins to make connections. As in other Concrete poems, its poetics suggest the logic of a game or puzzle. One reads them like a musical score. In fact, many of the poems make little sense except as performances; for example, the poem "cidade/city/cité" by Augusto de Campos is more interesting when read as performance of the overlapping languages an urban commuter encounters on a long subway trip rather than simply a long word on the page. Many of the visual cues, like color coding, suggest parts for multiple voices unavailable in poetry on the page. What is this logo a score for? How does one perform it as an iconic image?

At the highest metaphoric level, this multilingual poem summarizes all of the debates about logocentrism by putting its verbivocovisual relationships into play. It says that the God of our modernity exists in sign systems and codes. The God of the modern, multicultural urban world does not float in clouds; it sits at the center of semiotic codes. This poem is about the new god – the icon, logo, slogo god – and perhaps the clue to understanding its performance has more to do with networks, webs, and double-clicks than with modernist aesthetics.

Through its Concrete poetics, the logo also functions as a Visual poem with a conceptual coding of contemporary culture, as described by Claus Clüver:

> It has been argued ... that the most representative (and perhaps even the most exciting) art form of our age is the advertising logo. Why not create a logo advertising modern poetry, modern art, and the modern view of man as "homo semioticus," of man continually encoding and decoding signs, shaping his words by signs and in turn being shaped by them? (Clüver 1987: 34)

There is also a hint that *Codigo* is a self-canceling logocentrism. Marjorie Perloff (1991: 119) notes that although Clüver presents a worthwhile interpretation of this "especially pleasing and ingenious advertising logo," the conflation of advertising and poetry might be a "dead end" for Concrete poetry. Since advertising effaces allusions possessing the power of recognition, it does not serve the interests of poetry well. Perloff explains that *Codigo* functions like an advertisement for a literary magazine "because only that particular object has just this (and no other) emblem." In this sense, it looks like the kitschy personalized license plates, where the puzzle leads to a simple solution of recognition, as in the plate that Perloff describes, "JOG 2." The reduction of poetry to be as easily understood as airport or traffic signs "runs the risk of producing 'poems' that *are* airport and traffic signs" (ibid.: 120). The Concrete logo-poem here stands for an ironic mistake in the history of Visual poetry, an experiment that went too far. Following Perloff's warning against superficiality, this essay examines *the absurdity of the reduced poem as its positive value.*

At the Yale Symphosophia, Clüver, Perloff and Augusto de Campos asked me whose claims, from among this circle, the tone of my analysis supported. Here I argue that the Visual icon-poem presents a canceled tone and code that shifts undecidedly among the literal historical context and intention (Campos's reading), metaphor (Clüver's reading), ironic critique (Perloff's reading), and parody (read as mail art in an assembling). Circling around this iconic image suggests some clues about verbivocovisual relationships but does not produce any definitive clues about how to perform the image or even how to read the poem as a score.

I suggest that the tone of this poem, and many of Noigandres' works, is not simply a celebration or a dismissive irony. Instead, it involves a spectrum of tones overlapping and simultaneous, much like the visual and semantic aspects of the logo. That is, just as the visio-semantic poetics occur all at once, the tones of the poem are not singular. Again, few critics have commented on the tone of these poems simply because the formal, structural, visual, and cultural readings have proved so productive. It is the tone – not the didactic structural-visio-verbo-auratic-semantic tensions alone – that makes this image vibrate with potential. It is a zip code that marks a shift in tone for all codes, which are canceled by the shifting on-sending tone (metaphoric, ironic, parodic, etc.) expressed in this stamp. The play between god and code, self and bureaucracy, and word and image depend on shifting tone.

circle 2: post all poets
In 1953, Augusto de Campos's collection *poetamenos* ["Minus one poet"] became the "first manifestation of Concrete poetry." According to the poet this collection synthesizes lessons from the *Klangfarbenmelodie* ["Tone Color Melodies"] of Anton Webern and the ideogrammatic technique of Pound's *Cantos*. By borrowing sources from modernist art, the poets reinforce their poetry's artistic position historically within modernism, while details of the piece suggest an alternative reading. Augusto had planned to use "luminous letters that could automatically switch on and off, as in street advertisements," but "had no funds to do so"; instead he used colored lettering (cf. Campos 1973: n.p.). The colors in the poem indicate which voices should read in which sections. In 1955 Noigandres presented the *poetamenos* series at the Teatro Arena in São Paulo. They projected the poems on a screen while four voices read parts according to the color coding. In 1956 the poems appeared in the group's journal *noigandres 2*. Rather than resembling "street advertisements," the poems seem to have more in common with pop art's conceptual irony or twisting of popular culture. They are not simply tone color melodies. Their messages strike the contemporary viewer with unintended allusions to the American game show "Wheel of Fortune," with lighted letters whirling.

Given the poets' close ties to the modernist art of the Bauhaus, and with their manifestos advocating a structuralist brand of modernism, some critics have interpreted Concrete poetry to be an example of a tightly-constrained structural poetry with a singular meaning and definite effects. In their concern with pure form, the Concrete poets resemble other modernist artists. My position is that Concrete and Visual poems can function as conceptual games where the structure insists on a series of interpretations, rather than a singular meaning. Concrete poets did attempt to organize the most fundamental struc-tures and rules of poetics using layout, design, typography, and time. They employed this method not only to comment on poetic structure but also to create conceptual thought games.

Comparable to criticisms of modernism's use of reified conceptions of pure form, criticisms of Concrete poetry focus on the poems' attempt to represent static and idealized conceptions, as in silence. For example, Wendy Steiner (1982: 206) notes that Eugen Gomringer's "silencio" (cf. p. 402 of this volume) demonstrates the "dead end" of some Concrete poems. Roland Grass offers an interpretation of "silencio" that epitomizes the reified reading: "Eugen Gomringer, when he wishes to concretize an aural phenomenon like silence, relies on a spatial analogy" (1979: 189). Reading the poem's shape as an analogy for an idealized abstraction of "silence" makes the poem's meaning painfully obvious: silence is a lack of sound. The repeated word "silencio" surrounds an open space lacking words. If the poem offers a picture of silence, then it merely maps the concept of silence onto the words and the blank page. The poem does not engage our structures of language or thought but offers only a reified picture of silence.

Reading the poem as a conceptual game or score allows the reader to play through other relationships. Instead of repeated words describing a pre-existing blank silence, the poem also demonstrates that our concept of silence as blank space arises only from the surrounding words. Silence is born after writing. This interpretation does require our engagement with the design of the poem, which no longer mimetically illustrates the simple and banal idea that silence equals blank space. Instead, it sets up a tension between design and ideas, making possible a number of other possible readings: language, even the word silence, is structured around a lack, and words never fill that space. The blank space may not represent silence but an open space of imagination surrounded by silence; or, the reader is invited to fill in the blank space given the surrounding silence. Readings of Concrete poetry include more than semiotic and formalist solutions; the poem suggests a way to think through writing. Use of words opened poetry often unwittingly to alternative readings. A square box painted in a contrasting color to the background will inevitably create the expected visual effect. Words can too easily escape the rigid references required for formalist lessons. These poems do not privilege pure perception, but focus on the tension between meaning and visible arrangement. They represent concepts rather than things in the world. A reading of Concrete poems as conceptual games or scores links these poems to similar experiments in the last half of the twentieth century, for example in Fluxus and, later, in experimental multimedia journals.

circle 3: on-sendings

Codigo, beyond a reference to zip codes, resembles in shape a post office
cancellation on a letter. This poem appears on a journal cover precisely at the
height of the mail art movement and emblematizes many of the crucial issues
of mail art networks, a connection that receives no notice in studies of those
networks. Critics usually place Brazilian Concrete poetry in a modernist
lineage, which stresses internal formal relationships and structural grammar of
art and poetry, and they tend to read mail art and rubber stamp art in terms of
a post-modernism which stresses social relationships and anti-aesthetic
qualities. The few critics and participants of mail art and mail art assemblings
who discuss Concrete poetry at all dismiss it as part of an archaic interest in
strict rule-based formalist art. And, for their part, defenders of Concrete poetry
dismiss mail art and much of Visual poetry as sloppy, a-semantic, word salads.
The lines between modernist poetry and postmodernist conceptual art began
to blur when the Brazilians allowed semantics into the visual and aural formal
or structural issues. Once the Concrete poems opened the door to concept,
modernism could never return to purely formal or structural issues. Mail art
networks and assemblings grew at the unlikely intersection of mass media and
experimental artisanal art, between the codes of bureaucratic culture and small
intimate networks of artists and poets, an intersection crucial to understanding
Concrete and Visual poetry. This paradoxical mixture of impersonal code and
personal imprint will come to dominate the networked uses of multimedia
forms in the twenty-first century.

If *Codigo* functions as a score, then one might use it as a score for mail art
networkers. As a cancellation stamp, it asks the reader to participate in what
Ray Johnson called "on-sendings." An on-sending involves an artwork sent to
someone, who in turn adds to the work and sends it on to another participant
in the network. As an on-sending, *Codigo*'s meaning depends not on a particular socio-cultural context of production nor on an original intention, but on
a speculation on where it might go next and how one might change the network by using it in a certain way. How does the reader "return to sender" in
an on-sending? How do I as reader co-sign the signature poem of Concrete
poet Augusto de Campos?

circle 4: send-up

As in other circlings around this icon-poem, the reader inevitably reads it as
saying that codes, code systems, logos, and icons are the gods of contemporary
culture. Circling around again, another possible reading appears. Even God is
caught up in the code, and even the gods which we play as code makers and
poets are still caught in the code. I am humbled by the code-God that keeps a
vigilant panopticonic eye gazing at my every move as I continue to work on

Visual poetry that has not found a home in either art history or literary studies. The poem still appears to be a parody of poetry, even as it attempts to become canonized in the academy as part of the modernist tradition. Few have noticed its parodic tone under the weight of visio-verbal structural interpretations. Like an e-mail message, the Concrete poem, not an iconic representation of nature or the natural world, makes an argument against the absurdity of the norms used in evaluating poetry and scholarship. It makes its argument in the form of a concrete send-up: a parody. In that sense, the icon-poem supports Perloff's claim that they are too deceivingly simple. They are simple in the style of Jacques Tati or Jerry Lewis.

There is a fascination with rules, regulations, bureaucratic procedures not only in much of mail art networks and assemblings, but also in this icon of a postal procedure called cancellation. The parody of the poem cancels its message even as it, therefore, depends on that canceling to send it on. The canceled stamp appears on a letter sent on to its next destination. How then can one send on *Codigo* and to whom? What name should appear on the address? What is the zip-code? Because of its canceled tone, the Concrete poem offers a figurative connection to the explosion of visual literature in experimental magazines. Although one could find literal connections, the figurative link allows for a conceptual paradigm with which to read these often daunting assemblings. To read the specific codes and tones of multimedia magazines requires a figurative study of their antecedents, such as Concrete poetry and Visual icon poetry.

The experimental periodicals often associated with mail art networks, and sometimes called assemblings, use rather than reject the trappings and procedures of large institutional bureaucracies, corporate aliases, and the centralized efficiency and money-saving processes of collecting the pieces of the assemblage and sending it out. It is the Fed-Ex process in miniature: the process of shipping all the packages to one central location and then sending them out to the various destinations.

As a Concrete poem, *Codigo* remains on the page, an interesting puzzle but not a part of a social plastic art network. How can we send it on? Whom do we address it to? Who is the author of this poem, a proper name or a code? The network and assemblings frequently use corporate names, for example, International Society of Copier Artists, Private World, Blitzinformation, Administration Center, Museum of Museums, Artpool, Creative Thing, Postmaster, Ant Farm, New York Correspondance School and Buddha University, Image Bank, General Idea Group, and Sock of the Month Club. Perhaps the zip code will lead to a conglomeration of senders and receivers, a new corporate name for the icon of sending.

One last circle: the zip code tone

This logo poem emblematizes how our contemporary language and code systems meet the audience in their own homes, be they concerned with serious poetics, anti-aesthetics, or parodic prophetics. Is this simple logo also an emblem for my entire essay, narrative, and journey: a logo gazing at my life in language? A clue to a concrete language game? A marker for a moment in art and literary history? A score for mail art networkers? Or a stamp to be placed over all letters, changing their tone?

Where did this Concrete poem take me? How did it change me; how does it change its author? How do we receive its cancellation? This code was sent by Augusto de Campos. It is a poem of the network, larger than the International Concrete Poetry Movement. It is a network of semantics, of visual associations; of artists, poets, and critics; a network of circlings; and an excuse to look again. Where does this zip code sent by Augusto go now? Where is it now? What do I do with it now? I send it off again, to begin its journey anew. RETURN TO SENDER: Augusto de *Código*.

Bibliography

Campos, Augusto de
    1973   *poetamenos*. São Paulo, Edições Invenção. [1955]
Clüver, Claus
    1987   "Languages of the Concrete Poem." In: K. David Jackson, ed.,
             Transformations of Literary Language in Latin American Literature.
             Austin, Abaporu Press, 32-43.
Grass, Roland
    1979   "Concrete Treatment of Space." In: Richard Kostelanetz, ed., *Visual*
             Literature Criticism: A New Collection. Carbondale, Southern Illinois
             UP, 135-40.
Perloff, Marjorie
    1991   *Radical Artifice: Writing Poetry in the Age of Media.* Chicago,
             University of Chicago Press.
Steiner, Wendy
    1982   *The Colors of Rhetoric: Problems in the Relation Between Modern*
             Literature and Painting. Chicago, University of Chicago Press.

SWEDISH CONCRETE POETRY IN FOCUS

Amelie Björck

Even though Swedish Concrete poetry has had no direct impact on the international development of this phenomenon, I believe there is reason not to
overlook it even in that broader context. As early as 1954, Öyvind Fahlström
(1928-1976), Swedish poet and future painter, published a manifesto of
Concrete poetry. The manifesto, named "Hätila ragulpr på fåtskliaben (Hipy
Papy Bthuthdth Thuthda Bthuthdy)" after Owl's spelling attempts in *Winnie
the Pooh*, was not translated into English until it appeared in the anthology by
Mary Ellen Solt, *Concrete Poetry: a World View*, first published in 1968. Even
so the ideas put forward in Fahlström's manifesto cover most of the aspects
developed in the international movement of Concrete poetry.

Fahlström's very inclusive use of the term is, as we will see, in line with the
somewhat later attempts to define the concept of Concrete poetry – I refer
above all to Mike Weaver, whose ideas are also included in the Solt anthology.
There are thus many traits common to our Swedish Concrete poetry and that
of other countries. But the Swedish version of this poetic genre also combines
certain traits which are found less frequently elsewhere, traits which may
sometimes seem contrary to the purpose of Concretism.

Concrete poetry made a radical and resounding breakthrough in Sweden,
but its time of dominance was relatively short: after a few years the movement
seems to have disappeared almost totally. There are today few, if any, Concrete poets active in Sweden. Not many people are acquainted with this kind
of poetry, and even fewer like it and adhere to it. Even though Concretism in
an international perspective had active representatives in Sweden at an early
stage, it is not given much space in Swedish literary history. When mentioned,
it is also often in disparaging terms because of its "difficulty" and "anti-
literary" character.

It is my belief that regardless of subjective taste and attitude, the importance of Concrete poetry, including its Swedish representation, ought to be
recognized – at least as a sign of the emancipation within the art of poetry. In
this essay I will try to outline the specific traits of Swedish Concrete poetry in
order to cast some light on a field of research that is still to a large extent
hidden in the darkness of oblivion and neglect, even in its native country.

The Swedish Cultural Climate and the Birth of Concrete Poetry

When in the early 50s Öyvind Fahlström laid the foundations of the Swedish
branch of Concrete poetry he was fairly isolated – an outsider on the literary
scene. Nevertheless in this country such pioneers as Gunnar Björling and
Gunnar Ekelöf had worked on a literary and semantic renewal in various ways
as early as in the 30s. In the poems of Björling we find a broken syntax and a
language that is reduced to the core; in Ekelöf the poems are without metre or
capitals and filled with pregnant, surrealistically fragmented images.

The Swedish poets who, delayed by the war, made their début in the 40s –
poets such as Werner Aspenström, Karl Vennberg and Erik Lindegren – made
free use of the new ideas of modernism, especially Surrealism. It was only
then, that international influences could penetrate into the cultural life of Sweden more radically. However, in spite of the modernizations and breaks with
tradition, the Swedish poetry of the 40s is hardly characterized by a spirit of
revolution and progressiveness. The general feeling is rather one of pessimism
and profound existentialism in the wake of the war. This introspective climate
was to a certain extent still present in the 50s. At this time the ideas of New
Criticism also inspired a learned and academic interest in the esthetics of
language and the "typically poetical."

All this gave rise to a new, romantic tendency in poetry, and it was mainly
this estheticizing and fairly traditional poetry, with the popular poet Bo Setter-
lind as its chief representative, that Öyvind Fahlström turned against in his
manifesto of Concrete poetry. The manifesto encourages the creation of
Concrete poetry as an alternative to the "rough symbolic cryptogram, 'beautiful' romantic jargon, or desperate grimaces outside the church gate" (Solt
1970: 75). It also describes the rich selection of means and methods open to
the experimentally minded Concrete poet, a selection whose manifoldness
exceeds the limits of any narrow conception of Concrete poetry.

Fahlström's manifesto and his poems published in the journal *Odyssé* in the
50s were largely ignored by both public and critics. It was not until the beginning of the 60s that the time was ripe for Fahlström's ideas. By then the light
poetical expressions and the temperate climate of discussion of the 50s had
changed into a yearning for new and exciting experiments. It was not until
1966 that Fahlström published a book containing his manifesto and his Concrete poetry of the 50s. The book was given the title *Bord-dikter*, a contraction
of the words "bokstäver" (letters) and "ord" (words) into a concrete and
everyday concept: "bord" (table).

The foremost forum of the Swedish literary avant-garde of the early 60s
was the journal *Rondo*, belonging to the Bonnier publishing house. In *Rondo*,
from 1961 onwards, Concrete poems, Swedish ones as well as translations of

poems by for instance Gomringer, Heißenbüttel and Franz Mon, came to form an essential part of the contents. The fact that Concrete poetry was an international movement was an important inspiration for the Swedish poets. In his article "Bris," Fahlström (1961) gave an early survey of new, radical poetry in a global perspective, and mentioned more than twenty poets from all over the world. In *Rondo* and in other media, including the daily newspapers, there was also a continuous debate about the new poetry and related experiments in music and art, happenings of various kinds etcetera. A new interest was also shown in the provocative modernist predecessors, especially Dadaism and Futurism.

Several contributors and members of the staff of *Rondo* called themselves Concretists and were active as poets. Some examples are Leif Nylén, Bengt Emil Johnson, Jarl Hammarberg-Åkesson, Åke Hodell and of course Öyvind Fahlström, who was generally seen as the pioneer and nestor of the Swedish movement, although at this period he spent more time on the visual arts and, in the early 60s, had moved to the USA. Other poets worth mentioning in this context are Carl Fredrik Reutersvärd, Harry M Hällgren, Torsten Ekbom and Mats G Bengtsson. All of these published one or more volumes of Concrete poetry or prose during the first half of the decade.

The young Concrete poets formed a close-knit avant-garde – they even had a Concretist soccer team! They backed up each other against the attacks by critics from the outside, which were at times quite aggressive. The poets were inspired by an enthusiastic feeling of belonging to something new and revolutionary: the emancipation of language and the almost total renewal of poetry. Cultural life in Sweden in this period was marked by a dynamic openness, with many performances and happenings inspired by John Cage and American Neo-Dadaism. It was, in other words, a time of experimental border-crossing.

Despite the close connection among the poets, Swedish Concrete poetry is really a heterogeneous phenomenon. This may be seen as a natural effect of the lively and fertile experimental spirit of the 60s, but is actually encouraged and predicted already in the Fahlström manifesto of 1954. Concrete poetry in Fahlström's opinion is a concept to be generously interpreted.

The Heterogeneity of Swedish Concrete Poetry

Fahlström and the other Swedish Concrete poets do indeed show an open attitude in their renewal of poetry, its means and methods. They never believed in the intrinsic value of adhering to certain principles. In his manifesto Fahlström includes not only the foundations of a "purist" Concrete poetry, but suggests several types of experimental radicalism.

In the introduction to her anthology, Mary Ellen Solt refers to the English critic Mike Weaver who, in an article from 1966, describes Concrete poetry as consisting of three categories. He labels one of them "auditive [phonetic] poetry," since it is based on an "auditory succession" of sounds against a background of silence. Another type is "kinetic poetry," in which meaning gradually develops through a "visual succession." The sequential element in this mode of using language replaces the traditional structure of the discursive text. The third type recognized by Weaver is "visual poetry," which he defines, using the words of Gomringer, as "a constellation in space."

Throughout this paper we will see how the Fahlström manifesto "Hätila ragulpr på fåtskliaben" actually contains the prerequisites for all of the three categories of Concrete poetry, though presented in a very disorganized manner. In his article Weaver agrees that in practice the categories are not always separable: poets sometimes adopt the different approaches *in combination.* This point, which is also emphazised in Mary Ellen Solt's comment on Weaver, certainly holds true for the greater part of the body of Concrete poetry: not even Gomringer's constellations are *solely* visually elaborated.

The categories should thus be considered as abstractions, and as such they can be useful. The attribution then is due to the dominating trait of the poem, which in the case of Gomringer's constellations tends to be mostly visual. In a similar way a few of the Swedish Concrete poems actually come rather close to functioning as a constellation in space. These poems are of a size that can be grasped in a single look and can offer a simultaneous visual experience. They can be read in many directions and often invite the reader to a kind of intellectual game, taking place "inside" the poem as an interplay between form and content. These are the poems that, because of their convenient size, are most often presented in the anthologies.

The poet, critic, and co-editor Björn Håkanson, in his volume on new Swedish poetry of the 60s, names this branch of Swedish Concrete poetry "methodical" (Håkanson & Nylén 1966: 6), since it is often occupied with deconstructing and exposing the various possibilities and mechanisms inherent in language, such as sequence, repetition, transformation of words and puns. In an article in *Rondo*, Leif Nylén (1964: 30), the poet and editor of the journal, makes a comment on the same phenomena when he claims to see certain possibilities in a serial, mechanical moulding of language. He talks about "slicing up the stiffening surface of language and uncovering new layers in the body of language." (It is interesting to note how eagerly the poet uses metaphors when writing as a literary critic – in Concrete poetry the metaphor, as we know, is a rarity.) Nylén (ibid.) recognizes this more objective and formal tendency of what he calls "textual realism" in certain Swedish Concrete poets, like Carl Fredrik Reutersvärd and Åke Hodell, and in some of the poems by Öyvind Fahlström. Even though Leif Nylén is in general rather positive about this type of poetry, he also warns that these "linguistic demonstrations" may become "exceptionally boring literature in its non-humanistic, additive, monotonous structure" (ibid.).

Many contemporary critics reproached the Swedish Concrete poets for what they saw as emotional numbness, and expressed doubts about this suppressing of all linguistic magic for the benefit of "pseudo-science." One of the voices raised speaks about "the blue flower of romanticism planted in a test tube." This criticism, however, only takes into consideration a very limited part of the Concrete poetry, as manifested by Fahlström and his followers. In fact most of the Swedish Concrete poems are not methodical in kind.

Björn Håkanson embraces the wider spectrum, when, alongside his observations on the current of methodical poetry in the flood of the 60s avant-garde, he also comments on the even wider stream of what he calls "linguistic sensualism." This is a stream in which he spots the work of most of the Swedish Concrete poets, like Jarl Hammarberg-Åkesson, Bengt Emil Johnson and part of Öyvind Fahlström's production. The main thing for these poets, Håkanson writes (1966: 11), is *not*

> the material chosen to create an impression in the reader/viewer, or which of his senses the poet appeals to, but rather the mere fact that some kind of impression is made and that this impression is as rich and varied as possible.

These poems freely combine traits from Weaver's categories of visual, kinetic, and auditive poetry, and deliberately go against everything in the way of purity. In Fahlström's words, what is sought for is, instead of esthetic perfection, the highest degree of *impurity*. The linguistic sensual poem is not meant to be comprehended as a unified whole. In this perspective it appears as an unusual kind of hybrid.

According to Leif Nylén (1966: 64), one cannot deny that, in spite of the similarities in the wish to counteract the transparency in normal use of language by focusing on the material aspect and making it more independent, there are also crucial differences between Fahlström and Gomringer (the latter seen by Nylén as the father of "purist" Concrete poetry):

> Gomringer aspires to a rational, "objective," mathematical and technologically inspired art, a cool and harmonious purism that could even be called classicism. Fahlström's poetry follows a tradition of romanticism, demoniacal and boundless subjectivity, expressionism. The free "a-synthetic," "non-descriptive" principle is to Gomringer a neutral basis, an emotionally indifferent point of departure. To Öyvind Fahlström it is still largely a gesture experienced as an emotional "deformation."

In a similar manner, but expanding the discussion to a larger perspective, an article by the critic Gunnar Hagberg outlines two tendencies in the development of literature. One is based on empirical facts soberly noted: Realism – Naturalism – *nouveau roman* – the new simplicity (a type of Swedish poetry parallel in time to that of Concrete poetry). The other tendency is mystical, romantic, and visionary. Hagberg puts Swedish Concrete poetry at the end of this line of development, following the chain Plato – medieval mysticism – Romanticism – Rimbaud – Mallarmé – psychoanalysis – Surrealism – Ekelöf. Björn Håkanson joins the same line of thinking in his abovementioned text, when, among the predecessors of linguistic sensualism, he mentions the romantic Swedish poets Carl Jonas Love Almqvist with his series of "Songes" and Gustaf Fröding with his poem "Vallarelåt."

The two contrasting views of Swedish Concrete poetry that have been discerned above both have their foundation in the actual works by Fahlström and his followers. They clearly mirror the dualism between methodical constructivism and romanticism existing in Swedish Concrete poetry from its very start. Dividing poets into categories as being "methodical" or "linguistic sensualists" may increase the understanding of their poetry. At the same time one must be aware of the danger of looking at these categories as existing side by side without overlapping.

The linguistic sensual poem generally retains many of the constructivist qualities. Öyvind Fahlström's example makes out an instructive case. Some of his poems in *Bord-dikter* show a clear emphasis on the "objective" and constructivist tendency, concentrated on the use of method. The manifesto "Hätila ragulpr på fåtskliaben" contains an account of various structures and principles possible to use in the creation of Concrete poetry, and the use of rules is a general trait in Fahlström's work. But while he resembles Gomringer in the adherence to self-imposed rules, it is worth noting that most of his poems nonetheless convey the feeling of a highly charged and highly individual temperament, miles away from the perfection and calm of Gomringer. Thus, in the majority of the Fahlström poems the methodical traits co-exist with subjective, mystical, and expressive tendencies. The poet cannot or will not cut off the flow of the romantic-expressive stream, the linguistic sensualism, that characterizes so much of Swedish Concrete poetry.

As far as I can see, in the Swedish body of Concrete poetry, the more purist poetry is the exception, while it is the linguistic sensual tendency, with its vivacious spirit, that dominates, marking the activities of the movement as a whole. The fact that it also seems to give Swedish Concrete poetry its profile in an international comparison is another reason to take a closer look at this form of poetry, its special traits and its way of making an impact on the reader/viewer.

Due to the lack of space I will have to restrict myself in this text to one single example. I choose to look closer at an excerpt from a poem by Öyvind Fahlström called "Det stora och det lilla" ("The big and the little"), which was written in 1953 but not published until 1966 in the volume *Bord-dikter*. There is no existing English version of this poem, but hopefully my own rough translations will be of some help. "Det stora och det lilla" is a poem that offers a vivid example of the personal style of the Swedish nestor in the field. It also makes use of methods and shows patterns, many of which are suggested in

hastam hapar hava hetten höför haatt   håfå histi hacka huupp hänä
hooch håhå heller hisin hoko hifi hatta   håhå harda here^hasan huur hahaj hobot
hotjo hacka here   hastaaae hööa
tack karlar   karlar om världar   ljud av badkar som talar
med ljud av brassande våningar och myskdoftande falkar hängande-i kategorier om benen
konst salami två-tre karlar livs   marginal   konst tack två-tre svankig livs   marginal
           hajboet   kofittor
    cko cko cka cky cko cko cky cko cko cko cky cko cko cko cky
ur sina syner uppstår handelsmän för att göra hårda arbeten i livets tjänst
       och talar med hajar för att se vem de talar med
         står på en rasande primitiv matta
cko cko cke cka cka cke cki cki cki cka cka   stigande fallande
                                         skala

       med stjärnornas väldiga vo
      vo ly mma ssor buk tan de un der si na
     hu vu den hu vu den hu vu den hu vu den

mbo med skärnornas väldiga volummassor bultande under huvudet som björkris
     står han på sin a sis ta fri a fri mär ken fylls med buk tan de läsk pa pper
     för att bä ra hans o er hört ly hör da långa buk ta lan de lung or

cko cko cka cky cko cko cky cko cko cko cky cko cko cko cky

tack karlar
tack karlar garvarkluns som ett lik med ett köttben i munnen
cka-ka-cka
cka-ka-cka

min hjärna håller klockan med ett fast grepp
den är Massif Central överallt och där det finns tid och och luft
andra förändras oftare än garvare
garvarkung ett hårt slag med trum-
han sattes ner på havsbotten pinne mot trumpinne
så ljuva ja-andra-ma hajar försvinner med staga-
des med linor
klocka

Öyvind Fahlström, "Det stora och det lilla" [fragment]

Fahlström's manifesto – patterns that recur also in works by other poets of the Concretist group. I hope therefore, through the Fahlström poem, to be able to point out some of the main general tendencies in Swedish Concrete poetry, in order to give some guidelines on its ways of functioning in a larger view.

What are the characteristics of Swedish linguistic sensualism? As we shall see, the *extended* poem as a poetic form plays a vital role in creating the means for a vast elaboration of the visual and auditive rhythms and dynamics in the linguistic material. The redundance of material in this kind of poem also heightens the semantic intricacy, and all these elements put together vouch for an overall impression of sensual density, a point to which I will return in the closing comment. First, in the following section, I will examine some of the different aspects of the Fahlström poem one at a time, in an attempt to make a complex discussion as lucid as possible.

Special Traits of Linguistic Sensual Concrete Poetry

... the extended poem as a poetic form

If we bear in mind a visual memory of the Concrete poetry of Gomringer or the Brazilian Noigandres group – both early and internationally influential founders of the field – the different lengths of the Swedish linguistic-sensual poems may be their most striking trait. These poems do not only cover one entire page. One single poem, or a suite of poems, usually even extends over several pages. For instance, Fahlström's extended poem "Det stora och det lilla" covers no less than 16 pages. This extended form has not come about by chance – on the contrary, Leif Nylén sees this as a trait that is common not only to the genre of Concrete poetry, but to new Swedish poetry of the 60s in general (Håkanson & Nylén 1966: 14).

There are of course several objections to be made against the length of the extended poems. One difficulty is seen in my very choice of example. It is in most cases – especially in a context such as the present one – impossible to reproduce the poem in extenso. Cutting out a part of the poem naturally leads to a diminished impact. A more essential criticism is perhaps that a poem covering several pages is much more difficult to get a grasp of. This is especially important in poems where the visual shape is a vital component in the reader's impression.

The reader of Fahlström's, Bengt Emil Johnson's or Jarl Hammarberg-Åkesson's extended poems cannot possibly retain a simultaneous memory of the poem as a whole, which he/she can generally do with Gomringer's poems, for instance. Certainly most of Gomringer's poems are not to be perceived as static pictures, but have important rhythmic and dynamic characteristics. Still, the limited extension of the actual material renders the impression of controllable order, even when these rhythms and systems of transformations mentally suggest an eternal continuation. In this regard the "purist" poem has a potential function as an object of meditation, which the longer linguistic sensual poem lacks. The developing rhythmic patterns found there never even *seem* graspable to the reader/viewer, it is as if they are in a continous process of expansion, only repeatedly disrupted (or reinforced, whichever way we want to see it) by the turning of pages.

When Fahlström chose to call his new poetic form "Concrete poetry," he was inspired not only by Concrete visual art. Another and equally important source of inspiration was Concrete music, which, pioneered by Pierre Schaeffer, had gained ground in the 50s. The basis of Concrete, "direct" music is recorded auditive objects from everyday life: traffic and street noises, fragments of conversations, sneezes and so on. These sounds were manipulated in the recording studio and joined together in a kind of auditive collage. This procedure was seen by Fahlström as parallel to his own solidifying, "kneading" and rhythmization of language.

But when, in his manifesto, Öyvind Fahlström speaks about the possibilities of rhythmization, he does not only refer to the phonetic potential in language. All levels of expression in a poem can be worked on rhythmically and dynamically. The visual aspect as well retains a great importance in this kind of Concrete poetry.

Fahlström himself never clearly explained his concept of rhythm. For myself, when in the following I use this term in connection with the different aspects of the poem (the visual/acoustic/thematic), it denotes in all instances a way of structuring the material. This is achieved through varying and repeating elements, a method which influences the act of perception – the speed and intensity of reading, the degree of the reader's involvement in this act – on a physical, emotional and/or intellectual level.

... visual rhythm and dynamics

In spite of the already mentioned impossibility of getting a simultaneous overview of a linguistic sensual poem like Fahlström's, there are *parts* of the poem which must be visually experienced (thus defining the poem as belonging to Weaver's category of "visual poetry"). The non-traditional visual structure forms the basis of a "verbi-visual" (iconic) function.

Looking at the reproduced example from "Det stora och det lilla" we find some lines about "buktande volymmassor," "buktalande lungor," and "buktande läskpapper" (curving voluminous masses, ventriloquist lungs, and a curving blotting paper). These lines themselves are shaped in a curving form. At the same time the lines visually correspond to the bundle of "björkris" (birch twigs), another semantic element. The lower lines of the poem also have a very special visual appearance. By their spreading form they create associations with themes touched upon earlier in the poem: "ljud av brassande våningar" (sounds of apartments firing away), "ljud av badkar som talar" (sounds of bathtubs talking) – in each case the idea of sounds spreading. The word "munnen" (the mouth) to the left of the diverging lines becomes significant as the source of the spreading noise, when the poem is read in this manner. The sound of drumsticks also belongs to these auditive associations. One of the spreading lines goes like this: "garvarkung ett hårt slag trumpinne mot trumpinne" (king of the tanners a hard blow drumstick against drumstick). The explosive visual form of this part of the poem becomes iconic. The whole unit may lead the reader's thoughts to the hard sound of a blow, while the oblong forms of each line resemble the drumsticks themselves.

A different type of "verbi-visual" interaction, one that might be called "reading dynamic," is created when the structure of the poem causes a reading where the reader's eyes move in a way that corresponds to temporal and dynamic qualities in the semantic content itself. This is the case for example in the well-known poem "wind" by Gomringer (1960). There, the manifold paths of the reading resemble the whirling movements of the wind itself. A similar kind of iconicity may be discovered if we return to Fahlström's poem. The same spreading lines of his poem, which we have been talking about, also offer this kind of "verbi-visual" reading. If we choose to start our associations with the concept "klocka" (clock/watch), appearing there twice, these lines may turn into the hands of a watch, ticking onwards and moving at the same speed as the reader moves his eyes to the next line. The word "tid" (time) also appears in one of these lines.

Besides this type of reading-dynamic iconicity, in most linguistic sensual poems we also find rhythmic and dynamic qualities in the visual material that do *not* correspond to any specific theme of association, but have a vaguer and more independent function, conducing to the overall atmosphere of the poem. This rhythm does not necessarily work merely mechanically, by means of the reader's eye movement, as in the examples we have just seen; it may just as well arise through the reader's more or less conscious registration of variations and repeated elements in the visual material. But the dynamic impression is of course reinforced by the reader's actual movement over and between the pages. This is reminiscent of the category of Concrete poetry that Weaver calls "kinetic," based as it is on a serial succession.

If, for example, we leaf through the pages of "Det stora och det lilla," we find a rich spatial and rhythmic variation of a sprawling character. The poem is made up of words grouped together – verses of a sort, with varying size, concentration and complexity. Some elements, for instance small compact verses in the margins, recur several times, but not in any regular manner. Visually, this extended poem is put together fairly loosely as a whole. We get the feeling that it is caught in a high speed process of alternation, constantly changing appearances.

It is not until we start looking at the words themselves or the combinations of letters, that we find a certain unity in the poem. Some of the elements at this level reappear time after time throughout the poem. Even in the short part reproduced here we may discern this tendency. The beginning is for instance dominated by words beginning with an "h," later we find three times a line made up of the combination of the letters "ck" and a vowel, and so on.

The repetition of typographical elements or of words and syllables leads to a visual rhythmization closely associated to the auditive rhythm. This phonetic rhythm may at times be even more dominant than the purely visual one.

... auditive rhythm and dynamics
Several of Öyvind Fahlström's poems are meant to be read aloud, which is often the case with the Swedish linguistic sensual Concrete poetry. Some of the poems in the *Bord-dikter* collection are provided with instructions such as "line in bold type to be hummed" and "line with spaced-out letters to be hummed like a marching tune." In the part of "Det stora och det lilla" reproduced here we find the words "stigande fallande skala" (rising and falling tone). These words are part of the text, but may also function as directions for an auditive rendering of the poem.

The auditive structure of a poem is of course not only applied in the form of superficial appendices such as reading instructions or typographical variations; it is also a built-in quality of its language. Fahlström's composition is apparently methodical, using systems described in his own manifesto. By all these methods Fahlström tries to emphasize the auditive dimension of the text in order to create a beneficial resistance to easy reading. Repetition may be the most important of these methods, on the auditive as well as on the visual level. Fahlström does not, like some of his followers, work mainly with complete words. He often lets "kneaded," permuted words create rhythms in the text. The lines consisting of "ck" plus a vowel, already mentioned in connection with visual rhythms, are of course equally able to create auditive patterns.

The permutations of the words in Fahlström's poem are not wholly random. In some parts of the example foreign sounds have been inserted between syllables. Syllables or phonemes have also been switched around in a word, between words, or between lines. We also find an "h" plus a vowel and some other elements from earlier parts of the poem, contaminating and infiltrating into the first lines reproduced here. The sequence "hastam hapar hava hetten höför haatt håfå histi hacka huupp hänä hasan" can, if the foreign contamination is removed, be read as "stampar vatten för att få sticka upp näsan" (treads water to be able to get his nose up).

Yet another method mentioned by Fahlström in his manifesto is the use of a "logic of verbal similarity." According to this logic the relationships between words are based on an auditive similarity and not on normal, logical, semantic causality. Fahlström compares this method to associative systems of so-called primitive peoples, of children and of insane people. (He might also have mentioned the Dadaists.) For instance, it is the verbal similarity logic that gives rise to the development "buktande-bultande-buktande-buktalande" (bulging-beating-bulging-ventriloquist speaking), in lines 15, 17, 18 and 19 of our example.

These examples have shown that the auditive aspect is used to a great extent in the Swedish linguistic sensual movement. The acoustic structure of this kind of poem tends to be very intricate, as was the case with the visual elaboration of the text. The complexity is due to the multitude of rules, but also to their application to the rich language material of the extended poem. Instead of the rules being used in a clear and consistent manner, they are mixed together, creating a wild, unpredictable melting pot.

A good deal of the value of this type of poem lies in "verbivocovisual" interplay (a term frequently used by the Noigandres poets). Recitation alone for instance, apart from ruining the experience of engaging both eye and ear in itself, would also mean limiting the reader's chance of active participation in the choice of reading sequence and reading direction. A possible way of making use both of the visual and the auditive qualities of a poem is the reader's own slow, exploring recitation, or articulating but silent reading, while looking at the text. This way of reading will in my opinion lead to the most rewarding experiences.

Already at this stage we have been able to note that our example contains traits from all the three categories of Concrete poetry suggested by Weaver: the visual, the kinetic and the auditive category. All these aspects of language are being employed, turning the linguistic sensual Concrete poem into a highly explosive compound. Yet so far, we have not examined the semantic aspect of the poem, which is also elaborated into a complex structure by the Swedish Concretists.

... semantical structure
The linguistic sensualist poets work towards the same goals as the Concretists in general. They want to direct the attention of the receiver to language as an object, and make language free from conventional unambiguous referentiality through its emancipation from normal regular grammar, syntax, and logic. The main purpose of these manipulations, occurring simultaneously at all levels, is

to bring about a maximally rich and intense experience in the reader/viewer. Cutting loose from the normal way of using language in order to create an even richer way of communication is not an easy task. The resulting Concrete poems, both purist and linguistic sensual, have often been blamed by critics for going too far in semantic reduction. According to the critics, the content of the poem has been diminished to such an extent that its value disappears and the poem becomes worthless.

How one experiences a poem is of course a strictly individual matter. It is evident that many Concrete poems demand an enormous effort from the reader in order to function and create a rich experience. Semantic reduction is not, however – contrary to what is sometimes proposed – a goal in itself in Concrete poetry. This is made clear by its Swedish representatives, who never intend to deny the conventional meaning of the words. Fahlström has often felt misunderstood and forced to defend himself on this point. "I always speak about *language* as a concrete matter. Language is a store of conceptions tied to 'random' phonetic signs," Fahlström (1961: 28) writes.

In the case of Gomringer's and the Noigandres group's shorter constellation-like poems, it might be correct to say that the semantic element has been reduced, insofar as the poem is formed by an extremely limited material – often not more than a couple of words. But still Gomringer (1960, unpaged) comments that "the purpose of reduced language is not the reduction of language itself, but the achievement of greater flexibility and freedom of communication."

Obviously these poets, just like Fahlström, hope to give the single textual element greater importance and independence when it is emancipated from the limiting structure of normal syntactic and referential logic. In the free structure of Concrete poetry, where no prearranged pattern exists to guide and limit the experience, each word is given more scope for all its qualities – the visual and auditive qualities as well as the semantically associative ones. The content of the poem is thus not diminished, but rather extended. (This is further discussed in a study by Eric Vos from 1992.)

To generate this growth of fruitful associations from the relationships between the visual, auditive and semantic material, all these aspects must to a certain extent be structured – we have already discussed the first two. When it comes to the alternative *semantic* treatment, there are several methods proposed by Öyvind Fahlström in his manifesto and realized in his works. Some of these methods tend to break the poem apart rather than to unify it. The methods described by Fahlström are mainly intended to create a new experience far from the ordinary routines. Certain methods imply quasi-scientific regulations and may be seen as belonging to the "methodical" tendency within Swedish Concretism. Fahlström mentions for instance the possibility of forcing the reader to remain attentive by forming new words or by making old words take on new meanings. The play with homonyms also has an intellectual flavor – in the poem reproduced, there is for example the case "karlar" - "badkar/.../som talar" (blokes - bathtubs/.../that speak).

There are, however, other methods that must be seen as more characteristic of linguistic sensualism, since they are based rather on intuition and the use of emotional tools. Fahlström advocates the inclusion of words that are seldom used poetically – words that may have an everyday tone or that are generally considered banal or even repulsive. The contrasts heighten the effect of the poem. In the fragment reproduced from "Det stora och det lilla" Fahlström uses several unpoetic words – everyday words like "salami," "stamp," or "pork chops" or more formal words such as "categories," "marginal," and "traders" – side by side with poetical words such as "the stars" or "bottom of the sea." He also shocks the reader without hesitation by using really disgusting words such as "cow's cunts."

The contrast between the words in Fahlström's poetry is present not only in stylistics but also in content. Even though his manifesto makes little of Surrealism as a source of inspiration, there is in many poems an evident influence from Surrealism and its way of estranging a motive by creating new connections between objects and events. (Fahlström in fact had a period of Surrealist writing in his youth, before turning to Concrete poetry.) A line such as "falcons smelling of musk hanging in categories around your legs" (line 6), creates a vivid and surprising mental picture with a surrealistic, dreamlike character. In sentences such as this one Fahlström may allow himself to use correct syntax: the contradictions are found in the content. The fact that in certain parts of a poem Fahlström makes some motifs appear in readable sentences obviously does *not* give any guarantee as to any logic and "meaning" in the poem. A similar method frequently used by the linguistic sensual poets is the creation of new words by linking different semantic components that may give rise to many associations, but the meanings of which are uncertain.

So far we have not run into any semantic arrangements that contribute to the unification of the content of a poem. On the contrary, we have seen a conscious effort to create a wide and contrasting scope of associations. An extended poem would, however, not function at all if every element were absolutely independent and separate. The number of associations would be too great and impossible to handle. There must by necessity exist some kind of unifying structure.

In spite of the lack of complete logical chains, and in spite of the above-mentioned semantic manifoldness, the extended poem does allow a kind of theme to develop. This is due to the associative and integrating participation of the reader. The thematic aspect of the poem is difficult to describe and analyze. One reason is of course that it spreads over several pages which may not all be reproduced here. Another and more important reason is that what we are dealing with here is a non-discursive web of mementoes, whose interpretation is wholly dependent on each reader's personal, integrating, and intuitive associations, in which the visual, auditive and semantic aspects are finally inseparable.

The Fahlström poem "Det stora och det lilla" oscillates between objectivity and great intimacy in a very specific and personal style. It is permeated by a pattern of rhythmically returning themes of association that creates a repetitional structure. The temporal aspect of the poem – its sense of development – is contradicted by this repetition of content. Time and time again Fahlström returns to the same strangely hallucinatory motifs and expressions: "havet," "hajar," "hajbon," "hästar," "gelé," and so on (the sea, sharks, shark nests, horses, jelly) – it seems crazy and is crazy. Much of this could surely be seen as having sprung from unconscious instincts in the Freudian sense, though Fahlström himself hated all such psychologism. In some parts of the poem the sexual and perverted tone is quite obvious, in parts where a "he" and a "she" are mentioned together with words such as "het," "sväller," "mysk" (hot, swelling, musk). As noted in the section on the auditive aspect of Concrete poetry, Fahlström's poem also contains repeated auditive sequences that may be conceived as wild human groans and yells – this is really no poem for the drawing-room! It is impossible to reproduce the meaning of this poem in discursive words. (Reading the whole poem as a description of intercourse would surely be an exaggeration.) The only certain thing is that all aspects of the poem are combined in a brutal expression of a somewhat paranoid, highly charged experience.

Other examples of linguistic sensual Swedish Concrete poetry go even further, when it comes to narrativity and unifying traits. Jarl Hammarberg-Åkesson (1970: 66), one of the most important Swedish Concrete poets, and one of the few still active as such today, describes his endeavours to supply

the conditions for the reader's being able to experience the poem as a kind of "story." This may happen through descriptions of event and actions, but also through things happening to the word and to the text (words part, are stuck onto each other and mixed together in various ways and so on).

To a greater extent than Fahlström and most of the acknowledged Concrete poets, Hammarberg-Åkesson's poetry contains a basic structure of surveyable and unifying logic. His poems are not possible to translate discursively, yet his way of expressing himself is closer to normal language than Concrete poetry usually is.

The Overall Impression of Linguistic Sensual Concrete Poetry

In this final comment on the overall impression of linguistic sensual Concrete poetry, it is inevitable to get back to the earlier mentioned links to the romantic-expressive poetical tradition. While in the methodical or purist poem the "human touch" often seems to be wholly absent from the text, in the linguistic sensual poem there is no such strive for objectivity. The most obvious hint at this is the fact that we can sometimes find a subjective "I" in this kind of poem – as in the phrase "min hjärna håller klockan med ett fast grepp" (my brain is holding the clock in a tight grip) in Fahlström's poem – but, as we will see, the feeling of human presence is deeper rooted than that in the poem.

Sometimes the poem as a whole appears to be a kind of imprint of a mental "situational flow," impossible to comprehend and structure at an intellectual level. In this view it seems to come close to the technique of *écriture automatique* used by the surrealists, but the linguistic sensualist poet does not claim to be *true* to himself or anyone else – on the contrary he always manipulates the material expression in a most conscious manner, shaping it, kneading it and changing it, before handing it on to the reader for his or her *own use*. The lacking structures of logic and syntax are replaced by alternative structures in the material, and the deliberate obviousness, but yet complexity, of these very structures prevent the reader from passively abandoning him/herself to the text, forcing him/her to be an independent and actively participating subject. Instead of just mediating the poet's experience the purpose is to make the reader create his/her own "mental flow," and feel that the poem is "happening" here and now.

What the poet is doing, in other words, is to use tools and rules as and when he chooses in order to create a good starting-point for the reader's own exploration of a rich and redundant material. He shapes language at the visual, acoustic, and semantic levels, and in these structuring activities he lets his temperament and emotions play an important part. We have noted the sprawling, energetic, and chaotic temperament in the visual and auditive dynamics of the Fahlström poem, a temperament that also characterizes the semantic aspect, with all its disorganization and heated sexual strain. Thus, it is this – the feeling and atmosphere of the poem – that is its most important unifying factor. Nylén (1964: 27-28) speaks about Swedish Concrete poetry as "handwritten," saying that

> even if it does not immediately reproduce anything outside its words, even if it is without a correlate, it still develops as an expression of movement in language. Within the poem characteristic forms and movements arise, a way of discovering and using language that leaves the imprint of a certain individual, a poet's personality.

The lingering impression of the linguistic sensual Concrete poem, then, is one of emotional density, closely related to the (indirect) personal imprint of the author. This also forms the basis of the "romanticist expressionism" of this current of Swedish Concrete poetry, a poetry in which the author does not have to constrain himself – he creates his wild poetical hybrid and lets it expand and grow out over all the pages needed to create the right density. The length of the poem is of course an important condition for the rebellion he is undertaking against every kind of limiting convention.

The extended linguistic sensual poem of the kind that this paper has dealt with dominated the Swedish poetry of the 60s in this field – a field that Öyvind Fahlström initiated and named "Concrete poetry" already in 1954. This poetry indeed seems quite original, and it certainly adds some strong and colorful threads to the rich material of the international web of Concrete poetry.

Bibliography

Fahlström, Öyvind
1954   "Hätila ragulpr på fåtskliaben, manifest för konkret poesi." In: *Odyssé*,
        no. 2-3, 12-19. [Also included in the author's *Bord-dikter*. Solt (1970)
        offers an English version.]
1961   "Bris," in *Rondo*, no. 3, 24-32.
1966   *Bord-dikter 1952-55*. Stockholm, Bonniers.
Gomringer, Eugen
1960   *33 konstellationen*. St Gallen, Tschudy Verlag.
Hagberg, Gunnar
1964   "Sanningskravet i dikten." In: *Göteborgstidningen*, 15 September, 2.
Hammarberg-Åkesson, Jarl
1970   *Brev från Jarl*. Stockholm, Bonniers.
Håkanson, Björn & Leif Nylén, eds.
1966   *Nya linjer. Lyrik från 60-talet*. Stockholm, Bonniers.
Nylén, Leif
1964   "Textrealism." In: *Rondo*, no. 3-4, 26-31.
1966   "I denna fördömda liljebrasa (topp-timm)." In: *Bonniers Litterära
        Magasin*, no. 6, 64-66.
Solt, Mary Ellen
1970   *Concrete Poetry: A World View*. Baltimore & London, Indiana UP.
        [1968]

Vos, Eric
  1992   *Concrete Poetry as a Test Case for a Nominalistic Semiotics of Verbal Art.* Diss. University of Amsterdam.
Weaver, Mike
  1966   "Concrete Poetry." In: *The Lugano Review*, vol. 1, no. 5-6, 100-108.

AFTERIMAGES:
REVOLUTION OF THE (VISIBLE) WORD

Marjorie Perloff

In 1965, Ian Hamilton Finlay wrote to Ernst Jandl, "I am not considered to be a poet here ... [M]ostly, Scotch poets ... like to think they are *thinkers*, full of very *serious* thoughts about *serious* matters ... but 'thought' is not *intelligence*, and one *image* against another, can create something more subtle than thought." And he added, "[A]lmost any Scottish poem of the present is offered to one as a comment on life, an aid, an extension, etc. ... Hence we get inane critical remarks like: 'X has something to say' (which actually means, X's poems are crammed with jargon, about politics, hunger, Scotland, his love-life, or whatever). The notion that 'something to say' is actually a *modulation of the material* scarcely enters anyone's head" (Finlay 1994: 11-12).

The reference here is probably to Hugh MacDiarmid's notorious dismissal of Finlay's experiments in Concrete poetry as having "nothing in common with what down the centuries, despite all changes, has been termed 'poetry'" (MacDiarmid 1984: 703). Extreme as this sounds, it is still very much the Establishment attitude to a poetics that takes the visual (or aural) dimension of language as seriously as its semantic one. Even the more "advanced" poetry anthologies like Paul Hoover's *Postmodern American Poetry* and Douglas Messerli's *From the Other Side of the Century: A New American Poetry 1960-1990* do not include Concrete poetry like Finlay's, perhaps because such texts would be too expensive to reproduce side by side with more "normal" linear poems. The result, in any case, is that visual poetics has become largely the domain of the museum – the exhibition of artist's books, installations, art objects, laser works, and so on – rather than of the poetry world.

But there are signs that things are changing. For even as Finlay and his fellow Concretists are dismissed as "*not* poets," we are witnessing a quiet revolution of the visible word. The innovations of the Concrete poetry movements of the Fifties in Europe and especially in Brazil are now entering the poetic mainstream. Small presses like *tailspin, meow, leavebooks* – all three of these from the Buffalo Graduate Program in Poetics – are turning out dozens of visual and even tactile chapbooks like Kenneth Sherwood's *TEXT squared*, Michael Basinski's *SleVep*, and C. S. Giscombe's *Two Sections from Giscome Road*, not to mention the electronic transmission of texts via *RIF/T*, which now has a thousand subscribers. From Susan Howe's dramatically charged typography in *Articulations of Sound Forms in Time* (Awede, 1987) and *Eikon Basilike* (1989), to Christian Bök's "fractal" poems and poetic fractals in *Crystallography: Book I of Information Theory* (Coach House Press), to Johanna Drucker's desktop production of the computer-generated and hand-painted *Narratology* (both 1994), "one image against another" is "creat[ing] something more subtle than thought," as Ian Hamilton Finlay put it.

Meanwhile, Finlay's own particular tradition is being carried on by his son Alec's publication of Morning Star Folios. These are collaborations between artists and poets, published since 1990 in annual series of four issues.[1] At the outset, the folios tended to keep the verbal, visual, and even musical media distinct, as in *Heiligenstadt*, Friedericke Mayröcker's 1978 poem, illustrated by Wes Christensen's painting *An Mein Herz* (1987) and packaged with the score to Brahms's *Intermezzo*, which is the key to the poet's narrative. But soon Finlay was bringing together artists and poets who seemed naturally in sync, as in the case of Robert Creeley and Sol Le Witt (Fifth Series). A beautiful little folio juxtaposes, on its vertical front panels, a Le Witt abstract design in black and white with Creeley's poem "Echo," which begins "Find our way out / no doubts / or in / again begin." The panels then open to reveal on the recto another composition (c. 15" square) by Le Witt, a hexagonal maze that is the perfect visual "echo" of Creeley's poem, especially the stanza "Spaces wait / faced / in the dark / no waste."

The same series contains Ian Stephen's and Will Maclean's witty and charming artist's book *A Semblance of Steerage*. The only non-verbal image here is Maclean's semi-abstract cover drawing of a stylized rudder, captioned "*you learn to trust the keel that's under you*." But can we so trust? The eight accordion pages that follow each have three bands of text (top, middle, bottom of page). The top band is a one-line title (e.g. "RUDDER *for a* Mirror," "RUDDER *in teak*," "SEAN'S TILLER," "BEN'S RUDDER," "RUDDER to share"). The center of each page has a little free-verse poem, usually in the form of a proposition, as in

a semblance of steering
provides procedure

or:

an offcut rudder:
counterbalanced curves
for a wee keel

where "counterbalanced" describes the intricate sound structuring – itself a "semblance of steering" – of /k/ and /iy/ phonemes. The bottom band provides a kind of commentary on the other two: for example, the lineated text above is followed by a sentence in italics with justified margins: "(*this rudder, claimed by my son as it fell from another rudder under construction, has not yet found a vessel*)." But on the final page, the page has only a top and center band:

SKIN *of varnish*

**the sheen that seals the finish
on the diving blade**

where the pun on "finish" provides an apt conclusion to the book's nautical fantasy. The "diving blade" is what remains.

In Series 5/2 (April 1994), Alec Finlay gives us a remarkable collaboration between the Chilean poet Cécilia Vicuña and the Scottish Edwin Morgan called "**PALABRAR**mas / **WURDWAPPIN**schaw." The work consists of two square (5") pamphlets, the first containing an explanatory letter Vicuña wrote to "Eck" (Alec Finlay) together with a glossary and short poetic fragments. As the glossary suggests, Morgan provides the Scottish equivalents to Vicuña's Spanish paragrams. Thus the title "PALABRARmas," an elaborate paragram on the power of the poet's words ("palabra" = "word", "labrar" = "to work", "armas" = "arms", "más" = "more"), becomes, in a sly variant of the complex original, "WURDWAPPINschaw" (word weapon-show). Or again, the frontispiece couplet, quite formal in its articulation – "*Las palabras desean hablar / y eschucharlas es la primera labor!*" – becomes the down-to-earth "*Wurds wahnt tae spik! / Lisn! thon's yer furst wurk.*"

Vicuña's letter to Eck, partly written in short prose paragraphs, partly in phrasal units, separated by small cruciform designs, deserves to be cited at some length:

> In the Mayan letters Olson speaks of 'their leavings', (what the Maya left), but in Spanish 'sus dejos' would be 'their way of speaking', the delicate manner in which a mother speaks to her child when no one is listening, a form of being in sound ...
>
> And it is the double aspect of this 'leaving' that interests me, the fact that it is practical (utilitarian) and transcendent (full of other possibilities) at the same time.
>
> This is how I see our own words. Perhaps because I see Spanish from the point of

view of Quechua, and vice-versa, a word for me in any language is multidimen-
sional, and is charged with 'hidden meanings' as we can see ...

Vicuña's real obsession with verbal "leavings," she explains, began in London
in 1974, where she was living in exile after Pinochet's military coup. "This
time it was a new set of words":

> ver dad
> dad ver
> (truth: to give sight)

And she explains:

> Edwin Morgan's translations (so close to cons te llation,
> *latir* is the beating of the heart)
> is more than a trans
> it is an installation in the language of poetry.

"More than a trans": this surely is the point. Open the second folio and you
find, on facing pages, the words:

> **co**n**razón**   **her**ich**t**

Delete the "n" from "Con razón" ("with reason") and you have "corazón"
("heart") – an echo, perhaps, of Pascal's "The heart has its reasons," as well
as a representation of the familiar opposition of heart to head. In Morgan's
Scottish version, the "hert" ("heart") contains within itself that which is
"right." But the isolation of "ich" "(German 'I') personalizes that heart, even
as "her   t" points back to Vicuña. But then her paragram isolates the "co,"
suggesting that these poets are truly collaborators. Not a translation, as Vicuña
has said, but a "constellation" or "installation" in the language of poetry.
    Succeeding pairs like "**pen**sar / **pa**i**ense**" (with their play on "think,"
"sorrow," and "weight") carry on the poetic dialogue. And Morgan has an
uncanny way of letting the Scots dialect draw out the implications in the
Spanish words. On the final pages, Vicuña's

> **per**mite
> el **dón**

with its installation of "pardon" in the midst of gift-giving, finds a nice echo
in Morgan's

gie
for
gie

where the "gie" ("give"), repeated twice, takes precedence over the need for forgiveness. Where Vicuña stresses the need for "perdón," Morgan's response stresses the gift itself. A gift evidently "for" the reader.

If Vicuña and Morgan are still producing a fairly pure Concrete poetry, most visual writing today – I am thinking of Bruce Andrews or bpNichol, Karen Mac Cormack or Susan Howe – uses the resources of spacing and typography, phonetic spelling, rebus, and paragram so as to contest the status of language as a bearer of uncontaminated meanings and to question the one-way linear flow between poet and reader. In this sense, visual constellation (the lamination of the paradigmatic onto the syntagmatic axis) can produce what Steve McCaffery has called a "carnivalization of the semantic order." A stunning example of such "language graphics" is Joan Retallack's new book *AFTERRIMAGES*, whose very title ("AFTER" + "RIM" + "AGES") announces the possibilities latent in the most ordinary of words.

Newton, Retallack reminds us in her frontispiece, citing a reference in the OED, "suffered for many years from an after-image of the sun caused by incautiously looking at it through a telescope." But, speaking in the voice of her phonetic alter ego "Genre Tallique," the poet revises this linear Newtonian notion: "We tend to think of afterimages as aberrations. In fact all images are after. That is the terror they hold for us." Indeed, *after* – as in Wallace Stevens's "I do not know which to prefer / The beauty of inflections / Or the beauty of innuendoes, / the blackbird whistling / or just after," a passage which becomes, in Retallack's scheme of things, "*After* whistling or just_____" – is a basic, perhaps the basic "form of life" today, where ever image, event, speech, or citation can be construed as an "afterthought" or "aftershock" of something that has always already occurred. Hence Retallack's witty example (on the same page) from the Manhattan Project physicist Victor Weisskopff, who recalls that the explosion of the first atomic bomb was accompanied by a Tchaikovsky waltz, coincidentally being broadcast by a nearby radio station.

The *AFTERRIMAGES* sequence which gives the book its title has 34 pages, no two of which look alike. Each page serves as a kind of afterimage for the other, the lamination of citations from Chaucer's *Canterbury Tales*, from the notebooks of Leonardo da Vinci, Ovid's *Metamorphoses*, Lilly C. Stone's *English Sports and Recreations*, or from "Genre Tallique" herself, creating a set tantalizing "language graphics." Here is page 7:

vol low on radio • in Tangier

no smoke but smell of alarm

(see a pre-Socratic on fire in the mind)

nice being out here in the sun

(or St. Augustine on time)

±o = no future tense in dreams = o±
(poetry eludes genre as well)

sage of the ectopic eye

logical series of unsolicited occasions

_____

(see   i   in   e

        in   e   in

                    o

                    s w

        ec

        s

Ill. 1: Joan Retallack [from AFTERRIMAGES]

The poem's perspective is that of a "sage of the ectopic eye" (line 8). Displacement – again, afterimage – is the order of the day. "vol low on radio": the initial chiasmus followed by a rhyme, rather like the pop song that may be on the air, might be glossed by Wittgenstein's remark, in *Culture and Value*, that "Everything we see could also be otherwise." Fire (in Tangier? in the mind?) is announced not by smoke but by an alarm, the alarm gives rise not to sound but to smell, and the tenselessness of dreams and mathematical formula is, in a "logical series of unsolicited occasions," compared (in a tiny afterthought) to the genrelessness of poetry. And now, unsolicitated, the lines just proferred are written through (in the manner of John Cage, one of Retallack's chief mentors) to yield phonemic and morphemic after-echoes. The vowels *e*, *i*, and *o* are extracted from the displaced or "ectopic" eye in a spatial layout that makes seeing difficult. Then the "ec" is extracted as well, "topic" (not named) taking us back to the "topic" of pre-Socratics and Augustine above. But finally there is only the "s" of "unsolicited," and that "s" also attaches itself to "ec" in the preceding line to give us an X. "Unsolicited occasions," it seems, produce the most interesting new poetic formations.

Page 21, by contrast, has only a tiny morphemic afterimage – "s[   ]ent" with its visual reference to "silent":

---

your c u p i s l e a v i n g a r i n g o n *my* t a b l e

see RHYTHM and FORM p.5

(*Enna Labraid* etc.) quoted p.4, above,

translators note on the

fabled indifference of gods

here lies[   ]entire totem of body[   ]parts

silk pilfer nasturtium semiotic *ad sequitur*

see other *Italic Poetries* p.3

α) *H*yge sceal *heard*ra, *heorte* be cenre;

ß) (moping virgins [*versions*] of all genders [*genres*])

....

s[   ]ent

Ill. 2: Joan Retallack [from AFTERRIMAGES]

Here Retallack uses spacing and citation for effect: *"your* c u p i s l e a v i n g a r i n g o n *my* t a b l e" comically deflates the distinction (the obsession of two-year olds) between what's *yours* and what's *mine*. For one thing, if we're seated at my table drinking, say, tea, "your" cup is not really yours at all, because it comes from my set of dishes. Then too: "cupis" suggests "Cupid," "cupidity," "cupiscence," and so on. And cupidity is just what "you" are being accused of by the owner of the table. From here on the poem plays with mock reference, as in "RHYTHM and FORM," which might be the title of any one of a dozen handbooks on poetry, Old English saga and Latin verse, the language always running away from its source as in *"ad sequitur"* instead of non-sequitur, and the "moping virgins" – or are they "versions" – of gendres/ genres. There is always space for revision: the word "virgins," etymologically quite unrelated to "versions," does sound like it. Then, too, a virgin is known by someone's version of a particular woman's history. Might this *virgin* have *aversion* to sex? The message, in any case, has been "s[   ]ent."

Each of Retallack's poems plays with such versions, with the revisions of what she calls in one of her ideograms "c r e e p i n g l o g o p h i l i a" (p. 20). I conclude with a meditation on coincidence (p. 11; cf. Ill. 3).

Although she draws on remarkably varied sources (Chaucer, Mrs. Charles H. Gardner, the Vatican Library Book), all the "events" in Retallack's sequence go together; they really are a "thicket" (that etymologically rich word) of "CO...INCIDENTS." But the reader of the above poem can never know "what really happened"; Uncle Herbie's ominous "last words," for instance are followed by the line "but only one etc." where "one" (as opposed to "ten" in *"ten o'clock"* can refer to almost anything. Perhaps he only had "one hour to live" or even "one day"; perhaps "only one" person heard him, and so on ("etc."). William Carlos Williams wrote a poem called "The Geometry of Trees"; Retallack's poem refers to that title, embedding it in the phrase "nature's soft geometry." But line 7 also has an interesting repeat: "nature's soft" is grammatically like "geometry's trees," with the further anagram on *ress* and *strees*, two morphemes whose juxtaposition produces the afterimage *stress*.

"Strees" seems to contain the "riddle of the three sleeves." And that riddle actually makes good common sense: nature has a rinse cycle, culture a spin cycle. But what is it that comes out of this washing machine? Another "thicket" in the form of "TIGHT   LITTLE   GREY   CURLS." Those cycles embody the "rin" / "pin" of nursery rhyme: Rinny-Tin-Tin swallowed a pin. No wonder the after-echo in this poem is

cycl

GR

CO...INCIDENTS

Uncle Herbie's last words: *ten o'clock*

but only one etc.

(thik'it) /ME thikket (unattested) < OE oiccet
[*thiccet, thikket*] <oicce [*thicce*] thick. tegu-.
Thick. Germanic* *thiku.*[Pok.*tegu-* 1057.]

n a t u r e s s o f t g e o m e t r y s t r e e s

riddle of the three sleeves

natures/rin/secycle

cultures/pin/cycle

TIGHT   LITTLE   GREY   CURLS

---

cycl

GR

Ill. 3: Joan Retallack [from AFTERRIMAGES]

The cycle has run down, ending with the mere growl of "GR."

I am often asked whether poems like these can be recited, whether the poetry reading is still relevant, and how Retallack (or comparable poets) go about reading such texts. Clearly, the poet (or whoever recites the work) can activate what is a visual / musical score. But it may well be that oral performance cannot render the full pleasure of a text like the above. My own sense is that Retallack's are poems designed to be *seen*, that they require a viewer who will take in the visual play of the lines "natures/rin/secycle," "culturess/pin/cycle." Not quite concrete poems (for here not every word or phrase participates in the process of visualization and materialization), these "afterimages" represent the turn visual poetics is taking in the age of hypertext, the age of "random access mem-O-rees" (12). It is a turn that suggests a genuine transformation of poetry-as-we-have-known-it.

Note

1. They are available from Morning Star Publications, 17 Gladstone Terrace (ground floor), Edinburgh EH 9 1LS, Scotland for £20 per series, or through Small Press Distribution, Berkeley.

Bibliography

Finlay, Ian Hamilton
    1994   "Letters to Ernst Jandl." In: Alec Finlay, ed., *Chapman: Ian Hamilton Finlay Special Issue*, no. 78-79.
Hoover, Paul ed.
    1994   *Postmodern American Poetry*. New York, Norton.
MacDiarmid, Hugh
    1984   *Letters*. Ed. by Alan Bold. Athens, University of Georgia Press.
Messerli, Douglas ed.
    1994   *From the Other Side of the Century: A New American Poetry 1960-1990*. Los Angeles, Sun & Moon.
Retallack, Joan
    1995   *AFTERRIMAGES*. Hanover and London, Wesleyan UP.

MEMOIRS OF CONCRETE

CONCRETE STEPS TO AN ANTHOLOGY

Mary Ellen Solt

When Willis Barnstone asked me to guest edit a Concrete poetry issue of *Artes Hispánicas/Hispanic Arts*, I did not know enough to refuse. I had been writing and publishing Concrete poems since 1963, and my first book, *Flowers in Concrete*, was published that year, 1966. But working in isolation in Bloomington, Indiana, I was far removed from the centers of Concrete poetry activity in Germany, Switzerland, and Brazil. I had, though, met Ian Hamilton Finlay, who introduced me to Concrete poetry, in Edinburgh in August 1962. Finlay had founded the Wild Hawthorne Press with Jessie McGuffie in 1961 and had begun publishing the periodical *Poor. Old. Tired. Horse.* in 1962. The publications of the Wild Hawthorne Press immediately disturbed the literary status quo. Hugh MacDiarmid, Scotland's most renowned poet, had included Finlay in an attack upon his young compatriots titled *The Ugly Birds Without Wings*. And a rumor was circulating that Finlay, who was struggling to exist and to keep the Wild Hawthorne Press from going under, was planning to rain subversive documents upon the Writers' Conference during the forthcoming Edinburgh Festival, dropped from his Wild Hawthorne zeppelin.

Little did they know that soon to appear in *Poor. Old. Tired. Horse.* were some truly revolutionary poems from Brazil. Finlay showed me a small anthology titled *poesia concreta*, containing poems by the Noigandres Group of São Paulo. I was fascinated. So he gave me the address of Augusto de Campos to whom I wrote upon my return to the United States. Augusto immediately sent me a copy of *poesia concreta* with its minimal word images composed of black, lower-case letters in a Bauhaus style typeface, printed on pristine white pages. The book contained, also, a loose yellow page, folded to fit, titled *pilot plan for concrete poetry*, signed by three poets: Haroldo de Campos, Augusto de Campos, and Décio Pignatari. With the aid of a Portuguese-English dictionary, I managed to extract the delights of the poems, and I was intrigued by the concept of the poem as a three-dimensional, verbivocovisual ideogram set forth in the *pilot plan*.

From 1962 onward Finlay championed Concrete poetry in *Poor. Old. Tired. Horse.* He was in contact with European as well as Brazilian poets, so I had seen work by Eugen Gomringer, Ernst Jandl and others. Also my own Concrete poems had appeared in Finlay's periodical, in Belgium in the little magazine *Labris*, edited by Leon van Essche, Ivo Vroom and others, and in the United States in *Poetry*, edited by Henry Rago. And they had been included in Concrete poetry exhibitions in Spain and Italy. By 1966 Finlay was recognized as a prolific visual poet of remarkable talent and versatility. I had collected most if not all of his works. Also that year an Italian magazine *modulo*, edited by Arrigo Lora Totino, published a substantial international Concrete poetry number. Included were several poets whose work I had not seen before. And with the publication by Hansjörg Mayer in Stuttgart of a poster-size portfolio anthology *concrete poetry britain canada united states*, also in 1966, I discovered other North Americans working along Concrete lines: Emmett Williams, Aram Saroyan and the Canadian poet bpNichol. I had been in correspondence with Emmett Williams, who was collecting contributions for his forthcoming anthology.

In the spring of 1966, I met Mike Weaver at the Beinecke Library at Yale, where we were both reading William Carlos Williams manuscripts. I was aware of Weaver's work on Williams, but I did not know that he knew Finlay well and that he had organized the First International Exhibition of Concrete and Kinetic Poetry in Cambridge, England, in 1964. Also I did not know that he had edited, with Stephen Bann, a stunning presentation of Brazilian and other Concrete poetry for the November/December 1964 issue of the magazine *Image*.

During the summer Weaver visited me in Bloomington and gave a lecture on Concrete poetry at Indiana University. The content was essentially that of an article he had just written for the *Lugano Review*. There are, he said, three general types of Concrete poetry: visual (or optic), phonetic (or sound), and kinetic (moving in a visual succession). To illustrate the latter, he presented slides of Décio Pignatari's kinetic book poem **LIFE**. He stated further that Concrete poems can be classified generally as Constructivist or Expressionist, depending upon whether the words, set in sans serif type such as Futura or Helvetica, have been arranged in accordance with a scheme or system, which must be adhered to, or whether they have been arranged intuitively (or expressively) and set in a typeface expressive of particular content. Weaver emphasized, as did the Brazilian *pilot plan*, that in the fully-achieved Concrete poem: form=content/content=form.

Many of the poems Weaver used to illustrate his lecture were new to me. The kinship of the first Brazilian Concrete poems to the *Klangfarbenmelodie* of Anton Webern, mentioned in the *pilot plan*, became clear for the first time when he projected a slide of "lygia fingers" from the *poetamenos* series by Augusto de Campos (cf. Color Plate 4, p. 15). Color typography was used to indicate speech tone colors. Hearing the poems of Ernst Jandl and Paul de Vree for the first time revealed the almost limitless possibilities of a new sound poetry. Weaver allowed me to have the slides and tapes he had with him copied. Two slides showed poems that abandoned the usual white backgrounds: a poem by Haroldo de Campos, whose word play involved the French word *vert*, was printed on green, and Décio Pignatari's "beba coca cola" was printed on light brown. If I had not met Mike Weaver at this point in time, the presentation of Concrete poetry in *Artes Hispánicas/Hispanic Arts* would have been more limited in scope.

The next year, 1967, was devoted to searching for material for the magazine. Poets and editors I knew gave me addresses. Some material came in by way of the grapevine. It came pouring in from Europe, South America, Japan, Mexico and the United States. Joe Lucca, head of graphic design in the Fine Arts Department at Indiana University, supervised over-all design and layout, but much of the actual work was done by two MFA candidates: David Noblett and Timothy Mayer. They were wonderful to work with: young and full of energy and enthusiasm for the material. No decisions were made relating to presentation of the poems without consulting me. Barnstone was also closely involved and made excellent suggestions. It was his idea to ask the poets to send photographs of themselves. And he agreed that their manifestoes and statements, so essential to the understanding of the poetry, should be included. This would differentiate our anthology from the others and make it a source book of the international Concrete poetry movement. Some poets sent their own English translations, but many did not. I worked closely with translators: Irene Montjoye-Sinor, Hana Beneš, Marco Guimarães. Barnstone did the Spanish translations.

So many contributions were coming in that it became obvious that we were going to have a problem fitting them into one issue of *Artes Hispánicas/Hispanic Arts*. The magazine was published quarterly by the Macmillan Company for Indiana University from the William Byrd Press in Richmond, Virginia, noted for high-quality printing. Willis Byrd, director of the press, came to Bloomington to look at the material personally. He was as enthusiastic about it as we were, and suggested a double issue as the solution to the problem. Barnstone agreed. And both Willises agreed with us that the press should not reset the poems; that the typographical integrity of what the poets had sent us should be preserved. Also they granted our request to use color. This meant that works such as the beautiful collage poem by the now world-famous Czech artist Jiří Kolář could be rescued from the customary black and white reproduction that in no way does them justice. In a few instances the designers took the liberty of adding color. They enhanced the cosmic dimension of Augusto de Campos's complex ideogram "terremoto" by printing the poem in white letters on a highly-saturated blue square (cf. Color Plate 3, p. 14). The crystalline quality of the form of Haroldo de Campos's ideogram "cristal/fome" was thought to be more evident when the poem was printed in white letters on a skyblue background. And Décio Pignatari's anti-ad "beba coca cola" was printed white on red to suggest the actual advertisement.

When the magazine was published in 1968, its beauty exceeded all expectations. In the meantime Emmett Williams's major collection *An Anthology of Concrete Poetry* had been published in 1967. The two books made excellent companion pieces. Whereas Williams's anthology contained many more poets, and consequently more poems, ours included the manifestos that provided the theoretical foundation of the international Concrete poetry movement. And the luxury of the high-quality paper, printing, photographic reproduction and over-all book design made it possible to do justice to works such as Finlay's glass poem "wave/rock" and other types of poem objects. Guest editing *Artes Hispánicas/Hispanic Arts* was an exhilarating experience, because it was possible to be situated in Bloomington, Indiana, and to participate in a world-wide effort – propelled by the theoretical brilliance of Haroldo de Campos, Augusto de Campos, Décio Pignatari, Eugen Gomringer, and Max Bense – to restore the integrity and communicative potential of words by heightening their sign qualities.

A momentous event occurred in Bloomington in 1968 when Haroldo and Augusto came to Indiana University to speak and present their poetry. They were enthusiastically received, and we wore them out. This is not to say everyone in the literary establishment approved of Concrete poetry. They either stayed away or, if they attended, kept their objections to themselves. After a particularly session-filled day, Haroldo collapsed into a chair in our living room and exclaimed: "I resign from Concrete!" A very important consequence of the Campos's visit was that Claus Clüver discovered Concrete poetry.

Willis Barnstone persuaded the Indiana University Press to publish the magazine as a book. Bernard Perry, director of the press, formulated the title: *Concrete Poetry: A World View.* Design and format remained exactly as it was in the magazine except that John Vint, designer for the Indiana University Press, insisted upon using my "Forsythia" poem on the front of the book jacket for the hardcover edition and my "Moonshot Sonnet" on the back. He again used "Forsythia" for the front cover of the paperback. Certain flaws resulted from reprinting the magazine exactly, an economy measure. The lack of an index, for example, is most annoying. Somewhere along the line the negatives were destroyed because, when they were returned to the William Byrd Press, they were mistakenly filed with the magazine negatives, which are kept for a limited time only. Whatever misgivings may have attended the decision to publish the book, the Indiana University Press could be comforted by the receipt of three design awards for 1969. *Concrete Poetry: A World View* was copyrighted and published in 1970, the year the international movement of Concrete poetry peaked with a comprehensive exhibition at the Stedelijk Museum in Amsterdam, November 6 through January 3, 1971.

Consequences of the publication of *Concrete Poetry: A World View* by Indiana UP were immediately felt at the Unversity. Claus Clüver organized a month-long exhibition *Expose Concrete Poetry* for February 1970. The materials I had gathered for the anthology provided the bulk of works shown, but Tom Ockerse of the Design Program in the Fine Arts Department exhibited interesting new poems. Each week there was an evening program. Emmett Williams came from New York to present a reading of his book-length poem *The Boy and the Bird* in a program that included a dance poem created and choreographed by the Danish poet Vagn Steen and a performance of my *The Peoplemover: A Demonstration Poem*. The exhibition travelled to the Krannert Gallery of the University of Illinois at Champaign-Urbana. Doyle Moore of the Finial Press, noted for fine typography, organized the showing and presented some very innovative performances of Noigandres and other poems.

Because of the interest in Concrete poetry generated by *Concrete Poetry: A World View*, I was invited to join the Comparative Literature faculty at Indiana University in September 1970 to teach comparative arts and a course in Concrete poetry. When I retired in 1971, Claus Clüver took over the course, so it flourishes to this day. Over the years, in addition to Haroldo and Augusto de Campos, Emmett Williams, Vagn Steen, Eugen Gomringer, Ernst Jandl, Décio Pignatari, and Aram Saroyan have lectured and/or read their poems at Indiana.

THE RELATIONS OF HAROLDO DE CAMPOS TO GERMAN CONCRETIST POETS, IN PARTICULAR TO MAX BENSE

Elisabeth Walther-Bense

On July 7, 1959, Max Bense received a short note from a young Brazilian writer who came to Stuttgart to contact German poets. The note, in French, reads as follows:

> Je suis un ami d'Eugen Gomringer, lié au mouvement de poésie concrète du Brésil. J'aimerais beaucoup vous connaître personellement, et vous montrer des travaux de notre groupe. Est-ce que vous pourrez me donner un rendez-vous?
> Haroldo de Campos

> Nous sommes au Brésil très intéressés au sujet de votre nouvelle esthétique.

Since 1953, Max Bense, besides his professorship at Stuttgart University, had been a visiting professor at the Hochschule für Gestaltung in Ulm, where he met Eugen Gomringer, the secretary of Max Bill since 1954. Gomringer's *konstellationen* (*constellations*) of 1953 immediately interested Bense on account of his open-mindedness towards all literary experiments. In 1955, he presented Gomringer's manifesto of Concrete poetry "vom vers zur konstellation. zweck und form einer neuen dichtung" ("from verse to constellation. purpose and form of a new poetry") in the second issue of the new literary-cultural magazine *augenblick*, which he had founded with the publisher Karl Georg Fischer. Hence, Gomringer and Concrete poetry were not unknown to Max Bense when he received the mentioned little note, and having already met Décio Pignatari in Ulm, he was eager to become acquainted with another Brazilian Concrete poet. This first meeting with Haroldo de Campos was the beginning of a lifelong friendship.[1]

That meeting in July 1959 was so exciting, stimulating, and positive for both, I think, that Bense decided right away to exhibit the new literature of the Brazilian group at Stuttgart University. Already in September 1959, Haroldo de Campos announced a postal package with books, photographs, journals, reviews, a disk of their poems, and other materials, which were exhibited in the Winter term in the University Gallery, newly founded by Max Bense. A little catalogue with texts by Augusto and Haroldo de Campos, Ronaldo Azeredo, Gerhard Rühm, Helmut Heißenbüttel, Eugen Gomringer, Claude Shannon, Francis Ponge, and Max Bense himself was published.[2] It was the first exhibition of Concrete poetry in Germany, as far as I know. In connection with these texts, the circle "Geistiges Frankreich" ("Intellectual France") of the Studium Generale of Stuttgart University, under the guidance of Max Bense and myself, performed an evening devoted exclusively to the Brazilian poets, who called themselves Noigandres.

In 1960, because of the impossibility of continuing our periodical *augenblick* for economic reasons, Max Bense and I founded our *edition rot*.[3] Meanwhile, Noigandres, and Haroldo de Campos in particular, had published several theoretical articles in Brazilian journals, including Haroldo's "Kurt Schwitters ou o jubilo do objeto" in 1956, and his "poema concreta – conteudo – communicação" and "panaroma em português: joyce traduzido" in 1957. Augusto de Campos translated and commented on some pieces by Joyce under the title "Em Finneganscopia" in 1957, but most important was the publication of "plano pilôto para poesia concreta" by Augusto and Haroldo de Campos, and Décio Pignatari. Briefly and precisely, they pointed out their conception of Concrete poetry. The first sentence reads: "Concrete poetry: product of a critical evolution of forms." Their formal intentions included conceptions like "graphic space" as a "structural agent," and "space-time," known in physics since Einstein. Here they mentioned their literary forerunners, for instance Pound, Apollinaire, Mallarmé, Joyce, Oswald and Mário de Andrade, and Cabral de Melo Neto, but also modern musicians like Webern, Boulez and Stockhausen, painters like Mondrian, Bill, and Albers, and linguists like Fenollosa and Sapir. It is surprising, too, that theoretical conceptions of different sciences play an important role in this manifesto, with conceptions like communication, Gestalt psychology, pragmatics, phenomenology, cybernetics, coincidence, simultaneity, isomorphism, magnetic field, relativity, chance, feed-back, and so on. In 1958, Haroldo published his extensive article with the title "Poesia concreta no Japão: Kitasono Katue." Already indicated in the "pilot plan" was their "affinity to isolating languages (Chinese)." From the very beginning, their relations to Japan were very close through the mediation of their friend J. C. Vinholes, who lived in Tokyo at that time. Last but not least, I should mention two articles of Augusto de Campos which show the ability of Noigandres to utilize the conceptions of preceding poets and to combine them: "O lance de dados do Finnegans Wake" from 1958 and "Gertrude Stein e a melodia de timbres," from 1959.

Since January 1960, Noigandres, consisting of Augusto and Haroldo de Campos, Cassiano Ricardo, Décio Pignatari, Edgard Braga, José Lino Grünewald, Mário Chamie, Pedro Xisto, and Alexandre Wollner as typographer, utilized the term "invenção" to mark their texts in the *Correio Paulistano*. In February 1960, on the occasion of Max Bense's 50th birthday, Haroldo de Campos addressed the text "montagem: Max Bense, no seu quinquagésimo aniversario," dedicated to the "aesthetician, semiotician, and writer." In March and April of 1959, Haroldo had already presented Bense's aesthetics more extensively in the *Suplemento Literario* of the *O Estado de São Paulo*. At that time, several books and articles by Max Bense on aesthetics and text theory had already been published, for instance *Aesthetica. Metaphysische Beobachtungen am Schönen* in 1954 (*Metaphysical Observations of Beauty*; Spanish translation published in Buenos Aires in 1957), *Ästhetische Information* (*Aesthetical Information*) and *Rationalismus und Sensibilität* (*Rationalism and Sensitivity*) both in 1956, and *Aesthetik und Zivilisation. Theorie der ästhetischen Kommunikation* (*Aesthetics and Civilisation. Theory of Aesthetic Communication*) in 1958. Bense presented in these books aesthetical conceptions from a very modern standpoint, combining ontological and phenomenological with informational, semiotic, and communicational aspects. He distinguished the "physical state," which tends to entropy, from the "aesthetical state," which tends to negentropy or information, and therefore named his aesthetics "informational aesthetics," or later "semiotical aesthetics."[4]

The Noigandres poets were not only limited to literary, artistic, and scientific experiments which went on world-wide, and which they described and criticized, but were devoted in particular to the aesthetical foundations of art. Their dealings with Kurt Schwitters, James Joyce, Gertrude Stein, Ezra Pound, Francis Ponge, Stéphane Mallarmé, Guillaume Apollinaire, e. e. cummings, Arno Holz, in addition to Brazilian authors, their spiritual ancestors, all of whom they depicted *in extenso*, showed an open-mindedness for experiments in literature and art in general which one can really call "outstanding." But the Brazilian poets did more than continue the work of others; they were very creative themselves. They published in Brazilian journals, in periodicals, and later in their own review *invenção* and in many very finely designed books. I cannot list all their publications, but two of them must be mentioned here: *Teoría da poesia concreta. Textos, criticas e manifestos 1950-1960* by Augusto and Haroldo de Campos and Décio Pignatari, which first appeared in 1965, and *Metalinguagem: ensaios de teoría e critica literária* by Haroldo de Campos, from 1967.

It is not astonishing at all that after the first exhibition of Noigandres in 1959 in Stuttgart the correspondence between Haroldo de Campos, who was the spokesman of the group, and Stuttgart led to a very broad and intensive exchange of ideas. Max Bense's desire to know the members of the Brazilian Concrete group personally became still stronger, so he asked Haroldo to try to organize an invitation to Brazil for him. In February 1961, Bense received the desired invitation from the Brazilian government as a result of Haroldo's efforts.

Our first sojourn in Rio, Brasília, and São Paulo in October 1961 lasted two weeks. The day after our arrival in Rio, we already saw Haroldo and Augusto de Campos, and Décio Pignatari with their wives at our hotel, and got to know José Lino Grünewald and his wife Ecila. After one week in Rio, we flew to Brasília, where we met João Cabral de Melo Neto. While he showed us the new capital we had an exciting conversation about different literary questions, particularly about the work of Francis Ponge. From Brasília we went to São Paulo, where we met other Concrete poets at Haroldo's house, and also Alexandre Wollner, whom we knew from Ulm. We visited the Museu de Arte Moderna and became acquainted with Mário Pedrosa, its director. We also made the acquaintance of the group of Concrete painters in São Paulo. The so-called "pop-crete" works of Waldemar Cordeiro interested Max Bense so much that he wrote a little text for one of his catalogues. Back in Rio, we visited the studios of Aloísio Magalhães and Roberto Burle Marx. All artists urged Bense to commence new aesthetic research. The lectures that he gave in the Museu de Arte Moderna in Rio and the discussions with painters, designers, architects, and particularly with writers showed us an intellectually-stamped Brazil, which, of course, represented only one part of the entire society. There was after all still a large percentage of illiterates. Aloísio Magalhães and his collaborators had developed a program for alphabetization that interested us very strongly on account of our semiotic research. Max Bense, in his book *Brasilianische Intelligenz* (*Brazilian Intelligence*) of 1965, presented summations of these and other observations made during this and the following sojourns. Carmen Portinho, director of the Museu de Arte Moderna in Rio, and Mário Pedrosa invited Bense to give another series of lectures on his new aesthetics in Rio and in São Paulo in the near future. So we left Brazil, hoping to see our old and new friends again.

In 1961, Noigandres founded their review *invenção*, in which Haroldo de Campos published his essay "Majakowski em Português," comparing Maya-kovsky's concept of "novelty" with Bense's concept of "originality." Augusto and Haroldo de Campos had also written several times about Arno Holz, and had translated some of his texts. In a letter from December 1961, Haroldo told us proudly that he acquired the *phantasus* in the edition of 1916 from Insel-Verlag. He admired the poetical strength and modernity of Arno Holz. Then, I remember, he suggested that Max Bense should write his comprehensive radiophonic play "Wörter und Zahlen. Zur Textalgebra von Arno Holz" ("Words and numbers. On the algebra of text of Arno Holz"), relayed by Radio Stuttgart in December 1964, and in an altered version in October 1970. Haroldo also mentioned in his letter João Cabral de Melo Neto's *O cão sem plumas*, translated into German by Willy Keller, which we published in April 1964 as *rot text* 14. In 1962, Haroldo sent us Cabral's collected poems *terceira feira* with the remark: "Cabral, c'est un peu notre william carlos williams, un peu notre ponge." Haroldo esteemed Ponge very much, and, in 1961, published his fine essay "Francis Ponge: A Aranha e sua Tela," accompanied by his translations.

Meanwhile, we prepared *rot text* 7 with texts solely by Noigandres. It was published in February 1962 and contained poems by Augusto and Haroldo de Campos, Décio Pignatari, Ronaldo Azeredo, and José Lino Grünewald, "framed" between Helmut Heißenbüttel's foreword "Über konkrete Poesie" ("On Concrete poetry") and Haroldo de Campos's epilogue "Noigandres – konkrete texte" ("Noigandres – Concrete texts"), translated by Heißenbüttel. In the epilogue, Haroldo pointed out once more that "the Brazilian Concrete poetry is verbal-vocal-visual: it works with visual form, with sound and content of the verbal material. In this sense it is against pure typographical poetry, against sound poems, lettrism." Haroldo's short text ended with the sentence: "The Brazilian poetry, while being of such great importance to the semantic element..., recognizes the possibility of a verbal art which is revolutionary both in form and content. Complete isomorphy. Engagement." Max Bense esteemed this political behavior of Noigandres very much because of similar intentions in his own aesthetic and literary work. But he was also impressed by the quickness and precision of the way in which Haroldo followed the publications of Germany's literature and modern science. Haroldo's eagerness in reading seemed boundless. Hence, Bense gave him the nickname "locomotive of São Paulo." The exchange between Haroldo and Stuttgart deepened considerably during the time to come.[5]

Already in July 1962, shortly after our second sojourn in Brazil, Haroldo told us about the plurilingual poem by Décio Pignatari on Cuba that he denominated "engaged Concrete poetry." He also announced the translation of Bense's text on Brasília from *Entwurf einer Rheinlandschaft* (*Sketch of a Rhenian Landscape*) which was to be published in the second issue of *invenção* in 1962, and about the exhibition of Concrete poetry that J.C. Vinholes was organizing with the support of the German Cultural Institute in Tokyo. Haroldo himself was planning his trip to Germany in 1963 and sent us his later famous poem "forma e fundo" as well as his article about Arno Holz's *phantasus*. I already mentioned that the Noigandres poets did not deny their indebtedness to their "ancestors" but, on the contrary, dealt with them extensively. It is therefore not surprising at all to find traces of Mallarmé, cummings, and others in the politically engaged poem "Cubagrama" by Augusto de Campos.

As they often remarked, Haroldo and his friends understood Concrete poetry not as being visual poetry in the narrow sense of "Figuren-Gedichte," known since Greek antiquity. I have just quoted one of Haroldo's statements to the effect that the figure always remained secondary. Important were the words alone, the linguistic material, or the semiotic elements, that is: the words which possess their own reality, represent another thing (object or event), and serve to form texts or contexts. In Brazilian literature, he paid tribute to writers such as João Guimarães Rosa, Oswald de Andrade, João Cabral de Melo Neto and many others whom he admired and mentioned often in his letters or in conversation. Haroldo, in particular, was also very interested in other languages, and in translating from them. Besides Latin and Greek, he learned German, French, English, Italian, Spanish, Russian, Japanese, and Hebrew. Maybe some other languages, too. His goal was never to master foreign languages completely, but to be able to read literary texts and to translate them. It is always striking how critically he analyzed foreign literature without becoming a "negative" critic. He translated and published several texts by Max Bense, e.g. "Fotoestética" (20.2.1960), "Teoría do texto" (27.3.1960), "Textos visuais" (23. 11. 1961), "Max Bense sôbre Brasília" (*invenção* no. 2,1962), and "poesia concreta" (*invenção* no. 3, 1963), written by Bense to celebrate the tenth anniversary of Brazilian Concrete poetry. The German version of this last article was published two years later in the review *Sprache im technischen Zeitalter* (no. 15, July-September 1965). Haroldo also translated and published "Poesia natural e poesia artificial" (10. 10. 1964) and the little text for Waldemar Cordeiro's catalogue for the exhibition of his "pop-crete" paintings (*invenção* no. 4, December 1964). When Haroldo released his book *servidão de passagem* in 1962, Max Bense wished to publish the German version in our *edition rot*. Unfortunately, this plan could never be realized. But the mutual publishing of texts showed the real international behavior on both sides.[6]

In 1963, Julio Medaglia, who studied music in Freiburg, organized an exhibition of Concrete poetry at Freiburg University which was inaugurated by Max Bense. There is a little catalogue of this exhibition. Haroldo announced his coming to Stuttgart in January or February 1964. He also requested Max Bense to write a foreword for a book by Guimarães Rosa which was to be published by the editor J. C. Witsch in Cologne. Haroldo, together with Augusto, had translated up to that time some parts of *Finnegans Wake* by James Joyce, published under the title *Panaroma of Finnegans Wake*. Also, his article on Guimarães Rosa's "Linguagem do iauaretê" appeared, which was studied by Haroldo and myself for a translation into German.

At last, Haroldo's sojourn in Stuttgart was fixed for February 1964. He came for one month and gave five lectures on Brazilian literature, which were very well attended and very successful. For our students it was their first acquaintance with Brazilian literature, until that time rather unknown in Germany. Meanwhile, we had received Willy Keller's translation of Cabral's *O cão sem plumas* and prepared its publication. The booklet appeared as *rot text* 14 in 1964, soon after Haroldo's departure. At that time, the political situation in Brazil disturbed the intellectuals at home and abroad, so that also Haroldo, who intended to stay some time in Paris, Spain, and Portugal after his sojourn in Stuttgart, decided to return immediately to Brazil.

We learned that Anatol Rosenfeld had started to translate some parts of Haroldo's *Galáxias*. Already in 1966, we succeeded in publishing four pieces of this "book in progress," two in the translation by Anatol Rosenfeld, two others by Vilém Flusser. This book, without beginning and end in the traditional sense, has one solid repeated element on every page, either the "travel" or the "book." Haroldo noted that he worked out each page as intensely as a poem. In a letter of October 1965, he gave us most interesting observations about this work. A complete edition of the book *Galáxias* finally appeared in 1984. In October 1994, during the *Literaturtage* (days of literature) in Stuttgart, the Group Exvoco (Hanna Aurbacher, Ewald Liska and Theophil Meyer) performed *Galáxias* in the arrangement and notation by Theophil Meyer, and in the presence of Haroldo and his wife Carmen.

In spite of the difficult political situation of 1964, Haroldo succeeded in obtaining another invitation for Max Bense and myself from the Department of Architecture of São Paulo University. Bense was to give a series of six lectures on aesthetics and design, and I on semiotics. By that time, Haroldo, in collaboration with his brother Augusto, had published a book about Sousândrade, whom he considered to have been unjustly forgotten. In May 1964, he also published an interview with Max Bense entitled "A fantasia racional," to prepare our sojourn scheduled for September-October. But we then stayed only in Rio and failed to go to São Paulo for lectures; we had to return to Germany because of the sudden relocation of our Institute at Stuttgart University. It turned out to be our last trip to Brazil together.[7]

The exchange of ideas, papers, and books went on. In *invenção* no. 4 (1964) contributions by German writers such as Bense, Döhl, and Heißenbüttel were published. In 1965, Haroldo and his friends were planning a new review under the pertinent title "debabel," aiming to diminish the confusion of languages, i.e. the "babylonian confusion." Concrete poetry, mostly constructed out of few words, often by underlining even their letters, and without syntax, is very well suited to be understood and translated into other languages. It is for this reason that since 1953 Concrete poetry has developed all over the world, has become an international movement, often carried by the personal relations between the authors. In 1965, we organized a big exhibition at our University Gallery to show the internationality of Concrete poetry, with texts by authors

from many countries: Iceland, Scotland, Denmark, United States, Czechoslovakia, Belgium, France, England, Turkey, Mexico, Italy, Switzerland,
Austria, Finland, Sweden, Brazil, and Germany. Besides the catalogue of this
exhibition, the anthology *Konkrete Poesie International* appeared as *rot text*
21. It was one of the first anthologies of Concrete poems in the world.[8] In his
postface, Max Bense pointed out: "One is making something in the language,
one should do something with the language. Prose and poetry are conceptions
telling what can be made in the language, when it is already existing, when its
forms are known and given, can be used and worn out. Text is something
which is made with the language, that is, made out of language, but, at the
same time, changing, enriching, completing, deranging, or reducing it." At the
opening of the exhibition, some authors, especially from Scandinavia, were
able to be present, and so they met the German poets personally.

In the Spring of 1969, supported by a grant, Haroldo de Campos came back
to France for several weeks. He visited Francis Ponge in Nice and in Bar-sur-
Loup. He knew and admired the works of Ponge, as I already mentioned. But
Haroldo could not come to Stuttgart and we were unable to go to France to
meet him again. In our letters of this period two subjects prevailed: first, the
preparation of the Brazilian translation of Max Bense's *kleine abstrakte
ästhetik (pequena estetica abstracta)* by Jacó Guinsburg, Ingrid Dormien, and
Haroldo de Campos, and second, another trip to Brazil which – as I already
pointed out – could not be realized anymore. *Pequena Estética* was published
together with *Pequena Antología Bensiana* which was organized, presented,
and translated by Haroldo de Campos himself. The texts of the latter were
already published in Brazilian journals and periodicals. In his very profound
introduction, Haroldo showed the points of contact between Bense's aesthetics
and other aesthetical and text-theoretical conceptions of modern artistic
activities. He called attention to these points on account of obviously similar
intentions by his group and himself. This introduction with the fine title
"Umbral para Max Bense" remains until now one of the most important
analyses of Bense's aesthetics. *Pequena estetica* was published by the Editôra
Perspectiva, São Paulo, in 1971.

Only in January 1970, when Haroldo returned once again to Europe, was he
able to spend some days in Stuttgart. It was a very joyful and stimulating
reunion for all of us – as were all subsequent meetings, from 1976 to the
present. On the occasion of Max Bense's 60th birthday in February 1970,
Haroldo and Augusto de Campos, João Cabral de Melo Neto, and José Lino
Grünewald contributed to the Festschrift *Muster möglicher Welten (Pattern of
Possible Worlds)*, edited by Ludwig Harig and myself. In March 1970, Max
Bense, Eugen Gomringer, and Uwe Schneede, the director of the Kunstverein
Stuttgart (Association of Stuttgart's Artists), opened a very large exhibition of

Concrete poetry. Several other similar exhibitions were organized in other places, and by other persons, for instance one in Amsterdam by Liesbeth Crommelin.[9]

Today, one could think that Concrete poets are not as present in the "scene" as in the Sixties and Seventies, but Concrete movements and publications (books and magazines) exist and receive a new appreciation through current exhibitions and performances. Really, it seems to me that they are more alive than one generally supposes. In the Sixties, Concrete poetry was known to small circles only, but now it penetrates globally into the conciousness of a broader public. I wish to emphazise once more that the relations of Haroldo de Campos and his group to the United States, Japan and Europe, and particularly to Max Bense and other German Concrete poets played, without a doubt, an important role in this respect. But I also want to repeat that Concrete art and poetry always were and still are international "events," never limited to pure national circles. These new forms of literature developed all over the world almost at the same time, departing from the same forerunners such as Mallarmé, Joyce, Gertrude Stein, Schwitters, Hausmann, and many others already mentioned, resulting in similar texts.

In conclusion, I wish to quote a statement by Francis Ponge that Max Bense adopted as a motto for his book *Programmierung des Schönen. Allgemeine Texttheorie und Textästhetik* (*Programming of Beauty. General Text Theory and Text Aesthetics*) of 1960. It expresses also rightly the aim of Noigandres and of Haroldo de Campos, I think:

> In order not to pretend to be able to represent a reality of the concrete or spiritual world, a text must first reach the reality of its own world, that is the world of texts.

Notes

1. Likewise in 1955, Max Bense also met Helmut Heißenbüttel in Ulm, one of the first and later the most famous German Concrete poet who, in 1954, published his first book with the title *kombinationen* (*combinations*). The theoretical article "reduzierte sprache. über ein stück von Gertrude Stein" ("reduced language. concerning a piece by Gertrude Stein") was Heißenbüttel's first contribution to *augenblick* and was probably the first writing about Gertrude Stein actually published in Germany. Heißenbüttel attacked the partition between *form* and *content* in the literature of the nineteenth century and demanded from the literature of the twentieth century that it reduce content and disintegrate the form of its

traditional appearance. He also marked a new "speaking possibility" that has to be viewed in the reduction of and the retrospect to language itself.

Heißenbüttel's point of view came near to the conceptions of Haroldo de Campos and his Noigandres group. Heißenbüttel's call for engagement, or better, his political articulation, estimated by him to be legitimate in literature, was also close to Noigandres's mental outlook. I cannot enter into details here but want to stress that Heißenbüttel not only opposed the partition between form and content, but – and this is the case with Noigandres, too – neither did admit any difference between the textual forms or "textsorten" which Max Bense in his paper "Neue Textsorten" ("New kinds of texts") distinguished, for instance: semantic and non-semantic, predicative and mechanical, constructive and automatic, logical and stochastical, abstract and concrete, determined and randomized, high-entropic and low-entropic, reduced and complete, open and closed, homogeneous and heterogeneous texts, but also text-cuts, text-pieces, text-flow and text montages, and many other forms. The term "Concrete poetry," in my opinion, was to be enlarged to "Concrete literature" or "Concrete texts" – not all poets published only poetry, but also prose and theoretical papers, in short, Concrete texts.

2. Of course, Gerhard Rühm, Claude Shannon, and Francis Ponge figured in the catalogue but did not belong to the "Stuttgart Group" of poets (cf. note 3). Rühm – with Friedrich Achleitner, Hans Carl Artmann, Konrad Bayer and Oswald Wiener – belonged to the Vienna Group. Rühm's documentary *Die Wiener Gruppe* (*The Vienna Group*; published by Rowohlt, Hamburg, in 1967, rpt. 1985) enables us to get a good view of the Concrete aims of its members. But in spite of many similarities, they and other Austrian poets like Ernst Jandl and Friederike Mayröcker pursued intentions somewhat different from those of the Brazilian and the Stuttgart Group. Claude Shannon was not a poet at all, but a computer scientist or cybernetician, and Francis Ponge was an already famous and important French writer, whose visual texts were exhibited in Stuttgart earlier in 1959, presented by Max Bense.

3. The first booklet – or "text" – of this series was Bense's *Grignan-Serie. Beschreibung einer Landschaft* (*Grignan Series. Description of a Landscape*) which consisted of several short experimental texts. In September of the same year we published as *rot text* 2 Reinhard Döhl's *11 texte* (*11 texts*). They were montages of quotations by Reverdy, Breton, Schéhadé and Wittgenstein. When we came to know Döhl, he was still a student at Göttingen University. But in 1959, having published his poem "missa profana," he was indicted by the court on a charge of blasphemy. As he wrote to Max Bense, this occurred in his understanding due to the "strong influence of Catholicism over German political and cultural life." First, he was condemned, later acquitted by the Supreme Court, but he lost his private tutorship and was expelled from Göttingen University. With the support of Max Bense and Fritz Martini, professor of German literature, Döhl succeeded in getting himself enrolled at Stuttgart University, where he finished his studies and is even today professor of German literature. *rot text* 9, November 1962, was a collaboration between Döhl and Klaus Burkhardt and more "Concrete" than the earlier montages. Döhl's text *porträt - einwände* (*portraits - objections*) was not an

illustration, but rather the complement of Burkhardt's typography, reflecting the graphic patterns in the text. Burkhardt was a typographer and lecturer of typography at the Stuttgart School of Printing. At the time, he was fascinated by the typographic possibilities of contemporary texts, and he printed posters, postcards, and a series of 20 so-called *affiche* (one page of one author's text, folded in itself). In 1961, having finished this series, he printed Max Bense's *après-fiche* (*post-fiche*) as the very last one.

Another one of Bense's experimental texts, "Teile" ("parts"), was published together with Paul Wunderlich's indian-ink drawings *20 Juli 1944* (*July 20, 1944*) as *rot text* 4, 1961. This text was reproduced several times after this first publication. It was simultaneoulsy Concrete and political, referring to the attempt on Hitler's life and the death penalty of the German officers involved. In the same year, *haiku hiroshima* by Ludwig Harig appeared as the fifth text in the series *rot*. Harig was a very young writer from Saarbrücken, who, since 1956, had already written poems, reviews, translations and other texts for *augenblick*. He was influenced by Abraham Moles's *erstes manifest der permutationellen kunst* (*first manifest of permutational art*), which was published in a German translation as *rot text* 8 in 1962. Harig applied the technique of permutation in several books, in novels, stories, and poems. Later he wrote short stories, novels, and radiophonic plays which, though not being Concrete texts, were still experimental ones. He also wrote supplements to Max Bense's radio play *vielleicht zunächst wirklich nur. monolog der Terry Jo im Mercey Hospital* (*perhaps first really merely. monologue by Terry Jo in the Mercey Hospital*), which was published in 1963 as *rot text* 11. Bense's text was written in part by the computer and incorporated all kinds of text types into a new form of literature: automatic writing, montages, quotations from non-literary texts, i.e. from advertising, mathematics, scientific reports, and so on.

Our activities in Stuttgart in the early 60s resulted in the formation of the "Stuttgarter Gruppe" (Stuttgart Group). Harig, although not living in Stuttgart, was one of its early members (in fact, he still regards himself a member of the Stuttgart Group), as were Döhl and the now renowned typographer, printer, publisher, and gallerist Hansjörg Mayer. Mayer organized exhibitions of Concrete poetry and published portfolios of Concrete texts by authors from many different countries. The portfolio *13 visuelle texte* (*13 visual texts*) of 1964, for example, included works by Max Bense, Edgard Braga, Augusto de Campos, Haroldo de Campos, Reinhard Döhl, Helmut Heißenbüttel, Ernst Jandl, Hansjörg Mayer, Wolfram Menzel, Franz Mon, Décio Pignatari, Konrad Balder Schäuffelen and Pedro Xisto. In the same year, we published his *alphabet*, a typographical arrangement of letters, completed later by *typoems*, a catalogue of Mayer's exhibition in the Stuttgart University Gallery of December 1965, with an introduction by Max Bense and texts by Haroldo de Campos, Mathias Goeritz, Reinhard Döhl and Siegfried Maser, besides his own. In the same year, Hansjörg Mayer published the portfolio *konkrete poesie international* (*concrete poetry international*), with 13 texts by Carlo Belloli, Claus Bremer, Ian Hamilton Finlay, Pierre Garnier, Mathias Goeritz, Eugen Gomringer, José Lino Grünewald, Josef Hiršal, Diter Rot, Vagn

Steen, Paul de Vree, Oswald Wiener, and Emmett Williams. I also want to recall Mayer's series *futura* which consisted of single pages, folded in themselves, and dedicated each to one author. *futura* no. 3 of 1965 contains Max Bense's often reproduced poem *rio*, written on the occasion of the 400th anniversary of Rio de Janeiro in 1964. Another sheet, Max Bense's *rosenschuttplatz* (*dumping ground of roses*), was printed by Mayer, too. It was presented several times as a quasi-musical event, through Clytus Gottwald's musical notation, by the Group Exvoco.

In 1965, Max Bense and Reinhard Döhl presented their manifesto "Die 'Stuttgarter Gruppe' zur Lage" in the review *manuskripte*. There, they pointed out that in modern poetry the aesthetical morality, the aesthetical discussion (about language), and the aesthetical play have to be predominant. They distinguish six tendencies in modern poetry: 1. letters – arrangements of types – images of letters, 2. signs – graphical arrangement – images of writing, 3. serial and permutational realization – metrical and acoustical poetry, 4. sound – sonorous arrangement – phonetic poetry, 5. stochastical and topological poetry, 6. cybernetical and material poetry. In their understanding, the artist realizes situations on the basis of conscious theory and conscious experiment. Bense's and Döhl's conceptions were very similar to those of other manifestos, e.g. the "plano pilôto" by Noigandres of 1957 or the theoretical explanations by Gerhard Rühm in his book about the Vienna Group of 1967.

In the following years, many authors sympathized with the Stuttgart Group, for instance Helmut Geissner from Saarbrücken, Ernst Jandl and Friederike Mayröcker from Vienna, Konrad Balder Schäuffelen from Munich, Franz Mon from Frankfurt, Diter Rot from Iceland, Timm Ulrichs from Hannover, Johannes Ernst Seiffert from Japan (later Kassel), Friederike Roth from Stuttgart, Gabbo Mateen from Nürnberg, Carlfriedrich Claus from Annaberg, and the Czech writers Josef B. Hiršal, Bohumila Grögerowá, Vladislav Novák, Jiří Kolář, Karel Trinkewitz. Not all of them were pure Concrete poets; they published other kinds of experimental texts in the following years. Today, there are several Concrete, or better, experimental authors in Germany, like Jens Peter Mardersteig from Malente or Ruth Loibl from Rheinfelden, but after Max Bense's death in April 1990, the Stuttgart Group exists no more. Unfortunately, the experimental and Concrete poetry of Eastern Germany of those years was nearly unknown in the West and has only now been presented in several books and magazines.

4.	In 1964, Georg Nees, from Siemens in Erlangen, produced his first computer graphics and sent them to Max Bense, who became very enthusiastic about this new possibility, and displayed them in 1965 at the University Gallery. With the programs by Nees, and the theoretical aesthetical text "projekte generativer ästhetik" ("projects of generative aesthetics") by Bense, we published *computer-grafik* as *rot text* 19. Four years later, Nees obtained his Ph. D. with his dissertation *Generative Computergrafik* (*Generative Computer Graphics*). Max Bense, although extremely interested in this method to construct graphics, termed it "artificial art" to distinguish it from conventional art, and because of the opposition of some artists and art critics who would not accept artistic results obtained with the aid of computers. At the same time, Frieder Nake, a young mathematician of Stuttgart

University, produced computer graphics too, and Nees and Nake exhibited their work in Wendelin Niedlich's book shop in Stuttgart. Not only computer graphics but also computer texts were produced at that time, for instance by another young mathematician, Theo Lutz. Max Bense heard of these experiments and suggested that he take a repertory of 100 words from Kafka's *Schloß* (*Castle*), adding very simple syntactic rules to build phrases like "The castle is far," "The village is deep," and so on. In this way, Lutz generated some 1,000 sentences. Max Bense incorporated some of them in his *Vielleicht zunächst wirklich nur. Monolog der Terry Jo im Mercey Hospital.*

Although Bense often spoke of "the technical existence of modern man," and welcomed all experiments whatsoever, he refused persistently himself to use a personal computer or to handle any machine or engine other than his old type-writer. He has, for instance, never driven a car in spite of his famous text "Auto und Information. Das Ich, das Auto und die Technik" ("Car and information. I, the Car and Technics") published in the Swiss review *Du*, October 1970. Haroldo de Campos, on the other side, came into contact with electronic techniques in New York through Marshall McLuhan.

5.	In May 1962, we had the opportunity to visit Brazil for the second time. Among the artists we came to know better during this sojourn were Alfredo Volpi, the renowned painter whose work shows affinities with the Brazilian Concretist tradition, and Lygia Clark. Unfortunately, our planned lectures in Sao Paulo could not take place – but Max Bense's lectures in Rio were very successful.

6.	During our third sojourn in Brazil – visiting Rio, São Paulo, and Brasília in October 1963 – we had the privilige of meeting not only many of our old friends, but also the famous novelists Guimarães Rosa and Clarice Lispector, and the physicist/humanist Mário Schemberg, whose work was esteemed highly by Haroldo de Campos.

7.	In March 1966, Max Bense was invited to open another exhibition of Concrete poetry in Mexico City and to give a lecture on aesthetics and theory of texts at Mexico University. Mathias Goeritz, architect, historian of art, Concrete painter and poet, who died in August 1990, only three months after Max Bense, organized the exhibition, which was widely attended and discussed. In April 1962, Mathias Goeritz, under the pseudonym Werner Bruenner, had already published his renowned poem "oro" in the bilingual review *el corno emplumado*, dedicated to Concrete and experimental poetry. Goeritz was a real insider of Concrete art in general. In the Summer of 1966, Haroldo de Campos went to Mexico City, too, to contact Mathias Goeritz. After that visit, he went to New York to meet Roman Jakobson, with whom he had friendly connections for a long time. The friendship with Jakobson shows also that Haroldo always intended to combine poetical and theoretical acitivities. Another event in the domain of Concrete poetry was the lecture on Concrete poetry and aesthetics that Max Bense gave in March 1967 at the Goethe Institute in Paris, where Lily Greenham recited several Concrete texts. The traveling of Concrete poets in those years was considerable.

8.	In the following years, we published in our series *rot* other Concrete authors such as Konrad Balder Schäuffelen, Ludwig Harig, Hansjörg Mayer, Franz Mon,

Francis Ponge, Witold Wirpsza, Diter Rot, Timm Ulrichs, Reinhard Döhl, Friederike Roth, Gabbo Mateen, and Carole Spearin McCauley. Some experimental artists, like Mira Schendel, Aloísio Magalhães, Günter Neusel, were also presented. This list may show that until 1972 we dedicated our publishing activities mainly to Concrete and experimental literature and art. At the same time, some of the texts were also catalogues of exhibitions at the University Gallery.

9.   I wish to mention two more exhibitions of Concrete texts. The first, a very large one in February 1978, on the occasion of Max Bense's retirement, was organized by students of the Stuttgart Academy of Fine Arts. It was opened by Bense, and there was a performance of Concrete poems by the Group Exvoco. In September 1988, the last exhibition of Concrete poetry from our own collection was opened by Max Bense in the Stiftung für konkrete Kunst (Foundation of Concrete Art) at Reutlingen, a town not far from Stuttgart. There, too, books, papers, posters, and paintings, also by our Brazilian friends, were displayed. (After this event, we donated our collection to this foundation in order to facilitate access to those works for interested persons. In spite of our intentions, there is until now no public access to this collection, a fact about which I feel very angry, in view of students' interest in Concrete poetry.) With the opening of the exhibition, Max Bense brought his own activities in the field of Concrete poetry to a worthy end, I would like to say.

E.
THE YALE *SYMPHOSYMPOSIUM* ON CONTEMPORARY POETICS AND CONCRETISM: A WORLD VIEW FROM THE 1990s

Anne Tardos, *from "Amy Minden"* (1990)

THE YALE *SYMPHOSYMPOSIUM*
ON CONTEMPORARY POETICS AND CONCRETISM:
A WORLD VIEW FROM THE 1990s

[Editors' note: This closing section represents an attempt to recover the themes and issues raised in the round table debate at the Yale Symphosophia (cf. Preface), and to recapture the positive polemical and dynamic spirit of that discussion on theory, poetics, and practice of Experimental, Visual, and Concrete Poetry Since the 1960s, in order to demonstrate the vitality of experimental poetics. Thus, the statements reproduced below express personal opinions of and evaluations by individual participants in the Yale *symphosymposium*, not all of which are necessarily shared by the editors or other participants.]

Contemporary Poetics and Concretism

What dimensions of contemporary poetics are directly engaged with concretism?

Augusto de Campos   I see Concrete poetry as directly engaged with the practices of vanguard, experimental or – as it should probably more adequately be called – inventive poetry. I think that the task of Concrete poetry, after it appeared in the 50s, was to reestablish contact with the poetry of the vanguards of the beginning of the century (Futurism, Cubo-futurism, Dada *et alia*), which the intervention of two great wars and the proscription of Nazi and Stalinist dictatorships had condemned to marginalization. A similar movement occurred in the 50s in music, with the recuperation of the work of the Vienna Group (Schoenberg, Webern, Berg), the rediscovery of the great individual experimentalists (Ives, Varèse, etc.), and the intervention of new vanguard composers, from Boulez to Stockhausen to Cage. In terms of the poets whom Pound termed "masters," "diluters," etc., the practitioners of Concrete poetry situate themselves, or hope to be situated, programmatically, in the category of the "inventors," that is, those who are engaged in the pursuit of new forms.

E. M. de Melo e Castro   After more than 35 years, I think that Concrete poetry was not just one more avant-garde movement. Rather, it was the arriving at a radical point of view that concerned all the dimensions of modern poetry. So radical that it can be argued whether Concrete poetry belongs to poetry at all, being as it is an inventive criticism of all the dimensions of conventional literary writing.

In fact, Concrete poetry questions the very nature of the poetic image, confronting the verbal with the non-verbal, the symbol with the icon, time with space, alphabetic writing with the ideogram, the dressing with words of ideas and feelings with the nakedness of the stuff language is made of. The syllable, the word, verse, meter, accent, and grammar itself are all dramatically challenged by the agrammaticity of a spatial rendering of the possible meanings of the signs. Probability and unprobability thus become the key to the decoding of Concrete poetry, establishing ambiguity, plurisignification, and intersemiotics as the method of reading at the limits of communication.

Luciano Nanni   From an aesthetic point of view, I would say all art in general is directly connected to concretism. One could say that Concrete poetry reveals a way of being of the art work; a way of being that doesn't belong to Concrete poetry only, but, today, to every work of art of any kind.

Does not Concrete poetry realize its artistic specificity by negating communication? Does it not reduce communication, understood referentially, to its physical matter, to its concrete matter alone? And is it not only then, in the critical perspective and the practice that interprets it, that it returns to meaning, to the sign, but in a differentiated and polysemic way?

In sum, isn't this the function that contemporary aesthetics considers to be the specificity of the life of all works of art? Everyone has a way of proclaiming such awareness: R. Jakobson, speaking of the "ambiguity" of a work of art; J. Mukařovský, speaking of closed sign; R. Barthes of "plural language;" U. Eco of "a-communication;" S. Fish of works of art rewritten in a different way by various interpreters, and so on. But in spite of these differences of language, the concept remains the same, saying that the work of art is born as a sign (an historical object, as Prieto calls it), but functions today, again in the words of Prieto, as a physical object, a concrete object. Which does not mean deprived of thought, but rather that thought, present and working in it, functions in a presemiotic way, in the words of Hjelmslev, like matter *tout court* and not at all like matter already constructed into sign.

John Solt   The visual, how the poem looks on the page, the shape of the design as geometric or otherwise.

Claus Clüver   Any form of engagement with the materiality of the textual material, in particular with intersemiotic dimensions of textmaking; consequently, the production of texts that are highly self-referential, that involve the reader in questions of semantics, both on the level of minimal signifying elements and of syntax and structure; of texts that are primarily metalinguistic, metatextual, metapoetic; of texts that combine reduction of material(s) with semantic condensation/intensification; of verbal texts exploiting their aural-"musical" dimension or the visual-plastic-spatial dimension of their notation for semantic and not merely decorative purposes; of texts presenting themselves as spatio-temporal structures – visually, aurally, kinetically, and/or in performance; of intermedia or multimedia texts that have these qualities. Furthermore, any kind of textmaking that engages the reader in "operating" the text, in "game activities" – conceptual or physical.

Philadelpho Menezes   I consider "concretism" one of the trends of visual poetry, and "visual poetry" a part of a general "experimental poetry," where "sound poetry" must be included as another side of the same coin of contemporary experimentalism. In this way, I see Concrete poetry as a specific procedure of visual poetry that marks the last experiment carried out exclusively with the word. After the explosion of the verse and the word realized by the historical avant-gardes, concretism, as a late avant-garde, conceived a reorganization of the poem, based on a mathematical and geometric order and on a practice of similarity of verbal signifiers. Concretism represents a particular moment of the visual poetry in the first two decades of the post-war period when culture and society were searching for a new order of values and visions.

Concrete poetry, like the Concrete art of the 30s and 40s, offered a direction to rethink the relationship between poetics and mass culture, different from the historical avant-gardes. Futurism, for instance, aimed to do that by a utopian intention of transforming the cultural system, while Concrete poetry has opened itself to receive the influence of mass culture (and tried to insert its forms in it) without the intention of rupture. Another element can be added to explain the late avant-garde nature of Concrete poetry: the end of utopian purposes of the experimental poetics and the fast assimilation of the concretist procedures by advertising, universities, and museums.

Dick Higgins   Concrete poetry is one of the main forms of visual poetry. Its position within the whole has yet to be explored intelligently, and I had hoped this would happen at Yale; however almost none of the participants seemed to know of other visual poetries and therefore lacked the conceptual basis for doing so. "Concretism" seems to be a fiction invented by analogy with the many movements which end in "-ism," and it assumes that Concrete poetry is a movement and not a form. This is a moot point.

Harry Polkinhorn   I understand "concretism" to refer to the practices of some poets of the 1950s. In this sense, very little of contemporary poetic practice in the United States is directly engaged. Likewise, little in poetics has much to do with concretism. The political dimensions of the term poetics seen as a "systematic theory or doctrine of poetry" (Preminger), however, are directly engaged with concretism as an ideological construction. That is, in the ongoing cultural process of elevating some kinds of poetry (while suppressing others as irrelevant), concretism offers itself as a model for various more recent "schools" or "movements," such as Language Poetry, for example.

Charles Bernstein   "Concretism" suggests the radical materializing dimension within Concrete poetry, and I would say this work continues unabated in the poetry in North America often associated with L=A=N=G=U=A=G=E, the magazine Bruce Andrews and I edited from 1978-82. Certainly, we have many poets now working to make more concrete both the visual and sound dynamics of poems, though often in ways that would not allow their work to be categorized as sound poetry or visual poetry. (Some examples would be Susan Howe, Johanna Drucker, David Melnick, Jackson Mac Low, Larry Eigner, and Steve McCaffery.) Rather what has become inescapable is the fact of the poem, whether printed or performed, as a total sound environment; and, too, the fact of the poem, when printed, as wholly expressed in and through its visuality. In this sense, concretism, in its resistance to naturalizing poetic language, restores poetry to itself, to its medium. At the same time, recent work has also insisted on the social materiality of the poem, a rethinking of what the materiality of language is that incorporates the social and historical registers of words and their combinations not as tools toward extralinguistic expression or description but as artifacts that reflect, inflect, and inhabit the world. (Such social expressionism I associate, for example, with Hannah Weiner, Leslie Scalapino, Lyn Hejinian, Bruce Andrews, Ron Silliman.)

Steve McCaffery   I believe that aspect of contemporary poetics that might be termed the critique of voice is a central and persistent presence within concretism. It is important to distinguish vocality from voice. The latter, like the Freudian phallus, is to be understood less as a physical organ than an ideologically saturated signified fundamentally complicit with the logocentric tradition. A further dimension is the abrogation of linearity. The latter we have come to understand not merely as a spatial arrangement but as a way of thinking. A linked repudiation is that of grammar, of course, as an ideological governor of textuality. As also the break with linearity entailing the further break from lineal temporality, opening the poem up as a mediational or ludic space of indeterminate duration for the reader. A final dimension of contemporary relevance is the continued foregrounding of the materiality of the linguistic sign. All three dimensions mentioned might be considered as demythologizing, defetishizing positions.

On a negative note, concretism in some of its aspects can be seen as complicit with the objectification of the text, a reification of the inherent shiftiness of language into a linguistic object, literally framed and gazed upon. Perhaps the most enduring accusation against early Concrete is its failure to engage the social base of language as an interactive heteroglossia. This removal of language from active discourse and the living context of the sociolectic; this divorce from social utterance which instantly de-politicizes the work, remains the main issue in evaluating concretism's relevance or irrelevance to current cultural debate.

Finally, concretism is a fundamental force in the continual assault upon generic partition. I emphasize the word force as I do not admit concretism to be a genre spawned by high modernism, but a heuristic dynamism. This exploratory tendency naturally commits concretism less to advancing an aesthetic than to an active practice of the impermanent. Therefore requiring an engagement with social utterance.

***

Poetics After Concretism

Johanna Drucker Contemporary poetics seems to have moved far from the concerns of concretism as it was conceived within the two arenas of Brazilian and German/Swiss activity in the 1950s and 1960s. Contemporary visual poetry draws on some of the same sources within the early 20th century avant-garde, but also seems highly influenced by a collage sensibility from the visual arts, postmodern strategies of appropriation, and the synthetic mixture of elements (text and image, photography and writing, drawing and manipulations of layering, distorting, and so forth) made possible by electronic media.

Wladimir Kryksinski The heroic epoch of Concrete poetry seems to be over. Although there is no unifying poetics today, one has to acknowledge the fact that various contemporary poetics contain persisting and important elements of concretism. The concept of concretism being ambiguous and difficult to define on the basis of stable critical parameters, I would rather call these elements "concrete" operations: principle of repetition, permutational game of words, differential typographical game, inscription of the iconographic signs, manipulation of quotations or of quoted units. The "concrete" operations regularly occur in such poets as A. de Campos, H. de Campos, and D. Pignatari. Their present poetic practices tend to be more individualized than during the brilliant period of Noigandres. They both extend and, to some point, repeat the experimental poetry of Noigandres. However, Haroldo's recent poetic practice seems to return to the classical *topoi* (Homer) which, throughout his poetic discourse, undergo numerous permutational operations. The practices of the two Portuguese poets, E. M. de Melo e Castro and Ana Hatherly, are deeply grounded in "concrete" operations. (One must add Alberto Pimenta, Álvaro Neto [*Gramatica Histórica*] and some other writers.) Their writing is based on a strong foregrounding of language as a concrete material whose manoeuvrable elements are put into textual circulation: repetitions, permutations, language game, etc. The idea of experiment as a constant exploration of language in its numerous manifestations (grammar, syntax, semantics, morphology, phonetics, syntagms, paradigms, visuality) is at the basis of the writing practices of E. M. de Melo e Castro (see his quite remarkable *Corpos Radiantes*, 1982 and *O Fogo Frio do Texto*, 1989) and Ana Hatherly. The visual poetry of Ana Hatherly is "concrete" par excellence because it shows the tangibility of forms whose variations are given to be seen and understood as "poetry."

I would also like to consider several Italian poetic practices as being concretism-bound, for instance Sanguineti's *giochi verbali* (in *Straciafoglio*); Balestrini's poetics of prose-poetry in conjunctive manifestations (*Blackout*), of *neutralizzazione del materiale verbale*; decomposition, spatialization, repetition, language game, and "word" play in Porta, Giuliani, Pignotti, and many others. (Cf. R. Barilli: *Viaggio al termine della parola. La ricerca intraverbale*, Feltrinelli, 1981.) Finally, I would like to underline the importance of Enzo Minarelli's "concrete" poetic quests; his poetry draws strongly on such conceptions and realizations of concretism as: *poesia vincolata* (linked poetry), *poesia intersemiotica*, and *polipoesia*.

Marjorie Perloff   The Concrete movement qua movement may be dead, but its influence is, in one sense, more widespread than ever. The central notion of concretism – that language has a visual dimension and that the actual "look" of a poem on the page determines, at least in part, its meaning – is central to the visual poetics now ubiquitous. With computer graphics and layout possibilities, no poet can wholly ignore the role visual language plays (although some poets do write as if nothing has changed since the nineteenth century!)

Eduardo Kac   A holopoem is not a poem composed in lines of verse and made into a hologram, nor is it a concrete or visual poem adapted to holography. The sequential structure of a line of verse corresponds to linear thinking, whereas the simultaneous structure of a concrete or visual poem corresponds to ideographic thinking. As distinguished from traditional visual poetry, it seeks to express *dynamically* the discontinuity of thought; in other words, the perception of a holopoem takes place neither linearly nor simultaneously but rather through fragments seen at random by the observer, depending on the observer's position relative to the poem. Holopoetry belongs to the tradition of experimental poetry, but it treats the word as an immaterial form that can change or dissolve into thin air, breaking its formal stiffness. Freed from the page and other palpable materials, the word invades the reader's space and forces him or her to read it in a dynamic way. (See my essay in this volume, p. 247-257, for a description of the most important expressive possibilities of holopoetry, all unique to its grammar and only possible in part because of its specific behavioral space.)

Historical Precedents of Concrete Texts

How do you see the historical precedents of your own Concrete work? If you are not discussing your own work, please select a specific text on which to base your comments.

Luciano Nanni   It may surprise everyone, but I would like to point out my direct historical precedent as a concretist in the conception of writing found in Plato's *Phaedro*. Socrates says in this connection: "See, dear Phaedro, the shapes of writing are like those of painting: if you ask them they reply to you with a solemn silence." These words contain the whole idea of Concrete writing and its immediate visual valence. Here, to be sure, the concretism is a potentiality. My concretism and that of all the so-called Concrete poets and artists, is concretism put into effect, into practice. But in *Phaedro* I can see purer reasons for my work. Moreover, I would consider it my distinctive particularity to produce concreteness by frequently utilizing the Theuth myth (the Half-God, as is well-known, who gave writing to man and consequently became the archetype of writing itself) and its own image, variously significant and multiform.

Dick Higgins   One enterprise of mine has been to assemble a corpus of visual poetry going back to c. 1800 BC and continuing to the present. Not only every era but virtually every decade has impressed itself on the character of the works, but it is not for me as a working artist to point this out in detail; that is more the task of responsible scholars. I have also explored the history of the concept of intermedia itself (of which Concrete poetry is an example) and, with a friend, Charles Doria, translated Giordano Bruno's *On the Composition of Images, Signs and Ideas* (1591; New York: Willis, Locker and Owens, 1991) to this end. The history not only of intermedial works but also of the concept of intermedia will require the opinions and efforts of more than one person, however.

Augusto de Campos   For me, the dividing line for inventive poetic language in modern times is Mallarmé's work *Un coup de dés* (1897), a poem conceived intersemiotically as a fragmentary structure ("subdivisions prismatiques de l'Idée"), conjoining visual mural and musical score. With the acceptance of that work, it became possible to revisit the experiences of the vanguards of the beginning of the century and conceive of new elaborations. "Sans présumer de l'avenir qui sortira d'ici, rien ou presque un art," the last Mallarmé – from *Un coup de dés* to *Le livre* – catalyzes and spreads the principal future alternatives of poetic language. In his final period and in the subsequent developments of the historical vanguards, which will be recycled and radicalized by Concrete poetry, one encounters the formal presuppositions of the poetry of the Techno-logical Era, which greatly expands throughout the second half of the century. Besides Mallarmé and the historical vanguards, I would place as direct precedents Ezra Pound (the ideogrammatic method, the collage and metalan-guage of the *Cantos*), James Joyce (the vocabulistic kaleidoscope of *Finnegans Wake* and its textual polyreadings), cummings (the atomization and syntactical dislocation of his most experimental poems), and, on a second level, more idiosyncratic and less rigorous, the experimental, minimalist, and molecular prose of Gertrude Stein. In the special case of Brazilian poetry, the Sousândrade of *O inferno de Wall Street*, with its pre-collage epigrammatic mosaics, Oswald de Andrade and the "anthropophagic" instant-poem, the constructivist engineering of João Cabral [de Melo Neto]. In a transdisci-plinary mode, I would mention the transformations of musical language from Webern to Cage and of the visual from Malevich/Mondrian to Duchamp.

Wladimir Krysinski   Taking into account such poems by Haroldo de Campos as "Orfeu e o discípulo," "A naja vertebral," and "A invencível arma-da" [*Xadrez de Estrelas*], I should stress the importance of the historical prece-dents stemming from Mallarmé's and Apollinaire's specific poetics. What we see in these poems is a development of Mallarmé's poetics of spatialization and of constellation ("Orfeu" and "A invencível armada"), as well as Apollinaire's principle of *calligrammes* ("A naja vertebral").

Claus Clüver   I find it hard to distinguish between model and precedent except with regard to demonstrable familiarity. The work of the Noigandres poets was consciously modeled after the work of poets, visual artists, film makers, and composers, both national and international, and they gave ample account of these models in their prolific critical and theoretical writings, which included translations (usually with commentary), beginning in 1956. Undoubtedly, the key figures are those named in the "Pilot Plan." The texts documented (reprinted or simply listed) in the *Teoria da Poesia Concreta* (1965) refer primarily to work produced in the twentieth century (and Mallarmé's *Un coup de dés*). Of older poets, they published in the fifties translations of poems by Marino and English metaphysical poets (Donne, Marvell) and of a haiku of Buson; in 1960, of texts by Arnaut and Dante, of Lewis Carroll's "Jabberwocky," of Corbière, of Bashô; Arno Holz appeared only in 1962. All of these texts were chosen because they were seen to share qualities with aspects of the Concrete aesthetic and program; the date of publication is no indication of when the Brazilians actually came to know these poets and their work. (They had been early exposed to Ezra Pound's paideuma and his love for Troubadour poetry.) Knowledge of Mayakovsky and other Russian Futurist work seems to have arrived quite late; and yet I would count that work among the major historical precedents in this century, as well as the poetry of Wassily Kandinsky, "concrete" according to Hans Arp. We know that the Brazilians were not familiar with classical *carmina figurata* before 1959, but these and their tradition must certainly count among the historical precedents; one might be able to relate Augusto de Campos's *poetamenos* poems (especially "Dias") to Carolingian *versus intexti* (and then go on to point out the profound differences); all forms of labyrinth poems and similar patterns would have a distinguished place in the tradition of visual poetry that could be connected with the Noigandres work. Direct historical precedents in the visual arts would be constructivist or Concrete art; for song, the ancestry would extend to the Troubadours and (very importantly) to the traditions of Brazilian popular music. Given the importance of John Cage for their later work, one would also have to assign a significant role to Marcel Duchamp.

E. M. de Melo e Castro   Although at the end of the fifties the contact with the Noigandres Poets of São Paulo was decisive, I soon realized that there was a different historical set of reasons for Concrete poetry in Portugal and in Brasil. Portugal, on the Iberian peninsula and belonging to Mediterranean culture, is one of the birth places of baroque literature. Therefore baroque poetry, though not critically recognized for nearly two hundred years, is deeply inside our poetic culture. It was necessary to rediscover the Portuguese Baroque to come to the conclusion that the Portuguese experimental and visual Poetry of the 1960s had its roots in seventeenth-century baroque poetry much more than in the influence of the theories of Fenollosa and Ezra Pound on the Chinese ideogram. This is in short how I now see the historical setting of my own Concrete, visual, info and video poetry work.

Ana Hatherly   My experimental work was influenced by the study of Chinese calligraphy and oriental philosophy, specifically Zen Buddhism, but as most early Concrete poets I was also interested in modern linguistics, structuralism, semiotics, and information theory. As a Portuguese experimentalist my work of the 60s and 70s had particular anti-establishment overtones, dictated by the need to oppose the situation our country was in at the time. My interest in baroque poetics, which started as one more way of opposing anti-establishment values (baroque poetry was considered the most obnoxious thing ever produced by Portuguese culture) gradually became a major research project covering centuries of visual poetry. This involvement with ancient visual poetry was shared by some European and American experimentalists since the 60s, who published anthologies of visual poetry through the ages establishing a link with Concrete times.

My research project was centered in Portuguese visual poetry of the Baroque, a branch of the European trend at the time, but I did not just anthologize what I found in the libraries: I went deeper trying to understand its theoretical basis, and in my book *A Experiência do Prodígio* (Lisboa: Imprensa Nacional-Casa da Moeda, 1983) I included about a hundred examples of our visual poetry unknown until then, accompanied by their respective design principles, when available. Later I published several articles on the reading rules of Labyrinths and other visual poems in *Colóquio-Artes* 66 (1985); *Poemografias* (Lisboa: Ulmeiro, 1985); *Visible Language* XX.1 (Winter, 1986); *Colóquio-Artes* 76; *Casa das Musas* (Lisboa: Editorial Estampa, 1995). This research, which took me decades and still goes on, adding to the parallel work of colleagues in Europe and America, revealed a continuous flow of this type of poetry through the centuries, based on identical rules, establishing the visual text as one of the oldest and most persistent forms of poetry in the world. The purpose of my research, which I carried out as a sort of archeology of experimental poetry, was not to produce copies or remakes of those texts: what I really wanted was to understand the mechanisms of this type of composition, its rules, its metamorphosis through the ages and its contemporary rebirth. It was a most gratifying job, and it led me to go deeper and deeper into the heart of writing, reading, and communicating. I had done something similar previously with Chinese calligraphy, as I explained in *Mapas da Imaginação e da Memória* (Lisboa: Moraes Editores, 1973), but while Chinese calligraphy was part of a formative stage, the research of baroque poetics became a life-long project. Essentially what I have always been concerned with is the creative process and the mechanisms of communication. Probing the mechanisms of writing and reading led me to go deeper into the questions of legibility and illegibility.

A summary of my main thoughts on this matter, gleaned from my essay *A*

Reinvenção da Leitura (Lisboa: Futura, 1975), and translated into English by Prof. William Watt, was published in *Visible Language* XI.3 (Summer 1977: 307-20). In that essay I point out what was most meaningful to me in this matter at the time, and still is, because as the years go by I realize more and more how important these questions are for any creative mind. I am indebted to Concrete poetry theory, of course, but its influence in my work was limited. Other twentieth-century avant-garde trends and baroque poetics became more important.

Although I was interested in filmmaking for a while (I actually became a qualified film maker and even taught at the Lisbon Film School in the 70s), I have not yet done any videopoems or holograms or any experiments in that medium. I leave that possibility open.

Steve McCaffery   Key historical precedents to all my work were the theories of the Noigandres group and the linear alternatives offered by Gomringer's writing. From both I learned an important semiotic implication that form is relational, not essential; that form is fundamentally dialogic. These ideas were supported later in my discovery of the theories of Mikhail Bakhtin.

***

Beyond Historical Concrete

Philadelpho Menezes   I am very honored by the inclusion of my work in the "Konkrete Poesie - Zwei Generationen" anthology, organized by Eugen Gomringer (Hans-Peter Kaeser Typograf SWB, St. Gallen, Switzerland, 1993). It was published on the occasion of the 40th anniversary of the Concrete poetry movement, and my poems appeared as an example of a second generation of Concrete. But I don't see my work as concretism. I feel it more linked to a post-Concrete poetry that appeared in Brazil in the 70s and 80s, which I call "intersign poetry." It surpassed the structure of mathematical permutation or geometric arrangements of similar words that carried out the concretist variation of the Joycean verbivocovisual concept. Intersign poetry makes use of images (photos, drawings, numbers and mathematical notation, musical symbols, etc.) to construct visual poems that demand a "reading" (a decodification) of the semantic aspects of image and word. This can be observed in the work of poets like Villari Herrmann, Florivaldo Menezes, Ronaldo Azeredo. The last link (but not of small importance) with Concrete poetry is the conception of "ideogram," that is, a procedure of combining, in an nonlinear construct, different signs so that not only a visual form but also an ensemble of ideas and concepts can be produced. My first two books of poems (1980 and 1984) are totally included in this prospective.

My last poem-book (*Demoligues ou Poemas Arítmiticos*. São Paulo: Arte Pau-Brasil, 1988) retakes a trend of experimental poems elaborated only with verbal signs. They are disposed in the space of the page using elemental arithmetical variations in order to create paradoxes. So this book has more to do with concretism than the others. But my main research in these last four years is centered in sound poetry. Consequently the dialogue I am trying to establish is very far from Concrete poetry. Now I am referring to the work of poets like Fortunato Depero, Kurt Schwitters, Hugo Ball (of the historical avant-gardes), Bernard Heidsieck, Brion Gysin, Harry Polkinhorn, Enzo Minarelli (among the contemporaries).

John Solt   The Concrete "moment" (late 1950s to late 1970s) paid attention to the form and the relations between form and content in a new way. The narrative thrust until that time had been a dominant but superimposed element that took precedence in conscious and unconscious conceptualizing, but narrative in the Concrete moment collapsed into a residue which, when stirred (by reading), emerged as one imaginative possibility, spiraling out from within the poem. Concrete as such is no longer a dominant element of my work, but the effects of that moment are etched in the foundation of what I do.

Harry Polkinhorn   I don't see my visual poetry as "Concrete work." Rather, it is indirectly related to post-Concrete movements in visual writing, all of which grow not so much out of concretism specifically as out of the rich network of alternative poetries in which concretism participated, all of which explore page space as a signifying element.

Johanna Drucker   Though my own typographic work has been compared to the work of early 20th century artists within Dada or Futurism, I was more or less ignorant of those artists when I began working. I found as much inspiration in advertising graphics, commercial media such as tabloids and supermarket flyers, as in literary sources. Of course, once I began to study and understand the historical precedents, they became a valuable resource and point of reference as well. But my own experience convinces me that a visual sensibility need not develop only in response to the historical avant-garde in poetry or visual arts, but can be developed from a wide range of sources.

Eduardo Kac   Please let me make clear that my work is not concrete. Concrete poetry was a movement that started in the 50s and that achieved international recognition in the 60s. Concrete poetry had very specific stylistic parameters, as stated in the manifestoes and theoretical writings published at the time. I think there is a need to clarify the meaning of the words experimental, visual, and concrete. All vanguard movements and directions in this century were experimental, in the sense that they questioned the mainstream canon and experimented with new possibilities. Some of these new possibilities involved the use of images in poetry, or the creation of poems that were, themselves, images. Works thus produced fall under the category "visual poetry." Other equally significant directions of experimental poetry were not visual, or at least not primarily visual, as in the French Sound Poetry movement, for example. This century saw many movements and groups, as well as important individuals, in several countries, which developed their own poetics. I believe that they contributed equally to the larger debate on experimental poetry. Here is a partial list up to the 60s: France (Apollinaire, Cendrars, Birot, Lettrism, sound poetry, Oulipo); Italy (Futurism, Belloli, *poesia visiva*, Balestrini); United States (cummings, Giorno, Marcus, Kostelanetz, Language Poetry); Brazil (Luís Aranha, O. de Andrade, Concretism/Neo-Concretism, Poema/Processo), Chile (Huidobro, Parra, Deisler), Russia (Khlebnikov, Kamensky, Nikonova), Germany (Gomringer, Rühm, Dencker), Portugal (Almada-Negreiros, Sá-Carneiro, Pessoa, *PO.EX.*). I see the works of all these poets and groups as historical precedents to my work, at the same time that I clearly distinguish the innovative aspects of my own poetics. Since 1983 I have been developing a new poetics based on the exploration of the unique syntactical possibilities of holography, computer animation, and hypertext. I call my work Holopoetry.

Theoretical Underpinnings of Experimental Poetry

What are the theoretical underpinnings which distinguish your work from that of historical precedents or contemporaries? If not discussing your own work, please base your comments on specific poets and works.

John Solt   Intuition is the key. Rewriting the same poem is shunned in favor of the unknown. Logic is easily discarded, but so is illogic, if utter nonsense. How to use the style ("voice") developed over decades for aesthetic effect while breaking new ground to oneself in form and/or content is a perpetual challenge. Not paying attention to other people's theories and mythologies unless they come in eyeshot or earshot in a natural way.

Dick Higgins   Theory today is a more self-conscious enterprise than it was forty years ago. In preparing any critique of any avant-garde work I find there is too little consensus concerning meaning, especially regarding the appropriate use of particular forms, to apply semiotics, while deconstruction as an approach is an amusing pastime but no more. I find only hermeneutics works, and I mean specifically the Gadamer-derived work of Jauss and the School of Constance with its addition of an horizon of expectations and an horizon of poiesis to the body of possibilities. Further, I find I can use these myself as an artist in my various intermedial meditations.

Philadelpho Menezes   My theoretical underpinnings are semiotics (a mixing of Peircean semiotics and the European semiology), theory of communication, cultural studies, theory of culture (the debate of modernity and postmodernity, that I prefer to consider as a metamodernity). It is not specially different from the underpinnings that informed the theoretical approaches of my contemporaries, who are willing to elaborate their works critically. I try to fix a particular point of view in the conclusions that I risk to draw. I want to point out a special question that is related to technology. For me, most of the technological experiments in art, and particularly in poetry, are developed as if the single use of new techniques could lead to a new form of language and expression. On the contrary, what we see is that the technological poems only reproduce the old formula of permutation of words in an organized development that the concretism of the 60s produced on paper. In the field of sound experiments, the technological poetry makes evident a sort of epiphanic contemporary mysticism in art as if the nature of the new sound sign (or synthetic images, in the field of computer graphics, holography, and virtual reality) could reveal a kingdom of freedom in expression that should redeem us. It leads to a very repetitive procedure of technologic poems which obstructs the exploration of the real potentiality for a new poetry. I think technology must be thought as a transformed utopia. Technology accomplishes its expressivity as a means for poetry like a "heteropia," a utopia that realizes itself in another place, out of it but in indirect connection with it. That is, the language of technological poems is present out of the technological media properly. Intersign poems, published on paper (in the case of visual poetry) or produced and exhibited in low technology (in the case of sound poetry), expose more of the questions of high technology of language than the products of technological art.

Harry Polkinhorn   The "theoretical underpinnings" of my output are in fact not underpinnings but assumptions that are inextricably bound into the very fabric of the entire work in its social/cultural context. In this sense, my work comes out of post-structuralism's revalidation of the conflation of theory and practice, which then aligns me with certain impulses of the historical avant-gardes (Futurism, Dadaism, Cubo-futurism, Surrealism).

Charles Bernstein   I'm attracted to the idea of lines being a primarily visual feature of the poem – it's a modest way of designing (or arranging) how the page looks, an overlay – one more dynamic of the poem's multi-layered ecosystem.

Often I don't leave pauses for the line breaks when I perform a poem, which suggests that they are not principally related to the temporal sound text (or phono text). But then again, in performance, there are many more ways to cue different tones, voices, rhythms, beats, and phrasing than on the page, that the line becomes a crucial device for setting such things in motion. If the line is relatively independent of the phono text, then that's one of its great advantages, because you can play with the peculiarly visual space of the page, which is a particular feature of writing as opposed to spoken language or other non-verbal signifying practices. Given my interest in interruption (more than fragmentation), the line allows for a visual interruption of the phrase (or sentence) without necessarily requiring a temporal interruption, a pause: that's why I so often cut the line where you are least likely to pause (say between an article and a noun). When you break the line against the phrase, rather than at the end of a phrase, it's called syntactic scissoring; this preoccupies me because I can use it to set in motion a counter-measure that adds to the rhythmic richness of the poem: the main measure in the phrasally forward movement of the phono text, and the countermeasure of the syntactic scissoring of the visual text.

I'm mindful of Dennis Tedlock's useful discussion of the line as a device for registering oral dynamics of native American verbal art. Tedlock's use of the line in his translations/transcriptions is as far from traditional prosody as anything modernist poetry has come up with. Tedlock roundly condemns the use of prose to convey the hyper dynamic sound space of oral literature and has developed ways to cue not just different lengths of pausing, but also pitch, loudness, and other features of the phono text. I'm very attracted to the acoustic tactility both of the oral literature he is attending to and also his ways of transforming it into a multitextured writing. ("Writing wrongs speech," as Neil Schmitz puts it in his book on Twain and Stein.)

In creating an aural poetry, I think it's possible to have the resonant presence of language without hypostatizing a single speaker as the source of the language. Writing, that is, can become answerable to itself in ways that do not advance upon orality but are co-present with it. To do this, however, writing cannot revert to the conditions of orality, nostalgically imagining itself as secondary, as transcript of the voice, but rather must acknowledge its own materiality and acoustic density/destiny, its visible aurality.

Veil is my most visually oriented work. The visual emblem is produced by several layers of overtyping, so that much, but not all, of the freely composed writing is obliterated. One model I had was Morris Louis's "Veil" paintings, where successive stains of color occlude the inner layers, though at the edges the brightest of the suppressed underlayers of color shines through, ecstatically.

The sense of stain, as in soiling, and its associated sadness, is crucial; but also, as in biochemistry, the stain allowing you to identify otherwise invisible substances. In this sense, my poetry is an acoustic staining. That's why I'm inclined to dwell on (in) forms of damage, maladjustment, dislocation. This is not an aesthetic theory so much as an experiential dynamic – call it the everyday: that we have our misalignments more in common than our adjustment to the socially correct norms. Normalcy is the enemy of poetry – my poetry, "our" poetry.

The veil acknowledges the stigma that is our common ground, our point of adjacency with one another, our "us"ness. Here, *Veil* is related to a short book of my poems called *Stigma*, based on the title on one of Erving Goffman's resonant books on this topic.

The epigraph for *Veil* comes from Hawthorne's "The Minister's Black Veil," where the minister explains why he wears a veil: "There is an hour to come when all of us shall cast aside our veils. Take it not amiss, beloved friend, if I wear this piece of crape till then." Our bodies veil us from transparency (say, assimilation) and the veil acknowledges that: that we can't communicate as if we had no veils or bodies or histories separating us, that whatever communication we can manage must be in terms of our opacities and particularities, our resistances and impermeabilities – call it our mutual translucency to each other. Our language is our veil, but one that too often is made invisible. Yet, hiding the veil of language, its wordness, its textures, its obstinate physicality, only makes matters worse. Perhaps such veils will be cast aside in the Messianic moment, that utopian point in which history vanishes. On this side of the veil, which is our life on earth, we live within and among the particulars of a here (hear) and now (words that speak of and to our condition of everydayness).

Johanna Drucker   From the point at which I began to be acquainted with Language poets in the mid-1970s I felt an affinity with their experimental sensibility and appreciation of materiality but also felt an important point of distinction in my own interest in prose forms over poetic ones. In the 1980s, as a graduate student, I came under the influence of the usual critical theory texts from structuralism to post- as well as feminist theory and practice in experimental film and criticism.

***

Specificity of Concrete Poetics

Augusto de Campos   In view of the specific historical context in which it occurred, Concrete poetry obviously did not participate either in the ideology of Symbolism, which still underlies Mallarmé's poetics, or in the mecano-political Futurist utopias, or in Dadaist nihilism. Concrete poetry took a position as a poetics of objectivity, attempting simply to place its premises at the roots of language, with the intention of creating new operational conditions for the elaboration of a poem in the sphere of technological revolution. Technically, Concrete poets can be distinguished from their antecedents by the radicalization and condensation of the means of structuring a poem, on the horizon of the means of communication of the second half of the century. That implies, among other characteristics, the following: greater constructive rigor in relation to the graphic experiences of Futurists and Dadaists; greater concentration of vocabulary; emphasis on the nondiscursive character of poetry, suppression or relativization of syntactic links; making explicit the materiality of language in its visual and sonorous dimensions; free passage between verbal and nonverbal levels.

Poems such as "terra" by Décio Pignatari or "cristal" by Haroldo de Campos, from the 50s, or my "cidadecitycité" or "olho por olho" from the 60s typify these characteristics.

Concrete poets may be differentiated from other experiences (*zaum*, *lettrisme*, phonetic poetry) for not rejecting semantic values but rather placing them on equal footing with other material, visual, and sonorous parameters of the poem. They differentiate themselves from the "chance poetry" of Cage and others for not abdicating control of the structure of the poem, although allowing for chance interventions.

Willard Bohn   *Lettrisme* is different from Concrete poetry and in theory a rival. *Lettrisme* is a violently antagonistic movement that attacks the foundations of bourgeois society through the medium of the written word by reducing the letters of the alphabet to a series of phonetic or visual counters. By emphasizing the autonomy of the individual letter or sign at the expense of the larger word, it aims to destroy signification itself.

Haroldo de Campos   Concrete poetry, through its anonymous and plural group poetics, attempted to carry Mallarmé's project to its ultimate consequences by radicalizing the "verbi-voco-visual" up to its limits. Concrete poetry broke with residual discourses by converting itself into a "tension of word-objects in space-time," also producing unintentionally an intense, provocative, and instantaneous model of the *modus operandi* of the poetic function theorized by Jakobson. Structure became content and the "episte-mological metaphor," (to use Umberto Eco's term) of a world "produced" by the autonomous and self-reflexive poem.

We distinguish three phases in Concrete poetry. The first is the "organic phase," or "heroic phase," where there was a multiplicity of semantic elements. In fact, Concrete poetry was radical in its geometric phase, which we also called the "golden phase" – between 1958-60 – and it was minimalist poetry *avant la lettre*, even before the term existed. Concrete poetry adopted a polemical, almost terrorist attitude. We decreed the end of verse. There were Webernian and Mondrianesque poems, with moments of extreme bareness. That was the highest point of contention in Concrete poetry and the greatest approximation between occidental and oriental language. Japanese poets, with their ideogrammatic tradition, adopted gestaltic techniques of graphic organization from Brazilian Concrete poetry in order to reorganize poetry in Japanese. That is, we attempted to make an ideogram in Western poetry, and the Japanese "reideographed" their poetry with this Western example. There were only two ways for Concrete poetry to evolve: either it practiced an engaged poetics or it assumed total silence. The second phase, the "participa-tory leap," was announced by Décio Pignatari in 1963 at the Congress of Literary Criticism in Assis [São Paulo]. We opted to translate Mayakovsky, Brecht, with the idea that "without revolutionary form there can be no revolutionary art." Then, after the military coup of 1964, we went through a long period of suffocation. In spite of the impasse, we published the *Antologia da Poesia Russa*, and some book dealers were afraid to sell it.

Claus Clüver   These are samples rather than singularly precise instances: One could make a convincing argument that one of the closest precedents of Concrete poetry is the first of Anton von Webern's *Fünf Stücke für Orchester*, op. 10. Max Bill's work (much more than Mondrian's) would be another close precedent; the difference would be primarily in deciding what, if anything, is analogous in Bill's work to the important role played by verbal semantics in the poems, and most of the poems could not be reduced to the kind of structural formula that is Bill's concept of a visual idea. To Kurt Schwitters's "Gedicht 25," another close precedent, it is difficult to apply the concept of isomorphism that is so crucial to the Brazilians' Concrete aesthetic; its shape is clearly the result of its structure but makes it look like a visual poem, with mimetic implications that have nothing to do with its semantics. Isomorphism is a striking aspect of e. e. cummings's "bright" (translated by Augusto de Campos) – but the poem is still organized in stanzas, in contrast to the spatial syntax of the Concrete ideogram. The distance to Apollinaire's *calligrammes* is greater, through not as great as the "Pilot Plan" suggests. The strong affinity of the Noigandres poets' work to Kandinsky's prose poems in *Klänge* (1912) is on a more abstract, conceptual level and extends beyond the poetry of the fifties.

Steve McCaffery   When Concrete poetry appeared in Canada (circa 1963) it was not the emergence of a tangible movement, with a strong theoretical base – there were no manifestos for instance – but as a facet of marginalized publishing forces whose economy and productions were inseparable from low-budget publishing technology: mimeography. In the early venues: *Ganglia, Blewointment* linear texts coexisted alongside the Concrete work of Ian Hamilton Finlay and Jiři Valoch. Concrete was understood as one facet of the "new" and the "alternative" and did not manifest as pre-theorized but as a tactical insurgence into the dominant linear modes of lyric and narrative. In the case of bill bissett, bp Nichol, and myself, theories came *after* the fact and in so coming frequently precipitated revised agendas and altered directions. During the 60s and 70s we enjoyed and advanced what in Lucy Lippard's terminology might be called the dematerialization of the poem. It was less a Concrete poetry per se that was embraced, but rather concretism as a facet of what we considered "the language of revolution" which itself entailed a movement away from national themes and poetics towards the internationalism of an avant-garde and the global possibilities opened up by the rise of semiotics. Canada, then, did not produce an exclusively "Concrete" poet. The obsolescent Goliath, of course, was linearity. Less the literal, material line than linear cognition; the line as phenomenological ground, as an habitual mental given. The theories most amenable were Dom Sylvester Houedard's notion of the "borderblur" and Dick Higgins's concept of intermedia.

I personally worked at the unstable intersection oral/visual dimensions. What I grasped was the inherent performability of the "stable" visual or "constellated" text. Initially, because of the ideogrammic nature of early Canadian Concrete, this led to sound poems somewhat different from the Dadaists, producing chants and phonic structures that were the result of an initially visual and patterned poem. The resultant sound texts carried problematic notions of the subject and perhaps exemplified a belated Romanticism. What I relied upon was a familiar transit theory of communication in which "energy" (i.e. patterned vocal, buccal outlays) replaced "semantic" as the unit of message. (The connection here with Charles Olson's theory of proprioception and projective verse is not coincidental.) I later modified my notions of text-sound performance via Bataille's general economy and came to think of my work as a practice of outlay and expenditure.

Concrete Poets of the 1950s/1960s and Poetics Today

To what extent is the work you are discussing different from the work of the Concrete poets of the 1950s and 1960s? How?

Augusto de Campos   Now four decades since the first experiences of Concrete poetry, I would say that the 50s and 60s were the period of greatest orthodoxy of the movement, something like the serialization of all musical parameters proposed by European post-Webernian musicians. In the later decades there occurred a greater flexibility of poetic language in the sense of recuperation of phrasic structures (in relation to the elementarism of the first phase, with poems made up of only one word or of a few spatialized substantives) and of the inclusion of chance (with the interventions of Cage), but that flexibility always observed a compositional rigor and the principle of functionality or of the formal necessity of the poem. Such an opening became inevitable in view of the redundancy of process and of its degradation, brought about by the ineffectiveness of many realizations, especially in the area of visual poetry, characterized by a semantic insignificance analogous to many baroque graphic "labyrinths," which, with the superficiality of repeated graphic emblems, did not amount to more than the vacuity of epithalamian or funerial elegies. Such an opening should not be confused either with with the apparent complexity of the simply chaotic-surrealist texts that used graphic space without any satisfactory formal basis. Works of the 80s and 90s are, on the one hand, freer in relation to the orthodoxy of the first years and, on the other, more intensely participatory in the challenge of new technologies, which have produced digitalized poems, graphic and sound animation, and multimedia and intermedia processes. In this way, the "wishful thinking" of the 50s came about with computers, an ideal space for "verbivocovisual" adventures.

E. M. de Melo e Castro   Concrete, visual, spatial, and experimental poetry are of an international supra- or interlinguistic nature. Therefore it is very difficult to underline the differences among contemporary works that have similar theoretical roots and similar aims. Also, one of the questions more often discussed and a cause of misunderstanding is the relatively weak importance of the "I" of the Concrete and experimental poet. In fact this is one of the reasons Concrete poetry can't be considered as a kind of lyric poetry. But this is not an important problem, since I think that the subject of visual poetry is the questioning of the means of communication – verbal, nonverbal, or both. The poet as an individual being therefore a part of the communication system. A part that can be present or not in an explicit way in the poem itself. The poem being therefore the object of communication.

As for my personal experience, I began experimenting with words within the frame of verbal poetry in the 1950s, searching for an economy of language that very soon brought me to the transgression of grammar, experimenting with combinatory algorithms applied to verbal materials, words, and letters. Thus I went from the hypotaxe to the parataxe abolishing the difference between verbal and non-verbal and reaching a totally visual concept of invention. At this point, I realized that poetry is always on the limits of things: of what can be said, written, and even of what can be thought, felt, and understood. The next step was starting to experiment with the means of making poetry. Concrete poetry was for me not an arrival point but rather a starting one, or even better a launching platform.

At first I did Concrete poems by handwriting or using old typographical types. Later came letterpress techniques making the work easier. Soon it became evident to me that experimenting with letters and with different materials is the way to produce visual poetry. So I did poems in paper, in wood, in textiles, in stone and plastics. Now I use light to produce infopoems and video poems. My first video poem – RODA LUME – is from 1968, and since then I realized that heavy materials were coming to an end as a support for communication. The de-materialized virtual image is in itself a poetic image and therefore the poem should also be de-materialized. Video poetry became technically possible, and a new type of poem using the computer as a tool opened to a different notion of time/space/color and transformation.

Lello Voce   As I said in my essay on "Avant-garde and Tradition" (cf. p. 119), some contemporary poetry stresses technological means rather than message, meaning, communication. I am not convinced by such work (for instance Kac's holopoems or Melo e Castro's videopoems), because of its cool, technological reference. It glamorously misses the target of an anthropological effect, of contemporaneity, and brutally impoverishes gnosis, because it places its total trust in the technological means and in their power. The battle against "Star Wars" and the one against signed video clips (I'm thinking, for example, of those splendid and pitiless ones by Bruce Nauman) is, in a word, sensationally lost.

The apparent paradox that occured at Yale was that the "simple" readings of their own texts made by Steve McCaffery and Charles Bernstein were absolutely more successful in the determination of a possible space of contemporaneousness for what I would define as "post-sound;" and in some way post-technological poetry, or the video by Ana Hatherly (*Revoluçao*) dedicated to the mass movement which led Portugal to get rid of dictatorship (in spite of the fact that it was created with technologies that the author herself has defined by now as "archeological"), has lost nothing of its communicative and expressive pregnancy, or its "necessity," thanks to the skill, transmitted to the *medium*, of concentrating meanings with a very high content in the form of its own linguistic code: in spite of laser and CD ROM.

The case of Augusto de Campos and Cid Campos is very different as is the one of the three Japanese performers. The use of electronic media (videos, tapes) has been mixed with the use of the most traditional ways of music (from the thousand-year old plectrum of Fujitomi, Takahashi, and Nishimatsu to the bass guitar played with extreme discretion by Cid Campos) and has supported texts with remarkable aesthetic qualities. Moreover in the case of the two Brazilians, the performances of passages from ancient and modern literary tradition (from Bertrand de Ventadorn to Joyce) have joined expressiveness and very accurate philological intrigue, reaching really remarkable results. Another thing that I wish to underline is that in both the cases which I have right now mentioned, in spite of the mixing of different fields, it seems to me that the target of the performers is not absolutely synesthetic. I have already had a chance to express elsewhere my suspicion towards such poetics. I think that any field has all the others inside itself even though at levels of formal pregnancy that are hierarchically inferior: in short, it really is true that words have their own rhythm, music its own syntax, icons their own grammar, and verses their own iconicity, and could I be excused for the brutal simplification caused by the brevity of this short report. That doesn't obviously mean that performances in which different media and different performers take part are not practicable. What is important, in my opinion, is that we are conscious of the "interlinguistic" and not synesthetic valence of what we are carrying out: a dialogue, in a word, among different media, any of them being very deep in its own field, may be according to the postulate by Lotman suggesting that dialogue always comes before language without any illusion of reaching toward total art. On the other hand, it's not accidental that Augusto de Campos, with his brother Haroldo and with Décio Pignatari, is one of the fathers of Concrete poetry, the only "non-linear" poetic avant-garde in these last decades to direct its research towards the inside of its own field, deep inside its roots, to discover in the end that in the sign itself are contained those echoes of what is "different" from itself, echoes which some visual and sound poets were looking for outside.

Eric Vos   The most important issue at stake in the debate on "(new) poetics and (new) technologies" is the complex of interrelationships between potentialities of text (re-) production and poetical concerns; what counts is the way in which these influence each other. Neither of the two constitutes the "essential" characteristic of a particular type of work or an "essential" difference with other types of work by itself. (In fact, I don't believe that such "essentials" exist.) Which is also to say that the poetical impact of the technological aspect cannot be taken for granted, but should neither be dismissed too soon. And that ascertaining to what extent such work in the new media poetries differs from the Concrete poetry of the 50s and 60s depends, as always, on the interpretation of both poems and poetics, and particularly on the connections between these two that we care to observe.

John Solt   I recall and prize the excitement of the Concrete movement when breakthroughs into a new realm of poetry were achieved internationally. The need for new poetry was symbolic of the Futuristic age we were envisioning with psychedelics, rock music, the "out" jazz of John Coltrane, Pharaoh Sanders, etc. I absorbed that moment, but times changed and I am not hanging on to the experimentation of the 1960s and 1970s as a rigid orthodoxy. Rather, the Concrete moment is one facet of my poetry which ranges in content from narrative eulogies and one-line jokes to assorted play with warped imagery and inverted symbolic logic.

Dick Higgins   I produced my first Concrete poems in the fifties and in the sixties I was also active, through my work at Something Else Press, as a designer and publisher of Concrete poetry. My most recent visual poems date from 1993-94, so I am still active in the area. Thus, while I am conscious of the arts being in a more impoverished and threatened state today than they were forty years ago, which means that some forms and strategies must replace others, I am not conscious of any particular rupture. The advent of desktop publishing has slightly affected the economics of producing visual poetry, but not in any major way.

Philadelpho Menezes   Basically the Concrete poetry of the 50s and 60s is a poetry of the word. All other great matrixes of language (visuality and sonority) are submitted to the verbal one. The visuality of the Concrete poem of the 60s is the geometrical arrangement of the words in space. The sonority of the Concrete poem is the oralization of the words. What I nominate "intersign poetry" uses the semantic function of the visual signs (combined with verbal signs in visual poems) and the semantic function of sounds (associated to words in sound poems).

Harry Polkinhorn   I see the work of the Concrete poets of the 1950s and 1960s as manifesting a desire to establish geometric, at times minimalist, essentializing order or stabilizing control in the face of exploding social and cultural changes. In this connection, Concrete poetry came as an Apollonian corrective to the loosing of Dionysian forces which were transforming aesthetic production in Brazil in the late 1940s. In contrast, the dominant impulse in the historical avant-gardes and post-structuralism is away from traditional hierarchies that mediate social power and thus maintain the status quo, and in the direction of the transumption of these hierarchies once and for all.

***

Poetics Today

Haroldo de Campos   Viable poetry of the present is a postvanguard poetry, not because it is postmodern or antimodern but because it is postutopian. The totalizing project of the historical vanguards that, at its height, could only be sustained by a redemptive utopian, was succeeded by the pluralization of possible poetics. Today, the most promising poets of the new generation are those who are searching for a personal language while keeping in mind the constructive lesson of Concrete poetry, assuming the task of finding different dialectical options.

Johanna Drucker   Contemporary work, mine and that of others who make visual poetry, seems less exclusively literary in its sources than Brazilian concretism. Though the great moderns – Eliot, Stein, Pound, Joyce, H.D., Loy, and others are still major points of reference for many writers, they do not dominate the poetic landscape in the way they seem to have in the 1950s at the peak of high modernism.

Charles Bernstein   My work is "Concrete" primarily in the senses stated before; though as a visual outer limit of my poetry I do have a work in which the visual (over)inscription of writing makes the poem illegible (*Veil*, 1987). Certainly this work was influenced by poets such as Gomringer, Augusto and Haroldo de Campos, and other "Concrete Poets." When Bruce and I first started to think about editing L=A=N=G=U=A=G=E we certainly had such work in mind and especially had in mind the resistance to such visual concreteness among even the poets we admired among the New American Poets, as well as many of our contemporaries, who were interested in syntactic and propositional exploration and counterlogics but not in foregrounding the visual dimension of language. While we remained interested in the direct descendants of Concrete poetry in North America and Europe (generally labeled visual poetry), and such important projects as Dick Higgins's *Pattern Poems*, our own preoccupations were more toward acknowledging and extending the visual praxis of poetry in works where the visual dimension was not necessarily primary (for example extending "field" page scoring away from ideas of "breath" or process and toward ideas of design).

Luciano Nanni   I am convinced that the greater difference between my work and the concretism of the 50s and 60s is a firm push on the accelerator of "aesthetics" and the abandonment of ideology. As a consequence, a push on a-communication in contrast to the semiological residue that concretism, in some cases, was not capable of abandoning. An ideological valence always involves some content, and some content always demands, however little it may be, the presence of some communicative level. And then, I would say, the decisive renunciation of what in Freud's words we can term *in senso lato* the witticism. In some old works of art really gratuitous and nauseous. Which doesn't mean abandoning the explosive strength of the unconscious or the critical dimension of concretism as confrontation with the stereotyped life. The critical dimension remains, but in place of strictly political methods it is pursued through anthropological means.

Susanne Jorn   For me Concrete poetry is history. I don't write Concrete poems any more, and moved away from the "old" concept of concreteness as seen and heard at the Yale Symphosophia.

It started with poems written to the Icelandic artist Sigurjon Olafsson's (1908-1988) sculptures (*Tracks in Sand*. Reykjavik: Sigurjon Olafsson Museum, 1992), where I entered a three-dimensional sculptural space, having gone around the sculptures to see them from all angles. The poems depict this visuality, as I had the individual sculptures' form, color, material, texture, Icelandic light and darkness, and Nordic moodiness in mind.

After that, instead of having my texts illustrated, I wrote about other artists' work. At the Yale Symphosophia, I read examples of such writing from *Clairvoyant* (Copenhagen: Per Kofod, 1994), showing slides of the artworks at the same time. Here I also entered the artwork and did not come out until I had a visual text with me. Previously, illustrations by artists added visuality to the page. Now, this has been replaced with a facelift, because of a stronger and independent visuality in the text itself.

When I look at a Concrete poem the visualness is too obvious, less complicated than the one in visual poems of today. The visual realities, in other words, are created differently. Contemporary visual poetry has a picture-creating power in itself that Concrete poetry does not have. For me, this visual poetry is poetry in which pictures appear by a visual reading. If a poem consists of components, then it is here that the visual components are put together in a picture – creating the poem's space and text-sounds.

Wladimir Krysinski   Helmut Heißenbüttel's work is different from the work of the Concrete poets of the 1950s and of the 1960s insofar as it contains much less environmental, iconic, and joking elements. It draws much more on the systematic exploration of the relationship language-metalanguage and on the philosophical intertextuality or interdiscursivity, which means that the poet regards his discursive space as being retrospectively and potentially determined by the philosophical understanding of language and of society (Hegel, Wittgenstein, Bense, Adorno). The theoretical underpinnings which distinguish Heißenbüttel's works, particularly the series of his *Texte* are, on the one hand, Gertrude Stein's conception of verbal repetition and transformation, and, on the other hand, Wittgenstein's idea of language and of language game ("Das sprachliche Spiel"). At the same time what distinguishes Heißenbüttel's poetic concretism is the interplay which establishes itself in his texts between a "natural language" and "metalanguage."

Eduardo Kac   The poetic issues that holopoetry addresses are completely different from Concrete poetry, as I hope to have made clear. Consider the concept of simultaneity in Concrete poetry and the concepts of discontinuity and non-linearity in holopoetry. Contrast the rigid structures of Concrete poetry on the page with the immaterial and dynamic behavior of holopoetry. Think of the symbolic use of white space as silence in Concrete poetry and the interplay between presence and absence that help create the rhythm of holopoems. Compare the verbi-voco-visual reading of the Concrete poem, which has lead itself to oralization, and the irreducible holographic and interactive character of the holopoem, which cannot be performed acoustically. If Concrete poetry was a project for the new urbanized and industrial society of the post-war period, holographic (and digital) poetry is a project for the new electronic and virtualized world. I would like to point out that no poetic movement or direction should be regarded as more important than others. Each corresponds, in its own time, to issues relevant to contemporary life. The next century will know new and unprecedented poetics, further pushing the boundaries of this ancient art. Or, as Dick Higgins put it, "cultural innovation adds to the store of possibilities and does not simply replace some earlier mode forever."

Concretism : A Poetics or Formal Device?

Is there a poetics of concretism? Or is Concrete poetry a formal device rather than a conceptual premise?

Marjorie Perloff   Yes, I think there is a poetics of concretism, but in much discussion that poetics is too narrowly construed. There is a large literature on the semiotic of concretism, with all sorts of rules and regulations, whereas concretism is just a synecdoche for the larger category of visual poetry. I prefer to historicize concretism. That is: concretism was born after World War II in Switzerland, Brazil, and other non-first-world powers as part of the larger avant-garde "revolution of the word" that taught us that we can no longer take the printed page for granted. In the nineteenth century, the "look" of the poem was largely taken for granted, and the reader was given directions to read from left to right, from top of the page to the bottom. The typographic revolution of modernism changed this forever. By mid-century, with advertising techniques, billboards, magazine collage layouts, and so on flourishing, poets began to see that the possibilities for deriving meaning from the actual placement of words and letters were endless – that the *verbivocovisual* language of Joyce and Pound could be adapted to new ends.

Anglo-American culture is, however, very conservative when it comes to poetic developments. In Establishment poetry, the poem continues to be a print block with a beginning and end surrounded by white space. Its "layout" is wholly secondary to the "message" to be conveyed. Certainly, in magazines like *Poetry*, this is the case. At the same time, more and more poet-artists such as Johanna Drucker and Joan Retallack, Susan Howe and Charles Bernstein, are developing typographies that create intricate semantic fields. In the UK, the Scottish poets following Ian Hamilton Finlay are making interesting experiments, and in Canada Steve McCaffery, bp Nichol, and others have for years produced artist's books (poetry books?) and broadsides that are verbo-visual. So this is an exciting time for post-concretism, for visual poetics.

Nor is Concrete poetry just a formal device. To visualize the text or the page is to think of the language field differently.

Eric Vos   We should distinguish between what the question refers to as "a poetics of concretism" and a closed set of either "formal" or "conceptual" criteria for Concrete poetry. The first certainly exists, but the second is always questionable. I envisage the poetics of concretism from a semiotic point of view (one of the many relevant points of view that could be adopted) as a poetics of exemplification and repletion of the verbal sign. I use these terms as they are coined by Nelson Goodman (in his *Languages of Art* and elsewhere). "Repletion" concerns the number and variety of the features participating in the sign's referential function; a highly replete or saturated sign has many of such varied features. "Exemplification" means, briefly, that the sign functions as a sample of these features. Through these semiotic procedures, the Concrete poem intensifies – emphatically not: "reduces" – awareness of the various material and linguistic "properties" of the verbal sign (visual, aural, tactile, syntactic, semantic, pragmatic, kinetic) and of their interrelationships, and, most importantly, directs attention to the verbal codes and conventions in which such properties are constituted, by presenting alternatives for institutionalized practices of operating verbal elements, patterns, and methods.

This orientation towards fundamental verbal codes is one of the bases of concretist poetics, but it does not result in a fixed set of (semiotic) rules for Concrete poetry, since repletion nor exemplification can be closed off. They are context-, time-, and interpretation-dependent "premises" that can be "concretized" through a large variety of "formal devices." The exemplificative functioning of the Concrete poem does serve to distinguish it from some of its "visual" precedents, contemporaries, and successors, in which the verbovisual aspect serves either designative or connotative purposes (e.g. *carmen figuratum*, Apollinaire, Reinhard Döhl's renowned "apfel," and Marinetti's *parole in libertà* or Garnier's "Constructivist" poems, respectively).

Willard Bohn   The poetics of concretism has been repeatedly formulated and refined by, among others, Haroldo and Augusto de Campos, Eugen Gomringer, and Max Bense. Its value stems precisely from its conceptual bases.

Claus Clüver   In spite of the wide range of texts that I would include under the label, there is clearly a Concrete poetics, which I have repeatedly attempted to formulate (going beyond the Noigandres "Pilot Plan" that is too closely geared to the kind of text produced by those poets at that very moment). All of the qualities and "dimensions" I have listed earlier form part of that poetics; most of them have their own traditions and precedents, and many of them can be found, singly or in various combinations, in practices and theories of contemporary textmaking. If Concrete poetry were, on the other hand, a formal device I would not know how to formulate it, and whether to adjust the formulation more to the aural or to the visual aspects of Concrete poetry. The same question might be asked about Op art, and perhaps much geometric Constructivism in general. The Mondrianesque patterns we can now encounter on bathroom floors or pillow cases attest to the ease with which forms can deteriorate into formulas.

Caio Pagano   The fascination of the Concrete poet with words, vowels, consonants, the changing play of sounds (suspending meaning) is reminiscent of the composer who, not being concerned with meanings, creates separate forms based only on euphony.

The poet who dissects words and hangs out sounds like washed clothes listens as a musician. The invention of photography freed painting from the prison of repeating the real. The painter can work playfully with color and form, can compose. Music always enjoyed that privilege. Mallarmé seems to have had the same effect over literature.

Augusto de Campos   As I see it, Concrete poetry did not come about as a formal spatialization in the field of modern poetry, as one could speak of *carmen figuratum* in antiquity, but rather as a proposed radicalization of poetic language in which the visual aspects constitute just one of the relevant parameters. What Concrete poetry sought was to recuperate the specificity of poetic language itself, the materiality of the poem and its autonomy, beginning with a revision and radicalization of the methods of modern poetry and of the elaboration of a new creative project in the context of new media.

E. M. de Melo e Castro   To reduce Concrete poetry to a formal device is to miss the point both of its historical reasons and of its opening to the new poetics made possible by the technological devices that are transforming our perception of the world. We mustn't forget the advice given in the 1930s by Edmund Wilson in the essay "Is verse a dying technique?": "The point is that literary techniques are tools, which the masters of the craft have to alter in adapting them to fresh uses. To be too much attached to the traditional tools may be sometimes to ignore the new masters."

Concrete poetry is much more than a tool: it is a poetic conception. All my answers point in this direction. The above quotation should now be written as follows: the point is that poetics are conceptual premises which the masters of the craft alter following the dynamics of the new perception of the world. To be too much attached to the traditional poetics may be sometimes to ignore the new masters and the world we live in.

John Picchione   Concretism is a poetic form and a conceptual premise at the same time – all forms being never neutral and inseparable from ideological/conceptual ramifications. As such, Concrete poetry undoubtedly represents one of the most radical and innovative aesthetic expressions to come out of the latter half of this century.

The fundamental problem for me, whether we discuss Concrete poetry or any other literary/artistic production, is always one and the same: even the most visionary and revolutionary literary forms – after their initial impact wears off – will inevitably become worn out and hackneyed, thus losing their original force and vitality. Any innovation is destined to be absorbed by a process of normalization/legitimation which all avant-garde movements (if they have to be considered as such) must avoid at all costs. Maintaining the status quo is contrary to any experimental or avant-garde principle.

My questions are then the following: has Concrete poetry become a manneristic expression of itself? After decades of experimentation, have its forms become conservative, obsolete, sclerotic? Any true avant-garde movement must have the courage to negate itself. It must be capable of self-destruction, realizing the necessity to commit suicide by abandoning the forms which it has created. Resistance to this act means to give way to a mannerism which is bound to generate stereotypes and alienating forms which induce the reader to perform standardized and automatic reactions/interpretations.

These dangers have not always been avoided by experiments which find their humus in the experience of concretism. However, signs of revitalization are present. Augusto de Campos's performance at the Yale Symphosophia is a good example. His integration of verbal, visual, and musical media expresses the desire to create new forms and consequently new consciousness, new possibilities of meanings.

Harry Polkinhorn   As indicated, there is a poetics of concretism, the most significant dimension of which is ideological in nature. Formally, at the heart of this mechanism lies the belief that meaning is transmitted by art and that certain (concretist) forms transmit meaning better than other (linear or non-concretist) forms. However, a more comprehensive definition illustrates the political (power-based) workings of concretism, which sees itself as the new, final regulator of aesthetic value, the goal towards which the Hegelian process of cultural history was always already leading and beyond which it is impossible to move. In this narrow respect, then, concretism closes off, refers to the past, and wants to maintain a version of the genetic evolution of stylistic movements culminating in concretism.

****

Beyond Concretist Poetics

Dick Higgins   It should be clear that I regard Concrete poetry as a small part of a large picture. No doubt it has its ideological purposes and uniqueness but it would, I think, be a misprision to discuss it in isolation from sound poetry, aleatory poetry, and the other intermedial poetries with which it shares many strategies, purposes, and much of its history. Incidentally, many of its practitioners have worked in these other areas as well as in Concrete poetry. To discuss these issues requires a breadth of critical experience which is rather rare, and this is, I feel, one reason why especially in English there is so little adequate theoretical or critical literature on the matter.

Johanna Drucker   If there is a poetics of concretism, it derives from an emphasis on materiality (visual and sound values) which informs many poetic practices which would not fit under the rubric Concrete. The place of materiality within the production of poetic meaning is a fundamental fact of linguistic life – though oddly enough it continues to be repressed in much mainstream critical writing about poetry/prose. There are, of course, formal devices associated with concretism per se – and they are often borrowed without a clear understanding of their original function or conception – but to reduce concretism to a formal conceit is to miss the conceptual agenda underlying its operation – which was to make use of the formal means in a manner which was inseparable from the production of resonant and complex meanings.

John Solt   There still is a poetics of concretism, but its moment has passed. Most specialists now use the term "visual poetry," and no poet I know in Japan or the USA still uses the word Concrete except to refer back to the movement of the 1950s-1970s. The Concrete moment was so successful that it soaked through to the culture at large: words on paintings, although around since the early years of the twentieth century, are such a given of the contemporary scene that most viewers forget the contribution made by the Concrete poetry movement; likewise, advertisements and MTV videos often float words across the screen, which is an effect that would have been a part of Concrete poetry had the computer technology been available and the station started up during the years of the concrete heyday. In other words, Concrete poetry succeeded in making inroads into our consciousness, mostly through advertising, but the ideas that were new then are now second-nature to babies in diapers watching television. Should we bemoan the fact that the solid line back to Concrete poetry has become perforated and faded, and that few can trace it anymore? I think not, because the idea got across, so who cares about the fame of the movement as such? Bestowing credit where it is due is not really the point, except for academics who come after the fact and want to clean up for posterity.

Philadelpho Menezes   Yes, there is a poetics of concretism, and essentially it is a form of visual poetics. A formal device shows a conceptual premise. If the formal device changes, inevitably the conceptual premise has changed with it, and vice-versa. The formal device of Concrete poetry participates in the broader vision of art and world elaborated by Concrete art, from which Concrete poetry sprouts. Could anyone seriously ask if all non-figurative art after the 50s is a form of Van Doesburg's and Max Bill's Concrete art? When the formal device of visual poetry assimilated images (non-verbal signs) it reflected a new conceptual premise, and when the conceptual premise of visual poetry abandoned the rigid geometric construction of Concrete poetry and experimented with signifieds produced by non-verbal signs, as we see in the intersign poetry of 70s and 80s, it showed a new vision of reality and culture that requires those new formal devices.

Wladimir Krysinski   I do not think that there is a poetics of concretism. At any rate, it cannot be a normative poetics although, as a corpus of theory, it is comparable to the Futurist or to the Surrealistic manifestoes. Concretism is a movement or a tendency that can summarize its principles or maxims (such is primarily the function of the manifesto *plano-pilôto para poesia concreta*, 1958). However it is not a poetics based on specific rules for producing the artistic (in the sense of Yury Lotman) concretist text. It stems from the willingness to become a new poetry as a result of "critical evolution of forms" ("produto de uma evoluçao critica de formas").

Steve McCaffery   Is there a poetics of concretism? Let me move tentatively towards an eventual answer to this question by tracing the range of differences within the products of concretism. Canadian critic Stephen Scobie points out accurately the presence of two fundamental tendencies. One towards the "clean" and the other towards the "dirty." Dirty Concrete characterizes much of the British scene (for instance the work of Bob Cobbing, Paula Claire, Bill Griffiths, Clive Fencott, Chris Cheek, and Laurence Upton). Which can be described as a preference for textual obliteration rather than manifestation, and the use of found objects as notation for sound performance. "Dirty" also describes the productions of the majority of Concrete in Canada (the mimeographic overprinting of bill bissett, my own and Nichol's investigations into xerox disintegrations). In contrast, "clean" Concrete is epitomized in the spatialist texts of Pierre and Ilse Garnier, Gomringer's *konstellationen*, the semiotic texts of Décio Pignatari, and in much of the early work of the Campos brothers. It's important to grasp that this bifurcation is symptomatic of a difference in *tendencies*, a difference in approaches to and encounters with the materiality of language, and marks a sociopolitical distinction and not an aesthetic categorization. "Clean" isn't better than "dirty." I believe Scobie's schema can be amplified somewhat to include a different tendency towards openness and closure. It was the closure of the text, its reified condition as object, framed and/or paginated that was frontally engaged in Canada by the performed sound poem and its attendant cabaret sociology. The creative propulsion too was more emotive than rational with the resulting poems deriving from (to adopt a term of Johanna Drucker's) a poetic of effect rather than communication.

   In the case of bp Nichol the visual struggle (which was also a semiotic one) was to include aspects and codes from popular culture. Hence, his creation of "panelology" which employs the syntactic and grammatical conventions of cartoons and comic strips. Nichol's work drew the furious disapprobation of Eugen Gomringer who categorically dismissed it as not Concrete. (There were similar protestations from the Stedelijk Museum in Amsterdam which claimed that the hand-lettered work of John Furnival did not meet the requirements of a *Concrete* poetry.) By the early 70s the feeling had arisen that concretism had become overly precious and inordinately narrow in its range; that it had ossified into a school at the very moment it seemed to be opening up tremendous new territory. Perhaps this spirit of contestation with canonic Concrete (i.e. those poems that repeatedly appeared in European and American anthologies) can be demonstrated in two poems of mine which take a playful poke at Eugen Gomringer:

sound sound sound
sound   sound
sound sound sound

SILENCE SILENCE SILENCE
SILENCE   ping   SILENCE
SILENCE SILENCE SILENCE

The development of parodic and intertextual factors within the Concrete tradition still awaits scrutiny. (We find it not only above but also in John Furnival's "semi-idiotic" poems.) Perhaps we should consider less a poetics than a pragmatics of concretism.

Basic to any consideration of concretism is its articulation onto technological determinism. By this I mean the poem's cultural status as an always belated deployment of technological innovations developed in the non-artistic sphere, and a susceptibility to limitations established by the parameters of the technology itself. The issue of technological determinism is not new. There is for example the crucial instance of Neolithic cave paintings. It can be convincingly argued I think that Lascaux gave us not the first paintings but the first motion pictures. (Painted on a cavernous interior, devoid of natural light the caves could only have been illuminated by fire, whose flames would have created a flicker effect, combined with the naturally unsmooth surface of the walls, the effects are optical kinetics.)

To itemize the relevant technological changes might be interesting. The first, of course, came with the typewriter that allowed direct composition of metrically patterned and symmetrical poems. In fact, the first two decades of concretism are inconceivable without the typewriter. Then came dry-transfer lettering which facilitated the enormous typographic variation which Russian

silencio silencio silencio
silencio silencio silencio
silencio   silencio
silencio silencio silencio
silencio silencio silencio

Eugen Gomringer, *silencio* (1953)

and Italian Futurism achieved via the printing press and manual rubber stamps. Add to this the camera which allowed the emergence of the photo-poem; the tape-recorder giving birth to the audio-poem; the photocopy machine whose creative "misuse" was explored by myself, bp Nichol, and Bob Cobbing (among many others); videation which articulated text onto screen, and offered a radically different temporality than the time of paginated reading. And finally the computer with its ominous built-in obsolescence and annual improvements. One interesting effect of this technological change has been the disappearance of earlier technological instruments; the fabric ribbon manual typewriter, for example, whose range of misuses and creative effects were due to the mechanical imperfections and limitations that subsequent technology removed.

The key issue, of course, is not the material availability of technology but how it is creatively deployed. Bob Cobbing in his *Changing Forms in English Visual Poetry: The Influence of Tools and Machines* (London: Writers Forum, 1987) comments on the creative "misuse" of office machinery. (Cobbing's own first "duplicator prit" dates back to 1942.) I find Cobbing's practice and suggestions provocative, opening up the aesthetic of Concrete to the possi-bility of social critique. The pertinent strategy is to appropriate technology and force it to work against its own determined logic. One personal example of this attempt is my work in systematic disintegrative duplication. When one reproduces a reproduction of a reproduction, ad infinitum, the noise to signal ratio increases exponentially resulting in a final "copy" that has no visible resemblance to its original. While the actual product of this metamorphosis (i.e. the poem) can be judged aesthetically it is the procedurality of the method that reveals the logical aporia within the equipment that is most important. What Cage proved philosophically of silence (that it does not exist beyond Platonic ideality), disintegrative duplication demonstrates of the reproducible image. Significantly the procedure does not involve a willful deviation away from the paradigm of performativity of office technology, but reveals the contradictory nature of the machine by a systematic application of its rules and procedures. Against this is a more friendly or neutral approach to technolo-gical formats that would settle at programming a computer to generate a visual poem, as opposed to creatively work against its own capabilities. (Of the latter some interesting developments have been made by Toronto poet Darren Wershler-Henry in the area of translation via a limited vocabulary generated out of a spell-check program.)

Perhaps it would show more probity to admit the existence of two distinct traditions of concretism. What we might call a paleoconcrete and a technocon-crete, the former involving calligraphic, acoustic, and gestural modes; the latter technological production or supplementation. The latter might be divided into positivist and skeptical (as those who embrace the new technology and those who attempt to critique it in practice). There is a clear distinction along these lines in twentieth-century sound poetry.

Avant-garde Trends: Is Concretism A New Reading of Tradition?

Thesis: "Concretism, one of the most radical avant-garde trends of this century engaged in a critical reevaluation of the artistic object and its place in society, had a new way of looking at and reading tradition. It was a forerunner of later neo-baroque and post-modern trends."

Please give your evaluation or judgment of this artist's perspective from an artist's or participant's point of view, as it relates to your own work or poetics, or to your critical judgment of concretist experimentation.

Ana Hatherly   Being responsible for this statement, I will try to say what I mean by approaching separately its main points.

1. *A critical reevaluation of the artistic object.* The radical aspect of Concretism emerges clearly from the *Teoria da Poesia Concreta*, but its radicalism can also be assessed by the violent reaction it produced in the literary milieu when the Movement gushed out in the 50s in Europe and South America, and still goes on in many parts of the world. Why was Concrete poetry so shocking? One reason was no doubt the refusal on the part of Concrete poets to accept poetry as a purely discursive-lyrical-literary form of expression, proposing instead the poem as a magnetic field of verbivocovisual possibilities, implying a new trajectory from the word to the sign. Emphasizing the importance of the visual ideogrammatic nature of poem as a written text, this approach extended the boundaries of writing and reading beyond the traditional literary limits, re-establishing a long forgotten link between *ikon* and *logos*.

The antagonism on the part of the establishment to avant-garde action is a reaction to be expected, due to the intrinsic destructive-cleansing nature of avant-garde rule, intended to overthrow a *status quo* considered obsolete. Being a war-like or even terrorist-like form of action, it must necessarily create a climate of resistance on the part of those defending the dominant values at the time. This resistance to avant-garde proposals can assume several negative aspects, and Concrete poets, like other avant-garde groups before them, had to endure for a long time several forms of aggressive resistance implying a strong refusal of acceptance. But what characterizes the particular antagonism Concrete poets, and Experimentalists in general, had to face was based on the secret fear that, much more than Futurists or Surrealists, they not only announced but materialized the end of an era, the end of an idea of poetry as an artistic object, pointing to a future world where traditional values and even traditional media no longer would function. This had already been foreseen in the nineteenth century, but the new way in which poetry was presented by Concretism represented a greater threat. It did not announce the end of language, but it certainly announced the end of an established conception of language as an artistic medium. Concrete poets made it absolutely indispensable to rethink the function of poetry.

2. *A new way of looking at and reading tradition.* As I stated in my paper "Voices of Reading," Concrete poets were not antiquarians, but they did not shun the past: in fact they clearly stated the names and the works of the predecessors they most admired. In spite of their radicalism, Concrete poets did not make tabula rasa of tradition; they only rejected what they considered to be dead weight or dead branches in the bushy tree of artistic invention, thus allowing for the new ways to spring forth. Concrete poetry did not represent the end of a cultural tradition: it even created a new genre, as the recent M.A. dissertation by Pedro Alexandre da Cunha Reis (1994) clearly proved. Concrete poets updated poetry making, proposing a type of text in accordance with the actual reality of the second half of twentieth-century society.

3. *A forerunner of later neo-baroque and postmodern trends.* In retrospect, the particular way of confronting the present with tradition characteristic of Concrete and experimental poetics, made it possible for them to look at the past with cool objective eyes, not feeling obliged to follow or to accept anything just because it was traditional or modern, thus enabling them to refuse, reuse, or experiment at will with available or new sources or media.

Willard Bohn   I have no real quarrel with this statement as far as it goes, since it places Concrete poetry in an artistic and social perspective. To my mind, however, its significance is related above all to the linguistic arena. I agree that concretism is a revolutionary movement because it forces us to re-examine the foundations on which language is based and emphasizes the signifier at the expense of the signified. By stressing the materiality of the former, which acquires its own autonomy, it frees poetry from the demands of the latter or at least casts them in a new light. In short, Concrete poetry explores visual signification and revitalizes the verbo-visual relation implicit in the linguistic sign.

John Solt   Absolutely.

Haroldo de Campos   We believed that Concrete poetry could contribute to the renovation of poetic language in Brazil. Concrete poetry in Germany, the

United States, England, or even Japan was a vanguard movement and nothing more. In Brazil, it was also a cultural project that carried a certain weight. Concrete poetry spread through a musical movement, the *tropicalismo* of Caetano Veloso and Gilberto Gil. Concrete poetry also carried out a critical revision of the Brazilian literary past, awakening new theoretical and literary proposals, revealing new dimensions of criticism, such as semiology and semiotics. Translation became a mechanism of reading the past, exemplified in the *Re-Visão de Sousândrade*, produced by Augusto and myself after our experience of translating Pound. All this work in criticism, theory, and translation gives Brazilian Concrete poetry a dimension that was not present in other countries. I think that any Brazilian poet of today who has not considered our movement, whether negatively or positively, is someone who has not assumed an awareness of language. Brazilian Concrete poetry is still polemical. We are still attacked with the same fervor and impetus that we were in the 50s. I have said that Concrete poetry of the 50s and 60s, as an "experience of limits," did not close off poetry or entrap me; it taught me, on the contrary, to see the concrete in poetry, to go beyond the particularizing "ism," to face poetry transtemporally as a global, open process of iconic concreteness, composed in an always different way in the different examples of material language. Sappho and Bashô, Dante and Camões, Sá de Miranda and Fernando Pessoa, Hölderlin and Celan, Góngora and Mallarmé are in this sense, for me, Concrete poets (where the "ism" no longer has any meaning).

E. M. de Melo e Castro   Concrete poetry opens a different path to inventive communication, different from the continuity of the Western tradition of verbal poetry with its stress on meaning and feeling. That kind of traditional poetry can go on forever with little changes as long as Western civilization keeps alphabetic writing. But Concrete poetry is a sudden awakening of a different way of writing and reading that goes back to the visual roots of Mediterranean culture and to the moment when ideogrammatic writing gave way to the alphabet. In fact it was alphabetic writing that made it possible to interiorize the meaning of seeing and the function of the eye. Homer is said to be blind. This is a very meaningful myth: Homer was blind because he could not write or read: writing and reading alphabetically being a substitute for actually seeing. This opens to symbolic thought that which is the mainstream of Western culture. On the other hand, to see the ideogram or even syllabic writing is much more of a visual, iconic, and synthetic experience. To recover this original visual nature buried in the sources of our Western culture is a challenge for the poet of the second half of the twentieth century, faced as he is – as we all are – with the informo-society where visuality tends to be restored to a role of utmost importance.

To rediscover the meaning of seeing as a visual fact rather than a subjective and dreamlike fact is one of the achievements of the second half of the twentieth century, and Concrete poetry was certainly its forerunner, based theoretically on the work of Fenollosa on the Chinese written character, the ideogrammatic theory of Ezra Pound, the verbivocovisual proposition of James Joyce, and the theory of information. Nevertheless today, after the reappraisal of the systems of writing and reading, we can establish a theory of Mediterranean visual poetry from the Egyptian pictogram to twentieth-century visual poetry, including Concrete as a radical changing point. This tradition comes from the Greek Anthology, the technophagies from Alexandria, the Medieval *carmina figurata*, the visual combinatory machines of Ramon Lull, the cryptic tables of the alchemists, all being the deep inputs of the baroque poetry of the seventeenth and beginning of the eighteenth centuries.

Baroque poetry is therefore the nearest ancestor to twentieth-century Visual poetry: the calligrammes of Apollinaire, the words in liberty of the Futurists, the Italian *poesia visiva*, the constellations of Gomringer, Concrete poetry, Spatialism, and all kinds of visual experimentalism. All these "poetics" must be considered as the basis of the neobaroque trend that gives an adequate theoretical umbrella to the global, multisystemic, intersemiotic society we live in. Therefore I don't think that we are facing either the end of history or the end of language, but only the beginning of a possible new paradigm of writing and reading and of communication as a whole, a paradigm that is deeply rooted in our Western culture and from time to time makes itself visible to the eyes of man.

Ken Cox, a British Concrete poet from the 1960s, used to say that Concrete poetry is a gift from heaven: it opens the eyes of the people. One of the three original visual poems by Simmias of Rhodes (fourth century B. C.) is precisely the wings of an angel. But we do not live in an angelic society, far from it. Only we are now faced with the necessity to open our eyes and see the world as it is if we are to continue to live in it. When after the holocaust of the Second World War it was said that poetry was no longer possible, this must be understood today as a warning, a warning that a different way of invention and of survival is necessary: that a new paradigm of communication is coming along.

On the poetic and artistic field this has been felt since the end of the nineteenth century, along with the increasing importance of scientific discovery, technological sophistication, and the democratic diffusion of its effects on everybody's perception of the world. The idea of Mallarmé's galaxy is important since during the first half of the twentieth century creative writing was haunted by it. This galaxy includes the idea of the white page as a musical score standing before the poet as a challenge. This white page belongs to an ideal book the poet must write as his ultimate goal. But in the second half of the twentieth century things gradually changed. The poet is no longer faced with a white page. He faces a complex set of electronic apparatus and their multiple capacities to generate text and images in color and in movement. The poet is confronted with his own skills to operate with technologically-defined equipment. The page is no longer there nor is it white, not even as a metaphor. Also space is now equivalent to time, and writing is not a score but a dimensional virtual reality. Thus the idea of the book is coming to a crisis, as it is gradually replaced by other means of external memory, such as the videotape, the floppy disk, and even more by the CD ROM capacities, bringing such new possibilities for writing and reading as simultaneous space-time sequences, metamorphosis of signs and colors, and the navigation on the highways of global communication.

But the use of new technological devices by the poet should not be taken as just the use of different semiotic systems to translate our old experience and achievements to give them a new dressing. That would be to miss totally the point, as I believe by personal experience that technological means bring with them new possibilities for inventive work and even of a new poetics of verbal and non-verbal signs. The task of the poet is thus to explore this new frontier of invention, taking the respective risks of producing virtually a new art.

From what I said it can be easily understood that I cannot see any reason for the so called post-modernism, which seems to me an empty attempt to create a false period to characterize our poetic invention at the end of the century. What I see is a baroque reason, as occurred before in different times of history, now called rightly or wrongly "Neobaroque." To question the historical presence of Baroque in our time or in other times is a task completely outside the scope of these comments.

Augusto de Campos   I don't think that either of the expressions –"neobaroque" or "postmodern" – are sufficiently adequate to characterize the actual moment in its possible relations with Concrete poetry. The term "neobaroque" is too charged with historicity and could lead to confusions, if one considers that it usually takes in practices of Hispanic and Latin American poetry not connected to the poetics of concretism. As to "postmodern," it is a concept of indefinite contours, hardly defensible, to the degree that the presuppositions of "modern" are still in effect; it seems rather to be a label that serves as a pretext for eclecticisms of a conservative nature, actually pre- or antimodernist. I would stop at the first phrase of the thesis, adding in place of "It was a forerunner, etc." that Concrete poetry once again took up speculations of an experimental lineage in contemporary poetry, forming relevant presuppositions for the development of poetry in the context of new media that are growing in the technological phase of modernity. It constituted, at the least, an important movement for keeping alive the revolutionary ideology of permanent and autonomous experimentation and redefining vanguard action in the second half of the century, assuming this position under the category of "poetry of invention" (in contrast to the more palatable "expressive poetry") as a means of resistance against the massification and the banalization of literature imposed by the new means of communication and the stagnation of conventional literature.

***

Concretism and Other Avant-gardes

Marjorie Perloff This thesis seems slightly overstated. I'm not sure concretism was "one of the most radical avant-garde trends of this century" because it seems to me that concretism was a natural outgrowth of Futurist (both Italian and Russian) and French and German Dada developments. Marinetti was already a "concretist" in a sense; so was Schwitters. And certainly Khlebnikov and Kruschenykh did extraordinary things with "the word as such" and "letter as such."

Nevertheless, concretism can now be seen as a central forerunner of language poetry, performance poetics, and so on and, increasingly, intermedia works (for video, computer, etc.) are showing us that there's no clear dividing line between the verbal and the visual. So I think concretism was a very important movement still too little understood in the U. S. As technology and cybertext become more important, concretism will assume its rightful place in the culture. The danger, though, is that much visual poetics is no more than pretty, and if visual poetry is to succeed it must transcend the decorative function some of it now plays.

Claus Clüver There is little I would fully subscribe to in this thesis, except for its tone of positive assessment. Concrete poetry was radical in the sense of going to the roots of the verbal text as material sign (and thus "critically reevaluating the artistic object"); the major "radical" revolutions occurred in Europe earlier in this century, and Concrete poetry is one of the last of this century's avant-garde movements and by this very fact linked more to Modernism than to post-Modernism. In contrast to Italian Futurism and to Dadaism it did "look at" and reinterpret/reconstruct tradition, largely a different one than that which engaged contemporary mainstream poetry; and its very work helped change our own construction of the mainstream, although the shifts in the mainstream canon that have occurred cannot be attributed solely to the activity of the Concrete poets. It may be necessary to make a distinction between developments in Europe, in North America, and in Latin

America: the arrival of Concrete poetry in Brazil may constitute much more of a "ruptura" than that of its counterpart in Europe, and the concept and role of avant-gardism may also have to be assessed differently in Latin America. But the aesthetic ideals of the Concrete poetics are very much linked to those of Mallarmé and Pound, the Bauhaus and Webern (although this is too global a statement and does not, for instance, apply to the Wiener Gruppe or the Darmstadt group); its basic conception of the role of art and the artist is exactly what post-Modernism would challenge. It is the post-Concrete work of some of the same poets that links up with general post-Modern trends. (The concept of "forerunner" is critically of little use to me, and so is the concept of "experimentation.")

Dick Higgins   This loses me. Without knowing what the proposition says I cannot interpret it, and knowing what it says depends on knowing who said it and why. As it stands, the "thesis" is too laden with debatable points and ideas, to wit: "concretism" (I have already commented on that), "radical avant-garde" (this could be an oxymoron or not depending on context, plus it assumes that there is a huge army following its vanguard, which has not been the case), "critical reevaluation of the [place in society] of the artistic object..." (how so? isn't the publication of art multiples itself an even more radical act?), "looking at and reading tradition" (which tradition? rather few of the artists who have made intermedial work have had access to its historic precedents, especially from before the twentieth century), "forerunner of later neo-baroque and post-modern trends." (Fluxus group-secretary George Maciunas, back in the nineteen sixties, used to accuse me of making "neo-baroque theater," but I am not sure what this term means at this time; as for "post-modern trends," I do not believe that there are any, since "post-modernism" is over, so-called "post-modernism" solved nothing, and it was mostly a critical fashion, not something with any important basis in reality – my forthcoming book on this: "Intermedia: Modernism Since Postmodernism" should be out in late 1996 – I prefer to note the slow intrusion of a sense that radical change is necessary, that whatever we do as people or critics or artists *must* be improved upon if survival is to occur, which would make us, rather, "premillenarian," more than merely "postmodern.")

Having documented the existence of some 2700 visual poems from before 1900, in Egyptian, Cretan (Minoan A), Sanskrit and the Prakrits, Tamil and other Dravidian-languages of India and Sri Lanka, Chinese, Burmese, Korean, Annamese, Japanese, Arabic, Hebrew, Greek, Latin (including neo-Latin), Hungarian, Italian, English (of various origins), Welsh (Cymric), French, Spanish, Portuguese, Swedish, Danish, German, Polish, Russian, Ukranian, and a host of others, there are now a good many scholars who would find it preposterous to assert that Concrete poetry presents a unique formal statement. What is, however, unique to the Concrete poetry of the fifties and sixties is its application of the twentieth-century assumptions that each work should have its own form, that it should be somehow original. While a seventeenth-century German would read various assumptions and meanings into a poem which was shaped as a cross, a chalice, or a pyramid and would draw on these shapes to enrich his experience of the text, a Concrete poet (exceptions being myself and Gerhard Rühm, for instance) would find this derivative and perhaps naive. It is at this point that the discussion should begin, not from the excessive centering on twentieth-century experience which annoyed me at the conference. It should have faced forward and its trajectory should have been defined by more knowledge than was possible. The discussions after the sessions were sometimes more exciting than the presentations; one had the sense of there being a lot of unfinished business which might have helped us towards more of a consensus concerning Concrete poetry and all the intermedial arts so that the next step can be taken, which will be to define a corpus of excellent works to use as critical or artistic paradigms. One would like to see a second conference basically on the same subject as this but with a broader historical purview, yet one oriented towards defining some kinds of manageable foci for discussion, criticism, and even for heuristic purposes.

Philadelpho Menezes   The mathematical order of concretism, together with the idea of reduced elements in a clean and pre-programmed and absolutely planified construction, exposed in the theory and poems of concretism of the 50s and 60s, put Concrete poetry precisely on the opposition to an aesthetic of abundance, proliferation, and formal liberty that characterizes baroque. Concretism could be seen as a neo-classical poetry, never as a neo-baroque one. Concrete poetry has more to do with the international style and the conceptions of high modernism than the post-modern age. I think it is enough to remember that when the theory of Concrete poetry in Brazil appeared it emerged in direct dialogue with the construction of Brasília as a city heir of Le Corbusier's urbanistic conceptions. But some points link, evidently, concretism to post-modern culture: the relationship with the products of mass media; the re-evalution of the tradition of literature, making a synchronous reading of the past that interacts with the permanent present of the post-modern mentality; enthusiasm with regard to new technologies, showed already by the permutational structure of the poems, as conceived first in the *konstellationen* (1953) of Eugen Gomringer.

Harry Polkinhorn   Concretism did not read history in a new way. Even formally, its chief methodology had been explored earlier by artists as diverse as El Lissitzky, Jiří Kolář, González Estrada, Acuña de Figueroa, and Gama Lobo, among many, many forerunners one might mention. One needs to see the developments in Brazil as related to their European genesis, yet different from them, because Brazil was in a state of hyper-modernization during the euphoric, expansive 1950s, exactly the time when concretism proposed itself as a *de facto* state poetics or official political/aesthetic form perfectly complementing the impulses which were leading to the construction of Brasília and the entry of the country into the international community of nations. To ignore this dimension of the poetics of concretism of course leads to a concern with formal elements strangely disconnected from a mature version of literary or cultural history, thus concealing political aspirations which are then left free to establish concretism as somehow simultaneously "typically Brazilian" and the *dernier cri* of the international avant-garde. In my view, Concrete practice's greatest contribution was that for a short period during the 1950s it separated out the geometric/abstract/graphic dimension of poetry for exacerbated or hyperbolic treatment. Subsequent attempts to extend concretism into other, adjacent areas (sound, sculpture) either ended up moving beyond what might be defined as concretism as such or joined the many interesting failures which have dotted the landscape of poetic experimentation throughout the twentieth century.

Luciano Nanni   If the postmodern coincides with the crisis of ideologies and of "great narrations," its relationship with concretism, at least in my opinion, becomes obvious. The potential of "visual," the potential of "aesthetical," the potential creativity of the user (one who savors the art work), who is liberated from the obligatory chains of decodification and from communication in the strict sense of the word, producing in consequence the disappearance of mechanical man or, in the words of Marcuse, of one-dimensional man. These are some common traits. Concretism and the postmodern seem to me to be a happy pair. And if the postmodern has some merit in this connection (I think so), such merits belong to concretism too, which evidently worked toward the advent of the postmodern.

As for neo-baroque, I wouldn't know. It is still, for me, an obscure notion. If it is synonymous with postmodern (a free, non-ideological proliferation of worlds and forms without hierarchies and government control), I should have already underlined its positive angles. If instead it means something else, I would have to wait and take a sharper look.

Wladimir Krysinski   My evaluation of the thesis that "concretism. . . was a forerunner of later neo-baroque and post-modern trends" will be quite skeptical. The concept of the neo-baroque is highly problematic and debatable.

It captures just one of the aspects of some modern writings in their expansive development, that is to say, their exuberance which probably stems from the Surrealistic inspiration. The exuberant and subjectively-minded poetry of Pablo de Rokha, some poems by Neruda or by Vallejo, *Galáxias* by Haroldo de Campos, for instance, or *Bisbidis* by E. Sanguineti or A. Zanzotto's poetry may appear quite baroque at first sight, but under critical scrutiny, their formal, semiotic, and semantic specificities as well as their discursive finalities are of a different nature.

Does concretism lead to postmodern trends of contemporary literary discourse? Given the fact that postmodernism is to some extent an "anything goes" concept, I would not attribute to concretism the (problematic) merit of being a forerunner of postmodern trends. I agree, however, with the judgement that concretism was (or still is) "one of the most radical avant-garde trends of this century engaged in a critical reevaluation of both the artistic object and its place in society," and that it "had a new way of looking at and reading tradition."

Johanna Drucker   I don't think you could really tie the wide field of contemporary experimentation to concretism as a single point of origin – it simply did not occupy that position, nor do poetic activities develop in such a literal "lineage" as such a notion supposes. Certainly it is a known – if not always understood or attended to – element of late 20th century poetics. The evaluation of the relative "radicality" or lack thereof in Concrete poetry immediately raises questions about the bigger issue of the place of poetry within the culture as a whole. This has changed dramatically in the course of the 20th century. If "Marinetti" and "Futurism" managed to become household words in the 1910s – or at least, terms with a currency in the mainstream press – then the same could hardly be said of any area of poetic activity today when poetry is a tiny little circumscribed domain (of albeit significant experimental intervention in the normative mode of the symbolic – but one which hardly shows up in the blitz of the hypermedia infotainment culture industry).

Eduardo Kac   If the case in point is "experimental, visual, and concrete" poetry since 1960, it seems to me that the other terms of the equation, "experimental" and "visual," should also be discussed, rather than focusing on one particular movement. Mine is a pluralist view of the problem, one that is inclusive and not exclusive. As a poet and artist, I have an open interest in the problem of experimentation. This prevents me from focusing on a single group, and gives me a broader perspective on the diverse avant-garde scene. To me, the greatest lesson of the avant-garde poets, groups, and movements up until the 60s is not to be found on particular and specific results. I have no interest in duplicating anybody's results. With tolerant eyes, I see the lesson of the avant-garde as one of freedom, one that questions what has become accepted if not commonplace and that continuously opens up new alternatives. Some of the most interesting experimental work being done today in poetry can be found in the hypertexts of Rosenberg and Cayley, the videopoetry of Melo e Castro and Kostelanetz, or the digital animations by Bootz and Papp.

In regard to the thesis statement, I find the term "neo-baroque" a meaningless designation. "Post-modernism" is a troubled term. I can see the need to name the new period we live in, but the "characteristics" of post-modern art as discussed by theorists such as Levin, Paoletti, Connor, Jameson, Krauss, and Hasan, for example, are very problematic. There are three major problems with the term. First, it condemns the notion of avant-garde but nevertheless still proclaims, in a masqueraded manner, that there is a new (but not "innovative") way of creating art, based on appropriation, parody, gender, and race statements as content, and other strategies. Second, by trying to encompass all the current cultural manifestations it proclaims itself to be open to the multiplicity of media, styles, and ideas, but it fails to do just so by not including in the discussion artworks or concepts that represent a truly experimental attitude, such as digital, photonic, and telematic art. Third, post-modern discussions often ground their theory on works by modern masters, such as Joyce, Pound, Duchamp, etc. Clearly, "post-modernism" indicates a contradictory focus on the past, or recent past, while the new generations of artists and poets look forward to future challenges, discoveries, and inventions. I don't see how Concrete art was a forerunner of post-modernism, since Concrete art, as first created by Van Doesburg in 1930, purged all external influences in favor of highly self-referential mathematical structures. I don't see how it reevaluated the artistic object, since Concrete artists made paintings and sculptures that, except for their geometric abstraction, conformed to traditional materials such as oil on canvas.

Any attempt to define homogeneously the art of one's own time suffers of at least two problems: one is the human incapability of knowing everything that is produced in the present so as to discriminate (without the biased influence of the art market and related factors) what really is culturally relevant and what is not; the other is the impossibility of foreseeing how artists and critics of the future (even the near future) will rewrite the present according to their own interest. The examination of parts of the writings of some of the critics engaged in the "post-modern debate," including Steven Connor, John Paoletti, and Kim Levin, might lead us to believe that it might be premature to state that all the art of the present is an absolute reaction against the paradigms established in the first fifty years of this century.

The use of the art of the early decades of this century as a major point of reference, as in the word "post-modern," calls upon examination. The word "modern" comes from the Latin adverb "modo," that means "right now." Modern, therefore, is the epoch that is not defined by a name given by the past. A "post-modern" art would be a sort of "post-right-now" art, and its definition would be given by the kind of art being currently produced. So if one "right now" replaces the preceding "right now," wouldn't we be still in the same modern strategy, only this time not dictated by the artist's invention but by the movement of the taste makers through galleries, museums, and art magazines? This is not a simple issue exactly because everything is happening around us at this very moment, preventing historical objectivity. Physicists know well that to look at an "object" is to change it, and that if one chooses different measurement systems he or she will obtain different results.

One aspect of the problem is what object to look at in the eighties and nineties. The theoreticians of "post-modernism" have drawn their attention to the production of artists, like Schnabel, Salle, Clemente, Salomé, etc., who still use paint (not necessarily oil) and some support to apply it (not necessarily canvas) through some kind of instrument (not necessarily brush) or use some hard material (wood, plaster, steel, etc.) to create finite standing objects (sculptures, assemblages, mixed media painting-constructions etc.). One has to admit that it is very appealing to galleries, collectors, and museums to be able to purchase and display again "real art objects."

Another aspect of the problem is that the theoretical tools that are used are those that are very well known, those acquired in the study of the great masters of the past and the major "isms" since impressionism. Art criticism becomes a sort of deciphering exercise, where the understanding of the historical references made by the artist, or the straightforward race and gender references, are the focal point. Controversial subjects apart, no major risks and challenges are at stake.

Here we should ask: is it true that only paintings and sculptures referring to the past are being produced? What underlies the reference to painting and sculpture as if they were the only, the primary synonyms for art? Is it true that the advocates of post-modernism are ready to understand and analyze the experimental artwork that has been done in new media, like interactive installations, CD-ROM, holography, artificial life, virtual reality, and telepresence? What recognition can artists expect to gain if their works purposefully have no tactile appeal? Those artists are not the object of study of the theoreticians that favor neo-expressionist painting. And two of the main reasons are: first, contemporary electronic art (poetry included) escapes the "post-modern" framing; second, almost none of the "post-modern" art critics are intimate with the new vocabulary and the new structures created by current experimental artists.

Why bother studying the rich history of electronic art if one too quickly assumes that it has nothing to do with art? Why not just look at the past to find settled references that are easy to quote? Technology is being used by artists that experiment with new art forms at the same time that painters and sculptors look at the past to find quotable references. It is not possible, therefore, to analyze the complexity of contemporary culture without looking at these very different aspects of it.

There are no definitive answers to the question concerning our cultural situation. We should always be aware, however, that every conclusion is nothing more than the consequence of the selected object of study and, chiefly, of the analytical tools favored to understand it.

INDEX OF NAMES

ABSTRACTS

CRITICAL PERSPECTIVES ON EXPERIMENTAL, VISUAL, AND CONCRETE POETRY

Eric Vos

Introducing the articles collected in this volume, the author sketches a four-dimensional "space" of criticism and focuses on the interrelations between the various issues raised in the following chapters, in terms of these dimensions: historical position, language-related concerns, analytic and/or transgressive purport, and metapoetical reflection.

EXPERIMENTAL, VISUAL, AND CONCRETE POETRY
A Note on Historical Context and Basic Concepts

Johanna Drucker

The author discusses the artistic setting and "ancestry" of both European and Brazilian Concrete poetry, the similarities as well as distinctions between the two, and some of the post-Concrete, visual experiments that have emerged from them.

VOICES OF READING

Ana Hatherly

This paper discusses aspects of the relationship between creative writing and reading, showing how Concrete and experimental poets contributed to expand the traditional concept of the poem. Claiming that poetry was a verbivoco-visual-intermedia form of expression, they felt free to engage in all kinds of intervention and experimentation including a particular reconsideration of past trends. The Portuguese Experimental Group of the 60s and 70s illustrates this stand in a relevant way.

THE MOREMARROW TRAJECTORY OF OLIVEIRO GIRONDO

Jorge Schwartz

The purpose of this essay is to unveil the baroque profile in the poetry of Oliverio Girondo. Based on the statement by the poet himself that his work is in actuality made up of only one poem, we consider the different stages of poetic production as a totality, focussing especially on the last book, "En la masmedula" ["In the Moremarrow"], of 1954. The theory of the Baroque proposed by Gilles Deleuze in "Le Pli" supports our perception and description of the process of baroque poetics in the work of Girondo. The analysis of "Triptic II" is used to illustrate the poet's baroque procedures. The poem is viewed as a sonnet of vanguardist dimensions that returns to the classical theme of carpe diem (as found in Gongora, Quevedo, Sor Juana Ines de la Cruz, and Gregorio de Matos e Guerra).

SARDUY AND THE VISUAL TEXT

Roberto González Echevarría

This essay attempts to analyze Sarduy's passion for painting in connection with his practice as writer and painter. Considering three visual texts by Sarduy – a Concrete poem and two paintings – and confronting them with his major novels, the essay shows that there is a productive contradiction in his works between the spirit of the letter and the letter as material representations.

POETRY IN REVOLT
Italian Avant-Garde Movements in the Sixties

John Picchione

In the context of the Italian poetic landscape, the 1960s can be identified with an aesthetics of transgression which revolts against both the linguistic code and the dominant literary models. The major movement, *Novissimi/Gruppo 63*, aimed at destroying the conventional literary institutions without abandoning the linguistic medium. Other groups share the desire to transcend the semantic confines of the verbal sign, transforming it through iconographic and figurative compositions of numerous kinds. The Novissimi reject the normal linguistic code because of its reification and commercialization, and because of the conservative ideological implications it conveyed. Their alternative language, with its fragmentation of the syntactic and the prosodic levels, produces a blasphemous disorder, an impression of linguistic madness. Formal dissonances denounce the false harmonies and reconciling modes of bourgeois writing. The groups which have pursued a visual experimentation of poetry can be divided in 1) practitioners of Concrete poetry who explore the material base of language and the graphic possibilities it can produce; 2) poets who can be grouped in the area of symbiotic writing in which various elements (phonetic, graphic, spatial, etc.) interact, conditioning and modigying their ordinary meanings; 3) technological poets who make extensive use of extra-linguistic materials coming from images produced by the mass media. These materials are de-contextualized and de-mystified through the use of provocative collages. For all these groups, the revolution of poetic forms carries with it the hope of a social and political revolution. As such, they share with the historical avant-gardes the social critique, the subversive thrust, and the visionary-utopian activism. They aspire to bring about a new consciousness, a new society.

WHEN THE AVANT-GARDE REACHES ITS MASS
The *Novissimi* and the Political Situation in Italy: 1977

William Anselmi

In this paper I attempt to recuperate/reconstruct a specific period of neo-avantgarde praxis in Italy: 1977. By delineating this specificity I attempt to show how an elitarian/academic practice of working through language (Porta, Sanguineti, Balestrini) towards the totality of being, culminates in the seventies in a mass praxis of liberation, as shown in the album by singer/songwriter Claudio Lolli: *Disoccupate le strade dai sogni*.

AVANT-GARDE AND TRADITION: A CRITIQUE

Lello Voce

The author describes the attempt (of the Baldus group) to produce a complex and contemporary communicative project using a critical archeology of literary materials.

THE ENDLESS ENDS OF LANGUAGES OF POETRY
Between Experiments and Cognitive Quests

Wladimir Krysinski

The study is based on the assumption that "there is no end in contemporary art, but only an endless stream of new beginnings." It examines both the dynamics of experimental poetry (Haroldo de Campos, Helmut Heißenbüttel) and the necessity of such terms as "avant-garde," "transgression," "innovation," "experimentalism," and "the new." In light of analysis of the dynamics of experimental poetry it seems necessary to invest these terms with new contents. Several examples of these new contents are given.

HAROLDO DE CAMPOS' LITERARY EXPERIMENTATION OF THE SECOND KIND

Walter Moser

This essay deals with literary experimentation in general and in Haroldo de Campos' work in particular. There are two types of literary experimentation: the first type results from a transfer of the scientific concept of experimentation onto literature; it is result-oriented and aims at establishing a truth that would offer a basis for human emancipation; as such it takes part, as an instrument, in the metanarrative of modernity. The second type radically affirms the materiality of language; it is determined by its processual, ludic, and experiential aspect in relation to language; it therefore contains the potential to deconstruct the metanarrative of modernity. It is suggested that Haroldo de Campos' work, in its full extent and diversity, belongs to this second kind of literary experimentation. This reading offers a partial explanation of the controversies Haroldo's texts have generated.

PALABRÁS: THE HAROLDIC EMBLEM

K. Alfons Knauth

The poetry of the "universatile" Brazilian Haroldo de Campos can be seen as the verbal emblem of both an expanding and recurrent universe. Its basic principle is that of a neo-baroque "oxymoral": the intermediate "dis negpositivo" moving between the opposite poles of polyglossy and silence, the word and the world, Brazilianism and universalism, chaos and cosmos, lethal and fetal, atavism and avant-garde. Besides its general approach, the study is focused upon the specific emblems of auto referential language through which the overall "oxymoral" is articulated. They form a mobile ensemble of interfering emblematic fields, which are also the landmarks of this essay: Verbarium, Lapidarium, Herbarium, Aquarium, Planetarium, Sensorium and Bestiarium.

FROM HIEROGLYPHICS TO HYPERGRAPHICS

Willard Bohn

In order to enable language to recover its expressive power, the Lettrists argue that poetry has no need of words, which in any case have been hopelessly contaminated by bourgeois ideology. By emphasizing the autonomy of the individual sign, by reducing each letter to a phonetic or visual counter, they attack the traditional locus of meaning itself. While some of the Lettrists have concentrated on sound poetry, which is instantaneously accessible, others have experimented with the ideographic and/or the hieroglyphic rebus. Still others have focused exclusively on the sign's visual properties, on the free or restricted play of signifiers, whose significance derives according to the rules governing abstract art.

FLUXUS, EXPERIMENTALISM, AND THE END OF LANGUAGE

Owen F. Smith

Through experiments with language and its role as a vehicle for "event scores" and other Fluxus work, Fluxus artists have continuously investigated the constitution of meaning, as is demonstrated in this essay. It also discusses the close relationships between Fluxus and Concretism.

NONINTENTIONAL POETRY

Jackson Mac Low

A review of the author's major texts and scores, written by means of non-intentional methods, i.e. chance and other non-deterministic operations, whose aim is to display language in its concreteness.

A MINI-ANTHOLOGY ON THE STATE OF CONTEMPORARY POETRY (WITH SPECIAL REFERENCE TO THE USA)

Harry Polkinhorn (compiler)

A narrative of experimentation first points to the origins of a particular kind of activity in the natural science of the Latin Middle Ages, then turns to Zola's use of the term "experimentalism" to describe a kind of fiction in the late nineteenth-century. Understanding the diminishing role of the personal within a context favoring abstraction and generalization becomes crucial in charting the steady abdication of the former throughout the twentieth century. Institutional affiliations determine the contours of debates over experimental poetry.

Next the argument questions the nature of the split between a universalizing impulse in discourse on experimental poetry, and actual production of such work itself. A tentative definition is offered, based on the connectedness (of the known with the unknown) captured in the term "eros." Ultimately, no formalist definition of experimental poetry can be defended. In fact, the sheer heterogeneity and scale of production continually challenge the inherent reductionism of theory.

The argument is then completed by the inclusion of statements by five experimental poets and critics of such materials whose works have been in circulation for some time now: Michael Basinski, Jake Berry, Fabio Doctorovich, Jack Foley, and Karl Young. These statements provide a rich multiplicity of viewpoints (absent from the more unified viewpoint of the first part of the argument) by practitioners who are not institutionalized critics.

POLIPOESIA

Enzo Minarelli

This essay focuses on the history and theory of sonorous poetic experiments (vocalism in poetry) in the context of sign and sound, regulated and spontaneous play, and cold and warm means of communication. Sound poetry is viewed as a step toward total poetry.

VISUAL POETRY, VERBO-VISUAL WRITING

Lambert Pignotti

The theory of art pieces that refer simultaneously to writing and visual art is illustrated in this essay through the gastronomic sense and the author's "performances alimentari."

THE CRYPTIC EYE

E.M. de Melo e Castro

A statement by the Portuguese pioneer of experimental poetry on his recent work, involving a synthesis of language, color, and video images, followed by a suite of "infopoems."

KEY CONCEPTS OF HOLOPOETRY

Eduardo Kac

The basic principles and practices involved in the author's ground breaking work in holographic poetry are described in the form of a brief introduction and an illustrated glossary.

INTERSIGN POETRY: VISUAL AND SOUND POETICS IN THE TECHNOLOGIZING OF CULTURE

Philadelpho Menezes

This article discusses "experimental poetry" as a generic term that embraces a variety of visual and sound poetries. But it must be understood as referring to two different historical moments: first, the historical avant-gardes, and second, the contemporary period, in which experimental poetry is produced in a culture marked by new technologies. The features of recent technological poetry, free of utopic horizons, replaces old conceptions of aesthetics, which impedes the exploration of the potentialities of new technological means. An "intersign poetics" must be developed, so that the actual possibilities of these technologies can be made available to poetry.

CONCRETE POETRY: CRITICAL PERSPECTIVES FROM THE 90S

Claus Clüver

This study describes the development of both poetical and critical views on the basic tenets of concretism since the rise of Concrete poetry in the mid 1950s, with special emphasis on the Brazilian situation. In particular, it discusses the necessity to reconsider views on the demarcation of Concrete poetry, on its alleged rupture with poetic traditions, and on its relationships with "visual" and "experimental" poetries.

CONCRETE POETRY: A GENERIC PERSPECTIVE

Pedro Reis

The generic perspective has been somewhat neglected as a methodological possibility of situating Concrete poetry in the literary field. In fact, a large number of critics preferred to consider Concrete poetry as a movement, approaching it from the point of view of periodology. Yet genre attribution is a part of the process of assigning meaning to texts. It is, however, related to perspective and a change of perspective proves the existence of a plurality of generic logics. This implies the variability of generic identity at each moment of reception. In my reading, Concrete poetry may be seen as a kind of inter-media poetry, if we consider the concept of intermedia in a broad sense, as forms based on the miscegenation of elements. In fact, Concrete poetry is characterized by the interaction of several elements from several codes, so that it is important to point out its generalized intersemiotic nature.

CONSTRUCTIVIST POEMS

Pierre Garnier

A brief essay by the renowned inventor of Spatialism on geometric, constructivist poetry, illustrated by a series of new poems.

UNDER CANCELLATION: THE FUTURE ~~TONE~~ OF VISUAL POETRY

Craig Saper

This essay uses a close reading of the logo-poem, *Codigo*, as a pretext to present a narrative of how various contexts change the coding of visual poetry from formalism and structuralism to conceptualism and post-neo-isms, from histories of Modernism and the international movement of Concrete poetry to mail-art networks and send-ups of lyric poetry. The icon-poem presents a canceled tone and code that shifts among the literal historical context and intention of the poet (Augusto de Campos's reading), metaphoric interpretation (Claus Clüver's reading), ironic critique (Marjorie Perloff's reading), and parody (read as mail art in an on-sending). The essay uses these various interpretive contexts to read the poem as a performance score.

SWEDISH CONCRETE POETRY IN FOCUS

Amelie Björck

The manifesto of Concrete poetry published in 1954 by the poet Öyvind Fahlström presented the ideas, about a new and non-discursive way of using of language, around which a Swedish movement of Concrete poetry was formed during the 60s. Although the poetical production of the young poets involved was rather heterogeneous from the start, the major part of it is distinguished by certain traits, such as an extended form, causing a great visual, auditive and semantical complexity. The emotionally charged atmosphere, revealing the imprint of the author, is reflected in the label for this central type of Swedish Concrete poetry: "linguistic sensualism."

AFTERIMAGES: REVOLUTION OF THE (VISIBLE) WORD

Marjorie Perloff

This essay examines two types of post-Concrete poetry: the Morning Star Folios produced by Alec Finlay in Scotland (especially the collaboration between Cécilia Vicuña and Edwin Morgan) and the more sophisticated, complex visual poetics of the U.S. poet Joan Retallack. In both cases, verbal-visual constellations produce puns, *double entendres*, paragrams, and elaborate semantic complexity. I argue that such visual poetics is very much the wave of the future, that Retallack's "afterrimages" mark the direction in which experimental poetry is now moving.

CONCRETE STEPS TO AN ANTHOLOGY

Mary Ellen Solt

A retrospective view on the events that preceded and followed the publication of one of the pivotal anthologies of Concrete poetry: the author's *Concrete Poetry: A World View.*

THE RELATIONS OF HAROLDO DE CAMPOS TO GERMAN CONCRETIST POETS, IN PARTICULAR TO MAX BENSE

Elisabeth Walther-Bense

This essay presents a survey of the close personal and poetical relationships of De Campos and Bense, and of the German concretist movement, specifically of the Stuttgart group founded by Max Bense. It includes a detailed chronological account of German activities in the field of Concrete poetry, centered on the *ROT*-series.

CORRESPONDENCE ADDRESSES

- William Anselmi, Dept. of Italian, Carleton University, Ottawa, Ontario
  K1S 5B6, Canada
- Charles Bernstein, 215 W 92nd St Apt 5F, New York, NY 10025-7476,
  USA
- Amelie Björck, Södra Esplanaden 13 c, 22354 Lund, Sweden
- Willard Bohn, Dept. of Foreign Languages, Illinois State, Normal, IL
  61761-6901, USA
- Claus Clüver, Dept. of Comparative Literature, Ballantine Hall 402,
  Indiana University, Bloomington, IN 47405-6601, USA
- Johanna Drucker, Dept. of Art History, Yale University, New Haven, CT
  06520, USA
- Pierre Garnier, 80540 Saisseval, France
- Roberto González Echevarría, Dept. of Spanish and Portuguese, Yale
  University, New Haven, CT 06520-8204, USA
- Ana Hatherly, Estudos Portugueses, Universidade Nova de Lisboa, Lisboa,
  Portugal
- K. David Jackson, Dept. of Spanish and Portuguese, Yale University, New
  Haven, CT 06520-8204, USA
- Eduardo Kac, Dept. of Fine Arts, New Media Area,University of
  Kentucky, 207 Fine Arts Bldg., Lexington, KY 40506-0022, USA
- K. Alfons Knauth, Fak. für Philologie/Romanisches Institut, Ruhr-
  Universität Bochum, Universitätsstraße 150, 44780 Bochum, Germany
- Wladimir Krysinski, Faculté des arts et des sciences, Département de
  littérature comparée, Université de Montréal, C.P. 6128, succursale A,
  Montréal, Quebec H3C 3J7, Canada
- Jackson Mac Low & Anne Tardos, 42 North Moore St., New York, NY
  10013-2441, USA
- E.M. de Melo e Castro, Rua Maria 31, 2°, 1100 Lisboa, Portugal
- Philadelpho Menezes, P.P.S. Comunicação e Sémiotica, Pontifícia
  Universidade Católica de São Paulo, Rua Monte Alegre 984, 05014-901
  São Paulo SP, Brazil
- Enzo Minarelli, C.P. 152, 44042 Cento, Italy
- Walter Moser, Faculté des arts et des sciences, Département de littérature
  comparée, Université de Montréal, C.P. 6128, succursale A, Montréal,
  Quebec H3C 3J7, Canada

442

- Marjorie Perloff, Dept. of English, Stanford University, Stanford, CA 94305, USA
- John Picchione, Dept. of Languages, Literatures, and Linguistics, York University, 4700 Keele St., North York, Ontario M3J 1P3, Canada
- Lamberto Pignotti, via Cuma 2, 00183 Roma, Italy
- Harry Polkinhorn, P.O. Box 927428, San Diego, CA 92192, USA
- Pedro Reis, Dept. of Comparative Literature, Universidade Fernando Pessoa, Praça 9 de Abril 349, 4200 Oporto, Portugal
- Craig Saper, Dept. of English, University of Pennsylvania, Philadelphia, PA 19104, USA
- Jorge Schwartz, Departamento de Letras Modernas, FFLCH-Universidade de São Paulo, 05508-900 São Paulo SP, Brazil
- Owen F. Smith, Dept. of Art, Carnegie Hall, University of Maine, Orono, ME 04469, USA
- Mary Ellen Solt, 25520 Wilde Avenue, Stevenson Ranch, CA 91381, USA
- Lello Voce, Via Pescheria 21, 31100 Treviso, Italy
- Eric Vos, Haagwinde 12, 3755 TA Eemnes, Netherlands
- Elizabeth Walther-Bense, Dornröschenweg 67, 70567 Stuttgart, Germany

NEW LITERARY HISTORY

A Journal of Theory and Interpretation

RALPH COHEN, EDITOR

New Literary History focuses on theory and interpretation—the reasons for literary change, the definitions of periods, and the evolution of styles, conventions, and genres. Published quarterly in February, May, August, and November.

Prepayment is required. **Annual subscriptions:** $27.00, individuals; $79.00, institutions. **Foreign postage:** $4.50, Canada & Mexico; $11.30, outside North America. **Single-issue price:** $10.00, individuals; $26.00, institutions. Payment must be drawn on a U.S. bank in U.S. dollars or made by international money order. MD residents add 5% sales tax. For orders shipped to Canada add 7% GST (#124004946).
Send orders to: The Johns Hopkins University Press, P.O. Box 19966, Baltimore, MD 21211.
To place an order using Visa or MasterCard, call toll-free 1-800-548-1784, FAX us at (410) 516-6968, or send Visa/MasterCard orders to this E-mail address: jlorder@jhunix.hcf.jhu.edu

This is the fourth of four issues commemorating the twenty-fifth anniversary of New Literary History.

VOLUME 26, NUMBER 2
(Spring 1995)
What Difference Does Anti-Foundationalism Make to Political Theory? • Salome©: The Fetishization of a Textual Corpus • Derrida, Husserl, and the Structural Affinity between the "Text" and the Market • Codes of Law and Bodies of Color • Dorothy Wordsworth's Return to Tintern Abbey • Domesticating the School Story, Regendering a Genre: Alcott's *Little Men* • Research, Essay, Failure (Flaubert's Itinerary) • Demands of History: Narrative Crises in *Jude the Obscure* • Speaking about Genre: The Case of Concrete Poetry • Complementary Viewpoints: Some Thoughts on Binocular Vision in Mathematical Modeling and Latin Palaeography • Availing the Physics of Least Action • The Effect of Paternal Deprivation on the Capacity to Modulate Aggression • Not-Words

 Published by THE JOHNS HOPKINS UNIVERSITY PRESS

EA5

Studies in Twentieth Century Literature

Volume 20, No. 1 (Winter, 1996)

A journal devoted to literary theory and practical criticism

A Special Issue on

Dynamics of Change in Latin American Literature: Contemporary Women Writers

Adelaida López de Martínez, Guest Editor

Contributors include:

Pamela Bacarisse on The Novels of Josefina Vicens
Ksenija Bilbija on Laura Esquivel and Silvia Plager
María M. Carrión on Giannina Braschi's *El imperio de los sueños*
Sara Castro-Klaren on Feminist Literary Theory
María B. Clark on The Feminine Fantastic
Sandra Cypess on Griselda Gambaro
Naomi Lindstrom on Tamara Kamenszain
Doris Meyer on Victoria Ocampo
Kirsten F. Nigro on Women and Latin American Theatre

Also in preparation:
The Object in France Today
Martine Antle, Guest Editor
Contemporary German Poetry
James L. Rolleston, Guest Editor

Subscriptions:
Institutions—$20 for one year ($35 for two years);
Individuals—$15 for one year ($28 for two years).
Add $5 for AIR MAIL.

Michael Ossar, Editor
Eisenhower 104
Kansas State University
Manhattan, KS 66506-1003
Submissions in:
  German and Russian

Marshall Olds, Editor
1111 Oldfather Hall
University of Nebraska
Lincoln, NE 68588-0318
Submissions in:
  French and Spanish

Studies in 20th Century Literature

A journal devoted to literary theory and practical criticism

Volume 20, No. 2 (Summer, 1996)
Special Issue: The Object in France Today
Guest Editor: Martine Antle

Maryse Fauvel—Transparency and Pluralism
Dominique Fisher—From Object-images to Meta-objects
Jean-François Fourny—Fashion, Bodies, and Objects
Lawrence Schehr—Body/Antibody
Peter Shofer—What's Behind the Billboard
Monique Yaari—The Figure and the Great Divide

Essays also by:

Laurel Cummins—Reading in Colette
Barbara Klaw—On Beauvoir's *Tous les hommes sont mortels*
Elizabeth Mazza—On Redonnet's *Splendid Hôtel*
Juliette Rogers—On Colette's *La Naissance du jour*

Special Issues in preparation:
Special Issue on Contemporary German Poetry
Guest Editor: James L. Rolleston

Illness and Disease in 20th Century Literature
Guest Editor: Sander L. Gilman

Silvia Sauter, Editor
Eisenhower 104
Kansas State University
Manhattan, KS 66506-1003
  Submissions in:
  German and Russian

Marshall Olds, Editor
1111 Oldfather
University of Nebraska
Lincoln, NE 68588-0318
  Submissions in:
  French and Spanish

Subscriptions—add $5 for Air Mail
Institutions—$20 for one year ($35 for two years)
Individuals—$15 for one year ($28 for two years)

Neuerscheinungen:

Joachim Zelter
Sinnhafte Fiktion und Wahrheit

Untersuchungen zur ästhetischen und epistemologischen Problematik des Fiktionsbegriffs im Kontext europäischer Ideen- und englischer Literaturgeschichte

1994. XII, 349 Seiten. Kart. DM 168.– / ÖS 1310.– / SFr 168.–. ISBN 3-484-45032-0 (Studien zur englischen Philologie. Band 32)

Die Studie eruiert die Rolle des Fiktiven als ästhetisches und epistemologisches Problem in der europäischen Ideen- und englischen Literaturgeschichte. Das Fiktive ist nicht nur konstitutiv für die Literatur, sondern gleichermaßen für extraliterarische Welterklärungsmodelle, eine Prämisse, die gegen Ende des 19. Jahrhunderts in der Als-Ob-Philosophie genauso produktiv wurde wie im literarischen Werke Oscar Wildes. Die Studie skizziert zunächst die Bedeutungen und Bewertungen, die dem Fiktionsbegriff im Kontext verschiedener weltanschaulicher und ideengeschichtlicher Spannungsfelder zugeschrieben wurden: z. B. in der Ideologiekritik der Aufklärung und in der Wahrheitskritik der Gegenaufklärung. Sodann wird die zunehmende Problematisierung und Auflösung des Wahrheitsbegriffs in der Philosophiegeschichte verfolgt: von Bacon über Hobbes, Locke, Berkeley, Hume, Mill bis zu Vaihingers »Philosophie des Als-Ob«, ein Punkt, wo ein immer brüchiger werdender Wahrheitsbegriff der Fiktionsidee als unabwendbare Bedingung der Wirklichkeitserkenntnis weicht. Daraufhin werden die Rückwirkungen dieser Entwicklung auf die englische Literaturgeschichte aufgezeigt. Mit Wilde ist eine erste explizite Hinwendung zum Fiktiven als Kunst-, Lebens- und Erkenntnisprinzip erreicht. Im 20. Jahrhundert finden sich – nach einer langen Unterbrechung – erst bei Huxley Anknüpfungen an die Als-Ob-Philosophie und im Dramenwerk Pinters Steigerungen der Fiktionsidee, die sich dort zu einer umfassenden Bedingung der Welt und des Menschseins ausweitet. In Lawrence Durrells Romanwerk überschreitet der Fiktionsgedanke alle subjektiven und objektiven Referenzvorstellungen und steigert sich zu einer subjektlosen, objektlosen und abgrenzungslosen Unermeßlichkeit. Damit ist der vorläufige Endpunkt einer Entwicklung erreicht, deren Stadien und Zäsuren vom frühen englischen Roman bis zur postmodernen Literatur verfolgt werden.

Thomas Kullmann
Vermenschlichte Natur

Zur Bedeutung von Landschaft und Wetter im englischen Roman von Ann Radcliffe bis Thomas Hardy

1995. XI, 510 Seiten. Ln DM 168.– / ÖS 1310.– / SFr 168.–. ISBN 3-484-42133-9 (Buchreihe der Anglia. Band 33)

Ein herausragendes Kennzeichen englischer Romane des neunzehnten Jahrhunderts sind die zahlreichen Naturschilderungen, die nicht um ihrer selbst willen erfolgen, sondern der Verdeutlichung des zwischenmenschlichen Romangeschehens bzw. der Befindlichkeiten und Stimmungen der Personen des Romans dienen. Die vorliegende Arbeit versucht, diese Verwendungsweise von Naturmotiven als komplexes Zeichensystem bzw. Erzählverfahren zu beschreiben: Einzelne Naturphänomene aus den Bereichen Tageszeit, Jahreszeit, Landschaft und Wetter verbinden sich zu zusammenhängenden ›Naturbildern‹; diese treten auf unterschiedliche – ›motivsyntaktische‹ – Weise mit den Romangestalten in Beziehung und dienen – ›motivpragmatisch‹ – einem erzählerischen Zweck.
Neben die systematische Motivanalyse tritt die Darstellung literar- und kulturhistorischer Zusammenhänge: Nach einem Überblick über die literarischen Funktionen von Naturmotiven bis zum 18. Jahrhundert wird in textnahen Untersuchungen gezeigt, wie das ›Zeichensystem Naturmotivik‹ in der *Gothic Novel* (Ann Radcliffe, Charles R. Maturin) zur Ausprägung gelangt. Hierbei entwickelt sich aus der im achtzehnten Jahrhundert vorherrschenden moralphilosophischen Bedeutung der Landschaftsbetrachtung die Funktion einer erzählerischen Analogie für psychologische Phänomene, eine Funktion, die im frühviktorianischen Roman (Brontë Sisters, Charles Dickens) besonders deutlich wird. Einen weiteren ›Paradigmenwechsel‹ bringt die Evolutionstheorie Charles Darwins mit sich, die ihren Niederschlag in der Naturmotivik Thomas Hardys findet.

Max Niemeyer Verlag GmbH & Co. KG
Postfach 21 40 · D-72011 Tübingen

Critical Quarterly

Edited by Colin McCabe

'This is the only journal to remain faithful to the original spirit of cultural studies. It mixes 'high' and 'low' culture, criticism and creative writing without losing sight of political and social questions.'
Rosalind Coward

Critical Quarterly has been at the forefront of literary criticism since the 1960's and in the last ten years it has established an international reputation for its unique blend of fiction, criticism and poetry which mix together to reflect contemporary issues.

- -

ORDER FORM   CRITICAL QUARTERLY

Subscription Rates, Volume 38, 1996   ISSN 0011-1562

Institutional Rates, £57.00 (UK-Europe), $99.00 (N. America*), £64.00 (Rest of World)

Personal Rates, £31.00 (UK-Europe), $58.00 (N. America*), £37.00 (Rest of World)

Published in: April, July, October and December   *Canadian customers please add 7% GST

☐ Please enter my subscription/send me a sample copy

☐ I enclose a cheque/money order payable to Blackwell Publishers

☐ Please charge my American Express/Diners Club/Mastercard/Visa account

Card Number . . . . Expiry Date . . . .

Signature . . . . Date . . . .

Name . . . .

Address . . . .

. . . .

. . . . Postcode . . . .

Payment must accompany orders

Please return this form to: Journals Marketing, Blackwell Publishers, 108 Cowley Road, Oxford, OX4 1JF, UK.
Or to: Journals Marketing, CRIQ, Blackwell Publishers, 238 Main Street, Cambridge, MA 02142, USA.

Internet

Full details of Blackwell Publishers
books and journals are available on
the Internet.
To access use a WWW browser such as
Netscape or Mosaic, and the following URL:
http://www.blackwellpublishers.co.uk

**APPLY FOR YOUR FREE SAMPLE
COPY BY E-MAIL!**

jnlsamples@blackwellpublishers.co.uk

diacritics

A Review of Contemporary Criticism

Edited by
Jonathan Culler & Richard Klein,
Cornell University

Diacritics is the preeminent forum for exchange among literary theorists, literary critics, and philosophers. Each issue features articles in which contributors compare and analyze books on particular theoretical works and develop their own positions on the theses, methods, and theoretical implications of those works. Published quarterly in March, June, September, and December.

Annual Subscriptions:
$23.50 individuals, $59.00 institutions.
Foreign Postage:
$3.50, Canada & Mexico;
$8.40 outside North America.
Send orders with payment to:
The Johns Hopkins University Press,
P.O. Box 19966, Baltimore, Maryland 21211.
MD residents add 5% tax. Orders shipped to
Canada add 7% GST (GST #124004946.)

To place an order using Visa or Master-
Card, call toll-free 1-800-548-1784,
fax us at (410) 516-6968, or send Visa/
MasterCard orders to this E-Mail address:
jlorder@jhunix.hcf.jhu.edu

**March 1995
(Vol. 25, No. 1)
Latin American
Writers (special
issue):**
• Tracing a
Comparative
American Project:
The Case of Québec
and Puerto Rico
• Turks and Indians:
Orientalist Discourse
in Postcolonial
Mexico
• Grammar Trouble:
Cortázar's Critique of
Competence
• Interview with John
Rechy
• From *Autobiography:
A Novel*

 Published by
The Johns Hopkins
University Press